The War for Independence
and the Transformation
of American Society

Warfare and History

General Editor
Jeremy Black
Professor of History, University of Exeter

European Warfare, 1660–1815
Jeremy Black

The Great War, 1914–18
Spencer C. Tucker

Wars of Imperial Conquest in Africa 1830–1914
Bruce Vandervort

German Armies: War and German Society, 1648–1806
Peter Wilson

Ottoman Warfare, 1500–1700
Rhoades Murphey

Seapower and Naval Warfare, 1650–1830
Richard Harding

Air Power in the Age of Total War
John Buckley

Frontiersmen: Warfare in Africa since 1950
Anthony Clayton

Western Warfare in the Age of the Crusades, 1000–1300
John France

The Korean War
Stanley Sandler

European and Native American Warfare, 1675–1795
Armstrong Starkey

Vietnam
Spencer C. Tucker

Warfare, State & Society in the Byzantine World, 565–1453
John Haldon

Soviet Military System
Roger Reese

Warfare in Atlantic Africa, 1500–1800
John Thornton

The War for Independence and the Transformation of American Society

Harry M. Ward

University of Richmond, Virginia

First published 1999 in the UK and the USA
by UCL Press
11 New Fetter Lane, London EC4P 4EE

The name of University College London (UCL) is a registered trade mark used
by UCL Press with the consent of the owner.

UCL Press is an imprint of the Taylor & Francis Group

© Harry M. Ward 1999

Typeset in Bembo by Graphicraft Limited, Hong Kong.
Printed and bound in Great Britain by T.J. International Limited, Padstow, UK.

British Library Cataloguing in Publication Data
A catalogue record for this book is available from the British

Library of Congress Cataloging in Publication Data
A catalogue record for this book has been requested

ISBN 1–85728–656–1 (hbk)
ISBN 1–85728–657–X (pbk)

Contents

List of illustrations

Preface

This book assesses the impact of the War for Independence on the lives of Americans during the period of the conflict.

The Revolutionary War established a nation and confirmed American identity. The ideals expounded translated into guideposts for creating a Republican society, with emphasis on citizen responsibility and the promotion and protection of opportunity for freedom and equality. If societal reform seems minimal during the immediate war period, vistas were opened for continuity in progress. While the war during its span effected political reconstruction, stirred social mobility, brought economic self-sufficiency and expansion, and fixed in the American popular culture the "Spirit of '76," the war also had a negative side in the oppression of dissenting and ethnic minorities, further ingraining violence as endemic to the collective consciousness of the people, hardening class lines between the poor and the more affluent, bolting down more securely the institution of slavery, and accentuating even further sectional awareness and animosity. Yet most Americans united in spirit and action at least to some degree in support for the war. Like other wars in American history, however, there was the belief that the Revolutionary conflict could be easily won, making for less than adequate backing for the war effort and dissensions and frustrations. But total victory eclipsed in memory the dissonances. Largely overlooked in perceptions of the Revolutionary War is that during the war Americans were redefining themselves while forming expectations for the future.

Historians over time have searched for the meaning of the Revolution—its causes, objectives, and results. Historiography swerved from the celebratory tones of the nineteenth century to twentieth-century fathoming of the competing and conflicting forces that lay below the surface. "Progressive" historians exposed the theme of men on the make seeking to distract by a large war the underclass from their aspirations for a society more democratic and equal. From the imperialist historians there is the emphasis on colonies maturing economically and politically so that as a matter of course challenges rose against British rule. While historians have generally stressed the conservative side of the Revolution—the desire to preserve the entitlement of British Americans to the same liberties belonging to Englishmen in the realm—some recent historians have found much of the push toward rebellion in the persistence of constitutional crises depicted from the patriot view in libertarian rhetoric, influenced by the radicalism of English reformers.

Historians have taken as a cue for the study of Revolutionary society John Franklin Jameson's little book, *The American Revolution Considered as a Social Movement* (1926). Despite providing a peripheral and very insubstantial analysis in four short essays (on land, status of persons, industry and commerce, and thought and feeling), Jameson sounded the alert for the need for an examination of the social dimensions of the American Revolution. Valuable work has now been accomplished on fragments of community, such as the soldiers, women, family, African Americans, Native Americans, camp followers, and the "lower sort," namely laborers and craftsmen.

There is something about the social complexion of the American Revolution that invites chronologically open-ended treatment rather than consideration of the Revolution in its immediate timeframe and on its own terms. The war-and-society phase is all but passed over. There has long been a need to study the Revolution and its relation to society within the context of the war itself. This is a challenging task since trends and activity cannot be neatly boxed, with social change having roots before the war and extensions into the postwar period. But the climate of war and its particular effects on the lives of those who lived through it can be analyzed. To clarify and evaluate wartime development, however, it is necessary to carry the discussion in some instances, particularly relating to institutional factors, into the immediate postwar decade.

Americans had a wide range of war-related experiences. In this study, besides examining the home front and how lives were affected and the military–civilian connections, it is important not to lose sight of the aim of the rebellion—independence. This work elicits aspects of wartime society during the Revolution that largely have been neglected and thereby should stimulate interest in further investigations.

I wish to thank Jeremy Black for bringing me into the Warfare and History Series and for helpful suggestions. The staffs of the Library of Virginia (the Virginia state library) and the Boatwright Library of the University of Richmond afforded great assistance, and especially I thank Nancy Vick and Noreen Cullen of the interlibrary loan department of the Boatwright Library for their prompt help, even securing rare materials from various institutions.

CHAPTER ONE

A people in rebellion

American colonists on the eve of the Revolution shared a common identity that set themselves apart from Britons elsewhere. The New World settlers had forged a society and culture from multi-ethnic elements (English, Dutch, German, Scots-Irish and other Europeans), affected also by contact with native Americans and African slaves. A sense of destiny beckoned from the lure of a spacious frontier. The recent victory in the French and Indian War, the culmination of a long duel for a continent, left impressions of pride and invincibility. If challenged to defend against external encroachment upon their liberties, Americans were capable of translating their commonality into independence and union.

A revolutionary movement for the repudiation of parliamentary authority had formed during the decade since 1763. Protest forced the British government to retreat from levying taxes upon the colonies. Parliament, though insisting on plenary power in America, conceded to demands of the colonists to refrain from internal taxation and eventually also external taxes for revenue. Without new provocation the patriot cause seemed on the decline. But new parliamentary measures, in response to American reaction to the Tea Act of 1773, triggered a war.

"An Act to allow a Drawback of the Duties of Customs on the Exportation of Tea . . ." renewed the 3d. tea impost duty (first imposed by the Revenue Act of 1767) and aimed at ensuring a monopoly of tea sold in America by the British East India Company. With inland duties rebated in England, tea could be sold cheaper than before in America, interfering with merchants' profits made from retailing smuggled tea. Boston rebel leaders now saw the opportunity once again to exploit the "no taxation without representation" issue when East India tea arrived in Boston harbor. The destruction of the tea by a riotous assembly on the night of December 16, 1773 led to a get-tough policy from the home government. Because of the

1

impossibility of fixing culpability upon individuals parliament responded with punitive measures. More than submitting to a levy of import duties, colonists now faced strident curtailment of liberties.

The Boston Port Act (March 31, 1774), to be rescinded only if Massachusetts indemnified the East India Company for its loss of property, provided for the closure of shipping in Boston harbor. The customshouse was moved to Marblehead and the seat of the Massachusetts government to Salem. The British ministry calculated that severe measures against one colony would not arouse hostility from others, given the well-known sectional rivalry among the northern, middle and southern colonies. To compound the harshness of the Port Act, parliament also enacted the Massachusetts Government Act, intended as a permanent reform, which made councillors appointed by the crown rather than elected by the lower house of the legislature, forbade town meetings without approval by the governor other than for the purpose of annual election, and conferred on the governor authority to appoint all judicial and other officials, including sheriffs and jurors. The Administration of Justice Act, considered also one of the Coercive Acts, allowed crown officials indicted for capital offenses to be tried in England or another province. The three laws collectively underscored the far reaching powers of parliament as infringements on the fundamental rights of Englishmen. Edmund Burke, a member of parliament, correctly gauged the issue that would confront parliament as a result of passing the acts of coercion: it was no longer a question of the "degrees of Freedom or restraint in which they [the colonists] were to be held, but whether they should be totally separated from their connexion with, and dependence on the parent Country of Great Britain."[1]

"The Boston Suffering a Common Cause"

Colonists everywhere made the plight of Boston and Massachusetts their own. On June 1, 1774, "being the day when the cruel act for blocking up the harbor of Boston took effect," many Philadelphians, "to express their sympathy and show their concern for their suffering brethren in the common cause of liberty," closed their shops and refrained "from hurry and business;" muffled church bells rang throughout the day in the city, crowds attended religious services, and flags of ships in the Philadelphia harbor were hoisted at half-mast.[2]

The Boston Port Act caused "innumerable hardships." Provisions and other necessities could only be ferried into Boston by way of Salem or Marblehead, and other goods traveled a round about way by land through Boston neck. Wood boats had to load and unload at Marblehead. The inconveniences added to the price of commodities. "Our wharfs are entirely deserted," complained a well-to-do Boston merchant; "not a topsail vessel to be seen there or in the harbor, save the ships of war and transports." It was "no uncommon thing to hear the carriers and waggoners," who brought goods in by land, "when they pass a difficult place in the road, to whip their horses and damn Lord North."[3]

The interruption of commerce at Boston put mariners and laborers out of employment. Propertyless and as wage earners, these underclass workmen, one fourth of Boston's population, did not have the resources for survival as did merchants and established artisans. The Boston town meeting on May 13, 1774 formed a Committee of Ways and Means, which along with the Overseers of the Poor, was charged with finding aid for the newly unemployed. The Overseers of the Poor, after a few weeks, won exemption from this responsibility since they already had the burden of caring for the regular indigent. Thus the town government revamped the Ways and Means Committee into a Committee of Donations, which had the primary functions of receiving aid sent to Boston and establishing a work relief program. The Committee of Donations interviewed applicants for eligibility for public assistance. From funds obtained, the committee put the new welfare recipients to work repairing roads, making bricks at a new brickyard, cleaning docks, building wharfs and houses, and digging wells for use at fires. Moneys were also spent to set up looms for spinning and to buy materials to supply ropemakers, blacksmiths, and shoemakers. Some of those in the relief program complained because they had "to work hard for that which they esteem as their right without work."[4]

New England towns quickly came to the aid of "the industrious poor" in Boston, sending grain, sheep, cattle, codfish, and money. "United we stand—divided we fall," declared the *New Hampshire Gazette* of July 22, 1774. "Supplies of provisions sent from all the Colonies are pouring into Boston for the support of the suffering poor there," wrote Reverend Ezra Stiles of Newport, Rhode Island. "All the Colonies make the Boston Suffering a common Cause, and intend to stand by one another."[5] The Continental Congress several months later resolved that "all America ought to contribute towards recompensing" the people of Boston "for the injury they may thereby sustain."[6]

Substantial contributions flowed from local committees in New York, New Jersey, and Pennsylvania. Because of the difficulty of bringing commodities to Boston, goods were auctioned on the spot or carried to a New England port such as Providence and converted into cash or bills of exchange to be forwarded to Boston. Typical of cover letters accompanying gifts to the Boston Committee of Donations was that of a Bucks County, Pennsylvania committee, giving notice that it had resolved "That we hold it as our bounden duty, both as Christians and as countrymen, to contribute towards the relief and support of the poor inhabitants of the Town of Boston, now suffering in the general cause of all the Colonies." Philadelphia Quakers sent a total of £3,910 2s. Much of this money was dispensed

Figure 1 "Bostonians in Distress." A London cartoon depicts Bostonians caged because of the closing of the city's port in 1774. The nearly starving inhabitants are fed codfish supplied from neighboring towns. *Library of Congress.*

among the some 5,000 refugees who had escaped to rural towns, thus enabling them to purchase food and firewood.[7]

Southern colonists joined in the relief effort for Boston. Baltimore sent rye and bread, and Queen Annes County, Maryland, one thousand

4

bushels of corn. Twenty Virginia gentlemen at Williamsburg subscribed £10 each, and Alexandria, Norfolk, and at least nine Virginia counties gave assistance. The German and Scots-Irish farmers of Virginia's Shenandoah Valley sent many barrels of flour along backcountry wagon roads to Alexandria for shipment. Elsewhere in Virginia, Chesterfield County collected 1,426½ bushels of grain, and Henrico County provided a shipload of provisions. Fairfax County pledged £273 in specie, 38 barrels of flour, and 150 bushels of wheat "for the benefit and relief of those (the industrious poor of the town of Boston) who by the late cruel act of Parliament are deprived of their daily labour and bread . . . to keep that manly spirit that has made them dear to every American, though the envy of an arbitrary Parliament." Settlers in the Cape Fear region of North Carolina dispatched a sloop loaded with provisions; South Carolina supplied several cargoes of rice, and from Georgia came 200 barrels of rice and £122 in specie.[8]

The gifts to Boston were gratefully acknowledged by the Committee of Donations, which used the opportunity to stress the mutuality of interests of all colonies in condemning the victimization of the people of Boston by the British Coercive Acts. Even before resistance hardened, Americans united in sympathy.

Organization for Resistance

The united effort in providing material support for the citizens of Boston paved the way for the exercise of the popular will in the displacement of the established political authority in the royal and proprietary colonies. Massachusetts set the example by taking actions in violation of the Massachusetts Government Act. Town meetings convened in its defiance. Councillors and other officials appointed under the new system were intimidated to prevent them assuming office. Massachusetts also took the initiative to inaugurate an economic boycott of British goods.

On June 5, 1774 the Boston Committee of Correspondence, which had been in existence since 1772 when created by a Boston town meeting, drew up a Solemn League and Covenant, calling for merchants to pledge not to import British products after October 1, 1774. Many Massachusetts towns soon followed suit. Nine of 12 Massachusetts counties by the end of summer 1774 held county-wide conventions which issued declarations of rights and affirmed a boycott. A convention of Worcester County in late August proposed the convening of an extralegal Provincial Congress to act in place of the regular legislature. Mobs prevented holding sessions of the courts of common pleas and general sessions at Worcester, Springfield, Great Barrington, Taunton, and Plymouth.[9]

Mass meetings for the purpose of protesting against the Coercive Acts appeared throughout the colonies. In New York City, May 16, 1774, a large gathering voted to name 51 citizens "to be a Standing Committee" to correspond "with our sister Colonies," to take such "constitutional meas-ures" for "the preservation of our just rights," to maintain the "public peace," and to support the formation of "a general union . . . throughout the Continent." A Committee of Mechanics, consisting mainly of crafts-men, pressured not too successfully the conservative Committee of 51 to-ward radical action. No effort was made to install a boycott, the matter being left to a general congress in the future. The Committee of 51 contin-ued to direct the revolutionary movement in New York until spring 1775, when it was replaced by a committee of 60 persons, and then by another one of 100 members, and ultimately by a Provincial Congress. On July 19, 1775 a mass meeting in New York City elected delegates to a Continental Congress.[10] A large assemblage of Philadelphia citizens on June 18, 1774 gathered in the State House yard and chose 43 persons as a committee, which met in Carpenters Hall and adopted "six spirited resolves" denouncing parliament's usurpation of power. Mass meetings at Annapolis and Balti-more, Maryland, in May 1774 resulted in the establishment of committees of correspondence and a call for an economic boycott of Great Britain.[11]

During spring and summer 1774 seven colonies held provincial con-ventions or congresses. Virginia led the way in the use of a colony-wide convention to garner power away from the legislature, which would be similarly accomplished by other colonies in creating provincial congresses. When the Virginia General Assembly approved a resolution for observing a fast day on June 1 to show sympathy for the plight of Boston, Governor Lord Dunmore dissolved the legislature on May 26. The next day 89 of 103 burgesses met at the Raleigh Tavern in Williamsburg and proceeded to condemn the Boston Port Act and British taxation and to recommend a boycott of "all Indie goods and whatsoever but saltpetre and spice."[12] A committee of correspondence was formed to keep in touch with actions of other colonies and to promote the creation of a general congress. On May 30 a rump meeting of burgesses called for a convention representing all the colony to be held on August 1. The first Virginia convention met August 1–7 at Williamsburg, with delegates from 60 of the 61 counties. The conven-tion adopted complete non-importation to begin November 1 and, if this did not produce redress from the British government, also non-exportation commencing August 10, 1775. Counties were ordered to appoint committees to enforce the boycott and to keep merchants from raising prices. Delegates were elected to serve in the Continental Congress.

Maryland had the distinction of holding the first Provincial Congress, June 22–6, 1774, with 92 delegates from all the counties; trade relations with Great Britain were broken off, and delegates to a Continental Con-gress were selected. In July New Hampshire, Pennsylvania, and New Jer-sey followed with similar action. Seventy-one representatives from most of North Carolina's counties and boroughs met on August 25–7 at New Bern and decided to boycott East India tea immediately and other British goods after January 1, 1775; no slaves were to be brought into the colony after November 1, 1774.[13]

In Charleston, South Carolina's influential citizens, many of them members of the Common House of Assembly, had met periodically since 1773 to review British measures. From this arrangement came a meeting of a General Committee of 104 persons from the ranks of merchants, planters, mechanics, and backcountry settlers at the City Tavern in Charleston on July 6, 1774. The group considered what steps might be taken "in union with all the inhabitants of our Sister Colonies" to counter "the hostile acts of Parliament", but refrained from voting a boycott, waiting for such a decision by a general congress of the colonies. On November 9 the General Committee called for a Provincial Congress, which met on January 11, 1775, with a membership four times that of the legislature and representative of all localities of the colony.[14]

In most instances the extra-legal assemblies were created because governors had either dissolved or postponed sessions of legislatures. In Massachusetts, after Governor Thomas Gage had dissolved the legislature, delegates reconvened as a Provincial Congress at Concord on October 11, 1774. Upon removing to Cambridge the Provincial Congress dissolved itself and called for elections on February 1, 1775 to form a similar body. The provincial conventions and congresses brought more diverse social groups into government, especially from the backcountry in Pennsylvania and the Carolinas.

The new provincial congresses and conventions established colony-wide committees (or councils) of safety to perform routine government duties during the interim between sessions. More importantly, in some colonies these agencies exercised executive authority that had belonged to the governor, particularly with the outbreak of the war in supervising military affairs.[15]

Proposals for a general congress of the colonies to give direction to the resistance movement had been prolific from the first call by the Providence, Rhode Island town meeting on May 17, 1774, which was immediately endorsed by committees of correspondence in Philadelphia and New York and Virginia's extra-legal meeting of burgesses on May 27. The colonists had a recent precedent in the Stamp Act Congress of 1765. Benjamin Franklin, upon learning that the Virginia House of Burgesses in March 1773 had established a committee of correspondence to be in touch with measures taken by other governments, wrote from London that he was glad for this action, and hoped that other colonies would do the same. "It is natural to suppose," Franklin said, "that if the Oppressions continue, a Congress may grow out of that Correspondence . . . if the Colonies agree to hold a Congress, I do not see how it can be prevented."[16]

The delegates to the Continental Congress from 12 colonies (Georgia not represented) who met at Carpenters Hall in Philadelphia on September

5 to October 26, 1774, took charge of economic sanctions against Great Britain and military preparations. On September 17 Congress adopted unanimously the Suffolk County, Massachusetts Resolves presented by a local convention which had met in Dedham and Milton on September 6–9, calling for intercolonial action for alleviating "the distress" of the people of Boston. According to the resolutions of Congress, based on the Suffolk Resolves, the blocking of Boston harbor and all features of the Administration of Justice and Massachusetts Government Acts were contrary to the constitutional rights of British subjects and not to be obeyed. No taxes were to be paid until the "civil government" was again "placed upon a constitutional foundation" and economic sanctions should be levied against Great Britain. Militia commissions should be revoked and new officers elected by local citizens, and the people should "use their utmost diligence to acquaint themselves with the art of war" and "appear under arms at least once every week."[17] John Adams, reporting from Congress to his wife, Abigail, said that "the Esteem, the Affection, the Admiration, for the People of Boston and the Massachusetts . . . were enough to melt an Heart of Stone. I saw the Tears gush into the Eyes of the old, grave pacific Quakers of Pennsylvania."[18]

Congress, on October 20, adopted the Continental Association, signed by all delegates present. This declaration called for united actions by the colonies, with options "to establish such farther regulations as they think proper." After December 1, 1774 no merchants could import British goods or East India tea from any port of the world. For such cargoes that might arrive in the meantime merchants had the choices of either reshipment, storage, or public auction, with profits designated for relief of the Boston poor. After February 1, 1775 all goods from Great Britain had to be returned without unloading. To afford time for colonists to dispose of their own commodities, non-exportation would not go into effect until September 10, 1775. Citizens were obliged not to consume British products. All levels of government should "encourage frugality, economy, and industry, and promote agriculture, arts and the manufactures of this country, especially that of wool." There should be a moral imperative to the revolutionary movement, and therefore it was necessary to "discountenance and discourage every species of extravagance and dissipation, especially all horse-racing, and all kinds of gaming, cock-fighting, exhibitions of shews, plays, and other expensive diversions and entertainments." To effect this censorship, a committee was to be formed in every county, city, and town "to observe the conduct of all persons touching this association." Names of violators of both the moral and boycott sanctions were to be published in the newspapers so "that all such foes to the rights of British-Americans may be publicly known, and universally contemned as the enemies of American liberty; and thenceforth we respectively will break off all dealing with him or her."[19]

Figure 2 "The Alternative of Williamsburg." R. Sanger and U. Bennett, London, February 16, 1775. Persons signing the Association, are mindful of the barrel of tar and a sack of feathers on a gibbet. *National Archives.*

All colonies except New York and Georgia quickly implemented the Continental Association. The legislatures of the two colonies refused to act. But eventually New York backed the Association, and when the Georgia Provincial Assembly met in January 1775 it ordered that committees be established in every parish, town and district to enforce the Association.[20]

Implementation of the Association secured the revolutionary movement at the grassroots in two ways. All adult members of a community had to sign an Association agreement or face severe ostracism, and the proliferation of committees to enforce the Association made for broader political participation by citizens on behalf of the opposition to Great Britain. Persons throughout the colonies had to affix their signatures to such an agreement as used by one North Carolina community:

ASSOCIATION

We the Subscribers, Freeholders and Inhabitants of the County of *Craven* and Town of *New-bern*, being deeply affected with the present alarming State of this Province, and of all *America*, do resolve that we will pay all due Allegiance to his Majesty King GEORGE the Third, and endeavour to continue the Succession of his Crown in the illustrious House of *Hanover*, as by Law established, against the present or any future wicked Ministry or arbitrary Set of Men whatsoever. At the same Time we determine to assert our Rights as Men; and sensible that by late Acts of Parliament the most valuable Liberties and Privileges of *America* are invaded, and endeavoured to be violated and destroyed, and that under GOD the preservation of them depends on a firm Union of the Inhabitants, and a steady spirited Observation of the Resolutions of the General Congress; being shocked at the cruel Scene now acting in the *Massachusetts-Bay*, and determined never to become Slaves to any Power upon Earth, WE do hereby agree and associate, under all the Ties of Religion, Honour, and Regard for Posterity, that we will adopt and endeavour to execute, the Measures which the General Congress, now sitting at *Philadelphia*, may conclude on, for preserving our Constitution, and opposing the Execution of the several arbitrary and illegal Acts of the *British* Parliament; and that we will readily observe the Directions of our General Committee for the Purposes aforesaid, the Preservation of Peace and good Order, and Security of Individuals and private Property.

(May 31, 1775)[21]

With the committee system (committees of observation, inspection, or safety) inaugurated by the Continental Association, many more persons could now vote for and hold elective office than before. Political power shifted downward. The new committeemen came from all walks of life: obscure shopkeepers, farmers, and mechanics served along with wealthy merchants, large landholders, and lawyers. Typically, in summer 1775, the third Virginia Convention called for annual election of 21 freeholders in each county to serve as committees of safety. In Virginia and Maryland committeemen totalled about 1,100, and in Massachusetts, 1,600 in 160 towns, with expanded opportunity in all the other colonies as well. Including the increase in the number of delegates in the Provincial Congresses over the former legislatures, it is estimated by spring 1775 there were 7,000 additional officeholders in all the colonies.[22]

The committees had primarily an administrative function in getting everyone to back the boycott and in watching for and censoring disaffection to the patriot cause by word or deed. While courts under royal authority were not permitted to meet, the committees assumed certain judicial authority in their trying and punishing violators of the Association. Committee members made the rounds to inspect ledgers of merchants, and those charging excessive prices or who had trafficked in goods contrary to the boycott had to explain themselves before a full committee. So did those engaging in prohibited speech, with public apology being demanded. Unrepentent culprits had themselves singled out for ostracism—citizens were to avoid them and have no dealings with them. Names of offenders were published in newspapers. Worst-case scenarios involved heavy-handed intimidation and even tarring and feathering.

A usual inquisitorial proceeding was much like that of the case of Thomas Loosly, a Philadelphia shoemaker, who

> was brought to the Coffee House, and there being exalted as a spectacle to a great number of reputable citizens, he there very humbly and submissively asked and entreated their pardon and forgiveness for his illiberally and wickedly villifying the measures of Congress, the Committee, and the people of New England, sincerely promising that his future conduct should be just, true, and equitable, as should recommend him to the particular notices of all those whom he had so unjustly, falsely, and wickedly villified. On those assurances and promises, the company discharged him.[23]

Being branded, however, as one who was "inimical to the liberties of America" or a "wicked enemy of America and [to] be treated as such" (in the case of a Scottish schoolteacher in Westmoreland County, Virginia) meant that one had not much choice other than to leave his or her locality. An Exeter, New Hampshire committee of safety voted that if ostracism proved "ineffectual . . . an experiment ought to be made of Tar and Feathers."[24] Some committees more zealously kept inquisitional watch than did others on public morals; one casualty was an end to horse-racing, at least until toward the end of the war.

The effects of the economic boycott under the Continental Association were severe. A Philadelphia lawyer observed, as early as December 1774, that "every cargo arriving from Great Britain and Ireland, or the British plantations has been delivered into the hands of this committee, to be sold or stored," and "so great is the unanimity and prevailing spirit of the inhabitants, that no individuals have thought proper to refuse or decline a compliance with the self-denying ordinance of the General Congress."[25] From September 10, 1775, when non-exportation began, to March 16, 1776 only 32 vessels entered Baltimore harbor. South Carolina imports fell from a value of £378,116 in 1774 to £6,245 the next year.[26] Total value of imports from Great Britain declined from £2,953,000 in 1774 to £226,000 in 1775, and about nil thereafter. Colonial exports to Great Britain fell from a value of £2,457,000 in 1775 to £186,000 the next year.[27]

Great Britain retaliated in kind to the American trade sanctions. The New England Trade and Fishery (also known as the New England Restraining) Act of March 30, 1775 prohibited New England's access to the Newfoundland fisheries and confined its trade to Great Britain, Ireland, and the West Indies. A second Restraining Act of April 13, 1775 extended the same restrictive provisions to the other nine colonies. Congress, on May 17, 1775, interdicted "provisions of any kind" from going to British fisheries in North America and all exportations to Quebec, Nova Scotia, and Newfoundland.[28] Britain's Prohibitory Act of December 22, 1775 aimed at closing off all trade with the colonies. The mutual recrimination that had been brought on by the determination of Americans in their Continental Association contributed to a *de facto* status of belligerency between the colonies and the home government.

Call to Arms

From fall 1774 to spring 1775 efforts to secure munitions moved the impasse between the colonies and Great Britain into the arena of armed conflict. On September 2, a British detachment from Boston carried away 250 half barrels of powder and two cannon from the Provincial Powder House, six miles northwest of Boston. Soon rumors spread that a fight had taken place in Cambridge and six rebels killed and that the Boston garrison was marching into the countryside; British ships were reported to have bombarded Boston. The so-called "Powder Alarm" alerted 30,000 New England militia who prepared to march towards Boston. Governor (General) Gage wrote to the British Secretary at War, Lord Barrington, that "no People are more determined for a Civil War, the whole Country from hence to New York armed, training and providing Military Stores."[29] Before the false report of fatalities and the bombardment of Boston was defused, it had spread widely, stirring up a martial spirit. Upon hearing the rumor, Virginia militia on an Indian expedition in the Ohio country resolved to lend their services to the rebel cause. The "horrid News" had greatly excited the members of the new Continental Congress. "WAR! WAR! WAR! was the Cry," John Adams wrote to his wife, "and it was pronounced in a Tone, which would have done Honour to the Oratory of a Briton or a Roman. If it had proved true, you would have heard the Thunder of an American Congress."[30]

Patriots hauled off munitions from the king's stores. On December 9 and 10, 1774 most of the cannon at Fort George, in Newport Harbor, Rhode Island were seized and "conveyed into the Country," and on December 14, local citizens in Portsmouth, New Hampshire captured 200 barrels of powder belonging to the British army, transporting their prize to Exeter.[31] On February 26 an assemblage of militia deterred a British detachment under Colonel Alexander Leslie from destroying cannon at Salem. Fighting almost erupted in Virginia over Governor Lord Dunmore having royal marines carry off to a British ship 20 kegs of powder from the public magazine at Williamsburg. Patrick Henry rallied militia from Hanover and neighboring counties for a confrontation with the governor's little military force. The crisis diminished when Dunmore made recompense for the seized powder. Dunmore thereafter kept to the safety of the warship *Fowey* in Chesapeake Bay, itself indicative that Virginia was on the verge of armed rebellion. Militia in Massachusetts on April 19, 1775 resisted British troops sent to destroy munitions at Concord, resulting in the opening round of the war.[32]

As events progressed toward a military showdown that began on Lexington Green, the colonists realized the necessity of having their own military capabilities. Averse at the time to the idea of creating a patriot standing army which would cause further strengthening of British forces in America, the new makeshift governments searched for means of quick and effective military responses that did not require complete mobilization. The militia historically had enrolled all able bodied men, and service hardly involved more than attendance at an annual muster. Organizationally, the militia system was incapable of putting trained men instantly into the field.

To overcome this deficiency, the Provincial Congress of Massachusetts ordered the formation of volunteer independent companies to be in constant readiness. The Worcester County convention, representing 45 towns, on September 21, 1774 had provided the model. It established seven regiments of 1,000 men each who would "turn out twice a week to perfect themselves in the military art—which are call'd minute men . . . to be ready at a minute's warning with a fortnight's provision, and ammunition and arms." Each minute company contained 50 privates and a captain elected from the lieutenants and ensigns who in turn were elected by the men; field officers were chosen by the other officers. The Committee of Safety, created by the Provincial Congress, had responsibility "to alarm, muster, and cause to be assembled" as many of these voluntary troops as were needed for any situation.[33]

Most colonies, after the commencement of the war, followed Congress's directive of July 18, 1775 that one-fourth of "all able bodied effective men" between the ages of 16 and 50 "be selected for minute men, of such men as are willing to enter into this necessary service . . . to be ready on the shortest notice, to march to any place where their assistance may be required, for the defence of their own or a neighbouring colony."[34] New England incorporated this system, with enlistments in a minute-man company usually for about four months. Other colonies, after Lexington and Concord, provided for frequent drills of militia; in New Jersey militia trained once a week at Newark and daily in Cumberland and Somerset counties. In one village in northwestern Virginia the men mustered each morning at 5 a.m. to the beating of drums and "heroic Tunes."[35] New England towns also had "alarm companies," which in contrast to this designation, were the leftovers of militia, consisting of boys and old men and those otherwise exempt, such as ministers and magistrates, who were the last to turn out.[36]

Volunteer militia companies on instant alert were found in the other colonies outside New England, usually referred to as independent companies. The second Virginia Convention on March 25, 1775 called upon counties each to form one or more volunteer companies of 86 men, 68 of whom were to be privates. The minute and independent companies mostly disappeared as separate entities as war reached full scale by the end of 1775. The volunteer soldiers, if they so chose, wound up in regular regiments of the Continental army, and all militia were presumed to be on a readiness status. The third Virginia Convention in July 1775 dissolved its volunteer companies in connection with raising regular army units, but provided that 16 regiments of "minutemen," about 8,000 men, be selected groups of militia who received more training than ordinary militia.[37]

The activation of certain units of citizen-soldiers and the increased training and participation of militia in general during the period leading to hostilities and afterwards proved an effective way to enlist support for the Revolutionary War. As John Shy has written: "The broad popular basis of military organization forced thousands of more or less unwilling people to associate themselves openly and actively with the cause. In an age when single-shot muzzle-loaders were the standard instrument of coercion, sheer numbers were most important, and naked majoritarianism could grow from the barrels of muskets."[38]

Joining the War Effort

As radical patriot leaders strived to mould public opinion for separation from Great Britain and war, they found no greater ally than religion. By contrasting American morality and English corruption, patriot clergy evoked a sense of holy crusade. Traditionally New England clergy had backed defensive war—one in which Americans in 1774–5 were entering because of invasion of their liberties. Days of thanksgiving and of fasting and humiliation had long been a tradition in colonial New England. With the coming of the Revolution, New England preachers turned the annual spring fast day and fall thanksgiving day into occasions for religious patriotic oratory. Sermons delivered on annual militia days throughout colonial history appealed to the joining of faith and arms. Christian soldiers had driven out the Antichrist (the French) from the North American continent; now a new enemy had appeared.

Colonists observed special fast days to protest against the Boston Port Act. On May 17, 1774 Dutch Reformed congregations in New York and New Jersey kept a "Day of Fasting and Prayer" to express dissatisfaction with the Coercive Acts.[39] Upon news of the Boston Port Act reaching Virginia, Thomas Jefferson and seven other members of the House of Burgesses, wishing to arouse "our people from the lethargy into which they had fallen" and thinking "that the appointment of a day of fasting and prayer would be most likely to call up and alarm their attention . . . rummaged over for the revolutionary precedents and forms of the Puritans" and "cooked up a resolution, somewhat modernizing their phrases." The House of Burgesses, on May 24, scheduled "a day of fasting, humiliation and prayer" to coincide with the day that the Boston Port Act went into effect, June 1.[40] Governor Dunmore considered the burgesses's action an encroachment upon the executive authority and tantamount to "sedition," as it was the governor's prerogative to declare public observance days. The legislature, dissolved by the governor for its infraction, met on its own, and Virginia had taken a first step toward revolution. Similarly, when Governor Gage refused to proclaim a day of fasting and prayer, the Massachusetts clergy went ahead and did so for July 14, 1774, with ministerial groups in New Hampshire, Connecticut, and Rhode Island achieving the same. The South Carolina Provincial Congress decreed a day of fasting and prayer for the colony for February 17, 1775. The Continental Congress arranged for a national day of humiliation and prayer, which was observed on July 20, 1775 ("Congress Sunday") everywhere. Again, on May 17, 1776 another such day was kept by recommendation of Congress, to implore God's aid "to frustrate the cruel purposes of our unnatural enemies . . . it may please the Lord of Hosts, the God of Armies, to animate our officers and soldiers with invincible fortitude . . . and to crown the continental arms . . . with victory and success."[41] Thereafter, during the war, Congress declared regular annual fast and thanksgiving days.

Congregational and Presbyterian pastors especially proved to be effective agents for revolutionary propaganda. Clergy harped on three themes in their preaching: the wickedness of British measures and society; the need to adhere to Congressional measures, otherwise disunion would follow; and the defense of liberty required taking up arms. Preachers did not hesitate to include a political agenda in church services. Some New England clergy placed the Solemn League and Covenant, which declared a boycott on British goods, on the communion table, and at least one New England minister "told his people that they who refused to sign were not worthy to come to the table."[42] Typically Samuel Langdon, president of Harvard, declared in a May 1775 election sermon that "our firm opposition to the establishment of an arbitrary system is called rebellion, and we are to expect no mercy. . . . therefore we have taken arms in our own defence . . . Let us praise our God for the advantages already given us over the enemies of liberty."[43] Reverend David Caldwell of Guilford County, North Carolina, in a 1775 sermon titled "The Character and Doom of the Sluggard," told his parishioners that:

> I should have no difficulty in persuading you to shake off your sloth, and stand up manfully in a firm, united, and persevering defence of your liberties . . . and we expect that none of you will be wanting in the discharge of your duty, or prove unworthy of a cause which every patriot and every Christian should value more than wealth, and hold as dear as his life.

One British official remarked in September 1776, concerning his experience in Connecticut, that the "Dissenting Preachers . . . inculcate War, Bloodshed and Massacres, as though all these were the express Injunctions of Jesus Christ."[44]

Preachers were often successful recruiters for the army. One army corporal reported on a sermon by Reverend William Emerson of Concord in late April 1775: "He incoridged us to go And fite for our Land and Country: Saying we Did not do our Duty if we did not Stand up now."[45] Sometimes men signed up during church service, and occasionally a pastor not only recruited soldiers from his congregation, but marched away with them, himself joining the army. The most famous of the parson-soldiers, General John Peter Gabriel Muhlenberg, a Lutheran clergyman at Woodstock in western Virginia, preached his farewell sermon in his robes, which he discarded at the end of the service, revealing his army uniform; Muhlenberg recruited the eighth Virginia Regiment of German Americans, 300 of whom came from his congregation.[46] Two New Jersey Presbyterian ministers, in the pay of Congress, were dispatched to the North Carolina backcountry in late 1775–early 1776 to persuade the Scots and Scots-Irish settlers to remain loyal to the American cause and to enlist as soldiers with a $40 bounty.[47]

As war became reality, civilian volunteers provided necessities for the militia. During the early powder crisis of September 1774, "at every house Women & Children" made cartridges and bullets and baked biscuits.[48] The "first provisions" obtained for the New England militia army in the Cambridge area the day after the battles of Lexington and Concord were "all the eatables" that "could be spared" from the local households, "some carcases of beef and pork prepared for the Boston market," and "a large quantity of ship-bread" taken from British naval supplies.[49] A British ship surgeon wrote on May 26, 1775 that the American troops were "plentifully supplied with all sorts of provisions, and the roads are crouded with carts and carriages, bringing them rum, cyder, &c. from the neighbouring towns."[50]

Not until 1777 did Congress assume responsibility for supply of the Continental army, with purchasing through the military quartermaster and commissary departments. Provincial and state governments until that time had to round up war materiel the best they could, relying on slender funds to obtain goods at prices that guaranteed profits and encouraging production of essential items by various means. Localities offered premiums and bounties and also solicited donations. Virginia counties, in compliance with a resolution of the second Virginia convention of March 25, 1775, collected either by a small tax levy or by donations the equivalent of a half pound of gunpowder and one pound of lead from each taxpayer.[51] In early 1775 Northampton County, Virginia, and Chowan County, North Carolina, among other localities, offered cash bonuses to persons who made a certain amount of wool cards, gunpowder or other items within a stated time period. The North Carolina Provincial Congress in September 1775 offered premiums totaling £2,965 to promote local manufacturing.[52] Urban artisans found plenty of employment under government contracts, aided by seed money and guaranteed prices. Thus, for example, William Barry a potash-maker in Charleston, South Carolina, received a grant of £500 for equipment for making gunpowder and was promised 10s. for every pound of powder produced.[53] At the beginning of the war the provincial congresses and conventions established public arms manufactories, as in Fredericksburg, Virginia, and many small private ventures sprouted up for the making of weapons.

Following Congress's recommendation for development of self-sufficient industry, several attempts were made in 1775 in the cities to establish stock-company ventures for manufacturing. "The New York Society for employing the Industrious Poor and Promoting Manufactory" for making textiles and nails did not obtain enough capital to succeed, even with a subsidy from the New York City Committee of Safety.[54] The most ambitious and successful of such enterprises was the "United Company of Philadelphia for promoting American Manufactures," organized on March 16, 1775 and in operation by the end of April. Its purpose was not only to remove dependence upon Great Britain but also to provide employment for the poor. Newspaper advertisement for the project appealed to women who would have the "opportunity not only to help to maintain your families, but likewise to cast your mite into the treasury of the public good . . . strangers, who apply, are desired to bring a few lines, by way of recommendation, from some respectable person in their neighborhood." Two hundred persons invested in the company at £10 a share. The workers tended 400 spindles in the production of woolens, linen, and cotton cloth.[55]

A *rage-militaire* characterized the emotions of many Americans after Bunker Hill in June 1775. Citizens were eager to take up arms against the proven enemy. Volunteers made up a 15,000 man army besieging Boston. Congress created a Continental army, hoping for 75,000 recruits, a goal never even remotely achieved. An invasion of Canada began, and fighting erupted in Virginia and the Carolinas. The traditional aversion to a standing army persisted, and recruits were hard to find for the Continental army, though many persons were quite willing to engage in short-term militia service. The strict discipline of Washington's new army discouraged recruitment. Congress had to promise pay and bounties, creating a military force not so much out of patriotism as for hire. In spite of the difficulties of keeping a respectable army in the field, the stakes were high. Americans discovered that their lives changed; they were in the midst of war for a long duration, and extraordinary effort was required on the home front and in military service in order to achieve victory.

CHAPTER TWO

Reinventing the body politic

The civil war that erupted in 1775 progressed into a war for independence. The separation from ties to the British government, evident from the creation of the extra-legal local committees, provincial conventions and assemblies, and a Continental Congress, necessitated a transformation of the colonies into states. As Thomas Paine's *Common Sense* stated, it was an absurdity for a people, three thousand miles distant, to give allegiance to a monarchy that made war upon them or seem to support what was perceived as a decadent, corrupt political system of the mother country.

Responding to a petition for advice of October 18, 1775 from the New Hampshire convention, Congress, two weeks later, recommended to the colony's citizens that they arrange for "a full and free representation of the people" in assembly to "establish such a form of government, as, in their judgment, will produce the happiness of the people, and most effectually secure peace and good order in the province" during the duration of "the present dispute between Great Britain and the colonies." The next day the same invitation was extended to South Carolina, and on December 4 also to Virginia, where the royal governor, Lord Dunmore had declared martial law.[1] John Adams greeted Congress's decision with enthusiasm:

> Who expected to live and see the Principles of Liberty Spread and prevail so rapidly, human Nature exerting her whole Rights, unshackled by Priests or Kings, or Nobles, pulling down Tyrannies like Sampson, and building up what Governments the People think best framed for human Felicity.[2]

The remote possibility of reconciliation lingered until spring 1776. As the moment for declaring independence neared, Congress, recognizing that "the exercise of every kind of authority under the said crown should be totally suppressed," forthrightly in resolutions of May 10 and 15 called upon all colonies to establish state governments.[3] "A Revolution in Government" was "about to take Effect," wrote Congressman Oliver Wolcott of Connecticut; "There will be an instance Real not implyed or Ideal, of a Government founded in Compact, Express and Clear Made in its Principles by the People at large."[4]

While the Declaration of Independence prodded the American people into a common crusade and to lay claim to a new nation among nations, the challenge presented itself of reinstituting the body politic expressive of the liberties of the people. Americans could clear the government slate and establish a political order more to their liking than the one they had repudiated. "Few opportunities have ever been offered to mankind of framing an entire Constitution of Government, upon equitable principles," an anonymous writer noted in March 1776. "Perhaps America is the only country in the world wholly free from all political impediments, at the very time they are under the necessity of framing a civil Constitution."[5]

A New Social Contract

True to Lockean principles, American Revolutionary leaders believed in the right of a community to reinvent government from the foundations of an existing one. Government was to be instituted, not imposed. While the American Revolution went beyond John Locke's bloodless Glorious Revolution and severed all connections with the governmental superstructure, in reality the situation was much the same. The rebels merely had to reaffirm the best parts of their colonial constitutions, shearing them of royalist and other prerogative trappings. The Revolution meant that the colonists could proceed with an already established consensus regarding the viability of representative government.

The Massachusetts Constitution of 1780, which became the model of other states and even the national government for revising their constitutions, in its preamble defined a new social contract resulting from justifiable revolution, principles already announced in the Declaration of Independence. On revolution:

> The end of the institution, maintenance, and administration of government, is to secure the existence of the body politic, to protect it, and to furnish the individuals who compose it with the power of enjoying in safety and tranquillity their natural rights, and the blessings of life; and whenever these great objects are not obtained, the people have a right to alter the government, and to take measures necessary for their safety, prosperity, and happiness.

20

On the social compact:

> The body politic is formed by a voluntary association of individuals: it is a social compact, by which the whole people covenants with each citizen, and each citizen with the whole people, that all shall be governed by certain laws for the common good. It is the duty of the people, therefore, in framing a constitution of government, to provide for an equitable mode of making laws, as well as for an impartial interpretation and a faithful execution of them; that every man may, at all times, find his security in them.[6]

Americans preferred to put their full trust in the legislatures as the repository of the will of the people, while recognizing a need for minimal checks and balances on the lower houses of assembly by an upper house and an executive branch; the idea of an independent body, such as the judiciary, to decide on the constitutionality of laws was not yet generally accepted. There was an overriding fear of power distancing itself from the people, as the colonists had thought to have been the case in their relationship to the British crown and parliament. Patriot leaders felt compelled to cast about for a simple and refined political system that had guarantees for government to be held to constant accountability by the people, yet one that would not fall victim to the manipulations of powerful factions. A new contractual relationship between those who governed and the people would ensure safety for expression of the popular will. "A civil constitution or form of government," so read a resolution of the freemen of Lexington, Massachusetts, "is of the nature of a most sacred covenant or contract entered into by the individuals which form society."[7]

The most important ingredient of a new social contract was the preservation of the principle of popular sovereignty. Various writings as well as county instructions to delegates to the provincial congresses or conventions charged with the formation of state constitutions stressed the requirement to keep ultimate power with the people at large. "The people best know their own wants and necessities, and therefore are best able to rule themselves," advised the anonymous author of *The People are the Best Governors* (1776). "The more simple, and the more immediately dependent . . . the authority is upon the people the better, because it must be granted that they themselves are the best guardians of their own liberties."[8] Another anonymous writer of 1776 noted that the best government is that "which is most natural, easy, cheap, and which best secures the rights of the people."[9] It was important that the people themselves have the ultimate authority to make any corrections in government. The writer of "Four Letters on Interesting Subjects" (1776) wanted an elected "Provincial Jury" to have power to correct any "inroads" on a constitution, "but not to make alterations, unless a clear majority of all the inhabitants shall so direct."[10]

21

At the outset of constitution-making, Americans considered their choices for government as one that was republican, with indirect checks on the electorate, or a purely democratic solution. They rejected what they viewed as the only other alternatives—aristocracy, monarchy, or despotism. John Adams, who admired the checks and balances of the Massachusetts colonial government under a royal charter, strongly advocated republicanism and feared that state constitution-making would not go far enough in that direction. "The new governments we are assuming," he wrote to his wife in July 1776, "will require a Purification from our Vices, and an Augmentation of our Virtues or they will be no Blessings. The People will have unbounded Power. And the People are estreamly addicted to Corruption and Venality."[11] Carter Braxton advised his fellow delegates of the Virginia Convention, as they prepared to establish a constitution, that "however necessary it may be to shake off the authority of arbitrary British dictators, we ought, nevertheless, to adopt and perfect that system which England has suffered to be grossly abused, and the experience of ages has taught us to venerate." A "simple Democracy" existed only in theory and was "never confirmed" by experience.[12]

Americans, however, did use the term democracy to convey the meaning of the people's participation in government in an orderly way, as contrasted to mobocracy. A writer in the *Providence Gazette* of August 9, 1777 simply viewed democracy as a "form of government where the highest power of making laws is lodged in the common people, or persons drawn out from them." As formerly good Britons, American patriots, the more so those who already were ensconced in positions of leadership and social distinction, were apprehensive of entrusting too much power to the people at large, which might cause further revolutionary tendencies that would threaten social stability and property rights.

Thomas Paine, in his *Common Sense* of January 1776, called attention to the conception of republican government. To Paine, the "corrupt influence of the crown" had "eaten out the virtue of the house of commons" (the "republican part" in the British constitution). "It is the republican and not the monarchial part of the constitution of England which Englishmen glory in, viz. the liberty of choosing an house of commons from out of their own body—and it is easy to see that when the republican virtue fails, slavery ensues."[13]

American leaders began to perceive republicanism as a grade above democracy. Paine's *The Rights of Man* (1792) referred to republicanism as government designed to serve the "public good" and which "most naturally associates with the representative form." Although Paine favored a pure democracy, he recognized it was only feasible for small populations, and was "incapable of extension, not from its principle, but from the inconvenience of its form." Although Paine went further than most of his contemporaries in wanting to keep the state governments more directly responsible to the people, chiefly through unicameral legislatures, he appreciated the republicanism of the US Constitution: "By ingrafting representatives upon democracy we arrived at a system of government capable of embracing and confederating all the various interests and every extent of territory and population."[14]

A republic, from the Latin *res publica* (public affairs), was viewed more as an ideal than as a specific prescription for government. Generally the Revolutionary leaders sought to incorporate in their new governments three republican features: rule by the people within the bounds of laws, political virtue, and representation. To John Adams republican government was one "of laws, and not of men" and also "whose sovereignty is vested in more than one person."

As justification for a Revolutionary War, it was incumbent on political leaders to reconstruct governmental institutions on the principle of self-determination. A rule of laws and dedication to republican virtue would channel the people's will toward securing liberty and promoting public happiness.

Republican Constitutions

The Revolution would be consummated by the establishment and success of new governments. Reflecting the goal of the Revolutionary War to recover fundamental liberties, the new state constitutions recognized the people as the one source of power. As the New York Constitution of 1777 stated: "No authority shall, on any pretence whatever, be exercised over the people or members of this State, but such as shall be derived from and granted by them." Americans experimented with a principle new in history—government formed by constituent assemblies.

A constitution created by a people in special convention and ratified by the people at large was to become the hallmark of the American contribution to the process of government-making, although such development came gradually. Connecticut and Rhode Island continued to use their colonial charters, which had granted virtually complete autonomy. For the period of 1776–83, except for the Massachusetts Constitution of 1780, all of the new constitutions were adopted by existing legislatures, provincial congresses, or colony conventions during the regular course of legislation or by special constitutional legislative sessions. Four state constitutions went into effect before the Declaration of Independence: New Hampshire, January 16, South Carolina, March 26, Virginia, June 29, and New Jersey, July 2, 1776. By the summer of 1777 all the other states, including the territory of Vermont, except Massachusetts had finished the task of putting constitutions into place.

After a Massachusetts constitution framed by the House of Representatives in 1778 went down in resounding defeat by a colony-wide vote of 9,972 to 2,083, the legislature eventually called for a special constitutional convention, with its delegates to be selected by the freemen of the towns. The new constitution, prepared by 300 delegates, was ratified by a requisite two-thirds votes of the freemen, who balloted on each part of the constitution. With approval by the popular referendum, the Massachusetts constitution went into effect on June 15, 1780. The whole process established the principle that fundamental law must be separate from statute law. After the Revolution, other states, revising their constitutions, followed the example of Massachusetts.

The new constitutions sought to promote direct rather than virtual representation and to curb any despotic tendencies such as the colonists had experienced under the British parliament. To deter aggrandizement of power into the hands of a few, the new constitutions provided for frequent elections, tenure restrictions, and prohibition of plural office-holding. All legislatures were elected directly by the people, and the same for the upper houses (senates) save Maryland, whose senators were chosen by electors voted on in districts by the people. All members of the lower houses of assembly were elected annually, except semi-annually for South Carolina, Rhode Island, and Connecticut. Eight states also provided annual selection of members of the upper house; in South Carolina, Delaware, New York, and Virginia, terms ranged from two to four years.

Minimal checks were placed on the lower houses of assembly. Precipitous action by legislatures could be at least temporarily thwarted by a upper house and an executive (in a few instances). Senates also had legislative authority, but with the important exception of not being able to originate money bills. Pennsylvania had a Council of Censors, consisting of two members from each county, which was to meet every seven years to inquire into the state of the constitution and, if necessary, call a convention for drawing up amendments. The New York Council of Revision (the governor, chancellor, and two judges of the Supreme Court) could veto laws.

By creating weak executives, the constitution-makers indicated that they did not want to be too adrift from the principles of the British political system as they knew it at the time. Except for Pennsylvania, which had an executive of a 12-man council chosen from districts for staggered terms, all states had a governor. Eight governors were elected by the legislature (by joint ballot of both houses in New Jersey, Delaware, Virginia, and North Carolina) and by direct popular vote in New Hampshire, Rhode Island, Connecticut, Massachusetts, New York, and Vermont. In 11 states the governor had no veto, and in three others only a partial veto. Each state had a council to advise the governor. Six governors shared appointive powers with the legislatures. New York had a Council of Appointment, consisting of the governor and four senators who were selected by the lower house.

Legislatures elected the judiciary, except for Pennsylvania, where they were appointed by the Executive Council, and Maryland, where they were named by the governor with the consent of the Council. Judges served fixed terms in all states except South Carolina which based tenure "during pleasure" of the legislature, and in all states judges could be impeached and removed from office at any time. Despite dependency upon other branches, the idea of a detached judicial authority took hold. The Massachusetts Constitution of 1780 declared that "the legislative department shall never exercise the executive and judicial powers, or either of them; The judicial shall never exercise the legislative and executive powers or either of them: To the end it may be a government of laws and not of men." During the 1780s, Rhode Island, New Jersey, and North Carolina made partial strides in allowing for judicial review, whereby the high court of a state could render judgment as to the constitutionality of any particular legislation.

Besides the limited checks and balances, the constitutions had other conservative features, in the form of some semblance of property requirements for office-holding and the suffrage, for the purpose of involving only solid citizens in the governmental process and to retain a connection between government and the social structure. A governor had to have substantial property, as high as a value of £1,000 in North Carolina, £5,000 in Maryland, and £10,000 in South Carolina. Property requirements for legislators were about the same as voters, but were higher for persons serving in the senate. The idea of no taxation without representation, which had fueled the Revolutionary movement, and soldiers's claims that they deserved the right to vote were factors that made for liberalizing the suffrage franchise. Property qualifications for voting were reduced in North Carolina, New Hampshire, New Jersey, Maryland, and New York. Most states required a small amount of real estate, as did Virginia with 25 acres improved or 50 acres unimproved lands, or a certain level of property assessment or rent income. Six states dropped the freehold requirement *per se*, and simply allowed voting according to a fixed amount of taxes paid on real or personal property. Even then, exceptions were made; for example, Georgia gave the suffrage to anyone "being of any mechanic trade." In New Hampshire and Pennsylvania, all white adult males who simply paid a poll tax could vote. Although the beginnings were small, Americans during the war years began the march toward eventual universal suffrage.

Guarantee of Rights

Since the revolutionaries had made common cause in protesting against violations by the crown and parliament of basic rights of freeborn Britons, it was a foregone conclusion that provisions for instituting new governments should include guarantees of individual liberties. Eight states affixed bills of rights to their constitutions, and the others contained affirmation of certain common law liberties. Because the constitutions circumscribed the powers of government, there were no long listings of rights. The only rights common to all declarations of rights were trial by jury in criminal cases, the right to bear arms, and the free exercise of religion. Only five states, however, provided for the separation of state and religion. Freedom of the press was proclaimed only in six states.

A declaration of equality found its way into only three constitutions: Virginia, Pennsylvania, and Vermont. The Virginia Declaration of Rights, which was the first of its kind to be adopted by a state and served as a model for other state bills of rights, proclaimed that "all men are by nature equally free and independent, and have certain inherent rights, of which, when they enter into a state of society, they cannot, by any compact, deprive or divest their posterity; namely, the enjoyment of life and liberty with the means of acquiring and possessing property and pursuing and obtaining happiness and safety." The decision by states not to include references to equality in their constitutions was recognition that such provisions did not confer any legal status *per se* and that they might inspire disruption of the social structure.

Virginia's Declaration of Rights, drafted by George Mason, besides delineating the extent and role of government, guaranteed certain liberties, namely: the right to know cause of arrest and to confront accusers and witnesses, no self-incrimination, speedy trial by jury, no excessive bail or fines, no cruel or unusual punishments, freedom of the press, no standing army in peacetime, the right to bear arms in militia service, no general warrants of search and seizure, trial by jury in criminal trials and civil suits, "free exercise of religion, according to the dictates of conscience," and a general guarantee of due process—"no man be deprived of his liberty, except by the law of the land or the judgment of his peers." Notably absent from the Virginia document were the freedoms of speech, assembly, and petition, the rights to counsel, habeas corpus, and grand jury proceedings to bring an indictment, and protections against double jeopardy, *ex post facto* laws, and bills of attainder.[15] A factor in the states not having comprehensive bills of rights was the incorporation into their legal codes of a large measure of the English common law. With the war going on and the continuing problem of enforcing loyalty, states were reluctant to expand protection of freedom of expression beyond its narrow definitions in the common law.

Status and Power

For middle-class Americans the war was one of liberation, opening doors for political access and leadership. During the period leading up to the

Revolution younger and less affluent men had already begun to scale the ladder to political success and to challenge the hegemony of the old colonial elites. During the war itself the transformation became more pronounced. A broader distribution of wealth and population contributed to the change. The entry of many political leaders into national and state military service, whether in the field or the ever expanding staff bureaucracy, and membership in Congress and on the various state naval and war boards siphoned off many persons who would otherwise hold political office. War was a great leveler, presenting opportunities for persons to get ahead in private and political affairs. The ideology of independence sparked concern for the opening of the ranks of power.

High social status did not confer any special quality of character and republican virtue. There was a growing awareness that any industrious and upright citizen had as much claim to political office as did his so-called "betters." A writer in 1776 noted that "the rich and high born are not the monopolizers of wisdom and virtue; on the contrary, these qualities are often to be found among the middling class in every country, who, being less dissipated and debauched than those who are usually called their betters, apply themselves with more industry" and "in reality become better acquainted with the true interests of the society in which they live."[16] Legislatures now seemed to have a plebeian touch. A Virginian observed that the first House of Burgesses under the state's new constitution was "composed of men not quite so well dressed, nor so politely educated, nor so highly born as some Assemblies I have formerly seen."[17]

The proportion of wealthy delegates in the lower houses of assembly decreased dramatically. This change was owing to voters casting off deferential attitudes, the rise in economic station of many Americans, abolition of plural office-holding, creation of many new offices, and most importantly the increased size of membership in the legislatures due to the addition of new representatives from western counties. Jackson Turner Main has calculated the shift in wealth status in the legislatures from the late colonial period to the end of the Revolution. The percentage of wealthy persons in Massachusetts's lower house decreased from 17 percent to 8 percent and the number of the well-to-do from 33 to 17 percent for the period 1765–84. Similar trends occurred in other states; collectively for New Hampshire, New York, and New Jersey, the wealthy declined from 36 to 12 percent and the well-to-do from 47 to 26 percent, and for Maryland, Virginia, and South Carolina, collectively, the wealthy from 52 to 28 percent with the well-to-do, however, rising from 36 to 42 percent. In general, the yeoman-artisan "middle class" formed a majority of members of northern lower houses, and in the South, a strong minority. In the South, while the planter class yielded much power, their numbers decreased as the number of ordinary farmers rose. For example, Main cites a reduction of great landowners in the Virginia House of Burgesses from 60 to 50 percent, while the number of ordinary farmers rose from 13 to 26 percent (for the period 1773–85).[18] The importance of family ties declined. Newcomers to the legislatures nearly always had wide experience in community affairs and as local office-holders.

While senators had to own substantial property in the southern states, the size of individual holdings was much less when measured against that of persons in a similar position, namely the councillors of the prewar period. The change in the complexion of the senates paralleled that of the lower houses of assembly. Of the upper houses during the Revolution, only those of Maryland and South Carolina had a majority of men who were very wealthy. Elsewhere this class formed no more than one-third of members. Pronounced changes were in the kinds of occupations of members and the decline of persons representing old families. Generally, the "better sort"—large landowners, merchants, and lawyers—saw their ranks drastically reduced, being replaced by middle-class farmers. In Revolutionary Massachusetts the Senate had only one-fifth of its members from old families; before the war the council had one-half in this category. In New York the number of members from old families dropped to less than a third. There were more self-made men in the senates: for example, they were one in five of the membership in Massachusetts and even in South Carolina, two-thirds had parents who had not been prominent or were of humble origin. The majority of members of the upper house had fathers who had been ordinary farmers or artisans. One in five of New Jersey senators had started life without property. The effect of the war upon mobility, particularly with persons seeking out new available lands, is indicated by many senators having come from out of state, for example two-fifths of senators in New Hampshire and one of four in North Carolina. As to be expected with the relative social leveling in both houses of assembly in the states, new members had much less education than their predecessors.[19]

The disestablishment of the royal and proprietary governments and the election of state executives either by the legislatures or the people opened the way for persons serving as governors who were less than wealthy. James Kirby Martin has made a comparison of the wealth status of late colonial and Revolutionary executives for six states (Massachusetts, New York, Maryland, Virginia, North Carolina, and Rhode Island), finding that for all, with the exception of Rhode Island, there was a sharp decrease in the number of governors who were very wealthy and a corresponding rise of those who were well to do or were of average wealth.[20]

A new breed of governors emerged during the Revolution, men who had risen through the ranks by political astuteness and ability and who had broad public support. During the colonial period royal governors were usually persons who had influence in the English court and were often in financial trouble, hoping to recover their fortunes in America; 75 of slightly more than one hundred British governors of the North American colonies and the West Indies, 1689–1775, were sons of earls.[21] A small number of colonial governors had been professional military men.

Many new state governors (or presidents) had achieved high office because they had been patriot leaders on the eve of the Revolution and had substantial experience in the legislatures. Some held high rank in the Continental army or the militia. Revolutionary War governors who did military service are noted as follows, along with their gubernatorial terms: Massachusetts—John Hancock, 1780–85 and 1787–93; New York—George Clinton, 1776–95; Virginia—Patrick Henry (briefly a militia colonel), 1776–9 and 1784–6 and Thomas Nelson, 1781; North Carolina—Richard Caswell, 1776–80 and 1784–7, Thomas Burke, 1781–2, and Alexander Martin, 1782–4; and Georgia—John Houstoun, 1778, and George Walton, 1779–80. The "Spirit of '76" thrived long after the Revolutionary War and aided the election of heroes who had fought for independence to gubernatorial posts, most notably John Sullivan in New Hampshire, John Brooks in Massachusetts, Thomas Mifflin in Pennsylvania, William Smallwood in Maryland, Henry Lee in Virginia, and Isaac Shelby and Charles Scott in Kentucky.

A few of the war governors were from the most humble origins. George Clinton, son of an Irish immigrant farmer, went out at age 18 in 1757 as a steward's mate aboard a privateer. George Walton was a carpenter's apprentice. Walton, as did most of the others, found the legal profession the best route to high office. Patrick Henry was a successful country lawyer, and Thomas Burke, an immigrant from Ireland, gave up his medical profession to practise law.

The long-serving governors during the Revolutionary period were also among the most able—George Clinton and William Livingston (New Jersey). Both men expanded the power of their offices as governor and both built up a loyal constituency from the rank and file of voters. Livingston, son of a wealthy New York landowner and educated at Yale, was a veteran in New York's factional politics before moving to New Jersey. Clinton had the first viable party machine, championing when expedient the interests of the numerous small farmers while always looking after the concerns of lawyers and businessmen.

Despite the limits upon their authority placed by the state constitutions, the Revolutionary War governors enjoyed immense prestige. They exercised persuasion to prevail upon citizens to cooperate in the war effort and eased conflict among officials and military personnel. A letter from Colonel William Malcolm to George Clinton on behalf of a soldier stated that the person was in financial straits and "nothing will content him but an application to you, who he imagines knows everything and hath the power to do everything." Another writer referred to Clinton as the "guardian of the rights of the people."[22] No longer having a monarch, Americans viewed their governors as being representative of the people at large and the fountainhead of justice.

An Excess of Democracy

"The revolution has been accomplished," wrote a French traveler in America in December 1780; "it is like a newborn child, which must be nourished and reared." The Marquis de Chastellux feared that the new constitutions were too democratic, especially that of Massachusetts. Every taxpaying citizen "has a right to vote in the election of the representatives who form the legislative body which may be called 'the Sovereign.'" Although most citizens were "equally well-off," in time success in trade and agriculture "will eventually produce inequality in wealth," and hence the "balance of government" can only exist between the two extremes of aristocracy and anarchy.[23] To most Americans, during the war years, their experiments in self-government did not strike a balance in endeavors resulting in the public good. No one seemed pleased. Complaints persisted that the state governments neglected the war effort, recklessly tampered with property rights, enacted burdensome and excessive legislation, placed a dangerous reliance on majority rule, and submitted to the baneful influence of special interests.

The ideas that the new republican governments would continually be vigilant for the public's welfare and elevate only virtuous men to the key responsibilities proved to be illusory. Although men of distinction and ability surfaced in the executive, legislative, and judiciary branches, the nearly all-powerful lower houses of assembly drew from the people at large, who cared little about virtue. Laws were frequently changed. Failures to maintain the public credit diminished confidence in government. Insufficient curtailment of war profiteering aroused indignation among citizens and soldiers alike. The state governments during the war were destitute. Civilian morale was at a low ebb. Political leaders were reluctant to seek feasible remedies. Alexander Hamilton, who was exasperated with the "internal government" of New York, in 1782 complained that "here we find the general disease which infects all our constitutions, an excess of popularity. There is no *order* that has a will of its own. The inquiry constantly is what will *please* not what will benefit the people. In such a government there can be nothing but temporary expedient, fickleness and folly."[24]

Not only was it perceived that the emphasis on equality was the cause of evils in government, but the investment of the legislatures with such comprehensive powers was leading to a despotic rule by an unchecked majority. People felt victimized by the assemblies. James Madison noted several years after the war that the governors of the states were "little more than Cyphers" and that the legislatures were "omnipotent." Thomas Jefferson, in his *Notes on the State of Virginia* (1781), complained that "all the powers of government, legislature, executive, and judiciary, result to the legislative body." The concentration of these powers "in the same hands is precisely the definition of despotic government." Jefferson lamented that

"173 despots [the number of Virginia legislators] would surely be as oppressive as one. . . . An *elective despotism* was not what we fought for."[25]

The formation of political parties, which might have established clear lines of responsibility that was lacking in government, did not materialize. One exception, however, was Pennsylvania, where the Constitutionalists, who wished to retain the state's constitution of 1776, and the Republicans battled it out over issues. Political division overall pitted cosmopolitans versus localists. The former—merchants, large landholders, holders of the public debt, and urban artisans—favored stronger national and state government in order to protect their interests and to stimulate economic progress, while the latter, chiefly subsistence farmers of little education and new to government service, wanted, other than debtor relief and cheap money, the least government possible.

The shortcomings of the new state governments may be charged in a large degree to the wartime conditions, which called for extraordinary measures to harness financial, logistical, and manpower resources. The American Revolutionaries had a double burden: to meet the exigencies of wartime demands and to carry out untried experiments of self-government. After the war it was possible that moderate corrections in the political systems could have solved most problems rather than a rush to revise drastically the state and national constitutions to provide more concentration of power.

The crisis that appeared to exist as the war progressed was that anarchy was afoot and government did not function for the common good. Americans pondered the dilemma: liberty or order. As Edward Rutledge of South Carolina wrote to John Jay not long after the war ended: the people had become "the dupes of a word. 'Liberty' is the motto; every attempt to restrain licentiousness or give efficacy to Government is charged audaciously on the real advocates for Freedom as an attack upon Liberty."[26] David Ramsay, a congressman and Charleston physician, echoed the same sentiment: "This revolution has introduced so much anarchy that it will take half a century to eradicate the licentiousness of the people."[27]

Conservative leaders deprecated efforts by state governments to alleviate the plight of the poor. In all the legislatures "rag-money" groups were successful or struck fear among those who championed sound fiscal measures. George Mason lamented to a fellow Virginian, William Cabell, in May 1783:

Frequent Interferance with private Property & Contracts, retrospective Laws destructive of all public Faith, as well as Confidence between Man and Man and flagrant Violation of the Constitution must disgust the best and wisest part of the Community, occasion a great Depravity of Manners, bring the Legislature into Contempt, and finally, produce Anarchy & public Convulsion.[28]

31

Dillusionment with government further spread because of the multiplication and increase of taxes. Thomas Paine, in his *Prospects on the Rubicon* (1787), stated the obvious: "War involves in its progress such a train of unforeseen and unsupposed circumstances . . . that no human wisdom can calculate the end. It has but one thing certain, and that is increase of TAXES."[29] Tax resistance occurred in many states, with mob outbreaks in 1782–3 against tax collectors in Massachusetts being the most threatening protest. Taxes drained hard money from rural areas, and the situation was scarcely improved when Congress in 1780 prevailed upon the states to allow payment of taxes in specific commodities. It did not seem fair also that military officers at will could impress forage, livestock, and food for army use, giving only certificates which could not be redeemed until after the war. Despite heavy tax burdens, the states always fell short of sufficient revenue. They were often remissive in meeting requisitions placed upon them by Congress, and at the end of the war all Southern states were in arrears on this account.

Interstate rivalries added to frustrations with the new state governments and provided an impulse for a stronger national constitution. States discriminated against each other in trade. All states by 1786, except New Jersey, placed duties upon imports, though most were for the purpose of revenue only. New York, Massachusetts, Pennsylvania, Rhode Island and New Hampshire had tariffs protecting local industries. New York had entrance and clearance fees for goods going through its ports for Connecticut and New Jersey. A few states haggled over their boundaries and navigation privileges on rivers.

Much of the debate over the need for better government shifted to strengthening the Confederation (established March 1781), whether to confer on it extended powers over all matters pertaining to interstate relationships and which in certain areas would function directly upon all American citizens and not through the states. "This is the time of their political probation," declared George Washington in a circular letter to the states on June 8, 1783. "Unless the States will suffer Congress to exercise those prerogatives they are undoubtedly invested with by the constitution, every thing must very rapidly tend to anarchy and confusion."[30]

Besides Washington, nationalists in Congress and others let it be known the need for giving Congress more operable powers, especially with the growing deficiencies in pay and amenities for the soldiers and the disarray of public finances. As early as 1780 Alexander Hamilton called for a convention of delegates from all the states to redress "the evils arising from a want of power in Congress," and even an unlikely prospect, Thomas Paine, in a 1780 pamphlet, *Public Good*, advocated a national constitutional convention "for the purpose of forming a Continental constitution, defining and describing the powers and authority of Congress."[31] The government under the Articles of Confederation, however, would have to serve as a stopgap. Congressman John Mathews of South Carolina, in a letter to Washington of January 31, 1781, commented: "Tho' the powers of the confederation are very inadequate to a vigorous prosecution of the present war . . . it is better to have some authority to regulate us, than, (as for some time past has been the case,) to have none."[32]

What critics of the state constitutions viewed as an excess of democracy was just as evident after the war as during it. In 1787 James Madison presented a ringing indictment of the political systems. The states had failed to comply with Congressional requisitions, encroached upon federal authority by violating treaty powers of Congress, engaged in "unlicensed compacts" among themselves, discriminated in trade, and were deficient in providing guarantees against "internal violence." There was a want of sanctions to Congressional enactments. As to the states, Madison denounced the "multiplicity of laws"—"a nuisance of the most pestilent kind"—and the "mutability of laws," whereby "we daily see laws repealed or suspended, before any trial can have been made of their merits."

Above all Madison criticized majority rule without any checks or balances. Whenever "an apparent interest or common passion unites a majority what is to restrain them from unjust violations of the rights and interests of the minority, or of individuals?" Madison asked. The solution was an "enlargement of the sphere" of government, that of a national government covering a large territory and responsible to a wide constituency. Such a "modification of the sovereignty . . . will render it sufficiently neutral between the different interests and factions, to controul one part of society from invading the rights of another" and also "controul itself, from setting up an interest adverse to that of the whole Society."[33] Madison's prescription became at least a hopeful reality with the revision of the national and some of the state constitutions during the postwar period.

CHAPTER THREE

Loyal Americans

The American Revolution as a civil war meant divided loyalties. There were those Americans who desired to preserve their British citizenship and others who wanted a new political order separate from the mother country. To George Washington the Americans loyal to Great Britain were "Unhappy wretches! Deluded mortals."[1] From the opposite side, British General James Robertson had a similar view. "I never had an idea of subduing the Americans," he said. "I meant to assist the good Americans subdue the bad."[2]

For most of the war those Americans who were thought to be sympathetic to the British cause were referred to by the rebels as tories, royalists, the King's men and the like. Everybody opposed to the Revolution designated themselves as loyalists, and the term gained wide currency after the establishment of the Board of Associated Loyalists in New York in 1780.

Most estimates place one-third of Americans as loyalist, one-third on the fence, to be swayed by whomever was winning, and one-third rebel. Persons who decided to adhere to Great Britain faced ostracism, confinement, civil disabilities, and, on rare occasion, death. The easiest way to avoid detection and punishment was to take the patriot loyalty oath, which could be rationalized as a temporary expedient. If willing to keep to themselves, giving an appearance of being neutral and not aiding the enemy in any way, loyalists experienced relative unmolestation. For overt committal to the British cause there was but little recourse than to flee behind British lines or go into exile.

Choosing Sides

Throughout the colonies a variety of Americans had a predilection to side with the British cause. Individuals committed themselves out of conviction or self or group interest. A quantitative study of personal traits finds certain determinants. In comparison to the revolutionaries, loyalists tended to be older, members of the Anglican Church, more wealthy, holders of better jobs, residents of the east coast who depended on their livelihood from their connections with Great Britain, those who expected gain or protection from crown authority, those who had operations or dealings outside a colony, recent immigrants, those better educated and traveled, those more cosmopolitan in outlook, and those authority-and-order oriented.[3] Yet loyalists came from all walks of life. In Massachusetts, for example, of 300 persons banished in 1778, one-third were professionals, gentlemen, and merchants; one-third farmers; and one-third artisans, laborers, and a few shopkeepers.[4] Benjamin Rush, in 1777, differentiated loyalists according to conduct:

> There were (1) furious Tories who had recourse to violence, and even to arms, to oppose the measures of the Whigs. (2) Writing and talking Tories. (3) Silent but busy Tories in disseminating Tory pamphlets and newspapers and in circulating intelligence. (4) Peaceable and conscientious Tories who patiently submitted to the measures of the governing powers, and who showed nearly equal kindness to the distressed of both parties during the war. . . .[5]

While loyalists were everywhere, they were more concentrated in certain locales, usually in an urban context. Most New Hampshire loyalists were in Portsmouth. In Massachusetts, most were found in the Boston area, a good many of whom were wealthy merchants, whom Anne Hulton described as too "terrified to submit to the Tyranny of that Power they at first set up."[6] In Connecticut, loyalists were strongest in the westernmost seacoast country near New York City. Although Rhode Island, as General Nathanael Greene noted, had "only a shadow" of disaffection, loyalists were concentrated at Newport, which the British occupied from December 1776 to October 1779. Newport was a trade center and a political rival of Providence.

New York had well-defined and substantial sectors of loyalism. Besides New York City, which remained under British occupation during most of the war, loyalists were numerous along both sides of the Hudson River, from New York City to Albany. Such great landlords as Oliver DeLancey, the Van Cortlandts, Roger Morris, and Frederick Philipse held large land grants that had been bestowed by the crown, and their tenants were satisfied with rents that had long been frozen. Tenants of Livingston Manor, also along the Hudson River, were discontented with the feudal status of their leases obtained from the Whig Livingston family. Toryism moved westward along the Mohawk Valley through Albany and Tryon counties. Highland Catholic tenants of Sir John Johnson's estates carried on their traditional loyalty to the British monarchy. Loyalism in New Jersey held sway mainly in the three northern counties across from New York City, and in Pennsylvania, besides Philadelphia there were a substantial number of loyalists among the merchants and farmers in the counties bordering the Delaware River and along the Susquehanna River. Loyalists in Delaware were concentrated in the area between New Castle and Delaware Bay, and in Maryland, at Baltimore and Annapolis.

As to be expected, besides the frontier fringe, Virginia loyalists were most numerous in the port cities of Norfolk and Portsmouth at the mouth of the James River and the towns of Dumfries and Alexandria along the Potomac. Anglican clerics, merchant factors representing British and Scottish firms, and some tidewater gentry mainly formed the small core of Virginia loyalists.

Scottish immigrants scattered throughout North Carolina adhered to the crown chiefly out of fear of losing their lands that had been granted by royal authority and, from past homeland experience, fear of reprisal if they took the patriot side. Highland Scots had recently settled in the Cape Fear Valley and the central piedmont. Wilmington, a commercial port and for a while the staging area for British invasions in the South, had a large number of loyalists. Most of the same situation existed in South Carolina as for recently arrived Scots. Merchants and shopkeepers extending from Charleston to Ninety-Six in the interior provided loyalist support. Both German and Scottish farmers were apprehensive that they might lose their lands which had been obtained from the crown. The majority of Georgia's population of 20,000 had arrived after 1763. Most inhabitants lived in and around Savannah. Loyalists in Georgia were a majority of Scottish natives.

Ideologically loyalists believed that on the bases of mutual interests and a constitutional relationship the colonies belonged in the British empire. Loyalist writers stressed that a negotiated settlement could be easily achieved. But, on the negative side, they disparaged the revolutionaries as reckless, and expected anarchy or mobocracy would result from separation. William Smith, Jr, a New York councillor and later Chief Justice of Quebec, who delayed openly joining the British until 1778, argued that "neither of the contracting parties may dissolve this compact [between the colonists and Great Britain] as long as their joint aim in the union, to wit, their mutual prosperity, can be attained by it."[7]

Samuel Seabury, an Anglican rector in Westchester County, New York expressed a jaundiced view of social unheaval: "If I must be enslaved let it be by a King at least, and not by a parcel of upstart lawless Committeemen. If I must be devoured, let me be devoured by the jaws of a lion, and not gnawed to death by rats and vermin."[8] Peter Van Shaack, a New York lawyer and Whig leader who became a loyalist, feared the Revolution would lead to conditions similar to those of the English Civil War in the seventeenth century. Like others who disavowed independence he felt that the patriots had no concern for the public good and that their leaders only sought political advantage. War and independence, however, tolerated no dissent. A crusade for freedom waged by the majority required conformity, by which the ends justified the means.

The Price of Loyalty

Congress left to the states the treatment of loyalists. Two classes of loyalists were affected. Alien loyalists could be easily detected and deported under the customary rules of war. Ferreting out and controlling the activities and expressed opinions of native loyalists who were citizens of a state posed the greater challenge.

The Declaration of Independence removed any status for neutrality. English and Scottish merchants, as citizens of a country with whom the patriots were at war, had to foreswear allegiance to Great Britain and take an oath of loyalty to a state, or be expelled. The Virginia legislature on December 18, 1776 invoked the Statute Staple of Edward III (1353) compelling aliens with British citizenship to leave the state within 40 days after January 1, 1777. Ironically it was a British law that forced British citizens to leave. Most of the British and Scottish factors departed immediately, but some elected to stay and become staunch patriots, such as James Hunter and Duncan More of Fredericksburg and Robert Allason and John Carlyle of Alexandria. The departure of the British merchant agents created a void, opening up an opportunity for native entrepreneurs.

All state governments required oaths of allegiance and abjuration of crown authority by free males over age 16. The states implemented a congressional resolution that "the most speedy and effectual measures" be taken against any loyalists, such as disarmament, heavy bonds for good behavior, and, if necessary, imprisonment.[9] Town, county, and district committees everywhere directed enforcement. Persons summoned before the committees, who were deemed innocent of disloyalty, were given certificates and discharged. New York's Committee and Commission for Detecting and Defeating Conspiracies, consisting of seven persons, supervised district level boards, which had power of arrest and seizure of evidence and could call upon military assistance. In New York, from 1776 to 1779, 1,000 cases were tried, resulting in 600 persons being paroled on bond, while others were allowed to go into exile, and a few were confined; a number of cases were dismissed upon taking a patriot loyalty oath.

The institutionalized repression of loyalists served to diminish the likelihood of mob behavior, which had resulted in such actions as tarring and feathering, rail-riding, and destruction and theft of property.

Nonjuring loyalists endured civil disabilities. They were barred from office in all states, and disenfranchised in five. In most areas also they were excluded from practicing professions. Nonjurors could not serve on juries, acquire or convey property, inherit land, or travel at will. In extreme cases failure to take an oath led to banishment. North Carolina had a law for expelling nonjurors within 30 days. By an act to enforce "An Assurance of Allegiance and Fidelity" in South Carolina, a person who left the state to avoid subscribing to the oath faced the death penalty for treason if they returned. Nonjurors paid extra taxation. In Virginia they were assessed to double taxes in 1777 and beginning the next year, a treble levy. Thus the Sixth Lord Fairfax, proprietor of the five million acre tract in Virginia's Northern Neck, refused to take the required oaths. But Fairfax, an octogenerian and infirm, was not molested other than paying the tax penalties.

Loyalists who kept quietly to themselves or claimed immunity on account of their religious beliefs in areas where there was absence of military conflict came under little duress. They, however, underwent ostracism and close surveillance from neighbors. Other neutrals and loyalists lived in fear for their lives, and many found it expedient to become refugees behind British lines. In particular, those persons abetting or collaborating with the enemy, actions which constituted treason (see Chapter 4), eventually sought British protection. Most states provided for the death penalty for "adhering to the King of Great Britain." Because the warring armies often covered the same territory and were in close proximity to each other, any excessive bloodletting upon civilians would be counterproductive and provoke retaliation. Thus capital punishment used against loyalists was the rare exception, being reserved selectively for official spies and military defectors engaging in service with the enemy.

Americans who demonstrated loyalty to the British cause by taking up arms or going into permanent exile put their estates in jeopardy. From time immemorial governments have required forfeiture of estates of those committing actions tantamount to treason. The British military began the practice during the Revolution by seizing rebel property in New York City and South Carolina. From the beginning of the war military commanders on both sides seized ships, livestock, and other material used for the war. The American states first hesitantly employed confiscation primarily as punishment, but as the war lengthened, the process became a means to raise revenue for prosecuting the war. Interestingly, property belonging to American rebels was never confiscated in Great Britain.

Although a few states had begun the confiscation of property early in the war, it became a general practice after a Congressional resolution of November 27, 1777, which recommended to the states that they proceed as soon as possible "to confiscate and make sale of all the real and personal estate" of "such of their inhabitants and other persons who have forfeited the same, and the right to the protection of their respective states." The states were advised to invest the proceeds from sales of forfeited property in Congressional loan certificates, "to be appropriated in such manner as the respective states shall hereafter direct."[10] Once engaged in confiscation, however, the states preferred to apply the money gained to their own war debts.

Although everywhere estates of "absconders," those who had fled, were liable to forfeiture, the actual seizure and sale of loyalist property was relatively minimal. Through legal arrangements with kin or friends, loyalists were able to hold on to their estates. In Massachusetts wives and widows left behind could retain up to one-third of the estates of their loyalist husbands. States established commissions of escheators to determine the validity of seized property reverting to the ownership of a state. After a waiting period the escheated property was sold at auction.

Large-scale confiscation occurred in New York. The huge estates of loyalist landlords along the Hudson were seized. The 50,000-acre property in Westchester County belonging to Frederick Philipse, who went into exile, was offered for sale in lots of 500 acres or less, resulting in 287 new owners. The Dutchess County lands of Roger Morris and Beverly Robinson went to 401 tenants who purchased 455 sections of land. Tenants of these New York estates had pre-emptive rights of purchase; unfortunately many of them could not keep up with payments and lost their lands.

Although most states limited the amount of confiscated lands to be purchased by an individual, little redistribution of land from the wealthy to the lower classes occurred. Virginia limited sales to 400-acre tracts, but this requirement was honored more in the breach. For the confiscated property of 117 Virginia loyalists, there were 188 purchasers, with David Ross, a wealthy planter and iron manufacturer who served as the state's commercial agent during the war, acquiring one half of all the confiscated property. Similarly, in Georgia, property of 166 loyalists was sold to 188 persons, with one-third of the estates going to 12 purchasers. In South Carolina the real estate of 237 loyalists was sold in 200–500 tracts; there was no limit to the number of tracts a person could purchase, and some wealthy individuals wound up with large acquisitions of land, as did Benjamin Reynolds, who received 18 tracts. Confiscated estates sold usually at about one-fourth of their actual value. The total of sales from confiscated property in all the states amounted to £5 million. Little hard money was exchanged, as state-issued certificates were accepted toward purchases.

Loyalists under Arms

As the war progressed loyalists played a major role in military activity. The British provincial line, consisting of Americans enlisted on a regular army status, enrolled 19,000 troops (50 units and 312 companies), and another 10,000 served in loyalist militia or "associations."[11] Unfortunately for the British cause, full attempts to organize loyalists for military service came after the war was well underway. British military authorities finally recognized the key to securing territory and ultimate victory depended upon sizeable loyalist military support.

The initial reluctance of the British to engage loyalist troops was owing to various factors: British overconfidence and underestimation of the enemy; expectation of a short war; lack of military experience by loyalist enlistees; prejudice against loyalists achieving regular British military rank; the views of George III, whose approval was required, that incorporating loyalists into the military forces was too costly and would entail after the war provision for half-pay military pensions to loyalist officers. Not until 1779 did provincial officers who served as regulars receive the same pay and pensions as their counterparts in the British army. Shortages of equipment and transport and heavy-handedness of British foraging parties scouring the countryside discouraged enlistment in royal service.

Early British military objectives concentrated on keeping a well trained army in the field and confronting directly Washington's main army. With the British decision to step up a strong offensive and to secure large areas, especially in the South, from 1778 to the end of the war, loyalist military forces became a mainstay of the British campaigns. The hope was a change in the tide of the war favoring the British would further arouse loyalist citizens to arms.

Loyalist provincial corps served in all the colonies and in Canada, Nova Scotia, and the West Indies. The provincial corps were recruited early in the war, mainly from recruits in New York and New Jersey. Six hundred Virginians served with the British army in New York. By 1780, three-fourths of the Americans serving in these units were of European birth. Most effective of the units in the provincial line were the King's Royal Regiment (Edmund Fanning), New York Volunteers (Oliver DeLancey), New Jersey Volunteers (Cortlandt Skinner), Queen's Rangers (Robert Rogers and then John Graves Simcoe), Loyal American Regiment (Beverly Robinson), Royal Greens (Sir John Johnson), Butler's Rangers (John Butler), British Legion (Banastre Tarleton), and, in the South, King's Rangers (Thomas Brown).

One loyalist commander especially stands out. Colonel Beverly Robinson of the Loyal American Regiment might have become a patriot general. The son of an acting governor of Virginia, Robinson was a wealthy planter and friend of George Washington. While serving in the North during the French and Indian War, Robinson met and married Susanna Philipse, daughter of Frederick Philipse, owner of vast lands along the Hudson River. Defying a patriot oath of allegiance he fled to New York City, whereupon he raised loyalist troops, who assisted the British army mainly in attacks on American forts on the Hudson.

Much of the war was fought by militia. Loyalist irregulars joined in all the British campaigns, being particularly effective in New York, New Jersey, Georgia, and the Carolinas. New York frontier settlers aided John

Johnson's and John and Walter Butler's troops and Joseph Brant's Iroquois Indians in scouring the New York frontier. They were also a major factor on the British side at the battles of Oriskany and Bennington. Under commissioned British officers and provided with royal arms, the loyalist militia moved up and down coasts and inland valleys, provoking vengeance by patriot forces.

Loyalist militia conducted raids along the New Jersey coast, constantly engaging American troops. On December 27, 1780 General Henry Clinton established the "Board of Directors of the Associated Loyalists," which sought to provide direction of loyalist groups in their "self-preservation." The Board mainly supervised loyalist militia activity in the New York–New Jersey–Long Island coastal areas.

Provincial units of loyalists were major components of the British campaigns in the South. Colonel Thomas Brown's Rangers, many of whom were recruited from loyalist refugees in Florida, and Colonel Alexander Innes's South Carolina Royalists wreaked havoc in the Georgia–Carolina backcountry. Lieutenant-Colonel Banastre Tarleton's Legion performed valuable service as a detached van of Cornwallis's army despite its disastrous defeat at Cowpens. Both Tarleton's Legion and Lieutenant-Colonel John Graves Simcoe's Queen's Rangers were effective wings of the British army's invasion of Virginia in 1781.

The bitter partisan war that engulfed the Carolinas and Georgia in 1780–82 was largely a conflict engaging militia, irregular bands that were more apt to operate on their own than to assist directly British forces in the field. Carolina loyalist militia had been thoroughly disheartened by the defeat of loyalist militia, two-thirds of whom were Highland Scots of North Carolina, at the battle of Moores Creek, North Carolina, on February 27, 1776 at the hands of a rebel militia force led by Colonel James Moore. The British commitment, however, to an invasion of the South beginning in 1778 brought out a resurgence of local loyalist military participation.

Cornwallis, in command of the British southern invasion, was reluctant to raise "Provincial Troops of Dragoons" to police the interior because this would "open a door to endless applications & jobs, and cost a good deal of money & hurt the recruiting of the infantry."[12] Instead he authorized the collecting of 18 militia regiments constituting a force of 2,500 men. Major Patrick Ferguson, with seven such regiments recruited in the Ninety-Six district, met with total annihilation of his force at the battle of King's Mountain in October 1780. Other militia raised by local leaders were for a while quite successful in holding the rebels at bay, but were eventually beaten in a series of skirmishes. "Bloody Bill" Cunningham recruited a loyalist unit known as the "Bloody Scout," which brought terror and slaughter in Georgia and the Carolinas. Colonels David Fanning and Benjamin Cleveland, among others, with their partisan militia bands fought many small engagements with the rebels.

The Americans who left their homes to enlist in the provincial corps in the regular British military service had protection under the rules of war. The tragedy, however, chiefly in the South, occurred when local citizens, sensing the prospect of British success, turned against their neighbors, committing outrages upon life and property, which was met with by savagery inflicted by rebels by their own intent and in retaliation.

Loyalist Uprisings

While loyalists of western New York, coastal New Jersey, and the back-country of the Carolinas and Georgia took up arms to assist in British military campaigns, others were emboldened to engage in counter-revolutionary military activity in areas isolated from the war. The few loyalist uprisings not integrally connected with British military operations had common denominators in that there was expectation of eventual British assistance, inefficient leadership, and little or no bloodshed.

The landlord–tenant relationship on the great manorial estates along the Hudson River had always been a contentious one. Tenants, questioning the legitimacy of the landlord's holdings, wanted to escape leases and rent and to own their property outright. Riots broke out on the Van Cortlandt and Livingston estates in 1766, requiring militia and British troops to secure the peace. Robert Livingston and Robert R. Livingston, each a proprietor of a part of the 160,000-acre Livingston Manor, were zealous Whigs during the Revolutionary era, a fact that influenced their tenants to side with the British during the war. Tenants thought that a British victory would pave the way for their gaining full title to their lands. A reprise of the 1766 situation erupted in May 1777. Five hundred tenants on the Livingston Manor took up arms, expecting to join forces with General Burgoyne's invading army. Not only did the British army not arrive but the insurgents quickly met opposition from neighboring militia and some New England troops, backed in readiness by soldiers commanded by Generals Alexander McDougall and George Clinton. At the "Battle of Jurry Wheelers" on May 2, 1777 several insurgents were killed, but without loss to the patriots. Militiamen plundered the property of the loyalist tenants. Several hundred insurgents were jailed for a time, and two were executed—Aernour Viele and James Howetson, a retired British officer who had been attempting to enlist a loyalist regiment.[13]

In Sussex County, Delaware, May–June 1776, 1,500 loyalists, in communication with British men-of-war in Chesapeake Bay, took up arms. Congress quickly dispatched troops, and the loyalist resistance dissolved. In May–June 1778 Delaware loyalists led by Cheny Clows built a fort on the Chester River. Other would-be insurgents roamed the Eastern Shore "disrupting government" and seizing arms and supplies. Delaware and

Maryland militia forced the evacuation of the fort. Of those captured, several were sentenced to be hanged, but were pardoned. Clows avoided being apprehended until 1782; the next year he was executed for murder, which many thought had been caused by an accidental discharge of a weapon by another person. Also in Delaware in August 1780 about 400 loyalists, in what is referred to as the Black Camp Rebellion, disarmed patriot patrols. Rebel militia officers were robbed and kidnapped. The incipient rebellion was quickly crushed. Thirty-nine persons were indicted, and eight were sentenced to be hanged and quartered, but all were eventually pardoned. All three Delaware insurgencies had roots in protests against high taxes and intimidating behavior by patriot militia.[14]

Early 1777 500 loyalists of Somerset, Worcester, and Dorchester counties, Maryland, led by Hamilton Coletto, a physician, assembled and proclaimed allegiance to the king. Before any military action could be taken by the group, 200 Continental army troops and Maryland militia appeared. Unwilling to fight, the loyalists abandoned camp on April 10 and scattered. Most of the would-be insurgents surrendered, availing themselves of a pardon if so doing within 30 days. Thirteen captives, however, were imprisoned.[15] In Frederick County, Maryland, during June 1781, John Casper Frietsche, a harness-maker, encouraged by the prompting of an agent who had been sent to Maryland by the Board of Associated Loyalists in New York, went about the countryside trying to foment a loyalist uprising. Patriot militia made arrests, and the plot collapsed. Seven instigators were sentenced to be hanged, drawn, and quartered; four of the sentences were commuted, but Frietsche and two others were hanged.[16]

Many of the pioneer settlers along Virginia's southwestern frontier were loyalists. The population consisted chiefly of newcomers—Germans and recent immigrants from New York, Connecticut, and other eastern regions. Remaining quiet during most of the war, these small farmers became increasingly disgruntled over increased taxes that were to be paid in commodities and the instigation of military conscription. British victories in Georgia and South Carolina stirred them to action. During 1779–80 loyalists attempted to seize the lead mines in Montgomery County. Patriot leaders such as William Preston and William Campbell quickly brought local militia into action to thwart the loyalist's schemes.[17]

These loyalist uprisings all related to genuine grievances or roughshod treatment by patriot authorities. Their spontaneity was their downfall. Loyalists had little time to coalesce into fighting units. Patriot militia rallied to nip these would-be rebellions in the bud.

Diaspora

The war uprooted many Americans. Some 80,000 or more loyalists chose the protection of the crown and went into exile rather than face the stern retribution that awaited them from the watchdog committees, military forces, and fellow citizens. The British provided aid in the relocation of loyalists. A large number of American loyalists were persons who had served in British provincial military units, who expected land grants and pensions.

One half of American refugees settled overseas, and the remainder in Canada, New Brunswick, Florida, or Nova Scotia. New York supplied the largest group of exiles (35,000), with also a sizeable exodus from Massachusetts, Georgia, New Jersey, South Carolina, and North Carolina.

Many refugees from the early part of the war arrived in England, which received a total of 7,000 of these immigrants. Royal placemen, Anglican clergymen, and British citizens were the most likely to find sanctuary in England. The British government offered funds and pensions to loyalists who escaped to England, usually a standard allowance of £100 a year for colonial office-holders and £40–80 for others.[18] Unhappy in England and in search of greater opportunity, many of the refugees in England left for Canada.

Most New York refugees settled in Nova Scotia, New Brunswick (separated from Nova Scotia in 1784), and Canada. In the Deep South, refugees, seeking to replicate the plantation life that they had known, set out for East Florida, the West Indies, the Bahamas, and Bermuda.

The majority of loyalists entered British North America. The infusion greatly expanded the English-speaking population. Institutions could now be Anglicized, such as the establishment of elective assemblies. The loyalists of British North America promoted anti-American attitudes and the strengthening of ties to Great Britain.

By 1791, 25,000 loyalists had settled in Upper Canada (Ontario). Kingston (formerly Fort Frontenac) on the north shore of Lake Ontario received refugees mainly from Pennsylvania, New York, and Vermont. Other loyalists headed for Niagara and Detroit. The British government supplied provisions for three years and farm tools. By 1791 immigrants had taken up 3.2 million acres of land. Ten thousand refugees from the Mohawk Valley settled along the St Lawrence Valley in Lower Canada (Quebec was split in 1791 between Upper and Lower Canada).

Refugees from the evacuation of New York City in late 1783 poured into Nova Scotia. By 1784 there were 28,347 loyalists in the Nova Scotia population of 42,747. Three thousand exiles went to Cape Breton Island, and lesser numbers to Prince Edward Island. Of the Nova Scotia immigration, one-half went to the area of Port Roseway Harbor (Shelburne) and the other half to the mouth of the St John River (New Brunswick); 35 percent came from New York, 30 percent from the South, 20 percent from New England, and 15 percent from the middle states.[19] Ample landgrants were given to military veterans. The newcomers received provisions for one year, and their lands were exempted from quit rents for ten years.

The refugees in Nova Scotia experienced the most difficult times. Food and building materials promised by the British government were inadequate. The too few surveyors delayed land acquisition. Settlers fanned out to new locations. Law and order was a problem. In Halifax alone, in 1785, 20 persons were hanged, most for minor offenses; one black immigrant was executed for stealing a bag of potatoes. Without experience in farming or fishing, the new settlers had little success in obtaining a livelihood. By the mid-1780s many of the refugees left Nova Scotia for Great Britain, the West Indies, or returned to the United States. Storms destroyed the warehouses at Shelburne in 1798, and two years later it was a deserted city. The loyalists (half of whom were soldiers and their families) who settled in New Brunswick succeeded in farming.[20]

The flight of most black refugees had an unfortunate outcome, of freedom promised but denied. Of 50,000 slaves who fled behind the British lines, only 5,000 realized protected liberty. Many died of disease or were abandoned. Loyalist exiles took their slaves with them, with bondage simply a matter of relocation, and British officers, despite such proclamations as Lord Dunmore's in Virginia in 1775 or General Henry Clinton's Philipsburg edict of 1779 which pledged freedom to "every Negro who shall desert the Rebel Standard," often kept slaves as their own property or sold them to slave-owners. Yet many blacks took the road to freedom.

The end of the war saw a large exodus of blacks under British sponsorship. Nearly 6,000 slaves left upon the evacuation of Savannah in summer 1782, and 5,237 later in the year from Charleston. Nearly 5,000 blacks were sent out by the British during the invasion in Virginia leading up to Yorktown. Many slaves accompanied their loyalist masters from South Carolina and Georgia. By 1785, 6,540 slaves had moved with their masters from initial settlement in East Florida to different parts of the West Indies and elsewhere in the Empire.

General Guy Carleton, who had replaced Clinton as the British commander-in-chief in America, from his headquarters in New York City, was determined to honour the pledge of freedom to escaped blacks. An examining committee decided which blacks were free on the basis of the proclamations or as war prizes. Those in the New York City area who had spent a year within British lines were qualified for transport to Nova Scotia. From April through to November 1783, 3,360 such refugees were dispatched to that destination. Most of the blacks wound up at Birchtown (a township of Shelburne), with others going to Halifax, Digby, and other locations. The black communities were segregated from those of the whites. Blacks endured a horrible experience in Nova Scotia. They had to provide public labor to acquire provisions and tools that other settlers received free. The status of the black refugees was hardly more than that of peonage. Black villages were attacked and plundered.

English philanthropists, such as Granville Sharp and others, worked to establish a new homeland for the black Nova Scotians. The Sierre Leone Company was established to create a refugee colony on the west coast of Africa. In early 1792, 15 ships and 1,200 black loyalists departed from Nova Scotia for Africa, where they founded Freetown. The colony of Sierre Leone remained under the authority of the Sierre Leone Company until 1808, when it reverted to the crown.[21]

Compensation

The demonstration of good faith to those Americans who provided services to the British war effort or suffered losses in their adherence to the crown proved to be a costly venture for the British government. Aid for refugee resettlement came at a considerable sum. Special acts of parliament granted relief to loyalists on an individual basis. Pensions totalling £25,785 annually were sent to persons for loss of profession or income. Holders of large proprietary grants obtained partial reimbursement for lands confiscated and loss of rents; for example, the Penn family received £130,000; the trustees for the deceased John Carteret, Earl of Granville, for large landholdings in North Carolina, £40,000; and £13,758 went to the seventh Lord Fairfax, a small pittance for the loss of quit rents (sequestered by the state and abolished three years later) and control over ungranted lands of the Northern Neck Proprietary in Virginia.[22]

Five hundred officers of loyalist regiments received half-pay for life. Loyalist militia officers, however, with only a few exceptions, were denied this pension. The granting of military pensions stirred criticism because recipients included those who were commissioned but did not serve and persons who claimed activities unrelated but equated with military service.

In 1783 parliament established the Commission of Enquiry into the Losses, Services, and Claims of the American Loyalists. Eligibility for compensation rested primarily on claimants being able to show that they were "deprived of the means of subsistence by the loyal part they took in the Contest, and being thereby reduced to present distress." Claimants had to present documentary proof from patriot government or military records and depositions of witnesses to the depredations that they suffered. The great difficulty and cost of obtaining the required evidence deterred many persons from applying. The Commissioners carried on investigations until 1788, conducting hearings in London, Halifax, St Johns, and Montreal. Of £10,358,413 in total claims from 3,225 applicants, £3,033,091 was awarded toward the claims of 2,291 persons. Fifty-five percent of the compensation was in amounts of £1,000 or less. The commissioners were not very charitable toward the black applicants, only one of whom received any compensation for property loss, and several others gained annual incomes of only £5–20; the commissioners felt most blacks "gained their Liberty . . . instead of being Sufferers." Half of the claim applicants were farmers or plantation owners; 30 percent were merchants, storekeepers, or artisans; 10 percent were professionals, chiefly lawyers, doctors, or clergymen; another 10 percent were office-holders. Of the 3,225 applicants 468 were women.[23]

The Treaty of Paris ending the American Revolution called upon Congress to recommend that the states engage in no further confiscation of loyalist estates and return seized property or give compensation for it. Furthermore, "no lawful impediment" should be placed by the states for recovery of property. Congress, on January 14, 1784, requested the states to restore all properties and rights of loyalists. But state legislatures did not comply, citing war damages committed by British military forces and, for the southern states, the failure of the British government to offer indemnification for slaves who went off with the British. From New England to the Carolinas, especially embittered backcountry patriots supplied the pressure that prevented the free return of loyalists and the making of amends for confiscation. Several states passed trespass or new banishment laws affecting loyalists who sought to return and closed courts to litigation for recovery of sequestered property. In every state provisions of the treaty were ignored.[24]

By 1787 the states had repealed laws prohibiting the return of loyalists. Although confiscation laws were not repealed, some states, especially South Carolina, allowed legal action selectively on behalf of certain individuals to obtain compensation for loss of property.[25]

The war had caused the loyal Americans deprivation and severe stress that made them refugees from their homeland. In exile, the bitterness would be long-lasting. In the United States, however, by the 1790s differences were put aside, and many former loyalists not only had recovered full citizenship and social acceptance but also had achieved prominence in service to the new Republic.

CHAPTER FOUR

Constraints on liberty

The emergency conditions of wartime and the decision for independence tested the liberties that Americans had secured under their colonial governments and the British Constitution. During the war period, however, the states' legal systems were essentially identical with those of the colonial past. Significant reforms did not occur until after the war. Legal principles and procedures reflected British common law usage, and the states, as did the Pennsylvania legislature expressly, on February 11, 1777, allowed continuance of British statute law specifically relating to the colonies as long as it posed no conflicts with independence.[1]

In the prosecution of the war, the American revolutionaries did not seek to recast definitions of treason and sedition. The realities of a civil war, with citizens of different persuasions in areas controlled by one or the other contending armies, necessitated the mitigation of severity of punishments, otherwise there would have been an endless bloodbath of retaliation. The greatest abridgement of rights came during the first year of the war from governmental authority exercised by makeshift committees of safety, extra-legal provincial conventions and congresses, and implementation of martial law. Still, even when the Declaration of Independence put an end to the temporary governments, the regularly constituted authorities experimented to some extent with measures infringing upon civil liberty. But, in most instances the bark was larger than the bite. What is significant, however, is the rarity and selectiveness in repression of civil liberty. On the other hand, community ostracism, vigilantism, and military surveillance provided effective checks upon those who were disaffected.

Due Process

The war here and there brought sporadic encroachment upon substantive and procedural rights of the individual. Emergency measures, however, had impact on legal systems only in the short run.

Persons banished usually could dispose of their property before leaving.[2] Under the forfeiture laws, seized property was disposed of through a drawn-out process of *office found*, which through legal process established abandonment.

Anyone arrested on suspicion of disloyal activity generally had the privilege of posting bail until adjudication of his or her case. Upon a hearing or a trial, frequently surety bonds were deemed adequate to ensure that a person would not indulge in anti-Revolution expressions or conduct.

Persons were held incommunicado in order to deter their potential for giving aid to the enemy. The New Jersey Council of Safety traveled about the state, investigating alleged disloyalty and ordering sheriffs and militia to make arrests. Those at-risk loyalists were confined without bail at jails in parts of the state remote from the enemy. At Morristown, in July 1777, the Council of Safety directed the arrest of 48 persons in one day. Eventually courts disposed of the cases.[3] The New York committee "for detecting and defeating conspiracies" performed much in the same manner as the New Jersey Council of Safety, although it actually conducted trials and sentencing.[4] In Massachusetts, the Council had authority to issue warrants to arrest loyalists and to confine them to jail without bail until released by the Council.[5] During the British invasion of Virginia in 1781, Governor Thomas Jefferson ordered imprisonment of such persons in Gloucester and York counties suspected of committing treason or who were "disaffected to the Independence of the United States." The detention lasted for the duration of the emergency.[6] In confining loyalists for periods of time, a writ of habeas corpus was often bypassed. In the specific instance of apprehending Quakers in Philadelphia, the Pennsylvania legislature, on September 16, 1777, passed a law denying habeas corpus for the prisoners; even though the legislation violated common law protection and was also *ex post facto*, the Supreme Executive Council of the state upheld it as proper wartime measure.[7]

Governments during wartime always exercise authority to marshal resources required of armies. Congress and the states permitted impressment of goods from local citizens for an army's survival, followed by promise of reimbursement. The common law protections against invasion of privacy and use of property without consent, even the disposition of one's own dwelling space, was subjected to military priorities. Although the resistance to the British quartering acts was still fresh in their minds, the American leaders provided for requisition of billeting officers in private homes (see Chapter 6). Normally in warm weather when armies were in active campaigns, tents sufficed for officers and men alike. For army encampments at Valley Forge, Morristown, and elsewhere, officers sought quarters in homes of local residents.

Most citizens willingly let out rooms in their homes for officers' lodgings (according to British practice several rooms were required for generals). Where there was resistance to a request Congress and the states empowered military commanders, particularly Washington, to call on local magistrates to order appropriation of lodging space, which normally was forthcoming. An example of a state conferring authority for requisitioning quarters is a New Jersey enactment of March 24, 1778, which stated that with other space lacking a justice of the peace could "quarter and billet the remaining part in Dwelling-houses, Barns, and other Out-houses of such Persons in his Neighbourhood;" it was also "lawful for the commanding Officer of any small Detachment, or scouting Party, in Cases of Emergency to quarter and billet, *for a short Space of Time*, such Detachment or Scout in any Houses or Buildings as aforesaid."[8]

In December 1779, Nathanael Greene, serving as quartermaster-general for Washington's army, had difficulty in obtaining cooperation from Benjamin Lindsley, a justice of the peace in Morris County, for securing quarters for officers. Greene reminded Lindsley that as a last resort, the army could make use of quarters in the houses even without the consent of owners. The issue, however, became moot as Washington's officers found at least cramped lodgings.[9] On various occasions, dwellings were seized for officer billeting without consent, especially involving the property of Quakers and loyalists.

Bills of attainder (later forbidden to Congress and the states by the US Constitution) were passed by eight state legislatures. Although the process was used to attaint persons for the purposes of banishment and seizure of their property, normally bills of attainder were intended for legislative pronouncement of guilt of treason or other felonies upon designated individuals, carrying the death penalty and forfeiture of property. Four states enacted absolute bills of attainder, which allowed for no recourse through the judicial system, and four others provided trial by courts if the attainted person surrendered within a certain time period. The Massachusetts constitution forbade bills of attainder, and the New York constitution allowed them only during wartime.[10] Only one person was executed under a bill of attainder; the culprit had been a fugitive and had refused a court trial. In Virginia Josiah Phillips (see Chapter 5) was attainted for treason by the legislature; upon capture, however, he was tried by a court and convicted and hanged for murder rather than treason. The sparse use of bills of attainder was owing to their obvious violation of constitutional principles and fundamental liberty: nullification of separation of powers, *ex post facto*, double jeopardy, and denial of trial by jury.[11]

The states also used sparingly special courts of oyer and terminer. These tribunals heard cases that would normally be tried before a supreme

51

court of a state or colony. The oyer and terminer courts had no jury, and the judges were selected from the justices of the peace in the jurisdiction where the case was tried or from persons "learned in the law." At least four states authorized the use of oyer and terminer courts in treason cases. Adopted from English practice the special tribunals had been used during the colonial period, most notably in the condemnation of the Salem witches in 1692 and Jacob Leisler and Jacob Milborne for treason in New York in 1691. New Jersey used this method, as did Virginia, to prosecute many persons for treason at the end of the war. Virginia had long conducted slave trials in courts of oyer and terminer (in the deep South slave courts were similar). There was a reluctance of persons to serve on courts of oyer and terminer, not so much because they resembled Star Chamber justice of the Tudor and early Stuart monarchs in England, but because of resentment against the members of the supreme courts neglecting their duties by passing the troublesome cases to the local jurisdictions.[12]

Since the British army considered that the Declaration of Independence abrogated the judicial systems of the colonies it established martial law in areas under its sustained control. Six cities experienced British martial law: Boston, June 1775 to March 17, 1776; New York City, September 15, 1776 to November 25, 1783; Newport, Rhode Island, December 8, 1776 to October 26, 1779; Philadelphia, September 27, 1777 to June 18, 1778; Savannah, December 29, 1778 to July 11, 1782; and Charleston, South Carolina, May 12, 1780 to December 14, 1782. The Courts of Police in New York City exercised administrative and ordinance-making power as well as judicial authority.[13]

The revolutionary governments allowed military tribunals to try treason cases. The New York Provincial Convention required a review of treason convictions by courts-martial. It upheld the execution of 14 of the 17 persons condemned by courts-martial convened by Continental army generals Alexander McDougall and George Clinton and militia general Peter Ten Broeck.[14] In the bitter partisan warfare in the Carolinas of 1780–2, rebel drumhead courts-martial resulted in the summary execution of a number of loyalist militia prisoners of war, including nine captives at Bickerstaff's, North Carolina after the battle of King's Mountain in October 1780, and three persons were hanged from Rebecca Motte's gate by troops commanded by Lt.-Col. Henry Lee on May 12, 1781.[15]

Internment

Many persons during the war were not free to move about as they pleased. Prisoners of war on both sides, as terms of parole, were often required to reside in certain prescribed areas. Those of suspected loyalty had to stay in the immediate vicinities of their homes so as not to contaminate other citizens with their wrong-headed views or participate in a wide network of subversive activity. Of course, many loyalists were forced into exile. In war zones there were tight regulations affecting egress to and from enemy lines. In all, a substantial population endured restriction of their freedom of mobility.

Congress, from the start of the war, entreated states and localities "to arrest and secure" every person "whose going at large . . . may . . . endanger the safety of the colony, or the liberties of America."[16] States required persons moving about to carry a certificate attesting to their loyalty issued by some governmental authority such as Congress, a committee of safety, a local magistrate, or a military officer, and also indicating "whence he came and whither he was going." Innkeepers and the like could be fined for not asking patrons to show travel certificates. In Pennsylvania a newcomer without a certificate was taken to the nearest justice of the peace to swear an oath of allegiance; if he refused he was jailed without bond until he did.[17]

Primarily for military security, state governments required persons of suspected loyalty, such as neutrals, to remove a distance from their neighborhoods if located in war zones. The sending of loyalists to other states did not elicit goodwill from the receiving neighborhoods. During the early part of the war New York sent away loyalists for detention in Connecticut, Pennsylvania, Massachusetts, and New Hampshire; New Jersey exiled loyalists to Connecticut. Especially prominent loyalists were exiled out of state. Thus Peter Van Schaack, a leading New York lawyer and patriot-turned-loyalist, for refusal to take the requisite oath of allegiance, was packed off to Boston, eventually paroled to his home at Kinderhook, and, under the New York Banishing Act of 1778, forced to leave for England. Governor William Franklin of New Jersey and David Mathews, former mayor of New York City, were confined for two years at Litchfield, Connecticut. Some of the more dangerous out-of-state loyalists were incarcerated with Connecticut's "atrocious villains" in the abandoned copper mines at Simsbury, ten miles northwest of Hartford; the prisoners there made three spectacular escapes (1776, 1777, and 1781) during fires they set at the blockhouse over the prison's entrance.[18]

In 1776, with so many inhabitants on Long Island, especially in Queen's County, deemed "incapable of resolving to live and die freemen" and "inactive spectators," the New York Provincial Congress arranged with the authorities of several Connecticut towns to receive such persons; expenses for removal were to be paid by the New York government. Towards the end of the war the refugees were allowed to return. Their lot had been an unhappy one; the New York government only provided a small part of the compensation promised to aid in resettlement, and their properties on Long Island had been wasted chiefly by British military forces.[19]

Virginia interned prominent persons of suspected loyalty in western parts of the state, and once attempted en masse evacuation of two tidewater counties. The efforts were in response to the presence of a military force commanded by Lord Dunmore, Virginia's royal governor, in the lower Chesapeake Bay area. Dunmore actively recruited from native Virginians and slaves and ordered inhabitants to swear allegiance to the crown. Virginia authorities also feared that, with an anticipated Declaration of Independence soon to go into effect, a full-scale invasion of the new state would ensue. Certain Virginia leaders of questionable loyalty were ordered to depart from their homes. Ralph Wormeley, Jr of "Rosegill" in Middlesex County was caught in the removal net. One of the wealthiest planters and a member of the Virginia Council, 1771–5, Wormeley had written to his friend, John Randolph Grimes, who was in active service with Dunmore; the letter was intercepted, and the Virginia Committee of Safety decided that in it Wormeley exhibited an "inimical disposition" and a readiness to join the enemy. On May 15, 1776 the Virginia Convention ordered that Wormeley be confined to the far northwestern part of Virginia at Berkeley County where he had a plantation and that part of his father's estate in Frederick County, under £20,000 bond not to go beyond these limits. Not until 1778 was Wormeley released from these restrictions.

To further deny Dunmore's invading army an opportunity to capitalize on disaffection, the Virginia Committee of Safety, on April 10, 1776, directed "all the inhabitants of Norfolk and Princess Anne counties, at present residing between the enemy and our posts at Great Bridge and Kemp's Landing, and in a direct line from Kemp's Landing to the ocean be immediately removed to some interior parts of this colony." As John Augustine Washington put it, this meant "both friends & Enemies except such as are immediately under the protection of our troops" to move at least 30 miles from the enemy into the interior. Even women and children were included in the evacuation order because they "had learn'd the art and practic'd with address the Office of Spies." The Virginia Convention, on May 10, endorsed the order, and voted £1,000 to assist poor people in the removal and another £20,000 to provide material support to the refugees until they could produce corn. Because of the hardships and the costs, the evacuation policy was barely implemented. The removal order was soon amended to apply only to "all Enimical persons among which Neutrals are considered, and all such slaves of Military age whether belonging to Friends or Enemies." All livestock, however, had to be put out of Dunmore's reach. At the end of May, as Dunmore's little army and fleet cleared out of the Elizabeth River and Norfolk area, the evacuation order was rescinded. Virginians gave a sigh of relief when Dunmore's force completely left the state in August 1776. Faced with a similar invasion threat four years later as the war turned to the South, the Virginia Assembly conferred upon Governor Thomas Jefferson and the Council the authority to remove all such persons as they might decide in the event of a British invasion.[20]

As General William Howe's army in late August 1777 prepared to attack the rebel capital, Philadelphia, Congress advised the Pennsylvania and Delaware executives that all persons who were "notoriously defected" should be apprehended and secured until "such time as the respective states think they may be released without injury to the common cause." In accordance with this recommendation, the Supreme Executive Council of Pennsylvania ordered the arrest of 41 persons, mostly Quakers who were prominent merchants, and Congress directed that they be removed to Staunton, Virginia.[21] Despite petitions by the prisoners to Congress and the Pennsylvania government that the removal order was "arbitrary" and "illegal" and demanding a fair trial, 20 of the detainees, 17 Quakers and three Anglicans, were loaded into wagons and under guard made their way to Virginia, the destination now having been changed to Winchester. A mob pelted the group with stones as it passed through Reading. The detainees in Winchester were permitted to walk in part of the town during daytime. Congress refused to take charge of the prisoners, and in April 1778 the Pennsylvania Council ordered them to Lancaster, Pennsylvania, where they were soon released. The Pennsylvania government, however, required that the prisoners pay all expenses incurred by their arrest, detention, and "journey."[22]

Treason and Sedition

Citizens had to be careful that any of their actions could not be construed as giving aid and comfort to the enemy. Wartime bred measures to hold persons accountable for any behavior or expressions detrimental to the American cause.

The first legislation for the punishment of treason, in Congress' Articles of War, June 30, 1775, applied only to military personnel; no death penalty was provided. As the war became even more a reality, the need for treason laws affecting civilians was evident. The only such laws on the books, from colonial times, extended to treason against the king; now, in the irony of civil war, aid to the British sovereign itself was treason.

Two episodes early in the war dramatized the insufficiency in law that existed in punishing treasonable acts committed by citizens of the new United States. Dr Benjamin Church, chief surgeon of the army and a member of the Massachusetts House of Representatives, was detected acting as an informer for the British commander-in-chief in America, Thomas Gage. Although lacking authority to do so, Congress had Church jailed, and then, not knowing what else to do, permitted Church to go into exile; on his way to the West Indies Church perished in a shipwreck. The case of Thomas Hickey, a member of Washington's Life Guard, who was convicted by a court martial and hanged for "Sedition and mutiny, and also of holding a treacherous correspondence with the enemy," brought to light the complicity of David Mathews, mayor of New York City, and five other civilians. Nothing could be done with these culprits until after the Declaration of Independence and New York had a new treason law; this being the case in July 1776, the civilian traitors were sent to imprisonment in Connecticut.[23]

Congress, on June 24, 1776, recommended that the states enact treason laws, which should provide punishment for "all persons, members of, or owing allegiance to any of the United Colonies" who levied war against any one of the states, adhered to the "King of Great Britain, or others the enemies of the said colonies," or gave aid and comfort to the enemy.[24] By the end of 1777 most states had in place treason statutes that carried a death penalty. Congress persuaded the states to require the traditional colonial-English rule of two witnesses to an overt act for conviction of treason. Since, as Bradley Chapin has noted, a person convicted of treason is "civilly dead," the states confiscated property of persons judged to be traitors. Several states, however, prohibited "corruption of Blood," which prevented a person attainted with treason from transmitting property to heirs, and instead allowed for a widow's dower rights and provision for dependents.[25]

The states' courts accounted for only a few executions for treason. Courts-martial meted out the death penalty for a number of persons accused of treasonable activities, usually in the form of spying, desertion to the enemy's army after having been sworn into American military service, or aiding the enemy in areas under military jurisdiction. The states also preferred to exact the death penalty for crimes such as murder, burglary, kidnapping, counterfeiting, and the like, even though compounded with treason, rather than solely for treason. Of the 48 persons hanged for offenses other than treason in Pennsylvania, 1778–83, many could have been brought to trial for treason.[26]

Only one person, under sentence from a state court, was executed for treason in New England. Moses Dunbar went to the gallows on March 19, 1777 in Hartford for joining the British army, enlisting others to do so, and giving intelligence to the enemy.[27] Other than the military executions, four were executed for treason in Pennsylvania, and probably the same number in New York.[28]

Blood purges for treason almost erupted in New Jersey, Pennsylvania, and Virginia. A court of oyer and terminer at Morristown, New Jersey, in November 1777, sentenced 35 persons to death for treason. Two men, James Iliff and John Mee, were actually executed (December 2). The others received pardons conditional upon their enlisting in the Continental army.[29]

In Pennsylvania, 1778–81, eight proclamations of the Supreme Executive Council attainted 489 persons with treason, 80 percent of them for the period of the British occupation or immediately afterwards. Having already fled behind British lines, 386 of those cited did not appear to defend themselves in court. Only 16 of the 113 who surrendered came to trial, three of whom were sentenced to death. One of the three was pardoned due to insanity. Those who were hanged were Quakers: Abraham Carlisle and John Roberts. The former had served as a gatekeeper for Philadelphia during the occupation, and Roberts had recruited for the British army. Despite the fact that ten of the jury recommended mercy for Roberts and all of them for Carlisle, and that nearly 500 petitioners had appealed for clemency for the two men, the Supreme Executive Council denied pardon, and Carlisle and Roberts were executed on November 4, 1778. The Supreme Executive Council was determined to make examples of the two men in order to terrorize Quakers and others who might be tempted to collaborate with the enemy. Over 4,000 Philadelphians marched in the funeral procession for Carlisle and Roberts. Of 118 persons prosecuted for treason in Pennsylvania courts, besides Carlisle and Roberts, only one other culprit was executed, Ralph Morden.[30]

Recaptured slaves who absconded to the enemy or collaborated with them during the British invasion of Virginia in 1781 stood in peril of treason conviction. But any slave executions for treason were deterred by the case of Billy, a mullato slave belonging to the estate of John Taylor. Billy had taken up arms with the enemy voluntarily, and had been captured as part of a crew of a British vessel. Billy was sentenced to death, but was granted a reprieve by Governor Jefferson, while Mann Page, on behalf of the Taylor estate, appealed to the House of Delegates in June 1781 for a pardon. Both houses of the legislature jointly concluded that "proceedings against the said slave were illegal," and the treason conviction was dismissed. After all, a slave was not a citizen, and therefore could not commit treason.[31]

After the victory of Yorktown, Virginians, now confident of which was the winning side, called for vengeance against those who in any way had cooperated with the enemy. Numerous persons were rounded up and charged with treason; in most instances cases won acquittal or the accused persons, after a lengthy imprisonment in local jails, were discharged. Usually those convicted were sentenced to enlistment in the Continental army; needless to say most of them quickly deserted, a rather easy feat as the war was winding down. In June 1782 a court of oyer and terminer meted out six death sentences. The condemned appealed to the General Assembly which had the power of pardon in treason cases. A constitutional impasse ensued when one branch of the legislature voted for pardon and the other one did not. The Virginia Court of Appeals in *Caton* v. *Commonwealth*, establishing a precedent for judicial review, upheld the sentences of death. Not long afterwards, however, both houses of assembly granted pardon, ordering two of the condemned to leave the state and the others to be inducted into the army. John Holland, sentenced to death for treason, did not receive a pardon until May 1783.[32] Thomas Jefferson was proud that Virginia did not execute any of its citizens for treason. In his *Notes on the State of Virginia*, which he completed in December 1781, he commented that "it may be mentioned as a proof both of the lenity of our government and unanimity of its inhabitants that though this war was now raged near seven years not a single execution for treason has taken place."[33]

Various factors contributed to keeping the death penalty for treason at a minimum. Of course, there was the probability of retaliation by the enemy, who had captives in similar situations, if the severe rebel punishments were too common and indiscriminate. There were always such alternative punishments as fines, imprisonment, and banishment. Extenuating circumstances influenced clemency. Taking an oath of allegiance to a state might resolve any question as to one's loyalty. As Bradley Chapin states, pardons "were based on the assumption that traiterous acts of an accessorial nature resulted from misinformation. When given the facts, an individual would atone for his treason by loyal service to the state."[34] The states passed legislation establishing offenses such as misprision of treason, which called for less harsh penalties than did "high treason." Although misprision of treason in English law had meant non-involvement in an overt treasonable act or conspiracy, the states broadened this category to encompass the giving of limited aid to the enemy. Actually the misprision of treason laws left to prosecutors the discretion at what level a penalty might be sought. Treason was still treason, but degrees of it were recognized. States passed acts, such as did Virginia, that established culpability for actions that were "inferior in malignity to treason" but "injurious to the Independence of America."[35]

A Virginia law in 1776 set as penalties fines up to £20,000 and five years' imprisonment for any persons who "by any word, open deed, or act . . . maintain and defend the authority, jurisdiction, or power, of the King or parliament of Great Britain." Another Virginia act, June 1780, made every form of conduct that was favorable to Great Britain or harmful to the Revolution a misdemeanor, punishable by a fine of 100,000 pounds of tobacco or five years in prison.[36] Other states had similar legislation, which provided penalties of fines, imprisonment, or civil disabilities. As James W. Hurst comments, such statutes were "capable of being applied to sweep in all manner of incautious political talk in a time of stress."[37]

In March 1780, William Preston, who had been loyalist-hunting in western Virginia, asked Governor Jefferson what he should do with his prisoners. Jefferson informed Preston on the definition of treason as levying war against the state or giving aid and comfort to the enemy and that conviction on a treason charge required testimony of two witnesses or "voluntary confession." Jefferson advised, however, that "should your evidence . . . not be such as the law requires in cases of treason where the punishment is capital, perhaps it may be sufficient to convict them of a misprision of treason which is punishable by fine and imprisonment at the pleasure of the court."[38]

Congress entreated the states to take measures against persons who were "deceived and drawn into erroneous opinion respecting the American cause." All states by 1778 had punishments for disloyal speech or writing.[39]

Pennsylvania's sedition law of September 12, 1776 called for prosecution of persons who, in speaking or writing, attempted to "obstruct or oppose . . . the measures carrying on by the United States of America for the defense and support of the freedom and independence of the said states." Anyone so accused was to be put on bond by the nearest justice of the peace for future good behavior; those considered dangerous were to appear before three justices, two of whom, without a jury trial, could commit such persons to prison for the duration of the war.[40] Typical was a Connecticut law of 1776 which provided penalties of a fine, imprisonment, or disfranchisement for any one who wrote or spoke libeling Congress, the legislature, or the raising of military forces, or recognized the authority of the king or parliament over the United States.[41]

Penalties were light for casual seditious remarks. Many cases were in the nature of one brought before the county court in Louisa County, Virginia on May 15, 1777. Elkanah Baughman had to answer to the charge of "making expressions highly injurious and inimical to the Commonwealth." A jury found that Baughman had been "much intoxicated with Liquor" when he drank to the health of the king and damned Congress, and let the accused off with a five shilling fine, one hour imprisonment, and payment of the costs of prosecution.[42] Americans discovered that among everyday frustrations, war weariness, and fractious neighbors, a slip of the tongue could result in being hailed before a magistrate, and worse, being tried for seditious speech.

Freedom of the Press

"In establishing American independence, the pen and the press had merit equal to that of the sword," wrote David Ramsay in his military history of the Revolution, published a few years after the war.[43] Fortunately for the American cause, the vast majority of newspapers published during the war period (in all, 42 in 1775, 35 in 1780, and 41 in 1782)[44] were located in rebel occupied areas.

Freedom of the press had undergone a modicum of expansion during the colonial period. The important gain, occurring from the precedent set by the verdict in the John Peter Zenger case of 1735, had amended common law usage so that truth was considered a defense against a charge of seditious libel. Americans, however, during the colonial or Revolutionary periods, did not tamper with the doctrine of no prior restraint, whereby there was no set limits on expression but what was said was strictly accountable.

Wartime tested the latitude of expression of opinion, the degree to which one could impugn the motives of public officials and the civil and military actions and policies of government. While patriot authorities were more willing to afford protections to the press than to speech, the issue of balancing freedom of the press and security was a delicate one. Congressman Francis Hopkinson, writing in the *Pennsylvania Evening Post* on November 16, 1776, defended the freedom of the press, but argued that

> when this privilege is manifestly abused, and the press becomes an engine in the hands of an enemy for sowing dangerous dissentions, spreading false alarms, and undermining the defensive operations of government in an hour of danger, ought not that government upon the undeniable principles of self-preservation, to silence by its own authority, such an internal enemy to its peace and safety.[45]

The new governments, insecure and fragile, certainly did not want to encourage nurturing the seeds for their destruction. As evident in so much of the patriot Revolutionary rhetoric, liberty of expression meant liberty to espouse the cause of liberty.

Congress discovered it lacked authority to censor the press. Although extolling freedom of the press in America in its propagandist "Letters to the Inhabitants of the Province of Quebec" in 1774, Congress was sensitive to press criticism. Efforts, however, to hold its detractors to account failed. Congress tried summoning offenders before it to receive reprimands. Thomas Paine and John Dunlap, for revealing state secrets in their *Pennsylvania Packet*, made such an appearance in 1779, even though Congress could not compel them to attend. When Dunlap, a short time later, published an objectionable piece written by Dr Benjamin Rush, a majority in Congress voted down a proposed summons. Had Congress persisted in attempting to superintend press publication, without power of enforcement, it would have underscored its weakness.[46]

While zealously restraining free speech (of the new state constitutions only Pennsylvania had a guarantee for free speech), American leaders were reluctant to censor the press (only the New Jersey and New York constitutions did not contain a free press clause). Since the state constitutions merely cited "liberty of the press" without definition, the states could interpret the latitude of freedom of the press in any way they wished. The newspapers, however, gave little cause for alarm. Although at times critical of efforts at the prosecution of the war by Congress or the states, editorial opinion, usually reflected in letters to the publisher, consistently represented an unerring patriotic viewpoint. The potentiality of mob retribution upon wavering printers was in itself a powerful check. Prosecutions for criminal libel (chiefly involving defamation of individuals) proceeded, but only two states, Massachusetts and Pennsylvania, attempted prosecution of seditious libel during the war. In each instance grand juries failed to indict.[47]

The Pennsylvania case (1782) concerned a running fight between Eleazar Oswald, publisher of the *Independent Gazetteer*, and Chief Justice Tomas McKean. Oswald printed articles demeaning two army officers and also accusing McKean of speculation in soldiers' certificates. McKean had Oswald arrested, but the grand jury refused to bring an indictment. A reprimand of the jurors by McKean did not change their minds. McKean finally won out six years later when he had Oswald arrested and tried, without a jury, resulting in a conviction of seditious libel of the court.[48]

Legislatures took little action to muzzle the press. A case in point involved Isaac Collins, a Quaker publisher of the *New-Jersey Gazette* in Trenton. He printed a piece, entitled "Cincinnatus," which criticized Governor William Livingston and the College of New Jersey. The New Jersey Council, on October 28, 1779, demanded that Collins reveal the name of the author of the offending article. The lower house of Assembly did not support the Council's action, and the Council withdrew its order. The affair, states Collins's biographer, "set an early legal precedent for freedom of the press in New Jersey." Sometimes Collins published in his newspaper writings by persons of dubious patriotism, which policy served to instill in American journalism that an opinion in a newspaper need not reflect that of the editor.[49]

A printer faced a dilemma when the area in which he published suddenly was occupied by an opposing military force. Either he had to flee and set up elsewhere, as did several patriot printers when the British seized New York City and Philadelphia, or he could choose to remain and publish under different auspices. Benjamin Towne, who published the *Pennsylvania Evening Post* in Philadelphia, however, had it both ways. He opted to support the British cause while the redcoats held Philadelphia, and did not hesitate to print material that made the Americans appear as cowards. He was attainted a traitor by the Pennsylvania government. Amazingly after the British evacuation of Philadelphia, he simply recast his journalism to the American view, and miraculously escaped prosecution.[50]

The German press of Pennsylvania was divided in loyalties. Henry Miller's *Der Philadelphische Staatsbote* was pro-American. Miller, 77 years old, fled Philadelphia when Howe's army arrived. He returned to Philadelphia after the British left. Using a borrowed press and type, he reissued the *Staatsbote* for another year before retiring.

Christopher Sower, Jr and III, publishers of the *Germantowner Zeitung*, adopted a different course. The Pennsylvania Council of Safety in December 1775 ordered them not to publish "any political piece whatsoever." Upon the arrival of the British army in Philadelphia, the Sowers moved their presses to that city, and published *Der Pennsylvanische-Courier*, which found readers among German soldiers. Both Sowers were charged with treason by the Pennsylvania government. The elder Sower visited his homestead in Germantown, whereupon patriot militia forced him out of his house with only the clothes on his back; the estate was subsequently confiscated. Christopher Sower III moved to New York City with the British army, and set up printing there until the end of the war when he went to England.[51]

In all, 12 loyalist newspapers were published in cities occupied by the British: three in New York City (1776–83); one in Newport (1777–9); three in Philadelphia (1777–8); three in Charleston (1780–2); one in Savannah (1779–82); and one in St Augustine, Florida (1783–4).[52]

James Rivington, in his *New-York Gazetteer* at the beginning of war, tried to report fairly on both sides of the conflict, but this earned the antipathy of local Whigs. On November 27, 1775, a New York rabble leader, Isaac Sears, at the head of 75 horsemen from Connecticut, descended upon Rivington's shop and carried away his type and best press. Rivington quickly realized his peril, and left for England in January 1776. He returned in September 1777, and with the British army now in control of New York City, established the *New-York Gazette*, later renamed the *Royal Gazette*. Rivingston's newsheet relentlessly denigrated Congress and its officers and soldiers and exaggerated British military success. At the war's end Rivington shut down his newspaper, but was allowed to stay in New York City (possibly, as it has been alleged, because he had been an American spy all along), and finished his career as a bookseller.[53]

Other New York City printers faced intimidation during the period before the British occupation. Samuel Loudon, publisher of the *New York Packet*, printed a pamphlet critical of Thomas Paine's *Common Sense*. A dozen men broke into his shop and destroyed the plates and manuscript of the work in question. A notice was sent to each printer in the city that anyone printing materials offensive to "the rights and liberties of America" or "in favor of our inveterate foes" could rightly fear "death and destruction, ruin and perdition." Loudon weathered the storm, and, being the patriot that he was, re-established his newspaper at Fishkill during the British occupation, returning it to New York City afterwards.[54]

Only on one occasion did the military disrupt newspaper publication. On September 30, 1775, a landing party of seven marines and ten grenadiers from Governor Lord Dunmore's fleet anchored off Norfolk, Virginia entered the town and seized the printing press, types, ink, and paper of John Hunter Holt's *Virginia Gazette, or, the Norfolk Intelligencer*. Holt managed to escape but two of his journeymen were captured. Dunmore had been angered by what he considered the newspaper's misrepresentation of the facts and an article disparaging his ancestry; he also wanted a press for issuing propaganda. The mayor and council of the town protested that the raid was illegal, to which Dunmore replied that he was doing the town's citizens a favor. Dunmore used the press equipment to print proclamations and fleet records, and managed to get out an issue or two of the *Virginia Gazette*.[55] Dunmore's defeat at the battle of Great Bridge on December 9, 1775, his burning of Norfolk on January 1, 1776, and in a short time his withdrawal from the area put an end to the new loyalist newspaper.

Even as the war progressed pro-American publishers could feel the wrath of superpatriots. Mary Katherine Goddard and her brother William had to confront intimidation and threatened violence while publishing their *Maryland Journal* in Baltimore. While William was away, on May 29, 1776, George Sommerville visited Mary Katherine at the print shop and "abused her with threats and indecent language on account of a late publication in her paper." She complained to the Baltimore Committee of Safety, which had soldiers apprehend Sommerville, who was forced to apologize and was released on bond for good behavior.

On February 26, 1777 the *Journal* published an anonymous essay (actually written by Samuel Chase), which tongue-in-cheek advised Americans to make peace with Great Britain. A local Whig Club, whose members lacked a sense of humor, sent a delegation to Mary Katherine to get her to name the author. She refused. William was brought forcibly before the Club, and ordered to leave town within 24 hours and the state in three days. He went immediately to the Maryland Assembly in Annapolis, where he received legislative condemnation of the Club's actions as a "manifest Violation of the Constitution, directly contrary to the Declaration of Rights." William then printed a denunciation of the Club. Again ruffians, "a set of men not remarkable for their penetration and sagacity," assaulted William on May 25, and again he was ordered to leave town. Appealing to the Maryland government, William secured declarations from the Assembly and the governor condemning the Whig Club and promising prosecution if harassment continued.

Two years later the Goddards got into trouble again over freedom of the press. They printed General Charles Lee's "Some Queries, Political, and Military, Humbly Offered to the Considerations of the Public," by which Lee sought to settle a score with George Washington over Lee's being blamed for the ill success at the battle of Monmouth in 1778 and being subsequently forced out of the army. The essay was highly critical of Washington's military abilities. A mob led by Continental army officers seized William Goddard at his home, and gave him a drumhead trial out of doors under the threat of lynching. William had no choice but to print an apology in the *Journal*; this being done and the situation quieted, William printed a recantation of the apology. This time an appeal to the Maryland government brought no protection. Lee submitted even more vitriolic material, which Mary Katherine prevailed upon her brother not to publish, and the controversy soon subsided.[56]

The absence of measures to censor freedom of the press by the state governments during wartime was owing to the printers themselves embracing the American cause and respect for the freedom of the press clauses in the declarations of rights in the state constitutions. Printers avoided controversy by perfunctory reportage of war news, chiefly letters by American officers from the "front," and notices of military orders and state and congressional official actions. If no momentous strides were made for substantial libertarian changes, the wartime experience and the ideology of Independence opened the door for greater future protection of the freedom of expression and fundamental liberties.

CHAPTER FIVE

Revolutionary banditti

Guerrilla warfare played a major role in the military operations of the Revolution. Too often the hit-and-run tactics of units attached to an army or independent bands of irregular troops degenerated into wanton pillage. Banditti of dubious allegiance terrorized the countryside of the middle and southern states.

The armies, often stationary, frequently sent out patrols and foraging parties. Loyalist refugee groups and local rebel militia aided military forces in securing supplies, keeping lines of communication open, and cowering citizens of wavering allegiance.

Each side made strong efforts to rein in plundering by soldiers. Enlisted men were executed for stealing as little as a suit of clothes (as, for example, ordered by General Anthony Wayne in Virginia in 1781). George Washington knew that war was won to a large degree by military forces posing as protectors of the property and lives of inhabitants. General Henry Clinton and other British commanders did not need to be reminded of the difficulties of the British conquest of Ireland. Despite stated intentions and policy to treat the populace with respect, the military forces' commandeering of provisions and livestock in the countryside stirred great fear and resentment by the citizens. The breakdown of law and order in many areas because of war conditions and the partisan fighting between rebels and loyalists permitted even greater suffering at the hands of freebooters and robbers.

Criminals, such as horse and cattle thieves, counterfeiters, and highway robbers, had flourished in the late colonial period. The war, with the confusion and divided loyalties, presented the greater opportunity for brigandage.

Cowboys and Skinners

Bandits, irregulars, and British and American patrols scoured the Neutral Ground of Westchester County, New York. The Neutral Ground was a 20 to 30 mile stretch between the opposing armies. The British outer lines protecting New York City extended from Kingsbridge over Spuyten Duyvil Creek, separating Manhattan from the Bronx, through Eastchester and Yonkers to the Bronx River and down to Long Island Sound. American defenses in the New York Highlands projected southeastward from Dobbs Ferry on the Hudson to Mamaroneck on Long Island Sound. The western part of the Neutral Ground resembled a desolate wilderness because of the abandoned farms and the destruction of houses, barns, fences, and bridges for firewood. The horses and cattle roaming at large in the large eastern salt marshes and meadows offered a tempting target for marauders who could sell animals they rustled to either army with no questions asked.[1]

While the term "cowboys" was used to designate all marauding bands in the Neutral Ground, it specifically referred to those groups affiliated with British military forces. The cowboys were called such because the primary objective of raids was to secure cattle for the British armed forces at New York City. Most of the cowboys were members of James DeLancey's corps of light horse. DeLancey, a large landed proprietor in the Bronx and from one of New York's most prominent families, received a colonel's commission from the royal governor of New York, William Tryon, in 1777. Starting with a nucleus of 60 young men, DeLancey expanded his mounted corps to about 500, most of whom were refugee natives of Westchester County. From his base at his home, West Farms, in the Bronx, DeLancey directed raids and plundering expeditions in the Neutral Ground. DeLancey's cowboys served without pay or provision for clothing. Needless to say, "it was an established rule never to return empty handed." While officers were uniformed, most of the men were not.[2] Cowboys allegedly wrested information from their victims by torture, such as pouring hot coals into cupped hands, but they never had a reputation for murder. Actually, the wanton pillage and cruelty may be charged to those who were not members of DeLancey's unit but passed themselves off as such. At the war's end DeLancey claimed that the "irregularity" of operations in the Neutral Ground "originated from People who have no Connection with that Corps."[3]

Joseph Plumb Martin, a 17-year-old private from Connecticut doing a brief stint in Washington's forward unit of light infantry in the summer of 1778, was one of a small party sent to chase "cowboys" who had destroyed provisions collected by a rebel militia officer. Traveling at night through "fields and pastures . . . through swamps, mire and woods, endeavouring to keep as clear of the inhabitants as possible," Martin and his comrades captured 14 cowboys, whom they left in the custody of militia. On another mission, Martin encountered a cowboy who, "when we were boys" was "one of my most familiar playmates" and was a "messmate during the war in 1777;" Martin's opponent, who had since deserted the American army, had the chance to kill the young Connecticut infantryman, but did not.[4]

Skinners, whose loyalty to the American cause was dubious at best, acquired much greater notoriety than did the cowboys. Unlike the cowboys who had limited objectives and military association, the skinners were hardly more than parcels of bandits. It is said that skinners were so named because they looted everything, even skinning the clothing off the backs of their victims. The skinners caused no end of worry to American commanding officers in the Highlands. As late as March 1781, General William Heath, commandant at West Point, wrote to Governor George Clinton of New York that "the unbounded licentiousness of a number of persons who lurk the lines" had become "intolerable." Such persons, among whom "were deserters from the enemy, proceed below the lines by routes where they evade our guards, and there insult, whip, beat, and at some times almost hang till dead, the inhabitants, until they distort from them their money, &c." The

> wanton spirit of plundering which now prevails, will make more recruits for the enemy. . . . It will, besides, contaminate the morals of the whole adjacent country, will produce a disposition and thirst to plunder all ages, sexes and denominations—marked with such stains of abuse as will be a disgrace to our country, and our arms.[5]

The most famous exploit of skinners was the capture of the British spy, John André. Seven farm boys, most of them illiterate, set out from North Salem, Westchester County, toward Tarrytown with the intent of robbing cattle from British parties driving stock to New York City. Four of the group kept watch on top of Davis's Hill while David Williams, Isaac Van Wart, and John Paulding positioned themselves along the road below. Deciding upon another quarry, Williams, Van Wart, and Paulding intercepted André on his return from a conference with General Benedict Arnold. Searching for valuables they discovered in André's boots incriminating papers revealing the defenses of West Point. Hoping for a reward they turned their unfortunate captive over to American military officers.[6]

Beset by the constant depredations, the inhabitants who stayed in the Neutral Ground bore countenances of apathy and despair. Reverend Timothy Dwight, chaplain of a Connecticut brigade and later president of Yale College, was stationed at the edge of the Neutral Ground in 1777, and was shocked at what he saw in Westchester County. The inhabitants "feared everybody whom they saw, and loved nobody," and "all thought beyond what was merely instinctive had fled their minds forever." The houses were in a great measure scenes of desolation. Their furniture was extensively plundered or broken to pieces. The walls, floors, and windows were injured both by violence and decay, and were not repaired because they had not the means of repairing them, and because they were exposed to the repetition of the same injuries. The cattle was gone. Their enclosures were burnt where they were capable of becoming fuel, and in many cases thrown down where they were not. The fields were covered with a rank growth of weeds and wild grass. Amid all this appearance of desolation, nothing struck my own eye more forcibly than the sight of this great road, the passage from New York to Boston. Where I had heretofore seen a continual succession of horses and carriages and life and bustle lent a sprightliness to all the environing objects, not a single, solitary traveler was visible from week to week, or from month to month. The world was motionless and silent. . . .[7]

Long Island Whaleboaters and Marauders

Waterborne shore raids and small boat privateering were commonplace all along the Atlantic coast and its inlets and bays. Especially using British bases or the support of nearby British ships of the line, loyalist refugees made raids along Long Island Sound, eastern New Jersey, Virginia's Eastern Shore and Chesapeake Bay, and coastal South Carolina and Georgia. On Long Island, New York, however, rebel interlopers held sway. Whig refugees who had fled Long Island for Connecticut upon the British occupation of New York City and its environs returned to their homeland to plunder loyalists, who themselves were raiding Connecticut and New Jersey shores. Often no distinction was made as to friend or foe, and Long Island soon resembled the ravaged Neutral Ground across the western part of the Sound. Supplies for the British army and goods from the "London trade" unloaded from ships in Long Island waters also became objectives for marauders. What made the waterborne raids on Long Island different from those elsewhere was their inland penetration.

Whaleboat crews were well suited for conducting raids on Long Island. They had been organized as little companies for catching humpback and right whales which swam into inlets for mating and calving. With fewer numbers of whales migrating during the war years, crewmen had time on their hands. Twenty to thirty rebels could crowd into a whaleboat—a shallop of two sails and eight oars—and quickly cross from the Connecticut shore to Long Island, returning to hide in the shallow inlets from Greenwich to Norwalk. Major Benjamin Tallmadge, who, as Washington's intelligence chief, depended on open communication with his spies on Long Island, was disgusted with the wholesale pillaging on Long Island.

Persons from Connecticut, "some of whom under sanction of [privateering] Commissions," Tallmadge informed his commander-in-chief, "land on Long Island and plunder the inhabitants promiscuously." They act "most villionously . . . by lying on the road and robbing the inhabitants as they pass." One of Tallmadge's most valuable spy operatives "was the other day robbed of all his money near Huntington, and was glad to escape with his life."[8]

Besides the whaleboaters, American and British patrols roaming the island yielded to the temptation to plunder. Major Eli Leavenworth of the Connecticut Continental troops constantly had charge of a scouting party on Long Island, and acquired a reputation for extorting goods from the populace.[9]

British regular troops, except for a post on Lloyd's Neck on the North Shore between Huntington Harbor and Oyster Bay for the purpose of protecting woodcutters, were stationed no further west on Long Island than the towns of Flushing, Jamaica, and Newtown (Elmhurst), all today in the borough of Queens. But even these troops under the pretence of foraging parties committed extensive depredations. Judge Thomas Jones, himself a staunch loyalist, commented that the British soldiers "robbed, plundered, and pillaged, the inhabitants of their cattle, hogs, sheep, poultry, and in short of every thing they could lay their hands upon. . . . To complain was needless; the officers shared in the plunder."[10]

Judge Jones also condemned the "Honourable Board of Associated Loyalists" for their encouragement of whaleboat "predatory War" on the coasts of New Jersey, Connecticut, and "the easternmost parts of the province of New York adjoining the Sound." The intruders struck at night, and "brought off the cattle, horses, hogs, sheep, and poultry . . . furniture, household goods, negroes, wearing apparel, bedding, sheeting and linen;" they also "burnt houses, destroyed churches, and brought off a number of prisoners. This plunder was sold at vendue for the benefit of the captors." Ironically, rebel and loyalist whaleboaters going in opposite directions in the Sound looking for prey never attacked each other; indeed, at close range, they "hailed each other, gave three cheers, and unmolestedly proceeded on their different expeditions." These marauders "grew so civil to each other, that they mutually gave notice of the persons most proper to be made prisoners of, the situation of their houses, and where the most plunder was likely to be obtained."[11]

Lydia M. Post, a Long Island housewife whose husband was in the Continental army, recorded vignettes describing the terror experienced from "Runners" (whaleboaters) in her neighborhood. On one occasion "the Runners entered the house of John Wilson, and threatened, until the wife, to save the life of her husband, revealed the hiding-place. But it was too late; he died the next morning from a saber-cut . . . cleaving the skull. . . . The villains took a large sum of money, which was in silver coin, in bags under the hearthstone." Another time the Runners seized a man and placed his head "upon a block," while a person stood over him with an axe, "bringing it down every moment as if to sever his head from his body." The victim's wife rushed out and brought back forty pounds in money and placed her arm across her husband's neck; "the sight of the money" caused the intruders "to desist their threatenings." A Mr Lester was kidnapped, "blindfolded, taken to the harbor, placed in the light craft which they call 'whaleboats,' and rowed to the main shore, seven miles. The villains will sell him to the Whig Committee of Safety."[12]

Long Island residents learned to look after their own defense. According to Mrs Post,

The farmers have devised a scheme to make known through the neighborhood the presence of the "Runners." They are generally seen lurking about at twilight, spying the points most favorable for attack; if observed, they walk on in an unconcerned manner, whistling or singing. Sometimes they will stop, and inquire the way to some place; suddenly disappearing, they are unexpectedly seen again in the edge of the wood, or from behind a hay-stack in the field, peering about, terrifying every body, above all women and children. . . . We are on our guard; the "great gun" with which all are provided, is loaded and fired off. Pop! Pop! go the answering guns for five miles round; each house takes up the alarming tale, and thus it spreads, warning of impending danger, and frightens away the enemy, for that time at any rate.[13]

The predators Mrs Post most feared were "robbers" who "come over from the main shore in boats, and keep us in constant alarm! They belong to no party, and spare none: freebooters, cowardly midnight assassins, incendiaries, indiscriminate, bold, and daring."[14]

Neither the British nor the American military commands made any real effort to bring law and order into the no man's land of Long Island. Of more concern to the Americans were the staging bases for loyalist refugee whaleboaters who raided the Connecticut and New Jersey shores. The offending loyalist refugees had established themselves at two locations— one at Lloyd's Neck on the North Shore and the other at Smith's Point on the south side of the island in Suffolk County, 80 miles from New York City. Major Benjamin Tallmadge was entrusted with breaking up these two nests of marauders. During the night of September 5, 1779 Tallmadge and 150 dismounted dragoons crossed the Sound and catching the enemy by surprise destroyed their boats and huts, returning with prisoners without having lost a single man. Tallmadge duplicated this feat on November 23, 1780. Debarking from whaleboats, Tallmadge and 250 soldiers marched the width of the island to Smith's Point, and at dawn took 200 unalerted captives, the only ones missing in the round-up being 20 who were out on a plundering expedition.[15]

The Highlands Gangs

Bandit groups based in the Highlands west of the Hudson River had ample targets among the prosperous Dutch farmers in the "numerous rich and extensive" valleys of Orange County, New York, and upper Bergen County, New Jersey. Mountainous terrain afforded avenues of escape and hideouts. Favoring the British cause, the gangs found easy victims among the substantial patriot population of Orange County.

Of the Highlands outlaws, Claudius Smith, the "scourge of the Ramapo," has become a legendary figure. Smith was "a man whose abilities, if rightly directed, would have raised him to eminence and greatness."[16] He hailed from a mountain family of Smith's Clove, in the valley of the Ramapo River. He first came to notice when arrested for stealing oxen in July 1777. Escaping from jail, Smith formed a bandit gang with himself and his three sons—James, Richard, and William—as its nucleus. The gang specialized in rustling cattle and horses for sale to the British. William was killed by a posse in the autumn of 1778. With the gang accused of murdering Nathaniel Strong on October 6, 1778, Governor George Clinton issued a proclamation placing a $1,200 reward for apprehending Claudius and $600 for each of his sons.

Claudius Smith fled to Long Island where he found lodging near Smithtown. Major John Brush and an associate accosted Smith while sleeping. Smith was brought to Goshen in Orange County. Convicted of horse-stealing and highway robbery, Smith was hanged at Goshen on January 22, 1779. On the gallows Smith "kicked off his shoes, with the observation that his mother had often told him that he would die like the Trooper's horse with his shoes on, but that he would make his mother a liar."[17]

A remnant of the gang, led by Richard Smith, vowed vengeance. Murdering one John Clark in retaliation they pinned to the corpse a notice: "You are hereby forbid at your peril to hang no more friends to government as you did Claudius Smith . . . We are determined to hang six for one, for the blood of the innocent cries aloud for vengeance." Authorities, however, caught up with several branches of the gang. William Cole and Thomas Welcher were hanged at Hackensack on April 9, 1779, and James Smith and four others were executed at Goshen on June 8, 1779.[18]

Other Highlands outlaws worked more closely with the British. Thomas Ward, son of an ironworker at Smith's Clove and a deserter from the American army, plundered widely; "those associates with him were negroes, and vile creatures of his own race."[19] In November 1778 Ward and two other gang leaders, Wiert Banta and John Mason, led a group that stole into an American army encampment at Kakiat (now West Hempstead, Orange County) and carried away Colonel Joseph Ward, the mustermaster of the Continental army, and his deputy, Colonel William Bradford, along with muster rolls. Ward became a dashing hero of sorts, leading loyalist troops in a successful defense of Bull's Ferry, a post four miles above Hoboken, on July 20–1, 1780 against crack light infantry commanded by General Anthony Wayne and, on March 12–13, 1781, in a successful raid on Closter (in Bergen County, New Jersey), "a settlement," according to James Rivington, "abounding with many violent Rebels." Thomas Ward and Banta were awarded lands in Nova Scotia by the British government after the war. John Mason became so notorious in his plundering that the British imprisoned him in New York City, releasing him in January 1781 to carry General Henry Clinton's proposals to mutineers of the Pennsylvania line at Princeton. This proved a bad bargain for Mason, as the Americans hanged him as a spy.[20]

New Jersey Renegades

Not unlike other environs in proximity to New York City, New Jersey experienced brigandage committed by loyalist refugees and outlaws alike. Refugee raids into Bergen County and the waterborne incursions along the coasts kept rebels constantly on the alert.

Escaped prisoners of war from the Saratoga Convention army (as it passed through New Jersey to and from its internments in Virginia and eastern Pennsylvania), in making their way to British-held New York City, engaged in theft. Two persons sentenced to be hanged for the robbery and brutal assault upon General William Maxwell's father and brother at their home in Sussex County in May 1780 were thought to be escaped prisoners of war.

Horse thievery had become all the more a problem during the war, and New Jersey made it a capital offence. On June 15, 1780 four young loyalists from Staten Island, who had been about stealing horses, were apprehended hiding in a barn near Scotch Plains. One was killed while resisting. General Maxwell, commanding American troops in the area, instead of turning the captives over to civil authorities, sent them to Washington's encampment at Morristown. The three, including teenager Jonathan Clawson, Jr, were convicted by court-martial on June 18, and hanged the next day. Army surgeon Dr James Thacher commented on the pathos of the occasion:

> These unfortunate young men came to the gallows overwhelmed with the horrors of death. Their whole frames were thrown into a tremor, and they were tortured at the sight of the gallows and

halters. They had flattered themselves that mercy would be extended to them, and they would either be pardoned, or their lives be prolonged for a few days; but when they found the executioner was about to perform his office, their mournful cries and lamentations were distressing beyond description. It has some where been noted, that a girl walked seven miles in a torrent of rain, to see a man hanged, and returned in tears, because the criminal was reprieved; on the present occasion, a heart so full of depravity might have enjoyed an indulgence even to saiety.[21]

The Pine Barren region of Monmouth County and adjacent parts of Burlington County served as a refuge and a base for robber gangs. Ostensibly on the side of the British, these groups, each consisting of six to ten members, mostly deserters and fugitives from justice, paid little heed to loyalty distinctions among their victims. The gangs stole horses which they took to Sandy Hook or New York City for sale to the British army or civilians. Township tax collectors were likely prey. One gang leader William Giberson, Jr, was captured and marked for trial for high treason, but escaped; he survived, and went to Canada at the war's end. Two bandit leaders, Jacob Fagan and Lewis Fenton, and several followers, in 1779 were killed upon encounters with military units after authorities learned of their hideouts; other gang members were apprehended, several of whom were hanged. Joseph Mulliner, the best known of the "Pine-Banditti," who operated from a base along the Mullica River near Little Egg Harbor, was executed for high treason on August 8, 1781. A newspaper account noted that Mulliner "had made practice of burning houses," robbing "all who fell in his way, so that when he came to trial it appeared that the whole country, both whigs and tories, were his enemies."[22]

The cry of "Moody is in the Country!" sent New Jerseyans scrambling for safety. James Moody (1744–1809) and his following became the terror of central and northwestern New Jersey during most of the war. Eschewing personal gain, Moody adhered strictly to military objectives. He was a Sussex County farmer at the beginning of the war, and his refusal to subscribe to the patriot loyalty oath drew the wrath of local tory hunters. With 70 relatives and friends, Moody fled to British lines, and joined Cortlandt Skinner's New Jersey Volunteers as an ensign, later rising in rank to captain. Given a free hand, Moody quickly learned that for his hit-and-run operations in New Jersey small groups were most effective. He and his men robbed American army headquarters mail four times and destroyed a powder magazine in Monmouth County, carrying off its arms and ammunition to New York City. Moody conducted devastating raids on New Jersey farms and villages, captured American field officers, recruited for the British army, plotted to kidnap New Jersey officials, and almost succeeded in stealing the records of the Continental Congress. His remarkable feats and daring escapes are recorded in his "Narrative" (first published in London in 1783), which he wrote in support of his claim for loyalist compensation. The capture and hanging of his younger brother, John, in Philadelphia in November 1781 left Moody heartsick, and he went to England, where he stayed until moving to Nova Scotia in 1786. For his assisting Convention army prisoners to escape to British lines during the war, Moody is deserving of the sobriquet of "the Scarlet Pimpernel of the Revolution."[23]

The Doane Renegades

The Doane family members and their gang spread terror in southeast Pennsylvania. "Despite occasional lapses into conscientiousness," they became "near epitomes of evil. Pillage, robbery, burglary, incendiarism, threats of violence, violence itself, torture, occasional rape and even murder are listed on their unenviable records," writes John F. Reed.[24]

The core of the gang were the five sons of Joseph Doane, Sr—Moses, Joseph, Jr, Aaron, Mahlon, and Levi—and their cousin, Abraham Doane. The Quaker family hailed from the small farms of Bucks County. The Doane phenomenon began when Joseph, Sr refused to be taxed. Moses Doane, who had lived several years with the Indians in northeastern Pennsylvania, became the leader. At first the Doanes served as spies for the British army, and then entered the criminal world by joining up with other renegades to attack rebel farmers and rob tax collectors.

Very un-Quakerlike, the Doane gang did not hesitate to use torture to force victims to reveal the hiding places of valuables. Frequently changing hideouts in then forested Bucks County, concealing themselves in the numerous hillside caves, and when necessary fleeing westward or crossing the Delaware into New Jersey, the Doanes eluded capture throughout the war. Although looked upon with favor by loyalists because they usually attacked patriot families, the Doanes, nevertheless, on occasion made pro-British citizens their victims. The most profitable single take of the Doane gang was the robbery of £1,300 from the house of the Bucks County Treasurer, John Hart, in Newtown, Pennsylvania, on October 22, 1781. During 1781–2 it is known that they stole at least 200 horses in Pennsylvania, delivering most of the animals to Baltimore. Bounties placed on their heads by both the Pennsylvania legislature and the Continental Congress impelled the Doanes to flee to Maryland and then to the western Pennsylvania counties of Washington, Fayette, Westmoreland, and Bedford; the Doanes committed robberies wherever they went. Although the Doanes were relentlessly hunted, it took a while before they were brought to justice. The gang was again operating in Bucks County in 1783; in July of that year they staged six robberies, two of them on tax collectors. Moses was shot and killed by a posse on September 1, 1783. Mahlon escaped from a Bedford jail in 1783 and made his way to safety in New York City. Joseph, Jr, lodged in a Newtown jail under sentence of death, escaped in 1784, posed as a schoolteacher in New Jersey under an assumed name, and when found out, fled to Canada. Aaron, sentenced to hang for robbery, was reprieved because he had been tried without a jury; he, too, escaped and went to Canada. Abraham and Levi were hanged in Philadelphia on September 24, 1788.[25]

Swampland Bandits

Maroon settlements in swamplands served as jumping off places for marauders. Outsiders not familiar with a swamp's configurations were not likely to give pursuit.

Josiah Phillips and his gang who, during 1775–8 gave Virginia more trouble than since Bacon's Rebellion, found refuge in the heavily forested Dismal Swamp straddling Virginia's southeastern border with North Carolina. Phillips, a landless laborer from Lynnhaven Parish, Princess Anne County, upon receiving a commission from Governor Lord Dunmore in summer 1775, began his plundering. When Dunmore was forced out of Virginia, Phillips and his band, numbering up to 50 renegades, made raids in the lower tidewater counties of Norfolk and Princess Anne, escaping into the Dismal Swamp. The maroon population, consisting mostly of society's cast-offs and runaway slaves, shared Phillips' anti-property class bias and indeed provided him with recruits. Militiamen were afraid to enter the swamp, and most of those called up to go after Phillips preferred to pay a fine for non-service. The Phillips gang burned plantations, freed slaves, and carried off livestock and provisions, and on one of their sorties killed Captain Josiah Wilson of the Norfolk militia. Phillips had a price on his head and a legislative bill of attainder against him, under which he could have been summarily executed. Finally caught, Phillips and three others were convicted in court of robbery and hanged on December 4, 1778. Others of the gang would also be executed, including two runaway slave members. Despite the crackdown, remnants of the gang continued depredations through the remainder of the war, always retreating into the swamp after their robberies.[26]

The two counties of Virginia's Eastern Shore suffered from the marauding by "barge refugees" and runaway slaves, especially during the British invasions of the state. But the swamp inlets and numerous islands offered refuge also for "another sett of Villains no less dangerous than the Bargers, inhabitants of this County [Accomac]," wrote a complainant to Virginia's Commissioner of War in September 1781. "They would assemble six or eight together and Rob from house to house in remote places—Three of the latter class were caught . . . and hung by the Unanimous consent of more than a hundred of their neighbors."[27]

The Virginia government elsewhere had difficulty in breaking up robber gangs. Edmund Randolph, the state's attorney-general and who had just returned from serving as a delegate to the Congress, informed James Madison in August 1782:

> The laxness and inefficacy of government really alarms me. A notorious robber, who escaped from gaol about a twelvemonth ago, has associated in his villainies a formidable gang of blacks and whites, supposed to amount to fifty. They dispersed themselves . . . and have perpetrated some of the most daring and horrid thefts. An attempt has been often made to arrest this prince of the banditti, but it has hitherto miscarried . . . I live in the center [Randolph's home was just outside the then small town of Richmond, the new state capital] of the late depredations, and have no other hope to avoid their wickedness, than by the awe, which my office may create.[28]

Randolph's comment is fascinating, but unfortunately no clue or other record affords any explanation.

"Outlyers," loyalists who fled to the woods and swamps of South Carolina and Georgia, and other maroons caused great annoyance. The "small tory parties who live in swamps & make horrid incursions on the peaceable settlements neither give nor receive quarter," wrote Aedanus Burke, a South Carolina backcountry judge; they "sally from their swamps, & destroy our people in cold blood, and when taken are killed in their turn."[29]

Three hundred slaves, who had been arms bearers for the British army, elected to stay in America after the British withdrawal, styling themselves the "King of England soldiers." Taking refuge in swamps along the Savannah River, they constructed a fortified camp at Bear Creek on a parcel of land a half mile long and 400 feet wide. From their secluded retreat the maroons conducted night-time raids. At Mrs Godin's plantation they "carried off everything they could . . . all her Cattle, Sheep, Hogs [and] Horses."[30] Not until May 1786 did a militia expedition under Colonel James Gunn succeed in destroying the community and killing or wounding many of the defenders.[31]

Backcountry Banditti of South Carolina and Georgia

Many of the problems of the South Carolina backcountry during the Revolution stemmed from the lawlessness that had erupted in the 1760s among the "lower people" on the frontier fringe. Richard M. Brown has described these alienated and antisocial malcontents as consisting of "Crackers—motley Back Country ruffians . . . unfortunate small planters . . . hunters and squatters, absconded debtors, idlers, gamblers, and unsavory refugees from the northern colonies, settlers who had never recovered from the trauma of the Cherokee War [1759–61], deserters from military forces, and, often, Negroes, or people of mixed white, Indian, and Negro blood."[32] This assorted riff-raff resorted to widescale plundering and violence. Vigilante bands, calling themselves Regulators, during 1767–9 dealt crushing blows to the outlaws.

With no love for the dominant planter class, the poorer sort of South Carolina's backcountry made ready recruits for assisting the British military campaigns. David Ramsay, Charleston physician and historian, wrote that during the Revolution "a great proportion" of the people in the backcountry "was an ignorant unprincipled banditti; to whom idleness, licentiousness and deeds of violence were familiar. Horse-thieves and others whose crimes had exiled them from society, attached themselves to parties of the British."[33]

One mysterious figure, Joseph Cofell (also known as Scophol, Scofel, or Scovil) had considerable influence in arousing the maroon element of backcountry South Carolina to support the British cause. Little is known about Cofell. Before the war he had been an anti-Regulator leader. He served as a constable for the Orangeburg District, 1768–72, from which post he was removed by court order for "being guilty of evil Practices in the Execution of his Office." In 1773 he received whippings, once for cattle rustling and at another time for stealing chickens. The evidence for the theft of 38 chickens, Cofell swore, "was a dom'd lie, there were only sax and thirty, for I eat the guzzards."[34]

Cofell and his scofellites (eventually all backcountry loyalists were called by this term) formed the core of backcountry resistance to the Revolution. Initially the scofellites counted Cherokee Indians as their allies. Colonel Richard Richardson, in December 1775, defeated a group of backcountry loyalists at Great Cane Brake in Cherokee country, taking 136 prisoners, of whom six were "scopholite" officers (one of whom was "colored" and another, "mulatto"). Some scofellites were among "white Indians" captured in the Cherokee War of 1776.[35]

As the war progressed "the word Tory was erased from the lips of Carolinians, and replaced by the word, dreaded or beloved, Scofellite," writes the historian of the backcountry "maroons." "Whatever the chain of command of the British Regulars, most backcountry Loyalists of the deep South looked to Colonel Scofell as their leader and inspiration, for he was paramount chief of the maroons, the predominant Loyalist component."[36] The rebel General William Moultrie referred to "scopholites" as "some of the tories who were led by one Col. Scophol, Col. of militia, an illiterate, stupid, noisy blockhead."[37]

In 1778 Cofell collected about 500 loyalists in the Ninety-Six District of South Carolina and cut a plundering swath from the Savannah River to St Mary's in East Florida. Cofell's followers joined Colonel Mark Provost's British regulars in scouring the Georgia coast and participated in the plundering raids of Colonel Thomas Brown's royal rangers into the South Carolina and Georgia backcountry.[38]

Small bandit gangs of chameleonic loyalty as suited their purposes thrived in war-ravaged South Carolina and Georgia. William Lee was one of the many banditti. He had been sentenced to death for horse and cattle stealing in 1763 but was pardoned on grounds of insanity. Just after the war the South Carolina legislature offered a reward for his capture, declaring that he was one of the "most noted of the banditti who have so long infested the district of Ninety-Six."[39] Aedanus Burke also deplored the situation in Ninety-Six District at the war's end: the people were "worried and half ruined by a sett of horse thieves and outlying Banditti that constantly beset the roads, rob the inhabitants and plunder their dwellings."[40] Rebel militia bands like many of their loyalist counterparts degenerated into banditti, committing highway robbery and theft upon plantations, carrying away slaves, horses, cattle, and household goods and robbing people "in some instances [of] even the Cloaths on their backs."[41] General Nathanael Greene, from his camp on the Pee Dee River in South Carolina, in December 1780, rued the fact that "the great Bodies of Militia that have been in Service this year employed against the Enemy & quelling the Tories have almost laid Waste the Country & so corrupted the Principles of the People that they think of nothing but plundering one another."[42]

Daniel McGirth's unsavory group of loyalist irregulars looted widely in South Carolina and Georgia and, after the war, in northern East Florida. McGirth first entered rebel military service in South Carolina as a scout. When one of his officers tried to acquire McGirth's horse, the "elegant" Gray Goose, a quarrel ensued, and McGirth was sentenced to a whipping. While waiting to receive the second round of the lash, he escaped, proclaiming vengeance to all American patriots.[43] He linked up with bandit gangs led by John Linder, Jr and Sr, Belay Cheney, and William "Bloody Bill" Cunningham. After serving briefly with the British invasion of South Carolina in 1779, McGirth took his own mounted band off on pillaging expeditions, stealing horses, cattle, and, even though his own group was interracial, also slaves. The *South Carolina Gazette*, in 1779, called attention to

> a large body of the most infamous banditti and horsethieves that perhaps ever were collected together anywhere, under the direction of McGirt . . . a corps of Indians, with negro and white savages disguised like them, and about 1,500 of the most savage disaffected poor people, seduced from the back settlements of this State and North Carolina."[44]

Eventually posses forced McGirth and his gang to lay low in swamps. After the war McGirth took his forays into East Florida, where he had the benefit of the confusion that existed as the British transferred the territory to the Spaniards. The outgoing British governor, Patrick Tonyn, proclaimed McGirth "an outlaw, the Head and support of a degenerate Gang of high Way Robbers."[45] The new Spanish governor, Vicente Manuel de Zéspedes, relentlessly pursued McGirth and other banditti leaders. They were imprisoned at St Augustine. McGirth escaped and resumed his banditry along the Florida/Georgia border. Captured by Georgia militia in 1788 and 1792, for reasons unknown he regained his freedom. McGirth settled in Camden County, in the southeastern corner of Georgia, and may have resumed his outlaw career in this gangster infested area until his death in 1804.[46]

Various factors combined in the 1780s after the war to root out banditti from the South Carolina and Georgia backcountry. Special troop units were established in each jurisdiction to hunt down outlaws. In South Carolina the western districts were divided into counties, with each one having its county court and jail. Vagrancy laws were passed to govern "all suspicious persons," unlicensed peddlers, persons who traveled about making their living by gambling and horseracing, those owners of land who did not cultivate enough of it to support themselves and their families, and persons who could not produce certificates attesting to their good character from the jurisdictions from whence they came. South Carolina elevated the penalty for the first offence of horsestealing from whipping to death.[47]

A wave of new settlers penetrated into the backcountry. Emigrants from Virginia and the Carolinas flowed into Georgia during the 1780s. The expansion of tobacco agriculture into South Carolina and Georgia brought new plantations and also slavery.

What was happening in the South was occurring elsewhere. The spread of a settled population made for law and order. As the frontiers shifted westward, so did banditti. Not surprisingly, during the 1780s and 1790s, a new breed of cold-blooded murderers and robbers infested the Trans-Appalachian frontier.

CHAPTER SIX

Civilians and soldiers

American military commanders had the distinct advantage over their opponents of being able to avoid urban areas. It was enough of a challenge to exact discipline at campsites or on the march than to have to confront problems that result from soldiers stationed among civilians. Washington had to worry about his troops in urban environs only when the American army briefly occupied New York City in 1776. In the South, Continental and militia units were always afield, with the exception of troop concentration in Charleston during the British siege. British commanders faced a different predicament, having the bulk of their military forces occupying cities during long periods of the war. A nine-month sojourn in Philadelphia sapped the military readiness of Howe and Clinton's army.

The partisan warfare both North and South, with the attendant plundering, intimidation, and violence committed by militia and irregulars, took a heavy toll upon civilian populations. As far as the regular armies were concerned, there were plenty of problems affecting civilian–military relationships. Yet there was also a lighter side, involving social contacts between soldiers and civilians.

Crossing Military Lines

The demands of military security compromised freedom of mobility. The issue was especially a vexatious one for Washington, whose army lay close to British-occupied New York City. Various reasons led citizens to seek passes for travel into New York City: to visit kinsmen and friends or even a relative held as a prisoner of war, to secure debts, to conclude business matters, or, in the case of women, "for the sake of buying tea & trinkets." Washington particularly deprecated the "great part of the illicit traffic" carried on by persons obtaining passes.[1] Too easily persons traveling between the lines served as intelligence agents for the enemy.

Washington learned early the necessity of restricting passes. During the first part of the war, passes could be issued by Congress, the commander-in-chief, governors, general officers and commanders of staff departments in the Continental army, any member of a state legislature or council of state where the traveler resided, and even, when the army was in New York City, a three-man civilian committee. Complaints mounted that military commanders too freely delegated "to inferior officers their power to grant flags and passports." Subsequently passes were to be granted only by the commander-in-chief, a governor of a state, or a state legislature. The states also acted on the subject, with New Jersey having among the toughest regulations: passes could be obtained only from the commander-in-chief or the governor, and it was a penal offence to secure a pass otherwise. Offending magistrates in New Jersey could be fined £50 to £2,000.[2]

General William Maxwell, commanding American military forces in and around Elizabethtown, New Jersey, was rebuked by Washington for being too liberal in allowing persons to go into New York City. Replying to his commander-in-chief in December 1778, Maxwell pointed out that the responsibility lay elsewhere:

> I find it is your wish that the intercourse between the enemy and us may be as small as possible, yet you say I may permit so many of the Inhabitants to pass within the Enemys Lines as have written Licenses from the Congress, the Governors, or Legislative Authority. I am well assured your Excellency has no Idea of what number the Legislative authority of Pennsylvania has sent in to the enemy . . . . had they been properly sorted with a Man to each woman it would have made a good settlement for a new Colony.[3]

Visitation to army encampments required close surveillance. Of course, provision was made for women who attached themselves to various units in a support capacity and for all licensed sutlers. Washington also let it be known that "people who are innocently bringing refreshments to camp" should be "encouraged."[4] But suspicious persons, especially "country people or transient persons coming to or from the army" who "cannot give a good account of themselves" were detained in order to ascertain their status and intentions.[5]

One measure proved effective in screening out undesirable visitors: having "three intelligent well affected inhabitants" who were acquainted with the people of the neighborhood "stationed upon the roads leading into Camp" to give out passes "to those who may be safely admitted."[6] General Orders of August 1, 1781 stated that any persons without arms who were found at the front, flank or rear of the army and "who cannot give a good account of themselves" were "to be apprehended and committed to the Provost."[7]

While the liberal granting of passes for women to visit army encampments did not raise many hackles, increasingly female visitors came under suspicion. Philadelphia women entered camp under the pretence of visiting friends but actually had the intent of procuring goods at cheap prices from sutlers—items that were needed for the army. Washington also suspected that visiting women sometimes enticed men to desert. Thus Washington, with his army at Valley Forge, issued orders that women from Philadelphia "are not to be permitted to pass the first Guards without being informed they cannot return."[8] While the American army was in New York City, General Alexander McDougall typically was perplexed with Mary Debeau, who had gone to British-held Staten Island to see the mother of her husband, John Debeau, supposedly a member of an American militia regiment. Upon her return to New York City, McDougall had her "searched by matrons for Papers," but nothing incriminating was found. McDougall was certain "from her appearance and deportment" that Mrs Debeau was "a follower of the Enemy's army." Not content to let the matter rest, McDougall remanded her to a special city committee for further investigation.[9]

Ann Bates, a Philadelphia schoolteacher and married to an ordinance repairman in the British army, succeeded remarkably in gaining numerous passes to travel in American military sectors, from which she presented intelligence to the British in New York City. In the summer of 1778 she went from Philadelphia to Washington's encampment in the New York Highlands under a pass given by Benedict Arnold, the American commandant at Philadelphia. She visited the American encampment north of New York City twice more, posing as a peddler, and each time reported to British military authorities in New York City. In September 1778 she attached herself to a forward detachment commanded by General Charles Scott, and upon being recognized as a British soldier's wife, just in time managed to secure a pass from Scott to go near the British lines to fetch some items she had forgotten to take with her, and, of course, find refuge with the enemy.[10]

Protecting Civilians from Stragglers

Despite severe restraints and harsh punishments, some regular troops, when they thought they could act with impunity, engaged in theft and destruction of civilian property. The problem related chiefly to stragglers, those who strayed from main lines of marches and battle formations or even were so bold as to wander out of an encampment. They could always plead they were misdirected or lost or having been in pursuit of a military objective.

But staying detached from one's unit was absence without leave. Lieutenant William Feltman of the Pennsylvania line, while serving in South Carolina in January 1782, noted a not uncommon situation.

> After breakfast Lts. Doyle, McDowell, Allison and self took a walk to the country (about four miles) where we found a number of Carolina soldiers straggling through the country, which is against General Orders . . . We heard a musket fired, we pursued three of said soldiers and caught two of them, who had shot one of the poor negroes' hogs. We guarded them to camp and had them confined.[11]

Misdeeds of stragglers from the regular armies were almost wholly confined to common pilfering. Rapes on civilians by soldiers was an extreme rarity. In both armies, rape cases likely involved victims who were army wives and children and occurred within the area of a campsite. The few perpetrators of rape on civilians that show up on British army records were almost exclusively soldiers from loyalist regiments. The American propaganda mill and a congressional investigative committee tried to show the prevalency of rape by British and Hessian soldiers during the New Jersey campaign of 1776–7, but corroborative evidence is lacking.[12]

Early in the war Washington recognized the need for strict accountability of the whereabouts of all the troops. He entreated regimental commanders to hold unannounced musters three times a day and to punish immediately the delinquents. Soldiers' packs were to be regularly searched. One problem, too, was troops being distracted on a long march. The commander-in-chief informed General William Heath in May 1777 that he had learned "that the officers loiter away their time in a most scandalous manner on their march from Boston to Peekskill." In every little village on the way, "you find an officer and ten or a dozen men drinking and gaming in the public houses instead of prosecuting their march to the place of destination." Washington ordered Heath to "despatch an active, spirited officer, on whom you can depend, with orders to sweep every town between Boston and Peekskill of the officers and soldiers who are idling away their times in them."[13]

By a congressional authorization of May 27, 1778, Washington established a provost guard, consisting of one captain, four lieutenants, and 63 enlisted men, four of whom were "excarabineers" (executioners), selected from each of the brigades. Mounted, as "light dragoons," the unit closely resembled the modern "military police." It became known as the Maréchaussée (a French word for provost troops), recruited from among German Americans in Berks and Lancaster Counties, Pennsylvania and commanded by Captain Bartholomew von Heer, a Prussian immigrant. Washington made "former Prussians responsible for discipline within the army because they had little in common with native-born troops and had a fierce reputation for military order," writes Charles P. Neimeyer. Generally the duties of the Maréchauseé were "to watch over the good order and regularity of the army, in camp, quarters, on a march, to silence all quarrels, tumults and riots; detect and hinder every species of Marauding, prevent straggling and other unsoldierlike licenses among the troops."[14] General Orders of October 11, 1778 announced that the "Marechausie corps" was to "patrole the Camp and it's neighborhood for the purpose of apprehending Deserters, Marauders, Drunkards, Rioters and Straglers." Soldiers found beyond the nearest pickets on either side of the army or a mile distant from the centre of the army were to be taken into custody. "All Countrymen and Strangers that may be found near the pickets or in camp" without the proper passes and even persons with passes who hovered around longer than "a reasonable time" were subject to arrest.[15] Washington, however, cautioned his elite Maréchaussée team to "always remember that you are as carefully to avoid laying innocent free Citizens under any unnecessary restraint and inconvenience, on the one hand, as risking any mischief to the Army from ill-placed lenity on the other."[16] A special function of the mounted police corps was "to remain on the old Ground till the Colems & Baggage have Marched off in order to secure all such Soldiers as have loitered in Camp."[17]

Military Lodging among Civilians

Enlisted men were required to construct huts in which to live at American army encampments of long duration. Generals and field officers were expected to find quarters in the homes of local inhabitants, even if that meant commuting several miles to camp. Normally, as required by law in most states, local magistrates had to give their stamp of approval for requisitioning quarters in residences. But often a magistrate could not be found or approval was withheld, whereupon quartering was achieved solely by military order.[18] This was one of the ironies of the war as the colonists had protested against the British quartering acts of 1765 and 1774, which did not authorize billeting in occupied dwellings.

It was a disconcerting sight to witness several soldiers coming to one's home and chalking above the front door the name of a general officer. To 16-year-old Sally Wister the inscription of "[Gen.] Smallwood's Quarters" on the front of her house was not so bad because at least it "secured us from straggling soldiers." When the Maryland general arrived, however, he brought with him six aides, and horses, baggage, and wagons were crammed into the yard.[19]

Field officers did the best they could to find lodgings after the pickings by the generals. General William Maxwell had to get the quartermaster-general, Nathanael Greene, to remove a colonel and a major who had opted

for quarters that Maxwell had selected in the Morristown vicinity in December 1779.[20] But even then, some generals wound up with undesirable
space. General Samuel Holden Parsons, also at the Morristown encampment, complained to Greene: "I beg you to order me a large Markee and a
Stove as the last Resort I have to cover me; I cannot stay in this Tophet [i.e.
Hell] a Day longer. . . . The Room I now have is not more than Eight feet
Square for Six of Us; and the family worse than the Devil."[21]

Washington always needed ample quarters for himself and his "military family" and for Martha's visits. At Valley Forge he resided at the Isaac
Potts house, and finding the space cramped he built an adjacent log pav-
ilion to serve as a dining area. The bakehouse on the property was used as
an auditorium for theatrical productions and courts-martial.[22]

The British army in the cities had greater opportunity for lodging,
although the flood of refugees and usually a large prisoner of war population put a squeeze on accommodations. The fire in New York City in
September 1776 destroyed many structures. British soldiers in New York
City were billeted in vacant buildings, churches, and houses in designated
areas, while officers searched out lodging in residences. When necessary the
army required citizens to give up space in their homes. Those officers with
mistresses were expected to take up quarters in vacant houses.[23]

The situation was much the same in Philadelphia. The British, as did
the Americans elsewhere, marked doors of houses selected for officers'
lodgings. Quakeress Elizabeth Drinker voiced complaints: a "great number
of Foreign Troops" were quartered in her neighborhood, British soldiers
tore down her shed for firewood, and one officer "stole my servant girl
over the fence." Drinker had to accept Major Crammond as a lodger.
Though taking a liking to him, she objected to his late hours, finding space
for his three servants, and keeping three cows, two sheep, and fowl belonging to him. Her diary entry for January 19, 1778 noted: "This Morning our officer mov'd his lodgings from the blew Chamber to the little
front parlor, so that he has the two front Parlors, a Chamber up two pair of
stairs for his bagage, and the Stable wholly to himself, besides the use of
the Kitchen, his Camp Bed is put up."[24]

After the British evacuated Philadelphia, a mess had to be cleaned up.
Congressman Josiah Bartlett wrote John Langdon, Speaker of the New
Hampshire House of Representatives, in early July 1778 that "Congress
meets in the College Hall as the State House was left by the enemy in a
most filthy and sordid situation. . . . Some of the genteel houses were used
for stables and holes cut in the parlor floors and their dung shovelled into
the cellars."[25]

Although the American army was never stationed in Philadelphia,
enough soldiers and militiamen were there from time to time that much of
the billeting practices by the British were adopted. In 1776 Quaker meeting-
houses were used for quartering soldiers. The Pennsylvania Council of

Safety in January 1777 ordered the lodging of militia in "private houses of persons who had not declared for the American cause." Similarly, in January 1781, the Pennsylvania Supreme Executive Council directed that officers of the Pennsylvania line then in Philadelphia be billeted in the homes of Quakers and suspected loyalists.[26]

Spectators and Visitors

Civilians and soldiers often came into contact in pleasant ways. People turned out to watch military exercises, reviews, and parades. The spectacles frequently left impressions that American soldiers exhibited less than finished military deportment. Congressman John Adams described for his wife the march of Washington's army through Philadelphia on August 24, 1777. "Our Soldiers have not yet quite the Air of Soldiers," he said. "They don't step exactly in Time. They don't hold up their Heads, quite erect, nor turn their Toes, so exactly as they ought. They don't all of them cock their Hats—and such as do, don't all wear them the same Way." For the parade, Washington assigned officers to prevent the crowd from pressing against the troops and ordered that any soldier breaking ranks would receive 39 lashes "at the first halting place afterwards."[27] Janet Schaw, sister of a royal official, recalled watching an exercise of "bush-fighting" of about 2,000 troops in Wilmington, North Carolina: "It appeared so confused . . . I cannot say whether they performed it well or not; but this I know that they were heated with rum." Passing in review afterwards, the soldiers were "preceded by a very ill beat-drum and a fiddler, who was also in his shirt with a long sword and a cue at his hair, who played with all his might. They made indeed a most unmartial appearance."[28] Civilians enjoyed watching a mock battle between French soldiers and Colonel Christopher Greene's Continental regiment in Rhode Island on October 7, 1780.

Spectators caused soldiers themselves to raise their eyebrows. Lieutenant William Feltman, with Continentals commanded by Lafayette on the march just outside of Richmond, Virginia in late June 1781, observed that the local inhabitants

> sometimes come to the road side in order to take a view of us as we pass by, but a person can scarcely discern any part of them but the nose and eyes, as they have themselves muffed up with linens, &c., in order to prevent the sun from burning their faces (I mean the female sex). At the same time they will have a number of blacks standing around them, all naked, nothing to hide their nakedness.[29]

So many spectators crowded into the American trenches at the siege of Yorktown that Washington finally had to order that all civilians keep their distance.[30]

Army personnel, especially with the discharge of weaponry and artillery, joined with civilians in Fourth of July celebrations, and visitors to camp participated in special army festivities, such as observance of anniversaries of the French Alliance.[31]

In settled areas, soldiers at swimming occasionally affronted the sensibilities of the local populace. General Nathanael Greene, commanding the Brooklyn defenses on Long Island in May 1776, responded to complaints that some of his men had been swimming at the Mill Pond "in Open View of the Women and that they Come out of the Water and Run up Naked to the Houses with a Design to Insult and Wound the Modesty of female Decency." Thus "Expressing His disapprobation of such a Beastly Conduct," Greene promised severe punishment to anyone persisting in this behavior.[32] It became the practice of the army, concerned with safety as well as conduct, to permit troops to bathe only one day a week for less than a half hour in squads supervised by a non-commissioned officer.[33]

Officers stopped for refreshments and social visits at homes in the vicinity of a march or encampment. The young bachelor officers received close inspection by the young women of the household and neighborhood. Teenaged Sally Wister eagerly anticipated the visits. She was the daughter of Daniel Wister, a prosperous Philadelphia merchant, who with his family lived at the farmhouse of Hannah Fouke, 15 miles above Philadelphia, during the British occupation of that city. Sally, her sisters, and young friends put on their "dress and lips" for greeting the officers. Her best finery "for conquest" was to wear "a new purple and white Persian, white petticoat, muslin apron, gauze cap, and handkerchief."[34]

Sally Wister considered 24-year-old Captain Alexander Dandridge, a cousin of Martha Washington and brother-in-law of Patrick Henry, "the handsomest man I ever beheld." The ebullient Quaker girl had a less favorable opinion of two other Virginians, Lieutenants Lee and Waring. She "ridiculed their manner of speaking" and "took great delight in teasing them. They were not . . . first-rate gentlemen. But they are gone to Virginia, where they may sing, dance and eat turkey hash and fry'd hominy all day long, if they choose."[35]

A judgmental bias toward the opposite sex could go the other way, too. Several months before Sally recorded her impressions, Captain John Chilton of Virginia, writing from camp at Morristown, observed that

> these Jersey women are fond of Notions as they call our jimmy-
> lads and scarfs, and they like "a nice jiffer man." And yet, poor
> things, what with drinking tea (they are desperate people for tea)
> spoon victuals, and eating hot buckwheat cakes, there is hardly
> one above 16 that have their fore-teeth, nay that has a foretooth.[36]

Kinfolk and friends of soldiers were liberally allowed visits to camp. Of course, they were not always happy to hear "the foul language" of the average soldier.[37] Lieutenant Ebenezer Huntington wrote his grandfather, Jabez Huntington, from the Roxbury camp outside of Boston in February 1776 that "When Mamma was at Camp, I told her that I wanted some money sent to me, but have never received any."[38]

Visitors at camp observed parades, drills, and punishments. On the British side, Nicholas Cresswell, a traveler from England in New York City during May 1777, commented that he saw three Hessian regiments in review; they were "fine troops, but very slow in their motions when compared with the English." He was appalled to witness a Hessian corporal run the gauntlet of his regiment eight times; "he had upwards of 2000 lashes . . . not a single muscle of his face discomposed all the time. They appear to be a set of cruel, unfeeling people."[39]

Young women visited the American camps, even though Washington discouraged the practice. When the army halted at Germantown, Pennsylvania on August 3, 1777, Lieutenant James McMichael reported:

> The largest collection of young ladies I almost ever beheld came to camp. They marched in three columns. The field officers paraded the rest of the officers and detached scouting parties to prevent being surrounded by them. For my part being sent on scout, I at last sighted the ladies and gave them to know that they must repair to headquarters, upon which they accompanied me as prisoners. But on parading them at the Colonels marquee, they were dismissed, after we treated them with a double bowl of Sangaree.[40]

Officers' wives visited the army during the winter–spring encampments. Of course, many enlisted men's wives enrolled as camp followers. Few wives of junior officers visited the army. But the spouses of those generals and field officers who were financially secure often attended, even with their children in tow. The quartermaster department assisted in moving families to and from camp.[41]

At Valley Forge, many wives of general officers visited, including Martha Washington, Catherine "Kitty" Greene, Lucy Knox, Deborah Putnam, Molly Stark, and Lady "Kitty" Stirling. Martha Washington also stayed with the army at Cambridge in the autumn of 1775, at New York City in the spring of 1776, at Morristown in the spring of 1777 and the spring of 1780, and at Newburgh, New York in 1782–3. Sarah Livingston, Lady Stirling, wife of General Lord (William Alexander) Stirling and brother of the New Jersey governor, William Livingston, liked to go about the Valley Forge camp knocking on the doors of huts to distribute food and clothing.[42]

Washington allowed civilians with complaints to be heard at camp. Elizabeth Drinker and several friends went to Valley Forge and "requested an audience" with Washington to protest against the treatment of fellow

Quakers. The group waited with Martha Washington until "GW came and discoarsed with us freely, but not so long as we could have wish'd, as dinner was serv'd in, to which he had invited us." There were 17 officers besides George and Martha Washington at the "elegant dinner." All that Washington could do for the visitors was to grant them a pass to Lancaster, where they could be heard by Congress, which had taken refuge there.[43]

Military–Civilian Entertainment

Both American and British officers held balls to which civilian women were invited. During the occupation of Philadelphia, British officers presented a dance assembly every Thursday night, January 29–April 30, 1778. Rebecca Franks commented that at these gatherings she had "no loss for partners;" one night she danced with "seven different gentlemen, for you must know 'tis a fixed rule to dance but two dances with the same person."[44]

Beginning the social season in Charleston, South Carolina, a great ball was held at one of the mansions, at which time British officers and "elegantly attired slave women danced away the evening."[45] Even British officers on parole behind American lines staged dances. Thus Ensign Thomas Hughes reported form Lancaster, Pennsylvania in January 1780:

> The Mohairs (aliter Town Bucks) having hinted at giving balls—at which no British officers were to be invited—it was resolved to be beforehand with them; gave a hop last night at which all the ladies in town were present. It was an agreeable evening—had a supper and danced till three this morning.[46]

There were hundreds of dancing assemblies during the war, which were attended by army officers stationed nearby. The Marquis de Chastellux commented that the masters of ceremonies for those gatherings "are generally chosen from among the most distinguished officers of the army."

At the American encampment at Morristown, 1779–80, the Morristown Dance Assembly was organized, with subscriptions of $400 each from 34 officers. Dances were held in the vacant space at the commissary's storehouse and also at George O'Hara's tavern, across from the Morristown village green. At the first dance in February 1780, Washington, attired in black velvet, led off by dancing with the hefty Mrs Lucy (wife of General Henry) Knox; only 16 women showed up to dance with 60 men. Usually local inhabitants sent their daughters; the loyalist newspaper in New York City, however, derisively commented that "fifty females" were "picked up" for the Morristown dances. Still, the dancing assembly did contribute to matchmaking. There Alexander Hamilton began courtship of Elizabeth Schuyler, whom he married in December 1780; Elizabeth had come to

Morristown to visit her aunt, Mrs John Cochran, wife of the surgeon-general for the Middle Department.[47]

Music was essential for stirring an *esprit de corps* in the army, and military bands were popular with the general public. Every regiment in the Continental army had its drummers and fifers. Washington thought that the "music of the army" was "in general very bad," and he often included in his general orders instructions for strict times to practice. "Nothing is more agreeable, and ornamental," said Washington, "than good music; every officer, for the credit of his corps, should take care to provide it."[48] Washington, however, disapproved of having regimental bands because much of their expenses came out of the pockets of officers and the "invidious distinctions" over keeping bands produced an unhealthy rivalry.[49]

At least seven American military bands existed, the two best being attached to artillery regiments, and led by Colonels John Crane and Thomas Procter. Half of Procter's ten musicians were natives of Germany. The bands performed for holiday celebrations, marches, funerals, college commencements, Masonic functions, parades, dinner parties of officers, and dances. Two Hessian bands captured at Trenton were in much demand for military and public performances. Both performed at Independence Day celebrations in Philadelphia. One British band deserted and performed in Boston.[50]

Most of the 56 British regiments that served in America during the Revolution had bands. Regimental bands accompanying the French army performed for the public at Newport and also at Baltimore when passing through while on the march toward Yorktown. The French bandsmen, dressed in Turkish costumes, introduced Americans to the janizary (Turkish military) style then popular in Europe and to bass drums, cymbals, tambourines, and bells.[51]

The German bands, with their full complement of instruments, were always in demand for performances. One observer noted that a Hessian band provided "wonderful music" for a Masonic parade in New York City, for which the "musicians received good pay."[52] James McHenry, a former military aide to Washington, apparently succeeded in arranging with the Secretary at War for a Hessian band among the Saratoga Convention prisoners confined at Frederick, Maryland to be transferred in July 1782 to Philadelphia and to perform for a salary at the city's "play house." Washington observed that "if the Ladies should derive as much pleasure from the attainment of this Band, as I wish them, they will now be at the summit of happiness."[53]

A mark of an officer and a gentleman was cultural refinement. Staging theatrical events was a common practice by officers in both armies. The British had the advantage in the promotion of theatrical productions because of their occupation of cities. But American officers were equally enterprising. Plays were good for morale and gave opportunity for camaraderie sorely needed among the often fractious officer corps. Even back during the French and Indian War, at the frontier Fort Cumberland in Maryland, Washington's officers of the Virginia Regiment had put on Nicholas Rowe's *Tamerlane* for their own amusement.

At Valley Forge, the American officers staged Joseph Addison's *Cato* and another play at the bakehouse, and made plans for the production of four other plays, only to be interrupted by the army moving out of camp.[54] Several army officers, local residents, and college students at New Brunswick, New Jersey combined their talents to present their theater in "a spacious room, called Whitehall. . . . They played from Shakespeare and Addison."[55]

Congress took a dim view of military theater. Just before the war, Congress, in its Continental Association, had enjoined patriot Americans to refrain from "every species of extravagance and dissipation," including "plays." In October 1778, at the same time that some American army officers were staging a play at the Southwark Theatre "for the Benefit of Families who have suffered in the War for American Liberty," Congress again reiterated its condemnation of the theater, to the extent of declaring that "any person holding an office under the United States, who shall act, promote, encourage or attend such plays, shall be deemed unworthy to hold such office, and shall be accordingly dismissed."[56] This injunction appears to have ended only the thespian aspirations of American army officers for performing in Philadelphia. After Congress's prohibition of October 1778, Continental army officers staged *Cato* at New Brunswick, and there were also productions by military personnel at Portsmouth, New Hampshire, and Reading, Pennsylvania. Even in Philadelphia, in defiance of a powerful anti-theater constituency rallied by Quaker and Presbyterian leaders, citizens, including members of Congress, flocked to attend theatricals at the College of Philadelphia (in 1779 named the University of the State of Pennsylvania).[57]

British garrisons staged dramatic performances during the war at Boston, Portsmouth, New Hampshire, Charleston, South Carolina, Savannah, Georgia, and Charlottesville and Staunton, Virginia. During the brief British occupation of Boston, Faneuil Hall was turned into a military playhouse. The play season opened with *The Blockade of Boston*, a farce acted by British army officers and ridiculing George Washington and his troops. Other plays performed included Nicholas Rowe's *Tamerlane* and Mrs Susanna Centlivre's *The Busybody*. In New York City, casts of British officers and some New York loyalists and professionals (at least five of whom were women), aided by a 14-piece Hessian band put on 139 performances from 1777 to 1782. Proceeds from the sale of tickets for seating in boxes and the pit at 8s. each and 4s. for the gallery were used for the benefit of widows and orphans of British soldiers killed during the war. In 1783, Dennis Ryan and his American Company put on most of the theatrical performances in New York City, although at times including military players.[58]

During the brief British occupation of Philadelphia, military theater rivaled that of New York City. Productions, usually double bills, were staged at the Southwark Theatre weekly from January 19 to May 19, 1778. Major John André and Captain Oliver DeLancey served as managers, the former also painting scenery and the latter excelling as an actor. The two officers also organized the *Mischianza* of May 18, an extravaganza, lasting from 4 p.m. to 4 a.m., honoring the departure of General Howe for England. The spectacle included a regatta of decorated boats, a parade, fireworks and artillery display, a mock tournament of knights, dancing, and a midnight banquet with 430 place settings. Twenty-two field officers shelled out 3,312 guineas to underwrite the costs. A Philadelphia Quakeress lamented: "How insensible do these people appear, while our Land is so greatly desolated, and Death and sore destruction has overtaken and impends over so many."[59]

Elsewhere British military thespians were also active. "Gentlemen of the Garrison" staged plays in Savannah in September–November 1781. In Staunton, Virginia, in June 1779, "a group of English soldiers [prisoners of war]," wrote an observer, "has put up a Comedy House, where plays are given twice a week, and in which there are already three sets of scenery. . . . The officers lend the actors the necessary articles of clothing; drummers are transformed into queens and beauties. Very good pieces are performed." Because of the "satirical additions" to the plays, American officers did not permit their men to attend.[60]

Civilians and Military Authority

The war touched the lives of many Americans. Persons found themselves in war zones, as victims of depredations and impressments, and even subjected to military justice, especially during the early part of the war when the loyalist threat seemed rampant. As the war progressed, however, on the American side great deference was given by the military commands to the civil governments, although in the South during 1780–2 outside the cities there was difficulty in maintaining law and order under any constituted authority. Governor William Livingston of New Jersey, in February 1783, expressed pride that "perhaps no Army in the world has ever paid a more sacred regard to the civil authority than the American Troops have done throughout the whole Course of the war."[61]

During various periods of occupation, the British army established military rule in America's six largest cities—Boston, Newport, Philadelphia, New York City, Charleston, and Savannah. Military rule was the most mild in Boston and Newport, chiefly confined to enforcement of local ordinances that already existed. Unlike Boston, however, in Newport courts-martial tried criminal cases. During most of the period of the occupation of Savannah, royal civil government was re-established. The seven-year occupation of New York City witnessed a thoroughgoing displacement of civil government. The commandant for the city ran the government by proclamations. The Board of Police and the city Vestry enforced his orders. In 1780 a Court of Police was established to try most civil cases and minor crimes. The Chamber of Commerce decided on business disputes. British military administration for Philadelphia and Charleston followed much the same lines as that for New York City.[62]

Feeble attempts by the British were made to establish royally sponsored civil governments for New York and Georgia. General James Robertson, commandant of New York City since 1776, served as the royal governor of New York, 1780–2; actually the position was not much more than that of a figurehead, as the British control extended only to New York City, Staten Island, and tenuously to parts of Long Island, Westchester County, and the Bronx, and General Henry Clinton was reluctant to share power with Robertson. Judge Thomas Jones considered Robertson, who was in poor health, "the laughing-stock of the citizens" and one who, along with his cronies, squandered public funds on "strumpets, panderers, favorities, and pretty little misses."[63] The last royal governor of the colony of Georgia, Sir James Wright, at age 65, was returned to his office in 1779 after the British had recaptured Savannah. With the state's small population and the continuing warfare, the royal government was more elusive than real.

For American troops in the North, the civilian courts and legislatures kept the upper hand in checking soldiers' abuses of citizens. Often reprimands sufficed, for example when the Pennsylvania Council of Safety censured an officer for searching for deserters in a bawdy house.[64] In cases involving soldiers who had committed assaults upon civilians, local courts successfully claimed jurisdiction and meted out punishments. Congress frequently added its own reprimand and punishment of officers who transgressed civil authority. Congress's Articles of War (article 1, section 10) made quite clear the responsible jurisdiction for deciding cases concerned with a soldier's behaviour affecting civilians:

> Whenever any officer or soldier shall be accused of a capital crime, or of having used violence, or committed any offence against the persons or property of the good people of any of the United American States . . . the commanding officer and officers of every regiment, troop, or party, to which the person or persons so accused shall belong, are hereby required, upon application duly made by or in behalf of the party or parties injured, to use his utmost endeavors to deliver over such accused person or persons to the civil magistrates.[65]

Washington let civil prosecutions of officers and soldiers take their course. But he warned that civilians treating army personnel "in an improper manner" did so "at their own risque."[66] Regarding Lieutenant Patrick Carnes' improper seizure of forage, Washington ordered that Carnes "must be amenable to the civil authority." Above all, Washington insisted on harmony "between the Inhabitants and every part of the Army." When Captain Josiah Stoddard of the Second Continental Dragoons conducted a rescue of one of his men, who had been jailed in Norwalk, Connecticut, for assault on a civilian, Washington ordered the soldier back to the custody of the civilian authorities.[67]

One dramatic confrontation occurred when General William Maxwell lodged two loyalists caught delivering recruits to a British privateer in the army provost jail at Elizabethtown, New Jersey. Maxwell informed Washington of his action, and the commander in chief acknowledged that the two detainees obviously had "treasonable connexion and intercourse" with the enemy. A New Jersey judge issued a writ of habeas corpus, but Maxwell refused to accept the writ, and on the second attempt of a servor to deliver it, he took him by the neck and threw him out. Acting on the advice of Washington, Maxwell finally remanded the captives to the civil magistry. The case became involved in politics. Abraham Clark, who favored someone other than Maxwell to lead the New Jersey brigade, tried to get Congress to suspend Maxwell from command for having ignored civil authority. A congressional committee endorsed Clark's view, but Congress did not act on the recommendation.[68] Washington wisely ignored the controversy.

While the armies appropriated the use of buildings and quartered troops in private residences, often without the consent of the owners, it was the impressment of provisions, livestock, forage, horses, and wagons that incurred the greatest hardships because families might be deprived of all but the most marginal means of subsistence.

Normally supplies for the military forces were acquired by various means. Congress tried the hiring of merchants on a commission basis to buy supplies. Unfortunately this practice led to overpricing and inferior quality of goods. Deputies of staff departments also went about purchasing what was needed for the troops. Eventually Congress persuaded the states to levy "specific taxes" in the form of such commodities as beef, flour, forage, horses, pork, rum, and wagons, which would be forwarded to the armies. At the end of the war Congress turned supplying the armies over to contractors. With the very existence of military forces at stake because of scarcity of food and means of transportation, impressment of personal property was necessary.

Congress and the states had two requisites for employing impressment: authorization from a local magistry and full payment for goods received. Unfortunately magistrates were sometimes not around when needed or, insisting on the priority of civilians' rights, refused permission for impressment. Because of the depreciation of the Continental and state currencies and payment ultimately in certificates pledged for later redemption, farmers were reluctant to sell their commodities to the army. Forcible impressment was then the alternative. Governor Thomas Jefferson, with his state invaded by a British army in March 1781, wrote to General Lafayette, who commanded American forces in Virginia, that "In a Country whose means of paiment are neither prompt nor of the most desirable Kind, impressing property for the public use has been found indispensable."[69] Washington, to whom Congress several times entrusted plenary power for impressment in a declared military zone, deplored taking goods from persons without their consent. "By Military Impress," he noted in May 1781, "we are daily & hourly oppressing the people—souring their tempers and alienating their affection."[70] The commander-in-chief also feared that impressment set a bad example for common soldiers, encouraging them to plunder. Indeed, pilfering, which was strictly forbidden and severely punished, was enough of a problem as it was. When supplies ran out at the second Morristown encampment in January 1780, Washington refused to enforce punishment of soldiers for plundering the countryside.[71]

Impressment became more frequent from 1780 to the end of the war because of the deteriorating financial conditions of government. Communities were assigned quotas, and inspectors accompanied justices of the peace through the countryside inventorying and assessing chattel property. Soldiers were cautioned to leave enough items for the support of the affected families, and in Virginia could not seize more than 10 percent of the property.[72] Improper impressment carried a stiff military penalty. A court martial at Valley Forge tried Hugh Backer, a forage master, for taking a horse from Joseph Smedley without showing a warrant or giving a receipt. Backer was discharged from the army and compensation to Smedley for the loss of his horse was deducted from the pay due to Backer.[73]

Civilians often resisted impressment, turning to civil courts for redress and even engaging in sabotage, such as disabling army transport wagons.[74] Some states passed laws making impressment more difficult. Virginia during and after the Yorktown campaign prohibited all impressments except by warrant of the governor and during actual invasion.[75]

Although both armies followed the practice of reimbursement for impressed items, the urgency of war often led to neglect or violations of citizens' property rights; it was a principle of war to clear out all resources of an area before an enemy invaded it. The British hit-and-run forage expeditions in the middle states, the destructive war waged in the South by irregular units, and an army on the move living off the land were primary factors in forcible impressment. British commanders acted without the support of the local civil authority. The widespread desolation in the South conducted by Tarleton's Legion and similar units led one observer to remark that "Old England" had "descended" to "a mean, barbarous way of carrying on a war."[76]

Citizens, either willingly or under duress, who gave up supplies to the American army found great difficulty in receiving payment on the certificates presented them. Neither the army supply departments nor the national treasury had funds to redeem the certificates. Before 1780 the certificates drew no interest; starting in 1780 the certificates designated specie value and earned interest. Eventually the states accepted supply certificates for state taxes. States also had to redeem certificates that they had issued for supplies, and, in the case of Virginia, holders had to endure the slow process of verification of their claims by state and county courts. After the war Congress issued new certificates at 6 percent interest replacing the old quartermaster and commissary certificates.[77] Unable to pay off this debt on demand, the certificates circulated at much less than full value. The obligation for redemption passed into the national debt.

CHAPTER SEVEN

Recruitment and society

At the outbreak of hostilities, American revolutionaries from all walks of life took up arms to join with the embattled New England farmers to drive away the British "invaders." Within a year the *rage militaire* wore thin, and the rebels faced the reality of the need for durable and sustained armed forces. Victory depended upon a steady influx of common soldiers. Like all wars, from the view of those with the greater stake in society, the more common and lower-sort the soldier the better, to relieve the burden of combat from those who were the greater beneficiaries of the outcome. Men who signed on for specified terms of service in the army as privates or non-commissioned officers could expect few of the emoluments granted to officers, who came from a higher standing in a community and could resign their military commissions at will. The army witnessed wholesale departures from its ranks, and those who stayed among the enlisted men were those who were even more from the lower reaches of society and who saw in service an actual improvement of their own welfare.

Most Americans at the onset of the Revolution believed that a militia-based citizen-soldiery could rise to the challenge of beating back the intruding British forces. Every male, aged 16 to 50, was obligated for military service in defense of his state, as had been the situation in colonial times. Traditionally militia turned out for active military service in the field for only one or several months, and even if a militiaman volunteered to accompany an expedition outside his state, he could expect to return home in a short while. As the Revolutionary War became more intense and of long duration, recruits for the army were hard to come by. Those who initially served felt they had done their duty and that they were more needed at home. The solution for keeping an American army in the field involved the acceptance of two practices that transgressed upon cherished principles: the creation of a standing army and coerced service. In January 1776 Samuel Adams warned that "a standing Army . . . is always dangerous to the Liberties of the People;" soldiers "are apt to consider themselves as a Body distinct from the rest of the Citizens."[1] Opposed to a standing army in peacetime, Americans, to win the war, had to accept one in wartime.

Enlisting Common Soldiers

The birth of the Continental army occurred on June 14, 1775 when Congress voted to assume responsibility for the New England militia forces besieging Boston and to raise ten rifle companies (six from Pennsylvania and two each from Maryland and Virginia), which formed the first Continental regiment; the next day George Washington was named "to command all the Continental forces."[2]

During the rest of 1775 Congress called for regiments to be raised from every state and Canada, with enlistments expiring at the end of the year. Fortunately enough re-enlistments for one-year terms kept the army in the field, but it was becoming evident that a spirited patriotism could not solely be relied upon to win the war. Soldiers were expected to serve at long distances from their homes and with very little pay. In late 1776, Congress ambitiously called for the raising of 88 regiments of 728 men each, making a total of 63,000 troops. New enlistees would serve for three years or the duration of the war.[3] This provision itself was detrimental to attracting new recruits. The victories at Trenton and Princeton, however, provided enough stimulus for enlistments to keep the army intact.

The actions of Congress reflected a change of relationship between citizens and soldiers, an acceptance of a professional military force. Roger Sherman, in a congressional debate, berated the "long enlistment" requirement as "a state of slavery. There ought to be a rotation which is in favor of liberty."[4]

A contractual agreement between enlistees and citizens became paramount in the establishment of obligation to military duty. A soldier was promised wages, food, shelter, and a bounty paid in part at the time of induction and the rest at the termination of service. By mid-1777 patriotic zeal as a compelling factor for entering military service had all but disappeared.

Throughout the war recruitment for the Continental army lagged for various reasons. Word spread of the prevalence of disease, hardships, and harsh discipline of camp life. Inadequate clothing and food and the lack of freedom and privacy awaited enlistees. Some 10,000 New Englanders preferred the more profitable service aboard privateersmen to army life. But the chief deterrents to enlistment or re-enlistment in Continental service was insufficient financial reward and the competition from the states for military manpower.

Congress at first offered a $10 bounty for entering the army, and in September 1776 raised the amount to $20 for service of three years or the duration of the war; non-commissioned officers and privates were also promised one hundred acres of land at the end of the war (officers were entitled to a higher amount, for example a colonel, 500 acres). Congress's bounty increased to $200 in early 1779, with the same amount given for only one year's service by enlistees from Virginia, North Carolina, and Georgia.[5] The differentiation was considered necessary to spur recruitment in another Continental army, the Southern army, then in full battle against the British invasion in the South. Such a discrepancy along with the higher bounty offered to the later enlistees adversely affected morale of these already in service.

There was also the problem of states providing generous incentives for enlistments, placing them in competition with each other. Most injurious to the recruitment of Continental soldiers was the policy of states charging against their Continental army quotas persons who enlisted in state units. These troops were often sent to do duty with Continentals, but their enlistments were for short terms, no more than six, nine, or sometimes 12 months. Massachusetts, for example, in March 1781 had one-fourth of its army quota in service for six- or nine-month terms; most of these soldiers were assigned to home guard duty. Regardless of where these state levies were stationed they received bounties which were higher than that offered by Congress and usually also full issues of clothing; eight states during the war also provided land to their soldiers.[6]

The whole bounty system was counterproductive. Money due for Continental bounties was often slowly forthcoming or partially paid. General William Heath informed Washington in December 1779 of the "necessity of money to pay the continental bounty to reenlisted men, as many soldiers will not inlist unless they can receive their whole bounty." Heath also complained that the bounty given to Massachusetts troops enrolled for six or nine months was as large as the amount provided to three-year enlistees.[7]

Providing short-term recruits with "bounties before unheard of" and food, clothing, and pay superior to those soldiers already in Continental service, complained General John Paterson, served "little purpose than to have the populace to visit the army." Paterson, who commanded Massachusetts' short-term levies at West Point in 1780, informed General Heath that his troops "are mostly composed of nine months' abortions, sent here with bounties which ten times exceed those given for the war, naked, lifeless, and dead, who never saw action, and now counting days, hours, and minutes they have to tarry in service."[8] Captain Samuel Shaw of the Continental Artillery voiced a similar complaint:

The levies are almost totally unacquainted with service, and what is worse, by the time they will be good for any thing, their enlistments will expire. These short enlistments, and the amazing bounties given to the levies for six months, greatly discourage our veteran soldiery, and I fear that, if such measures are again repeated, the army will hardly be kept together.[9]

Washington protested vigorously to the state governments against the practice of dual enlistments and "the baneful Influence of advanced pay and bounty" offered to the short-term recruits; as early as February 1777 he noted that "the poisonous effects" had already "reached this Army." The commander-in-chief favored "Co-ercive Measures . . . to bring forth" required quotas of Continental troops from the states.[10] Even with the subsequent adoption of conscription, with inductees from the militia sent directly to the Continental army, the problems remained much the same.

The enlisted men of the Revolution had no prospect of a pension, an important inducement of military recruiting in later American history. Congress merely provided half pay for life to any soldier or officer who had lost a limb or was otherwise disabled so as to be unable to pursue a livelihood. Congress, reneging on an earlier pledge of half pay for life to officers, in March 1783 by the Commutation Act granted officers a flat pension of five years' pay at the end of the war.[11] Nothing further was done to secure veteran pensions until 1818 when Congress granted $20 and $8 a month respectively to those veteran officers and non-commissioned officers/privates who were in need of public assistance. In 1828 all who had served until the end of the Revolution received full pay for life. This provision was extended in 1832 to include all Continental and state troops who had served two years during the war. Of course most veterans had died by this time. Yet by January 1833, 24,260 of the late applications had been received; the average pension was $75.97 per year.[12]

Few soldiers realized their dream of acquiring bounty land after the Revolution. Joseph Plumb Martin, who enlisted as a Connecticut farm boy of age 15 and served during most of the war, lamented:

When those who engaged to serve during the war enlisted, they were promised a hundred acres of land, each, which was to be in their own or the adjoining states. When the country had drained the last drop of service it could screw out of the poor soldiers, they were turned adrift like old worn-out horses, and nothing said about land to pasture them upon. Congress did, indeed, appropriate lands under the denomination of "Soldier's lands," in Ohio state, or some state, or a future state, but no care was taken that the soldiers should get them. No agents were appointed to see that the poor fellows ever got possession of their lands; no one ever took the least care about it, except a pack of speculators, who were driving about the country like so many evil spirits, endeavoring to pluck the last feather from the soldiers. The soldiers were ignorant of the ways and means to obtain their bounty lands, and there was no one appointed to inform them.[13]

Those Who Served

"Poverty was endemic to the native-born soldier," writes the authors of a study of Maryland recruiting during the Revolution.[14] Even at the beginning of the war in Connecticut material benefits in joining the army outweighed the three shillings a day salary of a farm laborer. Besides pay of 40s. a month, with one month's salary paid in advance, a private received 52s. for a blanket, clothing, and a knapsack, 10s. for his weaponry, and food valued at 15s. a month. Along with a bounty, what a recruit received upfront would take a farm laborer up to ten weeks to earn, and meanwhile the new soldier had free food and clothing.[15]

Enlistment in the army appealed to many of the "swelling population of dependent poor" in New England—the unskilled and "loose people," new immigrants, former servants, and transients who went from town to town seeking employment. One-fifth of a New York regiment came from "the strolling poor."[16] There were also poor young men who were waiting for an inheritance or wanted to acquire a small nest egg from savings while in the army in order to make a start in life. Generally, the soldiers from any given state or locality who stayed on to fight during the war came from the lowest economic and social rungs of society. For one New England town, one author notes that enlistees, "as a group," were "poorer, more marginal, less anchored in the society."[17] A study of 710 enlisted soldiers of the New Jersey brigade indicates that 90 percent of them ranked in the poorest two-thirds of holders of rateable property, and half of the members of the brigade owned no property at all. One sample of a group of Massachusetts soldiers shows that only 10 percent of them owned any significant property after the war.[18] Many common soldiers also had no education; a majority of those from Virginia signed their names with an "X."[19]

The army further served as a welfare receptacle by taking in the very young or old and the infirm, a situation that frustrated General Steuben, who took leave from his inspector-general duties to superintend recruiting for the Southern army in Virginia in 1780–1. As Jefferson reported in December 1780, because "a very considerable proportion of the new Levies" were "totally unfit for service . . . being old men, boys or decrepid" Steuben had to refuse to accept such recruits into service or to count them toward the state's quota.[20] Steuben advised Governor Jefferson that there was in Virginia "as in every other State a great number of young fellows strolling about the Country, out of all manner of Employ who with proper management might be Inlisted . . . for very moderate Sums."[21]

Although there were specifications for enlistees as to height, age, and fitness, these were mostly ignored. Frederick Mackenzie, a British officer, in 1776 commented that not only did captive rebel soldiers appear not "to have washed themselves during the Campaign" and were poorly clothed, but "a great many of them were lads under 15, and old men . . . Their odd figures frequently excited laughter of our Soldiers."[22] When the French army joined Washington's troops on the Hudson in summer 1781, Claude Blanchard, a French commissary, commented that among the American soldiers "there were some fine-looking men; also many who were small and thin, and even some children twelve or thirteen years old."[23] General Heath, commanding at West Point in 1781, found that some of his new recruits were "totally unfit for service, men who are ruptured, infirm, old negroes, and some children."[24] It is estimated that one-tenth of New England recruits in 1781 had to be sent home because of their physical qualities.[25] But the persistently high number of men reported as "sick and unfit for duty" on Continental army musters suggests that many soldiers should not have been admitted into service.

Age-wise, Continental army recruits were not remarkably different from their counterparts during later periods of American history. Of the 1,068 soldiers of the Pennsylvania line whose ages are known, for example, only 1 percent were aged 54 or older (the eldest aged 73), and 11 percent were aged 17 or under (36 of this group were between the ages of 10 and 14); 55 percent were in their 20s.[26] Boys often served as fifers and drummers or as "waiters" to their fathers who had also enlisted; only a few of the youngsters were ordinary soldiers. The average age at enlistment of 396 troops was 23, with 42 percent younger than age 21.[27] One half of the soldiers in the New Jersey brigade were no older than age 22, with many of this group in their teens.[28] Ninety percent of the privates in the Virginia Continental line were under age 25, with the median being 20.[29]

As the American military forces became more professionalized, so did the public's perception of soldiers as forming a subcommunity. Certain kinds of people belonged in the army—the poor, unmarried sons of farmers, those of unsteady employment, common laborers, and even servants, apprentices, and slaves when given their master's permission. Northern states and Maryland (1780) permitted voluntary enlistment of slaves with their masters' consent. Rhode Island, New Jersey, Maryland, and Delaware allowed servants and apprentices to enlist on their own, with the state providing compensation for the loss to a master. Runaway servants and slaves were sometimes enlisted with no questions asked.[30] Washington was against enlistment of convict servants, fearing, quite accurately, that they had a propensity to go over to the enemy.[31] Using bounty money as well as some of their own, recruiting officers purchased indentured servants on condition that they enter the army. Nicholas Cresswell commented that in March 1777 he "saw a review of Captn. Wm. Johnston's company, a set of rascally servants and convicts, most of them just purchased from their masters. A ragged crew indeed!"[32]

The Continental army and navy had their shares of potentially dangerous persons who were expected to find redemption in military service—criminals, loyalists, prisoners of war, and vagabonds. It was to be a long-standing practice of American military policy until the latter part of the twentieth century to allow certain classes of offenders to choose between military service or jail. South Carolina provided for "idle, lewd, or disorderly" persons to be put into the army.[33] Most states, in varying degrees and instances, permitted commutation of certain felony and treason convictions in return for joining the army or navy. Persons hauled before the New Jersey Council of Safety for "suspicious Circumstances surrounding their Conduct" sometimes enlisted to thwart further investigation and probable arrest.[34]

While enlistment of British prisoners of war and deserters from the British army was encouraged during the early part of the war, it became evident that such recruits made unreliable soldiers who would take advantage of the first opportunity to return to British lines. Congress, in February 1778, prohibited the enlistment of enemy prisoners of war.[35] Congress, however, did make an exception by approving the enlistment of ten Hessian prisoners of war per American company. With George III preventing payment for rations for the captives, the cost was charged against the individual prisoners. Besides pay, Congress offered an eight dollar bounty and a promise of 100 acres to each Hessian recruit.[36] Since Hessian prisoners had the privilege of working as farm laborers for pay, the program to enlist them in the American army was not very successful.

If the observation of a Swedish colonel with the French forces at the siege of Savannah in 1779 that the American troops were "composed wholly of deserters and vagabonds of all nations"[37] was off the mark, substantial numbers of persons of foreign birth, nevertheless, served in the enlisted ranks of the Continental army. Most of the poorer recruits were foreign-born. Along with African Americans (10 percent of the army in 1778) and a few Indians, the mixture of Europeans definitely gave the army a mixed ethnicity. The largest numbers of foreign-born in the army were found in units from the middle states, due in part to the arrival in the years just before the war of Irish indentured servants and to a lesser extent German immigrants, some of whom were redemptioner servants. From 1760 to 1775, 221,000 immigrants, including those from Africa, came to America, with about 60,000 from Ireland (chiefly the Protestant Scots-Irish), 30,000 from England, 40,000 from Scotland, and 12,000 from Germany (the high tide from this source being a little earlier). The Bishop of Derry in Ireland lamented in 1775 that immigration from Ireland to the American colonies amounted to "nearly thirty three thousand fanatical & hungry republicans in the course of a very few years."[38]

One of four Continental soldiers were of Irish descent (mostly Scots-Irish Protestants, some Irish Catholics). Of the 102 privates and non-commissioned officers of a Maryland artillery company, one half were born in England or Ireland; of 299 of General William Smallwood's Maryland recruits in 1782, 40.1 percent were foreign-born, with 88 percent of these natives of England or Ireland. The median age for the foreign-born was 29, compared to age 21 for the native soldiers. Two-thirds of the Pennsylvania line were foreign-born, of whom one-half were Irish. Thirty percent of enlistees in Orange and Ulster counties, New York, in July 1775 were natives of Ireland. Of a sample of 146 non-resident enlistees in the New Jersey brigade, 32 were foreigners: including one from Canada, nine from Great Britain, one from Scotland, 16 from Ireland, one from France, and one from Holland.[39]

New England muster rolls do not reveal the national origins of Continental soldiers, but an estimate places the number of the region's foreign-born soldiers at 10 to 20 percent. Southern Continental army units also had sizeable contingents of Irishmen. Of Daniel Morgan's 418 riflemen, enlisted in western Virginia, 162 were natives of Ireland. General Steuben's Continental recruits assembled at Chesterfield County Courthouse, Virginia, in 1780–1 were 20 percent foreign-born, with 18 percent from Europe. A sample of several military companies recruited in South Carolina show that nearly half of the soldiers were Irish.[40]

German-born soldiers made up generally 12 to 15 percent of Washington's army. These enlistees in particular came from the valleys of the Pennsylvania, Maryland, Virginia, and Carolina backcountry. Although many Germans were pacifists or leaned toward loyalism, those Germans who supported the war made the most zealous patriots. As early as 1775 the German Society of Pennsylvania and the German Lutheran and Reformed churches issued manifestos declaring for armed resistance.[41] German American leaders sought out recruits from their countrymen-neighbors, as did Reverend (General) John Peter Muhlenberg, who enlisted most of the men of the church he pastored in Woodstock, Virginia. Captain Joseph Bloomfield, stationed with his third New Jersey Regiment in the Mohawk Valley in August 1776, noted in his diary: "attended & saw a ludicrous Beating up for Voluntiers by a High-German appointed Capt. who can neither read nor write. The oddity of the Capt., his officers & recruits with their dress excited the Laughter of all our officers."[42]

The Continental army had units enlisted exclusively among Germans, namely the First Pennsylvania Regiment, Eighth Virginia Regiment, General Casimir Pulaski's mounted Legion (after Pulaski's death in 1779 commanded by Colonel Armand Tuffin), and Major Nicholas Dietrich Baron de Ottendorf's independent Pennsylvania regiment, which merged with

Tuffin's Legion in 1780. One-third of Rochambeau's French army in America were German and Swiss.

Recruiting

At the start of the Revolution, officers at the company level received their commissions if they could enlist recruits to fill their units. Washington cautioned regimental commanders not to take "either Officers or Men into pay till at least fifty are ingaged to a Company."[43] To replenish the army with new recruits, Congress required regimental commanders (colonels) to detail officers to "recruiting service, to such parts where they are best known, and have the greatest probability of success." For each enlistee, a recruiting officer received 10s. in 1776, raised to $20 the next year, $200 in 1780, and 30s. in specie in 1781. Non-commissioned officers who assisted in the recruiting were entitled to half the sum given to the officer.[44]

Recruits considered their enlistments as legal contracts. Not only did they want to know the compensation, clothing, and equipment they were entitled to, they wanted to serve under officers whom they could respect. Recruiting officers, enlisting men for their own units, had to have an air of congeniality (though most certainly such familiarity would disappear after the recruit arrived at camp) and promotional ability.

Gaining the respect of would-be enlistees sometimes meant that a persistent recruiting officer in order to snatch his prey had to engage in a little rough-and-tumble. Captain Bernard Elliott in South Carolina, in 1776, had to prove his mettle in a boxing match with a local tough who would not serve under anyone he could whip.[45] Captain Alexander Graydon of the Third Pennsylvania Regiment, who was detailed to recruiting, "found it necessary, in common with my brother officers, to put my feelings most cruelly to the rack." Accompanied by a lieutenant, corporal, and a drummer, Graydon tried recruiting at Frankford, Pennsylvania. "A number of fellows at the tavern . . . indicated a desire to enlist, but although they drank freely of our liquor, they still held off." Tempers began to flare, and "the principal ruffian . . . squared himself for battle and advanced towards me in an attitude of defiance." Graydon hit the offender mightily between the eyes and "sent him staggering to the other end of the room." When the recipient of the blow "recovered," he "was as submissive as could be wished, and although he would not enlist, he hired himself to me for a few weeks as a fifer;" during this time "he bore about the effects of his insolence, in a pair of black eyes."[46] Shortly afterwards, Graydon and Captain David Lennox went to the Maryland Eastern Shore in hopes of recruiting unemployed "seamen or long shore men." A local gentleman at a tavern helped the Pennsylvania officers to recruit "a fellow, he said, who would do to stop a bullet as well as a better man, and as he was a truly worthless dog, he

RECRUITS.

London.Publifh'd Jan'.1.ˢ 1780.by Watfon & Dickinfon N⁰.158.New Bond Street.

Figure 3   Recruits for the British Army in America (1780). Americans (post-1776) had a similar view that enlistees for the Continental army were mostly decrepit. Engraving by Henry William Bunbury. *Clements Library, University of Michigan.*

held, that the neighbourhood would be much indebted to us for taking him away."[47]

Despite Captain Graydon's unpleasant experience in obtaining "liquor listees," besotting a prospect did produce results. All the recruiter had to do was slip some bounty money into a drunken fellow's pocket, and then lead him to a justice of the peace to be sworn in as a "soldier."

A successful recruiter carefully employed public relations tactics. If he was not already acquainted with a neighborhood, he would establish a presence among the local populace, attending dinners, barbecues, dances, and other social affairs. Hanging around the less respectable taverns he came into contact with single young men. Distributing broadsides or tracts displaying the rape-atrocities by Hessian soldiers or the murder of Jane McCrae by Indians attached to Burgoyne's invading army or the like were effective ways of reinforcing patriotism with desire for revenge. Recruiters promised the good life in the army—bounty money, pay, clothing, free food, and other amenities—without pointing out the harsh realities. Try as hard as he might, a recruiter faced a losing situation. "Regular soldiers had a bad reputation with the general public," commented a French officer on the American situation; "no enticement or trick could force solid citizens to enlist as regulars, inasmuch as they had to serve as militia anyway."[48] A recruiting officer reported to General Anthony Wayne: "I have been assiduous in my Endeavours to enlist, but all such as are fit for service are already engaged, the Others are only *Food for Worms*—miserable, sharp looking Caitiffs, hungry lean fac'd Villains."[49]

Naval recruits were also in demand. Ebenezer Fox described a magnificent naval recruitment in Boston, to which he yielded at age 16. The Massachusetts government had built a 20-gun ship, the *Protector*, to be used against the enemy, and recruits were instantly needed.

> A rendezvous was established for recruits at the head of Hancock's wharf, where the national flag, then bearing thirteen stripes and stars, was hoisted. All means were resorted to . . . A recruiting officer, bearing a flag and attended by a band of martial music, paraded the streets, to excite a thirst for glory and a spirit of military ambition.
>
> The recruiting officer possessed the qualifications requisite to make the service appear alluring, especially to the young. He was a jovial, good-natured fellow, of ready wit and much broad humor. Crowds followed in his wake when he marched the streets; and he occasionally stopped at the corners to harangue the multitude, in order to excite their patriotism and zeal for the cause of liberty.
>
> When he espied any large boys among the idle crowd around him, he would attract their attention by singing in a comical manner the following doggerel:
>> "All you that have had masters
>> And cannot get your due;
>> Come, come, my brave boys,
>> And join with our ship's crew."

A shout and huzza would follow, and some would join in the ranks. My excitable feelings were roused; I repaired to the rendezvous, signed the ship's papers, mounted a cockade, and was in my own estimation already more than half a sailor.[50]

Army recruiters used the same recruiting formula, even if less spectacular. John Claspy, a recruiting sergeant for the Tenth Virginia Regiment during 1777–80, recalled in a deposition he submitted in support of his pension application many years after the war:

> His destination always was where there were the largest gathering of the people in their civil capacity and where whiskey was most likely to induce them to assume a military one. He was always attended by his fifer named John Roe and his drummer named John Hart.[51]

The use of regular officers and non-commissioned officers for recruiting deprived the army of valuable manpower. Officers frequently cited intentions to recruit in order to gain furloughs, and upon returning home did little to pursue their duty. Fraud was prevalent. Officers drew bounty money to be given to enlistees, but often they kept part of the money for themselves or even all of it by reporting non-existent enlistees. Washington complained that much of the bounty money was "squander'd" away; "the pernicious practice of Gaming has been exceedingly injurious to the recruiting service."[52]

Obviously there was need for a less happenstance and more systematic method of recruiting. In July 1777 Congress took recruiting "intirely out of the hands of the Officers of the Army" and entrusted the process to the states. Each county or township became a recruiting district, presided over by two civilians appointed by a governor. Each recruiting agent was to receive eight dollars per recruit and five dollars for apprehending a deserter. By 1779 Virginia allowed the official recruiter, usually a county lieutenant (a civilian appointee), $150 for "each able-bodied soldier" he enlisted.[53]

Continental army officers and non-commissioned officers could still assist in recruiting, and many did. Each of the New Jersey regiments, for example, in 1780 had an officer assigned to recruiting duty.[54] Fraud did not end, but could be more easily checked under direct state supervision. William Davies, Virginia's Commissioner of War, in March 1780 nullified enlistments of recruits who had not received all of their bounty money.[55] Under the state system recruits were periodically gathered together and sent on to the army encampments. "We have an officer appointed who rides the circuit of the country once in two months," observed Governor Jefferson of Virginia, "to receive these men at certain places of rendezvous."[56] The delays from the time of agreement to enlist to being delivered to Continental army units encouraged second thoughts on the part of the recruit, and it was no wonder that some did not make it to the ultimate destination of an army encampment.

Conscription and Draft Resistance

Congress in 1776 assigned fixed quotas of troops to be supplied by each state to the Continental army. The states, in turn, set quotas for towns and counties. Far too many men upon completing an enlistment and returning home refused further military service. The states could not fill more than 50 to 70 percent of their quotas. Washington complained that the insufficiency of troops impeded "Opportunity of crushing the Enemy's power." Writing to Governor Patrick Henry of Virginia in May 1777, the commander-in-chief declared that "nothing less than furnishing our full Quota of Continental Troops, by any means . . . will ensure Success." Like Charles Lee, Washington felt that a uniform system of coercive enlistment for long periods would provide the best insurance for adequate manpower.[57]

To the former colonial Americans, coerced military service smacked too much of a standing army and also was reminiscent of the efforts of the British government before the war to impress unwilling citizens into the royal navy. Congress, to its credit, strictly prohibited naval impressment. But, if winning the war depended on conscripting citizens for the army then this was the price to be paid in defense of liberty. Conscription, only if it was democratic and did not affect one group of citizens more than another, was acceptable. Even Thomas Jefferson did not oppose a draft. "Our people even under the monarchial government," he told John Adams in May 1777, "had learnt to consider it as the last of all oppressions."[58]

On April 14, 1777 Congress recommended each state "to cause indiscriminate draughts to be made from their respective militia."[59] Massachusetts and New Jersey were the first states to use conscription. One-fifth of most militia units in Massachusetts were drafted in September 1776 for service in the Continental army until dismissed. The draft was largely used in Massachusetts for short-term service in particular campaigns; for example, one half of the militia from four counties served for one month with Gates's Northern army in September 1777. From July 1776 to April 1778, three-fourths of the town of Concord's quota was met by drafting through a lottery.[60]

Mindful of an army that seemed to be disintegrating at Valley Forge, Congress, on February 26, 1778, called upon 11 states (South Carolina and Georgia excluded) to draft soldiers from among the militia for service in the Continental army. The states, to avert semblances of creating a standing army, would provide for only short terms for draftees, usually as little as six or nine months, though occasionally 18 months. Persons selected would serve on a rotating basis and would come from all economic levels of society. States were required to appoint one or more commissioners to receive draftees at designated places of rendezvous and deliver them over to a Continental army officer, "who may be appointed by the Commander in

Chief." Draftees from the New England states were to rendezvous at Fishkill on the Hudson River; those from New York at Easton, Pennsylvania; New Jersey, Pennsylvania, Delaware, and Maryland, "at camp;" Virginia, at Alexandria and Sheperdstown, Virginia; and North Carolina, at Pittsylvania County Courthouse and Petersburg, both in Virginia.[61] By spring 1778 all 11 states had instituted the draft.

To determine who should be drafted, the states employed a system whereby the local militia was divided into "classes," according to one's standing relative to taxable property, thus making those from the upper and lower strata of society equally liable. One recruit would be drafted from each class in rotation until a quota was filled. Frequently a class tried to prevail upon an impressionable footloose youth to be the draftee, offering a bit of added monetary incentive and even engaging in intimidation. Maryland actually drafted vagrants. One New England farm boy told how he was "roped" into service:

> The inhabitants of the town were about this time put into what were called squads, according to their ratable property. Of some of the most opulent, one formed a squad; of others, two or three, and of the lower sort of the people, several formed a squad. Each of these squads were to furnish a man for the army, either by hiring or by sending one of their own number. . . .
>
> One of the above-mentioned squads, wanting to procure a man, the lieutenant told them that he thought they might persuade me to go for them, and they accordingly attacked me, front, rear and flank. I thought, as I must go, I might as well endeavor to get as much for my skin as I could.

Accordingly Joseph Plumb Martin signed up. "The men gave me what they agreed to . . . enough to keep the blood circulating during the short space of time which I tarried at home after I had enlisted. They were now freed from any further trouble, at least for the present, and I had become the scapegoat for them."[62]

Surely the draft, as Richard Henry Lee of Virginia expected, would bring a "number of our lazy, worthless young men" into the "service of their Country."[63] Sometimes a person was selected with the knowledge that he would be turned away upon reaching the rendezvous. In Craven County, North Carolina, for example, a draftee had only one eye and was the sole support of a "sickly wife and three small children;" elsewhere in the state men "having sore legs and ruptures which render them incapable of duty" were sent as draftees.[64] A Massachusetts draft in the fall of 1776 yielded several very old men and even a 69-year-old widow, Mrs Ann Prescott.[65]

Usually a lottery was used to select draftees. Militiamen assembled at a courthouse drew from a hat pieces of paper, each bearing the word "service" or "clear;" receiving the former meant that a person was now a draftee. In Virginia only unmarried militiamen over 18 years of age were eligible for the draft lottery.[66] Each draftee was presented with a bounty and clothing. North Carolina, for example, provided a draftee, who engaged for nine months' service, $50, plus $3 if he brought his own musket, and also a pair of stockings, a pair of shoes, two shirts, a hunting shirt, a waistcoat, a pair of breeches, a pair of trousers, a hat, and a blanket.[67]

Conscription of troops did not live up to expectations. Of Virginia's draft quota of 3,188 men in October 1780, for example, only 1,023 were raised; of these only 773 were delivered, and of the remaining 250, 58 were refused, 52 never left their counties, and 140 deserted.[68] Many factors impeded the effectiveness of conscription. If bounties were not fully provided for, the draftees were not sent on. Colonel William Davies, Virginia's Commissioner of War, complained that

> when a delinquent is condemned to be a six months soldier, he is struck off the militia roll; nobody takes the trouble or thinks it his duty to deliver him to the army; neither Government nor the army know anything of him or of his condemnation, and thus he continues, contrary to every kind of justice, in quiet repose at home, and not only contributes nothing towards the defense of the country, but does essential injury to it, by his example, his conversation, and the toleration he receives.[69]

A person who was drafted could simply satisfy his military obligation by paying a fine. Thus a draft notice informed a resident of New Salem, Massachusetts:

> To Mr. James Cook
> Sir. With the advice of the military Officers Selectmen and Committee of this Town you are Draughted to do Eight Months Service in the Continental Army from this Date; and you are to furnish your Self for Camp, and be in readiness forthwith to Muster and to march when and where ordered, or otherwise you are to pay a fine of fifteen pounds in Twenty four hours from the time of your being Draughted.
> New Salem April 17th 1778   Wm Page Lt[70]

For whatever the reasons a draftee did not show up at a rendezvous, he was not replaced. Militiamen were not to be put in double jeopardy.

Of course, there were many ways to avoid selective service. Two men in Prince William County, Virginia "cut off their fingers" after being drafted.[71] But self-mutilation was not really necessary. One could desert

113

before being officially received by the army, and most likely few questions were asked. Besides paying a fine, one could seek permission to be regarded as a hardship case. Numerous exemptions were granted to those persons in various occupational categories, including those involved in essential industries such as iron and arms manufacturing and milling, wagoners, tobacco inspectors, teachers, and students (at least at the College of William and Mary).

Draft laws permitted a conscript to engage a substitute to take his place. Here the selective service system gave advantage to the wealthy who could afford to obtain a substitute at almost any going price, whereas a poor man could not. It was common sense to purchase the "cheapest" substitute, from among the very old or very young, the infirm, derelicts, unemployed, servants, and, if one could get away with it, slaves. Many of these would be rejected by the army and would return home anyway. One half of the substitutes supplied by Culpeper County, Virginia were under age 20, with one being age 15.[72] Probably most states were in the same situation as New Jersey, in which 40 percent of the men raised by the draft from 1778 to 1780 were substitutes.[73]

Many localities ignored drafts called for by a state government. The stiffest draft resistance occurred in Virginia. By 1780, of the state's 72 counties, only 32 had tried to implement the draft.[74] No real efforts were made to prosecute county lieutenants or militia officers for not holding a draft. In those counties that did comply, the draft often met defiance. In Loudoun County, a draft on February 16 "was prevented by the violent & riotous behavior of the people." A jury convicted nine ringleaders and acquitted two; the sentences ranged from £3 to £50 fines and included 20 days in jail, but because the culprits showed "sorrow and Contrition of heart" the penalties were remitted.[75] Similar outbreaks during 1778 occurred in Westmoreland and Northumberland counties, with the rioters merely having to put up bond for future good behavior.[76]

Protests against the draft in Virginia during late 1780 and spring and summer 1781 veered toward the edge of insurrection. Successive British armies under Generals Alexander Leslie, Benedict Arnold, William Phillips, and Lord Cornwallis invaded the state. Many citizens were involved in militia call-ups to defend the state, and continued efforts to recruit in Virginia for Nathanael Greene's Southern army had little appeal. Virginia units had been captured at Charleston in May 1780 and routed at Camden, South Carolina three months later. Virginians had always viewed the Carolinas as a world apart and feared the malarial climate of South Carolina. Because many Virginia militiamen saw active duty against the invasion, being drafted and sent to the Carolinas amounted to double jeopardy. Ironically, the Continental troops in Virginia during the British invasions before the Yorktown siege consisted of most of the Pennsylvania line and a few troops from New Jersey and New England—not Virginians.[77]

The wave of riots in Virginia coincided with the new tax program of specific taxes (payable in commodities) and an extra 2 percent property tax to finance military bounties. Furthermore, the legislature in October 1780 provided for trial of draft resisters by courts-martial, consisting of militia field officers and captains.[78]

In Lancaster County in December 1780 a mob disarmed militia officers and seized "papers relative to the draft." John Taylor, the county lieutenant, held a court martial, and "many were condemn'd," but it was not within his power to arrest the riot leaders.[79] On September 14–15, 1780, in Northumberland County, 150 persons, representing about 25 percent of militiamen eligible for the draft, "entered into a most Criminal & unlawful Combination to prevent the due Execution of an Act of the last Session of Assembly for furnishing this States Quota of Troops to the Continental army." One officer was shot dead. To Thomas Gaskins it seemed that "almost the whole County was inflam'd." The rioters came from a cross-section of the population; they owned land on the average of 80–100 acres. Tempers cooled, and a court martial succeeded in sentencing many of the leaders to army service of 18 months.[80]

As the war heated up in Virginia, the state's Board of War, in March 1781, suspended the draft in 37 counties "from which a considerable proportion of Militia is absent on service."[81] Draft riots, nevertheless, broke out in counties still susceptible to the draft. The western counties of Augusta, Rockbridge, and Hampshire (in present West Virginia) had draft riots as did Richmond County and the two Eastern Shore counties of Northampton and Accomac.[82] The most serious of these occurred in Accomac County on April 23, 1781 when a mob of nearly 200 persons, "armed with Clubs swords guns and pistols . . . took possession of the Court house at the door of which they placed a sentinel with his Musket." The rioters stopped the draft by seizing the list of names for drawing. Several of the ringleaders had "capital estates." A court-martial did not try rioters until September 27, when resentment had simmered. Three of the leaders were bound over for trial for treason in Richmond; the others were sentenced to military service in the Continental army. Two of the leaders were released because of ill health: Robert Spiers, "a cripple with the rheumatism," and Solomon Bunting, "so ill of a malignant fever."[83] One witness signaled out Bunting as the chief ringleader, stating that Bunting said in inciting the riot:

> I shall mark them damnd sons of Bitches damnd shitten shirt tail'd sons of bitches and if a Clever company or parcel will Join me, says he I will go and wring their necks for them as I did my father's old Gander for eating up my corn. I'll wring their necks and turn their faces backwards upon which some of the Company made answer you'll have enough to Join you.[84]

Greenbrier County (now in West Virginia) in April 1782 had the distinction of having the last of the Virginia riots that prevented the draft.[85]

America's first experiment with the military draft thus fared badly. The problem faced by the revolutionaries was to a large degree remedied by the US Constitution and the Militia Act of 1792, allowing the federal government to order the call-up of militia. A national conscription of citizens directly, regardless of militia status, awaited its first trial during the Civil War.

CHAPTER EIGHT

Followers of the army

A variety of civilians attached themselves to the armies but were not officially entered into the ranks. Most were retainers, employed to perform services. Such were most of the women with the armed forces, although, in rare instances, a few, through deception, were carried as soldiers. Some officers had personal servants (usually male). Licensed sutlers set up shop in camps, and local citizens established markets in and around camp according to regulations. The staff departments, in addition to use of military personnel, had civilian employees as clerks, artisans, and teamsters and also contracted out for such services. Civilians were often hired for special army assignments and then released.

Women Camp Followers

Civilian women with an army traditionally have been dubbed camp followers. Except for the spouses of the generals and some of the other officers who spent long sojourns at camp in between campaigns, the women of the Revolutionary War armies were from the lowest levels of society, many of whom accompanied husbands with children in tow and were too poor to survive on their own. Women camp followers found employment in laundering and other support work; only a few served as cooks. It was a recognized principle of eighteenth-century warfare that armies performed at a higher degree of efficiency if women were present on a continued basis.

Both the British and American armies had large contingents of women. On May 20, 1777 the British army mustered 23,101 men, 2,776 women, and 1,904 children; on August 22, 1781 for those in and around New York City, 9,686 British soldiers, 3,512 non-military personnel in staff departments, 10,251 German troops, 3,615 women, and 4,127 children. The British army permitted six women per company. German troops had their women

117

camp followers; a Hessian officer in June 1777 noted the arrival of "over sixty amazons" at his unit, "whose acquaintance was soon sought."[1]

The American armies had no fixed ratio of women to men, although, less prevalent than those in the British army, the number of women in service of the patriot forces remained rather constant at about one to every 44 men. An estimated 20,000 women were camp followers of the American armies during the war.[2] Washington, however, recognized that occasionally "particular circumstances" made it necessary to admit more women to the army than usual. Some New York regiments were composed in part of "Long Islanders and others who fled with their families . . . and have no other means of Subsistence." Thus

> the lives of these Women; the suffering of their Children, and the complaints of the Husbands would admit of no alternative. The latter with too much justice remarked "If *pay* is withheld from *us*, and *Provisions* from our *Wives* and *Children* we must all starve together; or commit Acts which may involve us in ruin" . . . In a word, I was obliged to give Provisions to the extra Women in these Regiments, or loose by Desertion, perhaps to the Enemy, some of the oldest and best Soldiers in the Service.[3]

Women with the American armies performed chores ranging from sewing and mending uniforms to herding sheep and cattle. In doing work for hire, they had to abide by set fees; for example, orders of a New York regiment with Washington's army before Yorktown, in October 1781, declared that women were to be paid 2s. "a dozen for all articles which they wash . . . provided they find their own soape, or one and sixpence per dozen if the soape be found them."[4] Children assisted their mothers; thus John Geyer, age 11, after his discharge as a drummer, stayed on in camp to help his mother with the army washing.[5] Women received half rations, and children one-fourth. Seldom was provision made for living quarters, and women and children slept where they could. At Valley Forge, however, separate huts were provided. If a woman's husband died or was killed, she formed a liaison with another soldier. There are no records of fights over women attached to the army, but undoubtedly there were rivalries. An officer with the British army recorded that a soldier "shot himself last night in the rear of the camp. The discovery of a Connection he had with a married woman of the same Regiment appears to have been the cause of the rash action."[6]

The women camp followers, making no pretense of refinement, exhibited the coarseness of the rank-and-file men, matching them in drinking and cursing. One American officer in 1780 commented that the army women "were the ugliest in the world . . . their Usage dress etc every way" were "concordant with each other," some had "three & four children & few with none—I could not help pitying the poor innocent Creatures [children]."[7] Private Joseph Plumb Martin observed women tagging along with the baggage during the army's march. "A caravan of wild beasts could bear no comparison" with this group of women, "'some in rags and some in jags,' but none 'in velvet gowns.' Some with two eyes, some with one, and some, I believe with none at all. They 'beggared all description'; their dialect, too, was as confused as their bodily appearance was odd and disgusting."[8] Hannah Winthrop had much the same impression of the women accompanying captive Hessian troops as they marched near Cambridge, Massachusetts: They

> seemed to be beasts of burthen, having a bushel basket on their back, by which they were bent double, the contents seemed to be Pots and Kettles, various sorts of Furniture, children peeping thro' gridirons and other utensils, some very young Infants who were born on the road, the women bare feet, cloathed in dirty rags, such effluvia filld the air while they were passing, had they not been smoking all the time, I should have been apprehensive of being contaminated by them.[9]

To check venereal disease, women of the army had to undergo physical examinations. Thus a regimental order of July 1777 read: "That the Women belonging to the Regt be paraded tomorrow morning & to undergo an Examination from the Serjeon of the Regt at his tent;" married women however, were excepted, with their husbands "to undergo said examination in their Stead, all those that do not attend to be immediately Drum'd out of the Regt."[10]

Washington, who, as a proper Virginia gentleman, had little sympathy for the plight of underclass women in distress, was constantly vexed by having to tolerate them in the army. He lamented in August 1777 that "the multitude of women . . . especially those who are pregnant, or have children, are a dreg upon every movement," and he advised his officers "to use every reasonable method in their power to get rid of all such as are not absolutely necessary."[11] To put forward the best face of the army during its march through Philadelphia in August 1777, the commander-in-chief ordered all the army's women not to be seen with the troops—a directive that was not very effective.[12] The army women were forbidden to ride on wagons during a march.[13]

All civilians attached to the army had to abide by military regulations. Women belonging to both armies were subject to courts-martial on charges of disciplinary infractions or committal of crimes, which might include theft or enticement of soldiers to desert. Whipping and ducking were occasionally used as punishments; most likely a convicted woman offender was simply drummed out of the army.[14]

Women as Soldiers

Women camp followers remained in camp with the baggage as the armies went into combat. Yet some gave assistance during battle. In particular, women were allowed to serve with artillerists, who generally were positioned on high ground behind the attacking troops.

British Captain John André, reporting on casualties from a skirmish near New Brunswick in June 1777, said that the Americans "killed or wounded about twenty of our people and a woman, a Grenadier's wife."[15] Similarly, British Lieutenant Thomas Anburey, sent out to "reconnoitre across two ravines" in front of the British army after the battle of Freeman's Farm, September 19, 1777, "met with several dead bodies belonging to the enemy, and amongst them were laying close to each other, two men and a woman, the latter of whom had her arms extended, and her hands grasping cartridges."[16]

Women sometimes went into a battlefield after the fighting had stopped to pick up what valuables they could find. American army women stripped British dead after the battle of Bemis Heights, October 7, 1777.[17] With the southern armies frequently on the move, women camp followers at the rear with the baggage or on the flanks of a marching army, came under little supervision. In Cornwallis's army "swarms of beings—no better than harpies" broke off from the line of march "to distress and maltreat the inhabitants infinitely more than the whole army."[18]

Women served as water carriers during battle. Besides quenching thirst, cold water was needed to swab out cannon after firing. Two such female artillerists have become legends.

Twenty-five-year-old Margaret (Cochran) Corbin accompanied her husband, John, who served as a matross (cannoneer) in a Pennsylvania company of artillery. As the British army launched an assault upon the northern neck of Manhattan Island for the purpose of capturing Fort Washington on the Hudson River, John Corbin's artillery unit guarded against British approaches by way of Laurel Hill, overlooking the Harlem River. As the enemy pushed up the hill, Margaret's husband was killed by a musket ball. Taking over John's duties of sponging, charging, and ramming the cannon, Margaret Corbin performed with "skill and vigour" in operating an artillery piece. Badly wounded by grapeshot, with one breast mangled and one arm almost detached from her body, Margaret was made a prisoner of war. Paroled along with other captives, she received medical treatment at Philadelphia. Still crippled, Margaret Corbin was assigned, as the only woman, to the Invalid Corps stationed at West Point. The state of Pennsylvania offered her a small pension in 1779, and in the same year Congress granted her the same "half pay drawn by a soldier in the service of these States." Upon the disbanding of the Invalid Corps in 1783, Margaret resided for a while near West Point and then moved to Highland Falls. Her second husband, whom she married in 1782, was also an invalid. Unsuccessful in obtaining full rations, Margaret, nevertheless, was given a full allowance of rum or whiskey. Dying in poverty at Highland Falls about 1800, Margaret Corbin was later interred at West Point.[19]

The battle of Monmouth had an artillerist heroine, dubbed after the war as "Molly Pitcher." The actual identity has never been established, but a good case is made for Mary Ludwig Hays, whose husband, William Hays, a barber from Carlisle, Pennsylvania, served in the artillery. During the battle Mary busily carried pails of water. With the gun battery lined up in a hedgerow fending off a counterattack by British forces, William fell down, wounded and suffering from a heatstroke. Mary took his place, and continued operating the cannon for the remainder of the battle. She is most likely the person referred to by one soldier as the woman who "attended with her husband at the piece the whole time . . . a cannon shot from the enemy passed directly between her legs, without doing any other damage than carrying away all the lower part of her petticoat." William Hays died in 1787, and Mary subsequently married John McCauly. In 1822 Mary received from the Pennsylvania legislature a forty-dollar annuity for "services rendered" during the Revolutionary War.[20]

Deborah Sampson, who wanted to break loose from the humdrum farm and household life of rural Massachusetts, is the only woman known to have served an enlistment as a soldier enduring military duties and the rigors of camp, marches, and even battle. Tall at 5'8", muscular, and with a wide waist and long nose (one writer referred to her as "horse faced"), Deborah could easily pass as a soldier, especially since so many enlistees were mere boys. In May 1782 her first enlistment quickly ended. She was recognized while getting drunk on her bounty money just after she had signed up. A second attempt, shortly afterwards at a different location, as Robert Shurtleff, was successful. Deborah (Robert) engaged for three years or the duration of the war, and was assigned to a Massachusetts infantry regiment, keeping her breasts tightly taped helped to avoid detection. During her unit's fight with British dragoons between Tarrytown and Sing Sing, New York, Deborah suffered a sword wound to the left side of her head. In an ambush near East Chester, a musket ball pierced one of Deborah's thighs. Treated for the wound at a French hospital nearby her gender went undetected, and she rejoined the army before the wound healed. Transferred to Philadelphia as an orderly to Major-General John Paterson, Deborah came near to death with a "malignant fever." Dr Barnabas Binney, her attending physician, made the unusual discovery, but agreed to keep Deobrah's secret for the time being. Eventually as the war came to an end, Binney informed Paterson of Deborah's true sex. Paterson wrote General Henry Knox, commandant of the remnant Revolutionary army at West

Point, where Deborah was due to appear for a discharge. At West Point, Deborah paraded with the troops in female attire, and received an honorable discharge on October 23, 1783.

Deborah Sampson's fame began with a tribute to her published in the *Boston Gazette* on February 9, 1784. Though occasionally acting on a continuing urge to cross-dress, Deborah married Benjamin Gannett on April 7, 1785, and they settled down on a farm at Sharon, Massachusetts. A resolution of the Massachusetts Assembly granting her £34 to cover military pay not received noted that Deborah had "exhibited an extraordinary instance of female heroism by discharging the duties of a faithful, gallant soldier, and at the same time preserving the virtue & chastity of her sex unsuspected and unblemished, & was discharged from the service with a fair & honorable character." Deborah's story gained further attention when, in 1797, Herman Mann of Dedham, Massachusetts published a biography of her. The work was republished in 1866 by John A. Vinton, who supplied a sharp critical evaluation of the nearly fictitious biography. Congress, on March 11, 1805, placed Deborah on the Invalid Pension Roll, awarding her four dollars a month, later, in 1818, raised to eight dollars. In 1837, ten years after Deborah's death at age 66, Congress took the unprecedented step of voting her husband a widower's pension of $80 a month. Benjamin Gannett did not live to collect it, dying in 1837 at age 83. Congress then conferred upon Deborah and Benjamin's three children, as heirs, a lump sum of $466.66 to be divided equally among them.[21]

Anna Maria Lane and her husband, John Lane, were among New England troops under General Israel Putnam who linked up with Washington's army near Philadelphia after the battle of Brandywine. At the battle of Germantown on October 4, 1777 Anna Maria received a wound that left her lame for life. Whether she cross-dressed and enlisted as a soldier or simply remained in the status of camp follower is not known. She was probably not with her husband who was wounded at Savannah, Georgia. After the war John Lane was a member of the Virginia state guard, used for protecting the state's arsenals. John, Anna Maria, and their three children received daily military rations. Long after the war Anna Maria petitioned the Virginia government for a pension, stating that she was "very infirm, having been disabled by a severe wound, which she received while fighting as a common soldier . . . from which she never recovered." On February 6, 1808 Anna Maria and John Lane both were awarded pensions of $40 annually each for life by the Virginia government. Anna Maria Lane died two years later.[22]

A few women are known to have tried to pass as common soldiers. Expectedly, attempts to keep up a disguise were short-lived. Such was the experience of a runaway teenager who expressed a desire to join the army while at the camp of a detachment of a New Jersey regiment near Newark in November 1778. Lieutenant William Barton gave the "young Lad" some money and when he

told him to Come to my quarters he did so, I then Took an enlistment, and he remaind there Untill the next Day . . . at dinner he
was Calld in and desired to hand the Tankard to the Table he did
so and Made a Courtesy. . . . I was Inform'd of Several Circumstances which gave me reason to believe that it was A she.

A physician was called in, and "in searching" he

soon made the Discovery by Pulling out the Teats of A Plump
Young Girl, which caused Great divertion. She said the reason of
her behaving in the manner was, she wanted to marry A young
man and her Father would not Permit her, she remained at *my*
Quarters until the next morning, when I got Up; she Came to me
and said she Dreamd I had discharg'd her, I then orderd the Drums
to beat her Threw the Town with the whores march they did so
which was Curious seeing her dress'd in mens Clothes and the
whores march Beating.[23]

A female soldier known only by her alias of Samuel Gay was discharged
from the army. Anne Smith in spring 1782 enlisted as Samuel Smith, but
never lasted in service beyond first muster at Springfield, Massachusetts.
For her deceit she spent time in the local jail. A newspaper commented that
she would have gone undetected had she "had not the want of beard and
the redundance of other matters." Sally St Clair, who served as a soldier in
the Southern army to be close to her boyfriend, a sergeant, was killed
during the siege of Savannah.[24]

Prostitutes

The oldest profession thrived in locales where troops were stationed. Prostitution threatened an army's effectiveness by impairing its public image
(less than virtuous), seducing men away from duty, drawing on a soldier's
scant financial resources, and contributing to the spread of venereal disease.

From the beginning of the war, American commanders took precau-
tions against prostitutes entering military camps. General Artemas Ward,
commanding the new Continental army, on June 30, 1775, ordered that
"no lewd woman" be permitted among the troops, and "condign punishment" should be employed to rid army camps of all such nuisances. Washington engaged in similar action.[25]

The prevalence of camp followers afforded opportunity for promis-
cuity, even though many such women were with their husbands or had an
established relationship with a single soldier. The short rations for women
or the loss of a male companion from war-inflicted injury or disease were

factors that might lead a camp follower to turn to prostitution as a means for survival. The easy civilian access to camp meant that prostitutes could get in and out before being arrested. A military diarist in Washington's army commented: "Sergt. Bragg Brought Nancy into Camp at Night."[26] A court of inquiry for November 1, 1777 cited Major-General Adam Stephen for being "seen in open view of all the soldiers very drunk taking snuff out of the Boxes of strumpets."[27]

Prostitutes with the American armies, if found out, ran the risk of such punishments as having their heads shaved, "Being well Watred under a pump," and most certainly being drummed out of camp.[28] The latter ceremony, to the beating cadence of the *Whores March* rather than simply the *Rogues March*, reserved for persons dismissed from military service, was accomplished by leading the culprit to the front of assembled troops, and from right to left moving back to the rear and then to the entrance of the camp or garrison, whereupon the youngest drummer delivered a kick to the backside; the ejected person was then warned not to return upon pain of severe punishment.[29]

If prostitution could be regulated while an army was in the field or stationed in the countryside, it was entirely a different situation when troops were quartered in urban areas. Both the American and British armies had to contend with a large number of prostitutes in New York City. Commercial vice was especially found at brothels on the "Holy Ground" (so named because it was on land near St Paul's Church and owned by Trinity Church) and at "Canvas Town," between Great Dock and Canal Streets. Moreover, after the great fire of September 21, 1776 (493 houses destroyed, one-third of the city), prostitutes were among refugees from the area around Manhattan and derelicts of every kind who occupied the vacant burned-out buildings. During the long British occupation, Hessian widows or wives whose husbands had deserted, unable to speak English, had little recourse but to turn to prostitution.[30]

While Washington's army briefly held New York City, April to September 1776, soldiers consorting with prostitutes became a serious problem. Many troops were infected with venereal disease.[31] Colonel Loammi Baldwin wrote his wife in June that "the whores (by information) continue their employ which is become very lucrative." Baldwin noted that as an officer of the day, "in going the grand round with my guard of escort," he had broken up "the knots of men and women fighting, pulling caps, swearing, crying 'Murder' &c—hurried them off to the Provost Dungeon by half dozens, there let them lay mixed til next day. Then some are punished and some get clear—hell's work."[32]

The violence at the Holy Ground in late April 1776 proved to be a sobering shock. According to Lieutenant Isaac Bangs, "two Men were found inhumanly Murthered & concealed, besides one who was castrated in a barbarous Manner. This so exasperated the Men" that "they assembled and pulled down the Houses where the Men were thus treated, & with great difficulty the Guards dispersed them after they had leveled them to the Ground."[33] Solomon Nash wrote similarly that "several Limbs and heads of men were found at the Holey Ground which was supposed to Be Ciled by the hoars. The rifed men tore Down a hous. No man is Sufferd to Be there after Nine o'clock at Night."[34] With Washington's evacuation of New York City, the prostitution problem belonged to the British. Officers favored the better class of prostitutes; the common soldiers patronized the lower sort, who became known as "artillery wives." The sexual liaisons produced many illegitimate children, who were ineligible either for army or public support.[35]

Philadelphia, too, had its share of prostitutes. A civilian returning to the city just after the British evacuation gave his impressions, which were published in a Boston newspaper. "The females who stayed in the city while it was in possession of the enemy cut a curious figure," he said.

> I cannot yet learn whether the *cork rumps* have been introduced here, but some artificial rumps or other are necessary to counter-balance the extraordinary natural weight which some of the ladies carry before them . . . indeed many people do not hesitate in sup-posing that most of the young ladies who were in the city with the enemy and wear the present fashionable dresses have purchased them at the expense of their virtue. It is agreed on all hands that the British officers played the devil with the girls. The privates, I sup-pose, were satisfied with the *common* prostitutes.[36]

At the war's end, with the Continental army about to be disbanded, officers stationed at Newburgh, New York, "established a Seraglio at a place Vulgarly called Wyoma where we have super fine Kippen [soldier slang for prostitutes] immediately on application." Lieutenant Benjamin Gilbert, who recorded 15 visits to Wyoma in company with other officers, boasted that "we draw on separate orders, I make my returns once a week and receive a full ration without giving receipt for the same." Gilbert most likely overextended his credit for brothel services, for, in late August 1783 at a different duty station, he received "a disagreeable letter from Wyoma."[37]

Civilian Retailers with the Army

Besides civilians sometimes being allowed to hawk goods during visits to camp, sutlers, or self-employed peddlers, were allowed to set up shop, and at the outskirts of camp farmers established temporary produce markets.

Sutlers were usually limited to selling leaf tobacco, pigtail (tobacco in small twisted strands), soap, and alcoholic beverages. Rum and whiskey were most in demand, but a sutler's well-stocked inventory also included peach or apple brandy, cider, "strong" or "common" beer, and vinegar.[38] Sutlers's abuses of giving out too much drink to individual customers and charging excessive prices were prevalent at the beginning of the war, but were quickly reined in by Congressional and military authority. Complaints against sutlers had been rife. General Nathanael Greene with the army outside Boston in September 1775 said that because of sutlers the "troops are much Debauched" and "rendered undutiful."[39] General Philip Schuyler, commanding the Northern army, cited sutlers' "huts" as places where "mutiny, disorder and every vice takes rise."[40] Congressmen took notice of the problems caused by sutlers. Oliver Wolcott of Connecticut considered sutlers as "Harpies who for Triffles have stript" soldiers of their pay, and Matthew Thornton of New Hampshire contended that the "averice in the Sutlers has Slain ten Soldiers to the Enemies one."[41]

Sutlers had to abide by guidelines established by Congress. They could not sell "Rum or other Spirits" to a soldier without a permit from the commanding officer of his company; prices had to be posted; lists of debts soldiers owed sutlers had to be given to paymasters of regiments, with the amount of charges due sutlers deducted from payrolls; sutlers' shops had to close for business by 9 p.m. "or before the beating of the reveille, or upon Sundays, during divine service;" and importantly sutlers, as with other civilians attached to the army, were "subject to orders, according to the rules and discipline of war."[42]

The army itself established stiff regulations for sutlers. Prices were fixed. Sutlers were required not to sell any soldier more than "½ pint of spirits per day," and a liquor roll was maintained so that no customer would go over the limit.[43] "Strolling sutlers" had to leave camp upon penalty of their liquors being taken from them and distributed to soldiers without charge.[44] Sutlers assigned to a brigade or regiment could not sell to personnel of another unit.[45] Overcharging led to confiscation of liquor, paid for by the army "at a reasonable price," and the sutler being ousted.[46] More grievous offenses necessitated trial by court martial. Thus

> Andrew McCoy A Sutler brought before the Court for fraud & Extortion, the Court finds him guilty & Sentence him to Receive 100 lashes & be drummed out of the Camp & never permitted to Sell any more.[47]

Whenever drinking became excessive, commanders, on their own authority, barred soldiers from making any purchases of "spirituous Liquors" from sutlers.[48]

The farmers' markets set up near camp helped to plug a gap in the army's supply system. The quartermaster department determined where produce could be sold and set regulations for retailing to soldiers.[49] At

Valley Forge a market was held every Monday and Thursday on the east bank of the Schuylkill River; Tuesday and Friday near the North Bridge; and Wednesday and Saturday near the Adjutant-General's Office.[50] In summer 1781, at Dobbs Ferry along the Hudson, two markets were held, one for the American and the other for the French army. Washington cautioned that every retailer at "first coming" to the markets should have "a Certificate of Recommendation shew[in]g their Attachment to the American Cause and Interest. . . . that no Injury may arise to the Army from the Arts of Designing and evil minded Persons."[51]

Soldiers sometimes harassed "the country people who come to the market," such as stationing themselves on bridges and demanding tolls. The army could deal with this kind of behavior, but was powerless to prevent "unreasonable prices extorted from the soldier by the market People." Too often soldiers parted with their clothing, provisions, and accoutrements. Washington appealed to civil authorities to provide "a summary process before a Magistrate" upon any retailer receiving army property "by way of purchase or in exchange."[52]

Civilians for Military Hire

The war made for ample military employment of civilians with special skills. To meet the needs of the staff departments, besides drawing soldiers from the line whenever possible, the army enlisted persons into special adjunct companies and also hired civilians for clerical assistance and piecework. Thousands of civilians, in varied capacities, served with all the military forces, American and British.

The quartermaster department consisted of "three capital branches, Forage, Waggon & barrack departments. Besides whom there are several lessor branches such as the Artificers, Storekeepers, Expresses and fatigue men." The forage department had charge of gathering hay and other fodder; the wagon department had responsibility for all land transportation; and the barrackmaster department provided "barracks, quarters and Stores for all public purposes that has any relation to or connection with the Army."[53] The commissary of military stores department, in manufacturing weapons and maintaining arsenals, laboratories, and magazines, employed blacksmiths, armorers, carpenters, harness-makers, ironworkers, tinmen, and wheelwrights. Some of these personnel were in military service, some were not. The hired craftsmen made ten times the pay of army privates. The commissary departments of stores and provisions, issues (rations), and clothing engaged clerks, laborers, storekeepers, and coopers.[54]

Christopher Ludwig, appointed in May 1777 "Superintendent of Bakers and Director of Baking in the Grand Army of the United States," oversaw a far-flung operation that employed mainly civilians. In 1778 Congress enlisted a company of bakers to supplement Ludwig's staff. Baking posts were established at key locations and along lines of march. Ludwig had authority to license all persons baking for the army and to regulate their pay. He also had in his hire masons for the building of ovens. Ludwig's bakers in the field produced soft bread and those at camps, hard bread, which was more preferred by the troops.[55]

Complementing the use of civilians with special skills, the army had its own equivalent—artificers (craftsmen regularly enlisted). The Artillery Corps had two companies of artificers. Starting in 1778 some artificers engaged for the duration of the war; they received higher pay than the common soldiers. Although artificers "have always been upon a loose and uncertain footing," commented General Nathanael Greene in July 1779, they "are so useful and necessary" to the army's "operations that there is no moving without them." When the American army went on a contract system in 1782, Timothy Pickering, the quartermaster-general, dismissed from military service all artificers in his department.[56]

Shoemakers were retained by the army. Late in the war they were on a pay scale of 2s. for making a pair of shoes; 6s. for a pair of boots; and 6d. for half-soling shoes.[57]

Civilian carpenters signed up for a miscellany of military projects, including the building of barracks, fortifications, wagons, gun carriages, and boats. Master carpenters with the army were authorized to hire as many men as they needed.[58] To put an American fleet on Lake Champlain to contest an invasion of a British army flotilla in 1776, General Philip Schuyler, who commanded the northern department of the army, contracted with ship carpenters from Massachusetts and Connecticut. The workmen brought their own tools, and were formed into a company, setting up a shipyard at Skenesboro. In addition to these highly paid carpenters, privates with special skills of their own were pulled from the ranks to give assistance.[59]

Salaried staff department workers from time to time petitioned for pay raises and threatened to walk off their jobs. Unfortunately their Continental pay in currency depreciated in value, and Congress ran short on funds. A case in point in 1779 were artificers at Fishkill, New York; mostly carpenters and wheelwrights "employ'd by the day," they became "very clamourous about their wages." Nathanael Greene, then the quartermaster-general, warned the workers that if they left their posts they would be blacklisted from any further army employment. Eventually Greene, having investigated the expenses of these workmen and being convinced that they "mean not to abide a combination dangerous to the public service," relented and authorized wage increases.[60]

The constant need for prompt delivery of army supplies, usually picked up from a far-ranging countryside, required the use of civilian teamsters.

Washington discovered that taking "drafts from the line" to serve as wagoners left the army "in a reduced state;" so many men were assigned to teamster work that they amounted "to almost half the effective fit for duty. And what is worse, they scarce ever come back."[61] General Greene also deprecated the use of soldiers as teamsters; the practice led to "discontent" and loss of discipline. The soldier-teamsters "are greatly expos'd being Night and day without the common comforts . . . in a well regulated Camp. These hardships are multiplied by the abuse . . . from Officers of the Line," who "think every body has a right to correct a Waggoner."[62] A trial employment of a greater number of civilian wagoners, however, did not prove the remedy expected.

On May 14, 1777 Congress established a wagonmaster department as a subordinate unit under the quartermaster department. While some teamsters were still detailed away from their regular army duty and special enlistments of teamsters into the army were allowed, most of the carriers were salaried civilians—wagoners and packhorsemen.[63]

All kinds of difficulties beset the wagon service. Many drivers quit over insufficient salaries (given inflation and currency depreciation) or being paid in certificates rather than cash. Teamsters refused to carry supplies unless they received partial payment at the start of a haul and the rest upon delivery. Merchants and farmers outbid the army for services of teamsters.[64]

Teamsters were not always diligent or trustworthy. They refused to carry heavy loads, even jettisoning part of their hauls when roads were deeply mired in mud. To lighten loads wagoners drew off brine from the barrels of salt port, spoiling the meat. Many would haul only for a short run. The wagons were used to carry private goods. "The Waggoners plunder when ever they have an Opportunity," complained one deputy quartermaster. Teamsters were sometimes in league with dishonest military personnel and civilians to pilfer goods in transit. Barrels of meat and flour casks arrived at destinations as much as less than two-thirds filled. With little sense of urgency, wagoners frequently stopped at every town on a road to drink and gamble.[65] "The Waggon Conductors and Waggon Drivers Belonging to the army is the worst men I ever saw," commented another deputy quartermaster.[66] Any effort to bring teamsters under strict discipline was counterproductive because of the shortage of men willing to enter the wagon service and Washington could not spare persons for surveillance.

The wagon service was a test of endurance. While some wagoners made regular hauls from magazines and posts along main roads to encampments, many had to go deep into various unfamiliar neighborhoods to pick up supplies from farmers, even at times having to seek out magistrates to issue impressment warrants.[67] The army-issued vehicular and horse/oxen equipment was often faulty. As Jacob Weiss, deputy quartermaster-general, noted of the teamster articles he received in October 1778:

The Harness, Breast, and Tongue Chains . . . are most shocking Trash, no ways suitable for Continental Service . . . The Blind Bridles are not only base work, but come half finished, some wanting Reins, and others Forehead pieces and Throat Latches, The Breast and Tongue Chains, and Chains in general, are so badly made, that it would be running great Risks for Waggoners to steer their Horses in this Mountainous Country [Hudson River Highlands] without Danger of Killing them, and losing their own lives.[68]

There was a large turnover among civilian wagoners. Few engaged for more than a year. Henry Vanderslice, a 51-year-old former sheriff of Berks County, Pennsylvania signed up out of a sense of patriotic duty in March 1777 to become a wagonmaster of a brigade of 12 wagons, with 50 horses and 12 carters. Vanderslice and his four horse-drawn covered wagons crisscrossed New Jersey to bring supplies to Washington's army, hauling hay, oats, rye, wheat, beef, port, salt gammon, whiskey, baggage, guns, furniture, tools, and household goods.[69]

Eighteen-year-old Joseph Joslin of South Killingly, Connecticut tried his hand as a teamster in 1777, hauling barrels of flour, beef, pork, rum, hay, salt, corn, and iron between that part of Washington's army stationed on the Hudson and supply depots in Connecticut. His wagon could carry eight barrels of pork. Joslin braved all kinds of extreme weather, traversed roads "full of Brooks," hills, and swamps, subsisted largely on "stinking Pork," put in 13–14-hour days, and slept where he could, on the ground or haystacks or in stables and barns. Between teamster assignments he hired out as a farmhand. But Joslin soon had enough of army wagon service. His diary for November 28, 1777 reads: "I Don't intend to Drive a team for my Continent any more yet Sir goodby."[70]

Congress in 1780 adopted an army supply system whereby the states (under quotas) assumed full responsibility for providing the army with provisions and forage. Commodities, in some states raised by a "specifics" tax, were collected at state depots. Transportation within its borders was provided by a state. With reduced need for civilian teamsters hired by the army, Congress, as a cost-cutting measure, directed that the wagonmaster department's personnel be drawn entirely from the army. The state supply system soon proved inadequate, and the private contract program initiated in 1782 as its replacement also kept supply transportation by the army at a minimum.[71]

Civilian craftsmen, clerks, retailers, teamsters, and women camp workers all provided valuable services for the armies. Much of the experience was unsettling, such as wastefulness and strained labor relations, but at least was instructive for administrative, procurement, and support reform.

CHAPTER NINE

Non-combatants

Many Americans under obligation for military service avoided active duty. All male adult citizens were expected to appear at militia musters and to go with their units into the field when called upon. As the war progressed, draftees were taken into Continental army service. Besides those who were exempted because of occupational status or by providing a substitute, there were those who were counted out of service by their own voluntary decisions or by involuntary circumstances; all experienced some degree of inconvenience and hardship. Conscientious objectors, deserters, the sick, and persons under prisoner of war status formed a class of citizens in limbo, awaiting a future change of events.

Conscientious Objectors

Because of their small numbers and being intractable in devotion to their faith, most religious pacifists won exemption from military service with relative impunity. As long as they did not side with the enemy in word or deed and met compensatory demands instead of military service, they faced little ire or coercion from the community.

The right to refuse military service had been recognized in the American colonies and in England. But since everyone benefited from protection of life, liberty, and property in both peacetime and wartime, pacifists were obligated to contribute their share of the burdens for ensuring that protection through added financial assistance and personal service in lieu of military duty. Quakers and related small groups—Rogerenes, Nicholites, and Shakers—and German-speaking pacifists—Mennonites, Amish, Dunkards, Moravians, and Schwenkfelders—as organized religious bodies came under special government regulated exemptions; individuals of other religious orders not collectively pacifist seldom could claim any dispensation for their rejection of war service.

During the war pacifists who refused military duty were expected to pay special taxes and the costs for substitutes. The financial penalties for non-military service represented a double indemnity since fines were also levied upon pacifists refusing to take the test (loyalty) oaths required of all citizens. Refusal to pay the added assessments caused a liability to be satisfied by imprisonment or seizure of property. The commutation fee for exemptions from the draft varied among the states, from an annual fine of £10 in New York and Maryland to up to £500 in South Carolina.[1]

Most conscientious objectors other than Quakers, though adamant in not bearing arms, were willing to pay military fines and special taxes. A Schwenkfelder group pledged "to help each other to carry all fines in money that may be imposed on any of them or of their children on account of their refusal through conscientious scruples to render personal service in the war in which deadly weapons are carried and used."[2] North Carolina Moravians resolved in May 1778 that although they would not take up arms they would do their "share of the burden of the land in these disturbed times if reasonable demands are made."[3] John Ettwein, later the head of the Moravian Church, declared: "We will by the Grace of God seek the welfare of the Country . . . As long as we are protected we will pay Taxes & bear our Part of the public Burthren."[4] Mennonites and Dunkards took a similar position. Some members of these German pacifist sects, however, individually engaged in total non-compliance and experienced loss of property and brief imprisonment.

Quakers went the full distance in not having anything to do that remotely aided the prosecution of the war. Friends not only declined payment of the war fees and fines but also refused to drive their own teams when impressed for military use. Quakers, however, left to individual members whether to accept Continental or state paper money. Many did refuse. Even though non-acceptance of such currency was a capital offense in Pennsylvania, no persons were executed on this account.[5] Despite coming under disownment (excommunication) for accepting employment related to the war effort, many Quakers were willing to make this breach. One-fifth of Pennsylvania male adult Friends joined the army or assumed positions in government.[6]

Non-compliance with wartime assessments on pacifists in many instances resulted in severe punishment. In Pennsylvania officials could "break open any house, trunk, box, chest, closet, cupboard or other things" and seize any property desired. Livestock, farm equipment, grain, furniture, bedding, and clothing were among the sanctioned loot. Persons refusing military service could be fined one day's labor for each day not doing duty, and if unable to pay be jailed for up to four months. The whole scheme of the Pennsylvania coercive measures produced such hardships that occasionally riotous resistance erupted. In one instance a band of "memonests who pretend non resistance persive [passive] Obedience" forcibly prevented a milita detachment from arresting Samuel Albright for non-payment of the militia fines. About "12 men and a number of women Armed with Sithes, Coulters, & Pitch forks . . . struck one of the guard with a coulter, behind his back, which split his skul a bout 4 or 5 inches, the rest of the guard thought they were all in danger of their Lives." The guard fired on the rioters, wounding three of the ringleaders, "but having no more Ammunition . . . was Obliged to flee for their lives."[7]

Distraints (seizure of personal property) among Quakers, chiefly for military fines, were substantial. In Pennsylvania the estimated total value was £38,550; New Jersey £16,026 19s. 5d.; Delaware, £2,189 12s. 9d; New York, about £11,200; Maryland, £7,198 2s. 4d.; Virginia, £11,221 11s. 11¾d.; and North Carolina, £10,094 5s. 6d.[8]

While other sects were contending for their principles, the little group of Shakers made the most steadfast witness against war. Mother Ann Lee and her dozen or so followers of the United Society of Believers, fresh from England, had settled at Watervliet, New York, just north of Albany. Beset by rioters because of their anti-militarism, the Shakers refused protection offered by the authorities. Going the extra mile in resistance, the Shakers tried to persuade citizens from answering militia calls. In July 1780 half of the group were arrested, including Mother Ann, who spent the rest of the year in jail. The persecution of the Shakers attracted attention and won for them new converts.[9]

A few efforts were made to forcibly induct Quaker draftees into the army. Fourteen Quaker men of the Hopewell Monthly Meeting in Frederick County, Virginia were drafted and marched northwards to join the Continental army at Valley Forge. Kept in ranks at sword point and with muskets tied to them, the reluctant enlistees refused to draw rations. Half of the group on the way were sent back because of their poor physical condition. The others upon arriving at camp were ordered released by Washington. A Hessian major, Carol Leopold Baurmeister, commented that Washington's decision showed a sense of "great justice."[10]

William Davis, a Quaker from Virginia or North Carolina, was ordered "to join a Company of Militia who were to march to the barracks at Charlottesville to guard a number of British prisoners." Davis refused, and was apprehended and forced to go on the march. He did not answer roll calls because this would mean that he was a soldier. Davis ended up in a guardhouse, found guilty by a court martial, and endured 39 lashes of the cat-of-nine tails. Ordered to do duty again, Davis again declined. He then had a long "discourse" with the commanding colonel, who "in Some Meashure Excus'd himself for their Cruelty adding the Law obliged him to do as he had." Davis then returned to the guardhouse, expecting to be confined again, but instead was ordered away. He found lodging with some "Acquaintances" among whom he stayed until discharged. His "body was so tattered" that he was "not fit for much servis if I had been willing— was often threaten'd, and Endeavours used to get me to wait on the Sick which was offer'd at the first Saying it was Every good mans delight or duty to wait on the Sick. I let them know I Could not Supply the place of a Soldier Even to wait on the Sick."[11]

Dunkards and Mennonites skirted their consciences and served as teamsters hauling army supplies. This was not out of any sense of patriotism, but to protect their ownership of the wagons and teams that had been seized for military service and to make sure they were returned home.[12] Quakers refused to allow members to engage in this capacity or to hire out for any work with the army or to serve on privateers.[13]

From Christian obligation, the religious conscientious objectors performed humanitarian service, as long as they did so as civilians and not in a military capacity. Besides engaging in poor relief, religious pacifists volunteered for helping the military wounded and sick. Moravian John Ettwein served as chaplain of the Continental army hospital at Bethlehem, Pennsylvania. Quakers brought food and necessary items to wounded American soldiers after the battle of Germantown.[14] At the conclusion of the battle of Guilford Courthouse in March 1781, General Nathanael Greene, himself a disowned Quaker, called upon the Friends at New Garden Meeting House to administer to the wounded Americans. "I know of no order of men," said Greene, "more remarkable for the exercise of humanity and benevolence; and perhaps no instance ever had a higher claim upon you than the unfortunate wounded now in your neighborhood." The Friends replied that they were in dire straights due to plundering by both armies and many of their own were without food, but were determined to assist. The New Garden Friends buried the dead in their graveyards and nursed the wounded in their homes and meeting house.[15]

Deserters

To escape military service after being inducted into the army was a much more serious offence than avoiding it altogether. Once taken into the army the recruit or draftee came under the strict code of military justice as provided by Congress and the army itself.

Under the Congressional Articles of War of September 20, 1776 the penalties for all forms of desertion were either flogging up to 100 lashes or death. During the war of 546 court martial sentences handed down for desertion, 137 provided for death; only 40 were executed, and 70 received pardons.[16] Despite Congress's mandate as to the type of sentences, punishments less than death were frequently exacted, such as flogging, running the gauntlet, and riding the wooden horse (a culprit sitting on a sharp ridge with legs tied tightly and hands bound behind the back). In the heated war in the South, deserters taken in battle frequently met death from instant drumhead courts-martial.[17] Washington thought there was too big a gap between 100 lashes and death as punishment for desertion and wanted to increase the maximum flogging to 500 stripes, but Congress would not give its approval.[18] Although the viewpoint of the Marchese di Beccaria's *Essays on Crimes and Punishment* (1764) was beginning to have influence in America that certainty rather than severity of punishment was most effective, the American military leaders favored severity in sentencing. Thus there were so many pardons that punishment lost its deterrent value.[19]

Draftee militia who did not show up at Continental army rendezvous and militia who deserted when their units were activated posed serious problems for the states. Even though some states eventually adapted the Continental Articles of War for their militia, penalties for militia defection continued to be relatively light—fines, brief imprisonment, additional service, and demotions.[20]

Estimates put one-fifth to one-third as the proportion of troops in the Continental army who deserted.[21] A relatively small number of deserters were listed on the army strength reports, primarily in order to lessen demoralization among the rank and file. Many of the "sick absent," "on furlough," or "on command" were actually deserters.[22]

New recruits quickly discovered that the conditions of army life did not suit them. Repulsion at the frequent corporal punishment, the arduous military duty, lack of pay and food, contemptuous attitude of many of the officers, fear of combat, crowded and unsanitary camp life, rampant spread of disease, fear of capture by the British, enticement by the enemy, and opportunity to serve aboard privateers all were factors impelling soldiers to escape military service. Bounty jumping—collecting a stipend for enlisting with one unit and then deserting and signing up with another with no questions asked—accounted for many desertions. The inducement of receiving higher pay from one state line than that of another also caused desertion-reenlistments. Soldiers were motivated to desert or not return from furlough because of homesickness, the suffering of their families, and the need to attend to planting and harvesting of crops. Washington recognized this desertion problem early in the war:

> Men just dragged from the tender Scenes of domestic life; unaccustomed to the din of Arms; totally unacquainted with every kind of Military skill, which being followed by a want of confidence in themselves, when opposed to Troops regularly train'd, disciplined, and appointed, superior in knowledge and superior in Arms, makes them timid, and ready to fly from their own shadows. Besides, the sudden change in their manner of living, (particularly in the lodging) brings on sickness in many; impatience in all, and such an

unconquerable desire of returning to their respective homes that it not only produces shameful, and scandalous Desertions among themselves, but infuses the like spirit in others.[23]

Washington required his generals to tighten restrictions on camp life to prevent desertion. Frequent roll calls and keeping troops constantly employed deterred "Idleness and Dissipation which are too frequently and fatally attended by Desertion." Guards were so placed as to catch any soldier leaving camp without a pass. Most of all Washington insisted that recruiting officers bring enlistees "into Service, where they will be employed" as quickly as possible, instead of the new troops "loitering away their time in Taverns, and running from one offer to the next and receiving the bounty over and over again."[24]

Four times the commander-in-chief proclaimed amnesty for deserters who returned to the army within specified time limits, but these efforts produced little result. In November 1777 Washington offered £10 and payment of one shilling per mile for any soldier or civilian who brought in a deserter.[25] As an unfortunate drain of manpower, officers, usually by extended furloughs, were detained in their home neighborhoods to search for deserters.[26]

The states were negligent in the enforcement of their laws against desertion. The substantial fines to be levied on captains of privateers for receiving deserters in Massachusetts and Rhode Island were not much of a deterrent. Civilians caught in the militia drafts frequently ignored orders to join the army. In Virginia about half of those summoned appeared at the military rendezvous for induction.[27] William Davies, Virginia's Commissioner of War, in March 1781, complained to Governor Jefferson that "I have no doubt If every draft in future raises one third soldiers and two thirds deserters, the latter will soon become too formidable to be meddled with."[28] Indeed the draft defectors added to the numbers of deserters from the Continental army already in a community.

Because civilians were reluctant to report deserters, Congress recommended in July 1777 that the state executives establish districts over which a person would be appointed to supervise recruiting and to have "full power to take up and secure all deserters" and to require militia assistance if necessary. Congress offered a $15 reward to anyone capturing and securing any deserter.[29] Most states followed through with some provision to implement Congress's entreaty. Virginia had militia company commanders in each county appoint persons to search out deserters and to deliver them to a Continental officer; if this could not be accomplished within a 50-mile radius, then the detainee was to be lodged in a local jail.[30] The states had strict laws exacting penalties for harboring and assisting deserters. In Virginia, for example, an abettor faced military service equal to the time left unserved by a deserter; if women were involved they could each be fined

£50 or be imprisoned for three months. Toward the end of the war the Virginia penalty was a fine of 5,000 pounds of tobacco or six months in jail.[31]

The public made little distinction between temporary absenteeism and desertion. After all, furloughs were freely given, and long stays by officers at home were common. Citizens in general were apathetic about desertion. As the war progressed, so many soldiers came from the transient and lower classes that they were not known well enough in communities to be dubbed deserters. Most importantly, with the *rage militaire* subsiding and a wall of separation between soldiers and citizenry making for a mutual exclusivity between the two groups, the public was less concerned over apprehension or punishment of deserters.

An important factor abetting desertion was that if an absconder made it clear of the environs of an encampment undetected by patrols or a search detachment sent after him, he could count on slight possibility of being caught. Local justices of the peace and other officials at the county level preferred not to lend a hand, especially if a sizeable group of deserters returned home at the same time. Relatives and friends harbored and concealed deserters. Even when there were seizures by authorities, as Washington noted, "there have been many instances where Deserters . . . have been rescued by the People, and but very few where the Officers have received their aid and support."[32]

Large numbers of deserters found refuge in the backcountry. They absconded from the northern and southern Continental armies. Many of the escaped soldiers in the western hills and mountains became outlaws. Deserters joined Indians and Tories in frontier New York. President Joseph Reed of Pennsylvania wrote to Washington, in July 1780, that many soldiers had been lost because the "Land-Office in Virginia" had "afforded both an asylum and a temptation for desertion."[33] "Bands of Continental deserters" resided in the western mountains of Virginia (particularly in Botetourt, Hampshire, and Montgomery counties), Maryland, and Pennsylvania.[34] A good many of George Rogers Clark's troops on the western expedition of 1778–9 took leave as a Virginia legislative report noted, "with a view of making fortunes by land jobbing, and screening themselves as deserters."[35]

Deserters and Tories exiled from New York found a safe haven in the disputed territory between Lake Champlain and the Connecticut River, above the Massachusetts border. Here they mingled with distraught settlers who were struggling to defend lands granted to them by New Hampshire against efforts of New York to secure the territory. The rugged resistance of Ethan Allen's Green Mountain Boys culminated in the establishment of the independent state of Vermont in January 1777. Congress, determined to uphold New York's claim and to quash what seemed to be a conspiracy of some Vermonters to ally with the British, considered using the Continental army to bring Vermont to submission. The situation worsened. The

Tory Secretary of State of Vermont, Micah Townshend, admitted in April 1781 that "settlers flock daily [into Vermont] from the old Colonies; many also are deserters from the Continental Army, all fly from taxes or military service. No parties have as yet dared to come there for deserters."[36] Washington acknowledged that Vermont "gives protection, and is an asylum to all deserters."[37]

Congress ordered Washington to send a military detachment into Vermont to seize two ringleaders, Luke Knowlton and Samuel Wells. Troops from a Rhode Island regiment assigned to this task did not succeed in their mission.[38] Washington rejected a suggestion in a Congressional resolution to conduct an invasion of Vermont. Very simply, Vermonters would put up too much of a fight:

> The Inhabitants for the most part are a hardy race, composed of that kind of People who are best calculated for Soldiers: in truth, who are Soldiers; for many, many hundreds of them are Deserters from this Army; who having acquired property there, would be desperate in the defense of it, well knowing they are fighting with Halters about their Necks.[39]

Congress backed off from using force in Vermont, as long as there were not further "combinations or acts hostile to the U. States," and allowed for a negotiated settlement of the dispute over Vermont statehood.[40]

The Military Sick

Care for injured and sick soldiers enormously tested the resources of the army, and, with military treatment facilities overflowing with patients, civilians were expected to make available for medical use homes, barns, churches, schoolhouses, taverns, and any vacant buildings to serve as infirmaries. Sickness far more than service-related injuries reduced the fighting capabilities of the Continental armies.

Adding those who were "absent sick" to those cared for by the army medical program, at least one-fourth to one-third of Washington's army on the average were medically exempt from active duty. In July 1776, of 6,000 soldiers at Fort Ticonderoga, 3,800 were sick. In October of the same year in Washington's army out of a reported strength of 32,698 men, 3,392 were "sick present" and 4,878 "sick absent." As Washington's troops began their encampment at Valley Forge in late December 1777, 2,087 men were "sick present" and 5,008 "sick absent" out of a paper total of 25,985 men. Benjamin Rush, briefly the army's surgeon-general for the Middle Medical

Department, claimed that there were "now upwards of 5000 sick in our hospitals."[41]

Soldiers were most healthy when in motion rather than residing at camp. Being cooped up with 12 men in a smoked filled hut was an invitation for disease. The unsanitary and crowded hospitals contributed immensely to the spread of sickness. Smallpox (eventually all of the troops were inoculated), typhoid fever, typhus (or "camp fever," caused by lice), dysentery, and malaria took the heaviest toll among the soldiers. The Northern army in the Canadian offensive of 1776 was almost incapacitated by the prevalence of smallpox. Many soldiers were constantly affected with the itch, which, as General De Kalb noted, "attracts very little attention either at the hospitals or in camp. I have seen the poor fellows covered over and over with scab."[42]

Of 1,400 physicians and surgeons who served with the American armies, less than 200 had medical degrees (one half of these obtained abroad and the others from the incipient medical schools in Philadelphia and New York City).[43] Without knowledge of specific treatment of diseases, the best a physician could do was to prescribe bleeding, blistering, purging, sweating, or ingestion of herbal concoctions (some of which had worthwhile results such as the use of quinine from the cinchona bark). Laudanum (opium and saffron with canary wine) relieved pain. Unfortunately the available medical supplies fell far short of the need.

The army medical service became an extensive operation, including the use of civilians as nurses and orderlies in addition to physicians, surgeons, and a staff bureaucracy. Congress established a Hospital Department on July 27, 1775 during the siege of Boston. The first army hospitals were at Cambridge, Menotony (Arlington), and Watertown, Massachusetts. The largest military hospital during the war was at Fort George, which by October 1776 had treated 3,000 patients.[44]

Three kinds of hospitals received military convalescents: regimental, in the vicinity of camps or close to battlefields; field (or "flying" or "marching") hospitals near combat areas handling the overflow of patients, usually in huts constructed by the troops; and general hospitals, at a safe distance from the enemy. After the evacuation of New York City in September 1776, American military hospitals were set up at Stamford, Norwalk, White Plains, North Castle, Peekskill, and West Point. During Washington's retreat across New Jersey in late 1776, when one-third of the army was sick or wounded, military hospitals were established at Elizabethtown, New Brunswick, Trenton, Fort Lee, Newark, and Morristown. By the end of 1777 the Northern army had seven hospitals along the Hudson River, and Washington's army had set up 13 such facilities: three in New Jersey, nine in Pennsylvania, and one in Baltimore, Maryland.[45] In February 1777 Congress created three army medical districts: northern, eastern, and middle;

each department had a director-general. The district system was eliminated on September 30, 1780, and one director-general served for all the medical corps.[46] The British system, making use of urban buildings and hospital ships, also had a unified arrangement under one director-general.

Philadelphia, under the American occupation, received many of the wounded and sick from the military campaigns and army encampments in Pennsylvania and New Jersey. On December 6, 1776 the Pennsylvania Council of Safety created a five-man committee to provide care for "sick troops coming to the city from camp," making use of any empty houses and stores and other buildings" and employing "such discreet persons as to them shall seem meet." Besides the Pennsylvania Hospital, the Employment House (almshouse), Smallpox Hospital, Peel Hall (later part of Girard College), and privately owned buildings, including some 30 shops and houses belonging to loyalists, were used for the care of the military infirm. John Adams estimated that 2,000 soldiers died in Philadelphia during the winter of 1776-7. The dead were buried together, according to Dr James Tilton, "in large square pits, until nearly full and then covered over."[47]

The German-related religious groups in Pennsylvania endured substantial responsibility for treating military convalescents. Dunkards maintained a hospital at Lilitz. Lutheran and German Reformed churches at Red Lion and French Creek were used. The military forcibly appropriated the Quaker Meeting House at Uwchlan.[48]

When the army was at Middlebrook, New Jersey, it took possession of two churches in Somerset County. When it sought to use "the neighboring barns to accommodate our convalescents," a justice of the peace, Ernestus Van Harlingen, "laughed at the requisition" and threatened to jail any one who should take over "a Barn for the use of sick Soldiers." General Nathanael Greene, the quartermaster-general, intervened and saw to it that the army demands met with compliance, contrary to the opposition of the judge and "the people of the Neighborhood;" one of the barns appropriated for a hospital belonged to Van Harlingen.[49]

The Moravians at Bethlehem, Pennsylvania willingly opened their facilities for the care of army patients. The three-storey Single Brethren House on the average housed 500 patients. One of the church members recorded on December 6, 1776 that "the sick were brought here to-day in crowds. Their suffering and lack of proper care make them a pitiable spectacle to behold." On December 28 there were 700 convalescents at the Single Brethren House. On January 5, 1778 it was noted that "so many of our Single Brethren have been made sick by the stench from the Hospital, that they have been advised to keep away." Indeed, in early 1778 seven Brethren died from disease contracted from exposure with the sick.[50]

Army hospitals were breeding nests for disease, with the crowded and unsanitary conditions, no heat, contaminated water, and poor ventilation. The sick were not segregated from the wounded. The mortality rate was astounding. At the Valley Forge encampment of 1777–8 2,100 soldiers died at the camp hospital. Dr James Tilton commented that "many a fine fellow have I seen brought into the hospital for a slight syphilitic affliction" were "carried out dead of a hospital fever."[51]

Dr Benjamin Rush was disgusted with both the administration and the quality of care in army hospitals. The "great majority" of soldiers who died of disease caught the contagion in a hospital. On one of his inspections, he found 20 patients in a single room. Not only were there insufficient medicines, but patients had inadequate clothing and blankets. "Nothing but a miracle," Rush complained, "can save the life of a soldier who lies in a shirt and blanket which he has worn from four or five months before he came to the hospital." Rush noted that soldiers under age 20 and southern troops were most susceptible to the "putrid fevers." Many fatalities could have been prevented if there were proper sanitation. Rush recommended that the sick be dispersed among farm houses. "The air and diet of a farmer's kitchen are the best physic in the world for a soldier worn down with the fatigues of a campaign."[52]

Civilians often gave aid to the army convalescents. Women in Philadelphia contributed "old sheets and shirts" for the hospital sick.[53] Benjamin Rush informed John Adams in October 1777 that in Reading, Pennsylvania there were several hundred soldiers "who would have perished had they not been supported by the voluntary and benevolent contributions of some pious whigs."[54]

Women served as nurses in the hospitals. Their work, however, was largely custodial, much like that of a modern orderly, employed in such tasks as cleaning wards (including the sprinkling of vinegar three or four times a day), washing patients, and emptying "close-stools or pots as soon as possible after they are used, into a necessary house." Most medical work was performed by male surgeon mates, although in their absence women nurses could act in their place. Matrons were employed as supervisors of housekeeping services.[55] Washington thought that a minimum wage of a dollar a day was necessary to attract women as nurses. But Congress settled for less, granting nurses, in 1777, a base salary of 24¢ per day and one food ration (about the same compensation received by an army sergeant) and matrons 50¢ and one ration daily.[56]

On June 20, 1777 Congress established the Invalid Corps of eight companies, each consisting of five officers, five sergeants, six corporals, two drummers, two fifers and 100 men. Members were those who were disabled, but not so much that they could not perform useful duties. While one intention to use the Corps for military instruction did not materialize, its soldiers when possible were employed in guard and other camp work, such as cooking, dressing wounds, and packing supplies for shipment. Commanded during its whole existence by Colonel Lewis Nicola, the Corps was disbanded by order of Congress on May 1, 1783. The officers were allowed to retire at full pay for life, and the non-commissioned officers and privates became the responsibility of the states to serve as town or city police or guards of military stores. The costs of supporting those disabled soldiers were deducted from requisitions owed to Congress by the states.[57]

Prisoners of War

Prisoner exchange met many hurdles. As a result a large number of prisoners of war were kept for lengthy periods by both sides during the war. American-held prisoners fared better than their counterparts because of their wide distribution in rural locales distant from the war theaters, affording less supervision and opportunity to mix with civilians and gain employment. British-held prisoners were cooped up in urban areas. The mortality rate of British-held American prisoners was greater than the total of rebel soldiers and sailors killed in action. Captive officers from both sides did not endure the hardships of the prisoners from the enlisted ranks. Usually only officers were given parole.

During the early part of the war any equality between the belligerents as to the number of prisoners held was upset by the British capture of 1,000 American soldiers at the battle of Long Island and the 2,818 men who surrendered at Fort Washington. Along with the incarceration of certain civilians, 5,000 American prisoners were held in New York City by the end of 1776. New York became a "City of Prisons." Captives were crowded into three sugarhouses, dissenting churches, the closed King's (Columbia) College, City Hall, hospitals, stables, and the two jails—Bridewell and the New Jail or Provost Prison.[58]

Under the watch of provost guards rather than regular soldiers, the American prisoners in New York City suffered extreme deprivation. Samuel Young, one of 500 prisoners confined in a stable, noted that food was thrown to the prisoners, "as if to so many hogs, a quantity of old biscuit . . . some of it crawling with maggots, which they were obliged to scramble for . . . next day a little pork was given to each of them, which they were obliged to eat raw." There were no windows to keep out the cold, no clothing issued, and no water with which to wash; the captives slept on straw.[59] The *New Hampshire Gazette* of April 26, 1777 revealed that these conditions were not remedied:

> The enemy in New York continues to treat the American prisoners with great barbarity. Their allowance to each man for three days is one pound of beef, three wormeaten biscuits, and a quart of salt water. The meat they are obliged to eat raw as they have not the smallest allowance of fuel. Owing to this more than savage cruelty, the prisoners die fast, and in the small space of three weeks (during the winter) no less than 1,700 brave men perished.[60]

The worst of the prisons was the Provost, under the supervision of the notorious William Cunningham, known for his excessive brutality and who boasted that he himself was responsible for many prisoner deaths. During the winter of 1776–7 smallpox and other diseases from the prison compounds spread throughout New York City, inflicting many deaths and causing some citizens to flee in fright.[61]

Even more inhumane were the horrid conditions aboard the prison ships. By 1779, 14 prison vessels were anchored around the perimeter of Manhattan Island, at Wallabout Bay at the northern edge of Brooklyn, Paulus Hook (Jersey City, New Jersey), and on the Hudson and East rivers. Dysentery, smallpox, typhus, yellow fever, other infectious diseases, and malnutrition cost the lives of some 11,000 American captives aboard the "floating hells." Especially the *Jersey*, a converted worn-out man-of-war, which held 1,000 American seamen, had a high mortality rate. Captives were fed starvation rations, which even then consisted of food rejected by British military forces. The scant meat was usually spoiled and boiled in corrosive copper containers. Five or six captives died each day and corpses were hauled off for burial in shallow graves on the beaches of Wallabout; tides soon left the bodies exposed.

The inmates aboard the prison ships had little assistance from citizens of New York City. But for a while, "a very corpulent old woman" known only as Dame Grant rowed out to the *Jersey* every other day and offered at cost soft bread, fruit, sugar, tea, tobacco, pipes, needles, and thread to the captives. Unfortunately it was not long before she, too, caught the "fever" and died.[62]

Officers could sign a parole pledging their honor not to engage in hostilities until they were exchanged. They were either permitted to roam in a restricted neighborhood near their captors during daylight hours or, if they were more fortunate, return home.

American officers captured in 1776 had the liberty of New York City. In January 1777 they were moved to Kings County on Long Island and were lodged among the Dutch inhabitants. Two or three captives were assigned to a house. Officers had to pay for their board and room. Some married officers brought in their wives and families.[63] British officers paroled by the Americans generally had wide latitude as to where they could reside or travel, but seldom were they allowed to stay behind British lines or return to England.

During the Southern campaigns, the British adopted a more vindictive parole system than before. Upon the surrender of Charleston, practically the whole male adult population was placed on parole, and denied certain liberties such as the pursuit of one's profession and trade unless subscribing to an oath of allegiance to the British crown.[64] Some of the most prominent citizens were deported to St Augustine in East Florida. While the Continental army officers seized at Charleston were originally interned at mosquito-invested Haddrell's Point across the harbor, they were eventually permitted to return home. Such paroled officers hardly became second-class citizens. Brigadier-General Charles Scott returned to tend his farm along the James River in Virginia; ironically he was merely a spectator while the same British army that had captured him marched by his farm during the enemy's invasion of Virginia.

Militia officers captured at Charleston were not so fortunate. Colonel Isaac Hayne of the South Carolina militia was given the choice of being detained as a prisoner of war or parole upon swearing allegiance to the crown. With his wife and children seriously ill, Hayne chose the latter alternative. Considering that the terms of his parole ended with the British inability to conquer South Carolina, Hayne once again took up arms for the rebel cause, was captured, and hanged at Charleston on August 4, 1781, thereby setting an example for other militia who had violated their parole and in part providing retaliation for the American execution of John André.[65]

American captives were relentlessly recruited by the British. In particular seamen-prisoners, with the alternative of death by malnutrition or disease, escaped the awful severity of their confinement by signing on with the British navy. Washington was circumspect about bringing British captive soldiers into the American army; they could not be trusted and often deserted back to the British at the first opportunity.

Many deserters from the British army found their way into the interior and merged with the American civilian population. Nine hundred prisoners from Yorktown escaped on their march northward and were observed "strolling through Virginia."[66] Some of the British prisoners detained near York, Pennsylvania found American wives. It was said the local young women had "scarlet fever." At the York prison compound single prisoners lived at "Camp Security," inside a stockaded area, while married prisoners and their families resided outside the stockade at "Camp Indulgence."[67]

Hessian soldiers, with not much to look forward to back in the homeland, escaped in large numbers and settled among their German-American kinsmen. Five thousand Hessian soldiers stayed in America, some of whom were deserters and others who were discharged from service.[68] Including those who died from wounds or disease, more than one-third of the Hessian troops did not return to Germany.

Prisoners of war were allowed to hire out in a community, being paid with food and clothing and a small stipend. At first Congress prohibited this practice for prisoners of war in Pennsylvania, but then gave its approval, on condition an employer posted £1,000 bond as security that a prisoner would not escape and that $4 per month be paid to the Continental treasury.[69]

The German soldiers found ready employment. Some prisoners from the battle of Trenton indentured themselves to ironmasters in the German communities of eastern Pennsylvania. From this group, those who stayed on after the war, with the best land already claimed, set up farms in the mountains. Thus arose a saying among the earlier German-Americans, "Drau net die Let vum Barrick!" ("Don't trust the mountain people").[70]

John Jacob Faesch, a native of Switzerland, at his Mount Hope Furnace in Rockaway Township, New Jersey hired Hessian prisoners to work in iron mines and as wood choppers and furnace men; Faesch had a government contract to produce munitions for the American army.[71] Hessian prisoners hired out among the farmers of the Frederick, Maryland vicinity and Lancaster and Berks counties, Pennsylvania.[72] In western Maryland, a Hessian private noted in his diary on May 4, 1782 that "every night people depart from us . . . to sell work in the country."[73]

The release of prisoners of war held by both sides was delayed until long after the cessation of hostilities. Finally in January 1783 prisoners on the New York prison ships were discharged and allowed to go home. Washington and the new British commanding general in North America, Guy Carleton, met together at Tappan, New York on May 6, 1783 and concluded an agreement for the general release and exchange of all prisoners, which was accomplished by July 1, 1783.

CHAPTER TEN

The home front

The reality of war was inescapable on the home front. Ties of kinship or friendship with those who fought, food and fuel shortages, prices and wage inflation, taxes, currency depreciation, military requisitions, war profiteering, and conversion to war production involved the citizenry at large. Despite their remoteness from battlefield zones, many persons gladly did their part to enhance the survival of the Revolutionary military forces and probability of victory.

War Support Activities

Ersatz concoctions made up for scarce commodities. For household consumption, tea was brewed from sage, checkerberries, or balsamic resin; lye from walnut ashes substituted for salt; and the residue from boiled cornstalks took the place of sugar and molasses.[1] Ebenezer Huntington of Norwich, Connecticut observed in May 1779: "This whole part of the Country are starving for want of bread, they have been drove to the necessity of Grinding Flaxseed & oats together for bread."[2]

Although no rationing systems were firmly established, citizens were expected to observe limitations on certain items. In New England measures were passed limiting the distilling of spirits in order to conserve grain, and in Massachusetts only bakers could purchase grain or flour more than needed for family use and no one could stock up on provisions in excess of what was needed for one year.[3] The Boston town committee in March 1778 advised the consumption of meat at only two meals a day and to "avoid the Use of Poultry & every other Superfluity as much as possible;" families should have "two dinners per week on fish, if to be had."[4] In New York, families "well affected to the American cause" were given cards by local committees of safety entitling them to purchase three quarts of salt.[5]

Revolutionary War patriots on the home front held war drives. Women collected scrap metal, pewter pots and plates, and lead from window casings to be converted into bullets. Persons donated old handkerchiefs, bed sheets, and clothes for the making of paper and bandages and compresses for army hosptials.[6]

Women's associations solicited funds to assist soldiers of the Continental army. The most prominent of these was a committee of 39 women headed by Esther DeBerdt Reed, wife of Joseph Reed, President of the Supreme Executive Council of Pennsylvania. Volunteer collectors fanned out through Philadelphia and its suburbs in the summer of 1780, enlisting 1,645 donors. The committee presented Washington with $200,580 in paper money and £625.68 in specie for a total of $300,634. Mrs Reed suggested that the money be used as pay supplements to the soldiers, to which Washington objected because such grants would make the soldiers mindful of their own inadequate pay and the extra money would encourage gambling and excessive drinking. Instead the funds were used to purchase 2,000 shirts for the army.[7] Mrs Reed died in September 1780, and her role as leader in the women's association was taken by Mrs Sarah Bache, daughter of Benjamin Franklin.

The commander-in-chief praised the Philadelphia women volunteers. "The spirit that animated these women," he said, "entitles them to an equal place with any who have preceded them in the walk of female patriotism."[8] Eight hundred shirts went to the Pennsylvania troops at Morristown, and 200 were sent to the New Jersey Continentals stationed near Pompton, New Jersey; the rest were deposited with the army's clothier department at Newburgh, New York.[9]

Women's associations in New Jersey followed the lead of the Philadelphia volunteer group and also collected donations for the purchase of military clothing. "Ladies of Trenton," in mid-July 1780, sent Washington $15,480 that they had collected "to be disposed . . . for the benefit of the Continental Soldiers."[10] The New Jersey donations, however, came under criticism for being too little toward the fulfilment of the needs of the army. A writer in the New-Jersey Journal, probably an officer in the New Jersey brigade, complained that it was "below the dignity of a soldier" to receive "support from the hand of charity." It would be better to use the funds to establish a "foundling hospital" for the benefit of "orphans and children, born with the army, whose fathers have bled and died in the service." Funds could also be applied toward the education of such "orphans and indigent children" so that they could become good citizens.[11]

In Virginia Martha Washington, at the suggestion of Mrs Thomas Jefferson, led women volunteers in soliciting money for support of soldiers through collections in churches.[12] Maryland "Ladies" in the fall of 1780 provided shirts for the army.[13] General Lafayette, stopping in Baltimore on his way to assume command of Continental forces in Virginia, reminded belles of the city who held a ball in his honor that his army was in need of shirts. Borrowing £2,000 on his own account, the young Frenchman purchased cloth materials and "Sett the Baltimore Ladies At work for the Shirts which will be sent after me."[14]

Equally significant as the war drives that were conducted was that they were few and unsustained. Most civilians undoubtedly felt that the army through its various commissaries and procurement systems had the capabilities to attend to its own supply.

Poor Relief

The incidence of poverty did not subside with the Revolution. While skilled labor was in much demand due to the need for Americans to produce more of their own goods, such factors as the embargoes, the British blockade, war destruction of industrial plants, and the curtailment of the maritime industries contributed to enlargement of the numbers of employable poor. The wives and families of soldiers in the field and war widows and orphans constituted a new class of the poor. Despite the need for expanded relief, efforts were kept at a minimum. Limited programs of the colonial period continued much the same—"outdoor" relief (the occasional supply of feed and fuel) and "indoor" relief by boarding unemployable poor at almshouses and in the homes of citizens at public expense. The most obvious change in relief administration occurred in areas where the Anglican church had been established, with responsibility for care of the poor being transferred from the church vestry to county and town jurisdiction and support coming from regular taxation.

Private charity continued through donations from benevolent societies, such as the Union Society in Savannah, Georgia. Pennsylvania Quakers did more than their share in aiding the poor. Quaker groups distributed food, fuel, and clothing to the needy of all faiths. During the British occupation of Philadelphia when the poor were turned out of the almshouse to make room for soldiers, Quakers made available their meeting house on Market Street to the poor of the city and its suburbs.[15] On the rare occasions when there were surpluses of provisions, the armies made allotments of foodstuffs to the urban poor. The British army just before the evacuation of Philadelphia distributed wood and hay to the city's needy.[16]

Citizens volunteered to distribute food to the poor. The artist Charles Willson Peale, in July 1779, noted in his diary that he had spent a whole day in helping to deliver "in small quantities" some 15 barrels of flour and 20 barrels of bread. The provisions had been released from a storehouse of the Continental army, which at the time had the rare situation of a large amount of flour and bread.[17] More often than not, as in Philadelphia, with the need to supply Continental troops and militia, overseers of the poor and state authorities competed for the same available supplies in the distribution of flour and firewood, resulting with military requirements gaining the priority.

The plight of destitute families of soldiers elicited no response from Congress. Even Washington himself seemed to lack compassion. Writing to General William Maxwell in May 1779, he commented that all "the common soldiers of any country can expect is food and clothing. . . . The idea of maintaining the families at home at public expence, is peculiar to us, and is incompatible with the finances of any government."[18] The suffering of their families on the home front led soldiers to desert or at least not to re-enlist. An officer in the Connecticut line complained that:

> Not a Day Passes my head, but some Soldier with Tears in his Eyes, hands me a letter from his Wife Painting forth the Distresses of his family in such strains as these, "I am without bread, and cannot get any, the Committee will not Supply me, my Children will Starve, or if they do not, they will freeze, we have no wood, neither Can we get any, *Pray Come Home.*"[19]

A Georgia militia general, John Twiggs, echoed the same sentiment from his camp near Augusta in October 1781: "Many [militia] have left their families, in a condition truly deplorable, others have not at this moment the common necessaries of life."[20]

Local governments occasionally gave relief to soldiers' families upon their application for help. A few localities provided sustained assistance. Thus in Lynn, Massachusetts, in December 1777, a committee was established "to supply the families of those gone in the Continental service from this town."[21] The Pennsylvania Assembly voted aid to families of poor militiamen on active duty, not to exceed 10s. per week.[22] Some localities made provision for families of soldiers to purchase essential goods at lower than current prices.

Most states, but not Congress, made provisions for relief support for soldiers' widows and their families. For example, according to a Virginia law, the Hanover County court ordered that Mary Anne Jolly, a widow of a soldier, "who died in the service of the United States," be allotted four barrels of corn and "200 weight of Pork" annually for herself and her three children. The provisions were supplied by the state commissioners for the specifics tax.[23]

Wartime Production

Economic life experienced wartime adjustments. Non-importation at the start of the war, the British blockade, and the priority of military supply caused shortages of goods. Americans had to adapt production for different markets than before the war. Great Britain and the British West Indies were now closed to American shipping. New England was cut off from traditional fisheries and the carrying trade. Shipbuilding and related trades suffered, but losses were partially offset by privateering. The British bounties on lumber, indigo, and naval stores had ceased. In the South new markets had to be found for tobacco, lumber, and naval stores. Capital moved from the trade sector to domestic and war-related industries. Despite war adjustments, domestic production thrived in such diverse areas as clothing, flour milling, distilling, tanning, lumbering, and meat processing.[24]

The war set more Americans to making clothes. The textile manufacturing system underwent no reorganization, but the domestic output greatly increased. It was patriotic as well as a necessity to wear homespun clothing. Lieutenant Thomas Anburey, a British prisoner of war held near Charlottesville, Virginia, reported in 1779 that Virginians wore almost entirely clothing of their own manufacture.[25] Merchants made arrangements with households or groups for supplies of finished cloth. Societies were founded during the war for the encouragement of textile production.[26]

A French officer, Marquis de Chastellux, was impressed at the widespread involvement in making textiles. At West Hartford, Connecticut he noted that the "inhabitants engage in some industry in addition to their prosperous agriculture," fabricating "some cloths and other woolen stuffs." Chastellux went into a house "where they were preparing and dyeing" the cloth. "This cloth is woven by the country people, and is then sent to those little factories where it is dressed, pressed, and dyed." In nearby Farmington he also observed the manufacture of cloth and woolens. In one house even "the sons and grandsons of the family were working at the loom."[27]

The war had a mixed effect upon those earning a living by agriculture. Army purchasing absorbed surplus commodities, and flour milling expanded, but the effect of these advantages was offset by the depreciation of the currency and government certificates paid for produce, the shortage of credit, the high wages for agricultural workers, transportation difficulties in getting supplies to the army, and the disruption of trade eliminating profitable markets.[28] The Chesapeake area, which avoided military fighting during most of the war, suffered the least because of a shift, already begun before the war, to raising grain and livestock instead of tobacco. Fortunately much of the tobacco produced for export escaped the British blockade to find profits in European markets. Northern merchants supplanted English and Scottish commission firms in the tobacco trade.[29]

Farmers were hurt by government interdiction at various times on the export of provisions. Congress, from June 8, 1778 to January 1, 1779 installed an embargo on foodstuffs in order to guarantee supply for the army. States on their own set embargoes on such commodities as flour, leather, wool, cloth, and unshorn sheep. Penalties called for forfeit up to double the value of the restricted items. Farmers, considering themselves victims of price regulation and market interference by would-be monopolists, often withheld their products from sale.[30]

The war brought the iron industry out from under the restrictions of Parliament's Iron Acts of 1750 and 1757, which forbade the erection of new mills for producing finished iron or steel and export other than pig or bar iron. New plating mills, slitting mills, and steel furnaces were erected during the war. A sheet iron manufactory, established in Philadelphia in 1776, turned out camp kettles and other cooking utensils. Because of a decrease in the iron trade, owing to the war and European iron escaping the British blockade, commercial production of iron declined during the war, but the loss was balanced by demand for military production. Most commercial iron manufacturing was limited to serving needs of local neighborhoods.[31]

Of the minor industries receiving a boost during the war was salt-making. With outside supply all but cut off, many works for producing salt from sea water sprung up along the New Jersey coast; the industry aided iron manufacturing by the requirement of numerous iron salt pans.[32] Flour-milling made great strides, with Baltimore and Alexandria becoming centers for production.

The manufacture of weaponry and military equipment required much skilled labour. Carpenters and cabinetmakers built artillery carriages, tent poles, and boats, and blacksmiths made bayonets for muskets and engaged in arms repair. The army employed tailors to help it partially meet clothing needs, such as providing overalls.[33]

Iron foundries cast cannon, cannon balls, and shot. Ironworks owned by loyalists were seized and placed under government control. New powder mills were erected, and by 1780 Pennsylvania had 21 such facilities.[34]

Congress and the states established government-owned and -operated munitions plants. Congress had control over a foundry in Philadelphia, gun factories at Lancaster, Pennsylvania and Trenton, New Jersey, and magazines at Carlisle, Pennsylvania and Springfield, Massachusetts.[35] The states offered inducements for the production of munitions, including saltpeter and sulphur (both mixed with charcoal to make gunpowder), in the form of bounties, interest-free loans, premiums, and land grants for ironworks.[36] Among state-owned and -operated munitions plants where citizens could find employment were Virginia's gun factory at Fredericksburg and a foundry for casting cannon and cannon balls at Westham, near Richmond. Virginia and North Carolina had their own state lead mines. In Connecticut, each town without a privately owned saltpeter mill had to erect one, which was placed under the management of four selectmen.[37]

Many small, privately owned gun factories supplied arms to the military forces by contract. Such operations were handicapped by an insufficiency of skilled labor, the rising cost of materials, and labor discontent. General Adam Stephen, typical of proprietors of small gun factories, manufactured arms for the state militia at his plantation near Martinsburg, Virginia (now in West Virginia). Stephen's 30 employees, demanding higher wages, were frequently absent and engaged in slowdowns. Anthony Noble, the plant manager, complained that the workers "in general are a parcile of Villains, they are eternally a plotting, and throwing everything into confusion, and the more one hurries them the worse they are. I know no way to manage them, but to turn the grumbling rascalls out of doors."[38]

Wages and Prices

The war economy faced the challenges of spiralling inflation in the cost of labor and prices. Yet wages seldom kept up with real value because of the increase of prices.

Price inflation progressed throughout the war. A few examples illustrate the trend. By 1777 prices for West Indian commodities had risen up to 505 percent of their prewar level. In New England, beef which sold for 4¢ a pound in 1777 cost $1.69 per pound in 1780. Rents in Philadelphia, by 1780, were three times as high as before the war.[39]

Besides the shortage of goods, also fueling inflation was the increasing worthlessness of Continental and state paper money. Congress, finally on March 18, 1780, repudiated its currency altogether. The states had much the same experience—no wonder that many transactions were conducted by barter.

War profiteering artificially interfered with fair exchange conditions. Merchants used age-old devices to corner markets: forestalling—securing control of goods on the way to market; engrossing—purchasing large quantities of a commodity to create a monopoly for resale at high prices; and regrating—buying when cheap and selling when dear. States and localities experimented with measures curtailing such monopoly practices affecting essential goods and especially war supplies. Penalties included publication of names of offenders, refunds of excessive charges, fines, putting up security for future good behavior, and imprisonment. Enforcement, however, was minimal, and rarely did violators come under the punitive sanctions.

Conventions of towns, meeting independently in Massachusetts, New Hampshire, Rhode Island, New York, New Jersey, Pennsylvania, and Delaware, ordered wage and price controls.[40] But it was soon evident that effective regulation required statewide and interstate codes.

A convention of delegates from the four New England states and New York, meeting in Providence in December 1776, drew up a comprehensive program for price and wage regulation to be implemented by each participating state. The preamble of the document stated the urgency: "the avaricious conduct of many persons, by daily adding to the now exorbitant price of every necessary and convenient article of life and encreasing the price of labor in general, unless a speedy and effectual stop be put thereto;" failure to take regulatory action "will be attended with the most fatal and pernicious consequences, as it not only disheartens and disaffects the soldiers" but also "distresses the poorer part of the community by obliging them to give unreasonable prices for those things that are absolutely necessary to their very existence."[41] The convention fixed prices on 27 necessary commodities and wages for labor. Wholesale prices on imported items should not exceed 250 to 275 percent of the original costs, and retail markups should not be more than 20 percent. Wages for mechanics, craftsmen, and "other Labour" was "to be computed according to the Usages and Customs that have heretofore been adopted and practiced in different Parts of the several States compared with Farming Labour." Congress by a close vote rejected the Providence program.[42]

The New England states, nevertheless, quickly passed legislation adopting the provisions of the Providence convention. The regulations were to be administered by specially appointed town committees, and strict penalties were provided for deviation from the legal rates. The other states, however, refused to adopt the Providence guidelines. In New England the difficulties of enforcement soon became evident. Too many people disobeyed the laws, many towns neglected to appoint the price fixing committees, and there was a threatened breakdown of distribution of goods. Another interstate conference, consisting of representatives from New England and New York, met in Springfield, Massachusetts on July 30–August 5, 1777 and tried to amend the process, but in frustration called for an end of the wage and price regulations; in the fall, the New England legislatures repealed their whole price fixing programs.[43]

A conference of delegates from the mid-Atlantic states meeting in York, Pennsylvania in March 1777 came up with a program for fixing prices and wages. But the scheme did not materialize; the delegates were divided, with New Jersey, New York, and Virginia in favor, and Pennsylvania, Delaware, and Maryland in the negative.[44]

With the failure of interstate regulation, Congress decided to use its influence. On November 22, 1777 Congress called for three regional conventions: at New Haven (all the northern states from New England to Delaware); at Fredericksburg, Virginia (Virginia, Maryland, and North Carolina); and at Charleston (South Carolina and Georgia). The conference at New Haven, the only one of the three to be held, reported in January 1778 the recommendation for increases above 1774 levels: wages for laborers and farm workers at 75 percent, craftsmen at 25 percent, and prices for manufactures and domestic produce at 75 percent. Although other states that had been represented at the New Haven meeting passed the wage and price scales, Massachusetts, New Hampshire, and Rhode Island did not. Congress, therefore, in exasperation, on June 4, 1778, called for the repeal of all price fixing measures: "Limitations upon the Prices of Commodities are not only ineffectual for the Purposes proposed, but likewise productive of very evil Consequences to the great Detriment of the Public Service and grievous Oppression of Individuals."[45]

One final effort for interstate regulation occurred. New England and New York delegates, assembled at Hartford in October 1779, again proposed price and wage systems for the states to adopt and called for a meeting in Philadelphia of representatives from all the states north of North Carolina. The Philadelphia convention of January–April 1780 endorsed the Hartford program, with two states, however, not participating in the final sessions. Only several states briefly installed regulations, but, with other states refusing to go along, the new enactments were repealed. The Philadelphia convention marked the end of attempts of general financial regulation.

Wage and price fixing was doomed to failure. Lacking a strong national government, there could be no general administration or enforcement of codes. Many Americans viewed price and wage fixing as contributing to redistribution of income, discouraging agricultural production and commerce, and exacting greater hardship upon poor and honest citizens than upon war profiteers. Special interests—farming, merchandising, trade, and labor—wanted protection at the expense of others. It was also learned that checking inflation discouraged production.

Whereas price and wage regulation proved futile under civilian authority, the armies had some success. The American quartermaster department set maximum prices for purchases by the army and maximum wages for civilian personnel attached to the military forces. British commanders in areas under British occupation issued regulations that set prices for both the civilian sector and the army commissariats. Certain commodities could only be sold by special permission. Monopoly practices were forbidden upon penalty of confiscation.[46]

Food and Price Riots

Crowd actions protesting hoarding and exorbitant prices were common wartime occurrences. While undoubtedly some economic riots went unrecorded, at least 40 are known. Women were in the majority of one-third of the mobs. Rioting, writes Barbara Smith, was a kind of "resistance and revolution opened for women, not as republican wives or mothers but as social and economic actors within household, neighborhood, and marketplace."[47]

The earliest food riots involved the scarcity of salt. Armed bands from Virginia's piedmont region descended upon river towns in the fall 1775 to seize salt from merchants' storehouses. A resident of Henrico County noted that inhabitants were in constant fear of having their houses searched by "the upland people." Salt was essential to the diet of livestock and for preserving meat. It was a bitter irony that the poor people in the lowland regions who were being raided for salt could not afford to keep livestock and depended on salted fish for their principal food.[48] Salt riots also occurred in the fall of 1776: on November 20, Nicholas Cresswell reported a "great Disturbance for want of Salt" in Leesburg (Loudoun County), Virginia and during October and November rioters seized salt in Dorchester County, Maryland. Crowd action in Ulster and Dutchess counties, New York forced merchants to sell salt at a fair price.[49]

In most instances, merchants confronted by crowd action submitted to demands to lower prices or make goods available. When offending merchants were not persuaded by popular pressure, violence resulted, with mobs breaking into a store, manhandling the proprietor and seizing the quantities of the commodity desired. Most often rioters considered their forays as enforcement of regulations established by governmental authority.[50]

During 1776–7 groups of housewives in Ulster, Dutchess, and Westchester counties, New York besieged storehouses, forcing merchants to sell tea at reasonable prices.[51]

Price gouging had citizens of Boston up in arms. On April 19, 1777 a "concourse of People to the amount of 500" took to the Boston streets, led by a disguised figure, who styled himself "Joyce, Jr." The mysterious stranger seems to have appropriated the name of Cornet George Joyce, who commanded the troops who captured Charles I in June 1647 and was afterwards one of the king's executioners. The actual identity of Joyce, Jr has never been established but is thought to have been John Winthrop. Joyce, Jr had first appeared during the intimidation of the Boston tea consignees in early 1773 and early 1774 and had headed a "tar and feathering committee" in 1774. Joyce, Jr, "mounted on Horse back with a Red coat, a white Wig and drawn Sword, with Drum and fife following," and his cohorts seized five monopolists, put them in a cart, conducted a symbolic hanging, and then drove the cart westward out of town to Roxbury, where the victims were unceremoniously dumped, with the warning that return to Boston would be upon pain of death. Joyce, Jr "then ordered his Gang to return which they did immediately without any disturbance."[52] A "notification," from Joyce, Jr published in the *Boston Gazette* on April 21, warned merchants that they must sell goods "openly and publickly" and at "Prices stipulated by Law" or face "condign Punishment."[53]

Rioters made off with sugar from storehouses in Salem and Beverly, Massachusetts in the summer and late fall of 1777. At Hartford, during August 1777, "a corps of female infantry met at Lyon Tavern, and "with a Flank Guard of three chosen Spirits of the male line," marched one mile to East Hartford, where they took sugar that had been reserved for the army.[54] Abigail Adams wrote to her husband of a similar situation in Boston during July 1777. "There is a great Scarcity of Sugar and Coffe," she said:

articles which the Female part of the State are very loth to give up, especially whilst they consider the Scarcity occasioned by the merchants having secreted a large Quantity. There has been much rout and Noise in the Town for several weeks. Some Stores had been opend by a number of people and the Coffe and Sugar carried into the Market and dealt out by pounds.

The fury came to a high pitch when some 100 women descended upon the store of Thomas Boylston, "an eminent, wealthy, stingy" bachelor, who refused to sell coffee at the regulated price. The women demanded the keys to the warehouse store, which Boylston refused, "upon which one of them seazd him by his Neck and tossd him into the cart." Boylston now consented, and the women "opend the Warehouse, Hoisted out the Coffe themselves, put it into the trucks and drove off." Abigail further commented that Boylston had been spanked by the women, "but this I believe was not true. A large concourse of Men stood amazd silent Spectators of the whole transaction."[55]

The female riots brought in persons from all socio-economic levels, including some of the destitute poor. The protests followed the traditional patterns of crowd action during the colonial period in that they served as an extra-legal arm of the community, focused on a single objective, and had the approval of persons in authority. Unlike rioting during the French Revolution, as Linda Kerber notes, the Revolutionary War economic riots were less frequent and violent and aimed at luxury goods, such as tea, coffee, and sugar rather than bread.[56]

Steep increases in the price for food and currency depreciation in 1779 had citizens of Philadelphia on the edge of riot. "The Bell-man went about the City," wrote Elizabeth Drinker in her diary of May 26, "desireing the people to arm themselves with guns or Clubs, and make a sarch for such as had sent away Flour, Gun Powder &c out of town."[57]

Off-duty militiamen paraded in the streets of Philadelphia on October 4, 1779 protesting against prices and lenity toward loyalists. While the marchers were passing the home of James Wilson, who as a lawyer had represented merchants accused of violating price controls, shots rang out between the militiamen and 24 persons who had gathered inside Wilson's house. Six were killed and 19 wounded in what became known as the "Fort Wilson" riot. The city's First Troop of cavalry and Continental dragoons under Colonel George Baylor apprehended 27 of the marchers, who were jailed for a while and released without facing further prosecution.[58]

The Revolution, of course, had its share of other kinds of vigilante action, mainly conducted against reputed loyalists. In Philadelphia, just after the victory at Yorktown, a mob went on a rampage of vandalizing homes, concentrating on those belonging to Quakers, for not having illuminations in celebration of the British defeat. "Many women and Children," wrote Mrs Drinker, "were frightened into fits, and tis' a mercy no lives were lost."[59] Although laborers occasionally marched in protest or drew up petitions for redress from government, strikes were rare. One that got out of hand was a protest for higher wages from 150 sailors in Philadelphia on January 2, 1779; the sailors took to the streets and then boarded ships, unrigged them, and held guards captive. Continental soldiers put an end to the commotion; 15 strikers were arrested and fined.[60]

Changing Attitudes

"Although war gratifies the army, it embarrasses and often exasperates that countless multitude of men whose minor passions every day require peace in order to be satisfied," wrote Alexis de Tocqueville in his appraisal of American democracy.[61] War becomes less a glorious adventure as victory becomes elusive and people attend to their daily pursuits. American citizens during the Revolution not only grew tired of the war but became apprehensive of its effect on democratic society and institutions. During the protracted war people began to question the value of what was to be gained. There were those who feared that the war itself was corrupting the republican virtue on which Americans had justified the rebellion.

Both the Americans and the British had expected a short war. Even when this was not accomplished prevailing opinion on both sides held that the conflict would soon be concluded, if not on the battlefield, then by a negotiated truce or peace. But the less than full commitment to the war by both sides made a long war inevitable.

The British relied on too large a gamble, that the rebellion could not be sustained, and, with a favorable turn of events, citizens would rally to the British cause. But challenging this expectation was the growing reality that without further large-scale commitment the British cause was doomed. Washington adopted Fabian tactics, knowing that if the British could not win the war, they would lose it.

Most Americans felt that because the British government had not demonstrated much of a will to fight or had given full commitment to prosecuting the war in North America any peace settlement would secure at least in large measure independence. Adding to frustrations was Congress's cavalier refusal to treat with the Carlisle peace commission of 1778 or to follow up on peace initiatives other than diplomacy with the objective of British unconditional surrender. Thomas Jefferson, in 1779, commented that "we have lately been extremely disturbed to find a pretty general opinion prevailing that peace and the independence of the thirteen states are now within our power, and that Congress have hesitations on the subject, and delay entering on the consideration."[62]

The year 1777 marked the beginning of pronounced disillusionment with the war. British Captain James Murray remarked in the fall of that year that "the novelty" of the war "is worn off and I see no advantage to be reaped from it."[63] Washington and his officers expected that victory at Brandywine would bring the war to a halt. In General Orders of September 5, 1777, Washington declared that the British "will put the Contest on the event of a single battle—If they are overthrown, they are utterly undone—The War is an at end."[64] Robert Hanson Harrison, Washington's secretary, expected such an engagement "will establish our Liberties."[65] This would have been undoubtedly the case, considering the American capture of Burgoyne's army at the time. Even the American defeat at Brandywine did not diminish expectation of a near end of the war. Edmund Pendleton, Speaker of Virginia's House of Delegates, commented that the battle "having reduced their numbers much more than ours, they can't wish to continue the War for the sake of repeating such Victories, two or three more of which would ruin them."[66]

The war proceeded, nevertheless, without much vigor. The British invasion of the South hardly amounted to much more than a strategic defensive, and the bloody partisan war that developed in that region further underscored the futility of any British offensive. American commanders Nathanael Greene in the Carolinas and the Marquis de Lafayette in Virginia avoided major battles. In the North, the war definitely stalemated from 1778 to its end. In the minds of civilians the war had might as well be over.

Americans sensed a decline in virtue. Both soldiers and civilians felt disappointment in government ineptness and war profiteering. The army considered it was betrayed because Congress and the states did not live up to their responsibilities in making adequate provision for sustaining the troops, and Congress delayed pay and reneged on its promise for officer pensions. Major Samuel Shaw wrote to his parents from the American encampment at New Windsor in June 1779. "I wish seriously that the ensuing campaign may terminate the war," he said. "The people of America seem to have lost sight entirely of the noble principle which animated them at the commencement of it;" the "patriotic ardor which then inspired each breast . . . has given place to avarice, and every rascally practice which tends to the gratification of that sordid and most disgraceful passion."[67] Colonel Ebenezer Huntington deplored the public's neglect of the army. "I despise My Countrymen," he declared. "I wish I could say I was not born in America, I once gloried in it but am now ashamed of it."[68] The Rev. Ewald Schaukrik, in December 1780, from British occupied New York City, echoed the same frustration: "The general language even of common soldiers is, that the war might end, would have been ended long before now, if it was not for the great men, who only want to fill their purses."[69]

Civilians also believed that war profiteering impeded a successful conclusion to the war. Dr Robert Honyman, a physician in Hanover County,

Virginia, lamented that "every class & rank of people are so totally engrossed with schemes & projects for making money that every other consideration holds but an inferior place. Never were people so entirely infatuated by the rage of amassing . . . every other principle & Spring of action is swallowed up by this."[70] Mann Page, Jr, a Virginia planter, complained in April 1779: "All is still & quiet, except the bustle which the busy sons of avarice make in their pursuits. An universal thirst after riches has seized upon all ranks of people, and public virtue seeming to be rooted from their Breasts by that sordid passion."[71]

The frustrations over the effects of the war on the quality of American life coincided with despair over American military capability and a desire to conclude as quickly as possible an honorable end to hostilities. To bring the state governments and Congress to their senses and instill energy in the prosecution of the war, some citizens and military personnel felt conferring dictatorial power on George Washington might help; after all, Congress had already on several occasions in 1776 and 1777 granted Washington wide discretionary authority for impressment of provisions and other articles within a stated radius of the army and for a specified duration. President Joseph Reed of Pennsylvania informed General Greene in September 1779 that "some officers of considerable rank have pressed the General to assume dictatorial authority . . . Necessity may, perhaps, plead for such a measure; but certainly such power should be received from other hands."[72] A New Jersey lawyer, William Peartree Smith, declared in April 1783: "All the inferior wheels will run into Confusion, and by and bye, some Master Hand will seize it. So did a Cromwell; and if this should become necessary . . . God grant it may be the man who merits from the Country he rescued—a DIADEM!"[73] Lewis Nicola, the army's commander of the Invalid Corps, wrote to Washington on May 22, 1782 suggesting the nation would be better off with Washington as a monarch. The commander-in-chief was not at all amused and sternly advised Nicola that "if you have any regard for your Country, concern for yourself or posterity, or respect for me, to banish these thoughts from your Mind."[74]

The Virginia legislature, in December 1776 and June 1781, debated a resolution proposed by George Nicholas that a temporary dictatorship be established, preferably in the person of Washington or Greene. The resolution when it was last debated came within a few votes of being adopted. Patrick Henry supported the idea of a dictatorship, and to the mind of Thomas Jefferson, was the person behind it.[75]

The extent to which even some staunch American patriots would go to end the war is seen in a remarkable petition to the Virginia legislature signed by "numerous persons" of Prince George County in June or July 1781. Cornwallis's army had cut a swathe through the county, taking slaves and destroying property, including the courthouse. The petition asked for an "accommodation" as soon as possible with the enemy, even acceptance of a ceasefire on any conditions that Cornwallis might state. The petition cited the benefits the colonies had enjoyed under "the Parent Country" and bemoaned conditions during the American rebellion.

> Countenanced and protected, by their armies, and their Fleets we fear'd no foreign Enemy, our burthen of Taxes was light our Commerce profitable, and while their Power secured us from abroad, plenty reigned and our Internal wealth and numbers increased even beyond our most sanguine expectations. How different is our present situation, Warring with one of the greatest Powers on Earth, our Country greatly depopulated, our paper money from the extraordinary demand of government, and immense quantities Emitted, depreciated to a value which threatens total annihilation, that abundance of provisions formerly in our Trading Towns for Exportation, wholly exhausted, the means of being supplied, with arms ammunition and Clothing from abroad absolutely cut off and no credit, or fund by which these great and growing Evils, these pressing wants are likely to be supplied. . . . With an Enemy at our Doors . . . we confessedly in want of soldiers to oppose them without money or credit . . . We your petitioners Humbly pray . . . that the seeds of Passion Private resentment and of Prejudice being expunged from our breasts, cool deliberate thought, Universal Benevolence and Brotherly love may again take Place that the solid and Permanent Happiness of our Country be established in the Bonds of amity and Peace and that discord, Bloodshed and Misery, may once more as they formerly were become strangers to this Happy Land.[76]

To civilians and soldiers alike, if the war lasted longer than it should have, in the end it was worth the wait, being settled entirely according to the American terms. Putting the republican house in order, however, was still an unfinished task.

CHAPTER ELEVEN

Women and family

Revolutionary War experiences affected the quality of life for women and the bonds of family relationships. While substantive reforms in the legal status of women would be slow in coming, continuing well into the twentieth century, the Revolutionary War years bred a questioning disposition and assertiveness among women that would serve them well in the future. The process for wider participation in community life, definitely in evidence by the mid-eighteenth century, accelerated. Ideas of equality and the desire for inculcation of republican virtue into the American character aided in loosening the restraints on women's roles and diminishing patriarchal authoritarianism in family life. But the war also had a negative impact. The recognition of women as the prime nurturers of virtue within the family contributed to the definition of women's sphere as more firmly lodged in the household. As Sylvia R. Frey and Marian J. Morton have noted, there was not much challenge in seeking to liberate women from the household, only what they did there, in "contributing to republican stability by rearing virtuous citizens."[1]

"Revolutionary ideology gave women ways to resist norms," writes Joan R. Gundersen. "But it also made them more vulnerable to charges of individual responsibility. Women's restrictions and vulnerability eventually outweighed any opportunities."[2] David Ramsay had much the same view with regard to Revolutionary South Carolina: "When the war was ended and their husbands and fathers were by its ravages reduced in their circumstances," women, "aided by their economy and retirement from the world," sought "to repair the losses."[3] Women, however, particularly in the North, continued, as before the war, to enhance their position in the household, with husbands moving their businesses and shops out of the home and into the marketplace. In the South among upper-class women the trend for giving women a freer hand in the domestic realm was less in evidence; with

163

the tightening of reins over slavery, the whole patriarchal system became even more entrenched.

Legal Status of Married Women

The ideals of equality and freedom proclaimed by the Declaration of Independence challenged the legal disabilities governing women's status under existing laws. Abigail Adams, learning that her husband, John, and other members of Congress had "declared for independency," in her famous letter of March 31, 1776 chided her husband that in the shaping of new codes of laws he should "Remember the Ladies." She pleaded: "Do not put such unlimited power into the hands of the Husbands. Remember all Men would be tyrants if they could. If perticular care and attention is not paid to the Ladies we are determined to foment a Rebellion, and will not hold ourselves bound by any Laws in which we have no voice or Representation."[4] John Adams light-heartedly replied that "We know better than to repeal our Masculine systems," but in deference to Abigail's sensibilities he admitted that "We dare not exert our Power in its full Latitude . . . We are the subjects." Men "have only the Name of Masters," and they should preserve this distinction, otherwise they would be subjected "to the Despotism of the Petticoat."[5] John Adams's concession that women influenced the actions of men, however, evaded the real issue: that women, married or single, were denied not only full rights as citizens but also unfettered self-determination affecting their everyday lives.

More seriously, in a letter to John Sullivan of May 26, 1776, John Adams explained his opposition to awarding women the right to vote. Applying the same criteria as he did to men without property, Adams regarded women to be in a status of dependency and hence without a will of their own. Women's place was as nurturers in the home.[6]

Colonial laws regarding person and property substantially reflected English legal principles. Women's marriage status conformed to *feme covert*, whereby a married woman is under the protection or cover of her husband. A husband could not grant property to his wife because such would violate the wedded union. Nor could a woman testify against her spouse in court for any harsh treatment because there could be no contrary testimony between husband and wife. A man, however, could devise any or all his property upon his wife by will, with coverture ending upon his death.

Despite coverture, restrictions upon married women were sometimes circumvented, without formal legal sanction. Women occasionally owned and administered property outside the marriage agreement and engaged in business independently, although the husband by law had to give his consent for any *feme sole* transactions. For example, Abigail Adams purchased property in Vermont on her own while her husband was in Europe. Of course, women could enter into prenuptial contracts by which their property brought into the marriage remained under their sole control. Increasingly by the end of the eighteenth century married couples agreed to maintenance of separate estates; there were also settlements giving a husband joint control of a wife's property.[7] No intrusion upon coverture as such, however, was made during the war or its immediate aftermath.

Under law, a woman could enjoy her dowry (property she brought to a marriage), although it was technically under the husband's control. Upon the death of her husband, the widow was entitled to hold for life this property and any of that property of her husband that would complete the dower (that amount of a husband's estate prescribed by law as a life estate for the widow).

During the Revolutionary era the dower right eroded. Normally a widow was afforded one-third of the estate for life use. If the husband died intestate, she was entitled to one-third of personalty after debts and one-third life interest in realty. A widow could also contest a will, claiming one-third of the estate. Increasingly states made provision for widows to have a share in an inheritance equal to that of a child; thus if there were more than two children a widow would receive less than one-third of the property. The end of primogeniture (in intestacy, all the estate going to the eldest son) during the Revolutionary era in states which hitherto had this requirement did not materially affect the widow's dower, as in any case she had life use. Most states immediately after the Revolution gave daughters, in an intestate situation, a share in real and personal property equal to that of the male heirs. Married daughters also fared better. Although a married woman had to surrender ownership of inherited personalty to her husband, she had ownership of inherited realty both during her marriage and after her husband's death.[8]

Divorce

The war itself had little impact on filing for divorce. For those new states still under Anglican influence, for a while it was not allowed. Elsewhere, few divorce applications referred to wartime stress, and those that did resulted from the birth of illegitimate children by the wife while the husband was away in military service. Importantly, however, with the disestablishment of the Anglican church and also the influence of republican ideology with greater emphasis placed on marital fidelity, changes in divorce law occurred.

In colonial New England, where marriage was considered a civil contract, divorces were awarded by the courts, but on narrow grounds. In areas where there was an Anglican establishment absolute divorce was impossible, particularly because the colonies lacked the spiritual courts which, in England, were required to adjudicate divorce proceedings. Legal separation, however, was freely granted. With the disestablishment of the Anglican church in the southern states and New York, the way was cleared for civil authority over divorce. Where no absolute divorce had been permissible, remedy could now be granted, depending on the state, either through a legislature acting on a private bill for divorce or through court action. With the Revolution, all states except South Carolina provided for absolute divorce. New York's first divorce law of 1787 granted absolute remedy for adultery only through chancery court.[9] Despite reforms, obtaining a divorce in states that required legislative action, such as Virginia, was a prolonged and cumbersome process, necessitating the presentation of a petition, a legislative committee conducting hearings and review of evidence, and finally action by the whole lower house of assembly.

In Massachusetts more women than men sought divorce. One study for that state shows that the rate of success for women filing for divorce because of adultery increased from 49 percent for the period 1692–1774 to 70 percent during 1775–86; the rate of success for husbands improved only slightly from 66 percent to 73 percent.[10] The Pennsylvania legislature conferred only 11 divorces in 35 cases heard from 1777 to 1785; 9 of 23 men who applied were successful, and 2 of 12 women. The procedure usually took from one to two years. The Pennsylvania Divorce Act of 1785 shifted the adjudication of divorce suits from the legislature to the courts; grounds for divorce now consisted of bigamy, impotence, desertion for four years, sexual incapacity, adultery, and cruelty.[11] Other states also added to the category of grounds for divorce, as did Massachusetts by a law of 1786, which allowed divorce for impotence and having a spouse sentenced to prison for seven or more years.

Working Women

Besides engaging as civilian auxiliary helpers at army camps and as nurses and providing economic war support on the home front, women followed the trend set in the late colonial period of taking on work other than as homemaker. Economic opportunities for both single and married women expanded during the Revolutionary War years. Nothing much changed legally, but there was a wider latitude for women to assume business and career roles.

As in the colonial period no restraints were placed upon single women from entering any occupation. Married women technically needed the permission of husbands to expand into economic endeavors unrelated to family subsistence.

Increasingly married women assumed greater responsibility for managing the business affairs of the family, serving as deputy husbands. The war left many wives alone to look after a farm or business in the place of a spouse who was away for long stints of military duty or for other reasons. Normally a married woman would act through a power of attorney to represent her husband in business and legal transactions. Sometimes women merely had informal agreements with their husbands to act independently in economic matters. But even then a wife's role as deputy husband would be impeded unless she had the requisite legal authority. A Massachusetts law of November 21, 1787 recognized that there were occasions when a married woman might be destitute because an absent husband had neglected to make arrangements for her to assume responsibility over family property. The Massachusetts Supreme Judicial Court was therefore authorized to grant permission to such wives to dispose of real estate within a marriage.[12]

The average farm wife during the war kept busy with domestic duties, gardening, and assisting in tending livestock and poultry. She prepared clothes through the various stages, for example the shearing of sheep or harvesting flax, weaving of thread, and cutting garments. With a husband away in the army she assumed additional farm work. Elizabeth Adkins of Culpeper County, Virginia in a pension deposition long after the war recalled that in 1775 her husband "was gone all summer and she had to plough, and hoe his corn to raise bread for the children."[13]

Women retailed produce from their farms and gardens. Janet Schaw, visiting Wilmington, North Carolina in 1775, observed a woman who had a garden, "from which she supplies the town with what vegetables they use, also with mellons and other fruits." She also made "minced pies, tarts, and cheesecakes and little biskets, which she sends down to town once or twice a day, besides her eggs, poultry, and butter, and she is the only one who continues to have Milk."[14] The war heightened a broader awareness for the marketability of surplus foodstuffs of small farmers. During the latter part of the war army contractors roamed the countryside, offering high prices for food and equipment.[15]

Widows and wives as household heads took on boarders. Many single women were in the workforce. Carole Shammas has found that in Philadelphia in 1775 about one half of women aged 15 years or older were not part of a male-headed household. Fifteen percent of unmarried women lived at home with parents or siblings, and the others were self-supporting or in indentured service. Many single women worked as maids.[16]

The boycott of English goods during the war made Americans fully reliant on homespun or other domestically produced clothing. Thomas Jefferson commented during the war that "the wife weaves generally and the rich either have a weaver among their servants or employ their poor neighbors."[17] Some women found employment in textile workplaces, one of the largest being the American Manufactory in Philadelphia, which set about 400 women to spinning cloth.[18]

By the 1770s, writes Laurel Thatcher Ulrich, New England's "distinctive household production system was fully in place." Female weavers steadily encroached upon the domain of male artisan weavers. Daughters, self-employed in weaving in households, became virtually self-supporting, and in some situations controlled their own earnings. Women developed a reciprocal exchange of labor, aiding each other at the various tasks in producing cloth, such as carding, combing, spinning, reeling, spooling, warping, and weaving. "Household production shaped female consciousness and reinforced habits of neighborly exchange," notes Ulrich. Hannah Adams realized the profitability in adjusting her textile work. "During the American revolutionary war," she recalled, "I learned to weave bobbin lace, which was sutable, and much more profitable to me than spinning or knitting, which had previously been my employment."[19]

Women worked for wages and in some instances in their own establishments in a variety of trades, including as ironmongers, cutlers, brew masters, soap-makers, bakers, printers, horse-shoers, tallow chandlers, tanners, and netweavers.[20] Martha Ballard of Hallowell, Maine, in her diary entries not long after the war, mentioned women in her locality employed as diarywomen, nurses, spinners, weavers, dressmakers, a bonnet-maker, a chair-caner, and midwives.[21] On the eve of the Revolution several women took over publication of newspapers upon the death of their husbands: Ann Timothy, the *South Carolina Gazette*; Anne Catherine Green, the *Maryland Gazette*; and Clementia Rind, the *Virginia Gazette*. Mary Katherine Goddard, while her brother was away serving as a surveyor, published the *Maryland Journal* from 1774 to 1784. Elizabeth Holt succeeded her husband, John, upon his death in 1784 as publisher of the *Independent Gazette* in New York City.[22] There were women retailers, especially as operators of millinery and women's clothing shops and taverns. One-fifth of licensed tavern-keepers in Pennsylvania and North Carolina were women.

Outside urban areas trained physicians were scarce, and many doctors served in the medical departments of the army. Of course, medical needs were served by home remedies and the assistance of apothecaries. Some women practiced as physicians, basing their talents upon experience and knowledge from medical books. Margaret Morris, a widow of Burlington, New Jersey, had a reputation as a "skillful doctor." She treated patients daily, and at one time 30 persons for smallpox. Her diary entries show that she provided relief for such maladies as rheumatism, ringworm, whooping cough, dysentery, and the "itch." Even out-of-town strangers came to Mrs Morris's home seeking care. On July 14, 1777 she noted that "some of the gondola-men and their wives" were sick, and since there were no doctors in town they visited her. Morris diagnosed their ailment as "the itch fever" and "treated them according to art."[23] Mrs Mary Elmendorf, who lived along the lower Hudson River, administered to patients in Ulster County, New York and also in adjoining areas of New Jersey and Pennsylvania.

Margaret Vliet Warne of New Jersey passed herself off as a doctor and surgeon and "rode through the country ministering to the sick and wounded soldiers and their families without price."[24]

Independent Minds

The ideology of Independence and Republicanism offered expanded intellectual development for women. Even as the female role in the domestic sphere was being reinforced, it was recognized that women were entitled to cultivate their own minds and that they should set an example in guiding their husbands and children along the path of republican virtue.

The opportunity for the expansion of women's intellectuality was aided by the rapid advancement of literacy during the late eighteenth century. While the gap in the literacy rate between men and women remained substantial, particularly in the South and among poorer people generally, women were catching up to the literacy level of men. Female literacy in New England and Pennsylvania climbed from about 60 percent in 1775 to above 90 percent by 1820. The progress of literacy moved more slowly in the South. Virginia, for example, by 1800 had only a 70 percent literacy rate. Generally, by the 1780s 75 percent of Americans were able to sign their own names on legal documents.[25]

By the time of the Revolution already small academies for girls and some co-educational schools had been established throughout the colonies. Most were boarding schools or in home-site settings. Girls were admitted to the Boston public schools on a regular basis in 1789, and by the School Act of that year girls and boys were to study the same subjects. What is most significant of the Revolutionary era is that the curriculum for females broadened to include most of what was being taught to males, although women's academies also often had practical subjects such as needle crafts.[26]

Proposals for educational reform advocated the same quality of education for both sexes, at least through the elementary level. Thomas Jefferson recommended the creation of district, tax-supported schools that would provide elementary education to "all the free children, male and female:" the curriculum to consist of "reading, writing, and common arithmetick" and some introduction to "Graecian, Roman, English, and American history."[27]

Noah Webster's "On the Education of Youth" (1790) declared that in any "system of education" embracing "every part of the community the female sex claim no inconsiderable share of our attention." A broad education for women was necessary because they should be able "to implant in the tender mind" of a child "sentiments of virtue, propriety, and dignity;" also women's "influence in controlling the manners of a nation is another powerful reason" for women's education. Young women should be taught facility of language, arithmetic, and "Belles-lettres learning," which "seems to correspond with the disposition of most females." Because a woman's "real merit is known only at *home*," music, dancing, and drawing should "hold a subordinate rank" in women's education.[28]

Benjamin Rush, in essays written in the mid-1780s, noted that the "peculiar mode of education proper for WOMEN in a republic" should be instruction "in the principles of liberty and government" and "the obligations of patriotism." Rush thought that the essentials for a woman's education consisted of the English language, writing, knowledge of bookkeeping (so as to "assist her husband"), a broad sampling of science, history, poetry, and moral essays, study of the Christian religion, and, for a little polishing, music and dancing.[29]

Abigail Adams believed that if women received an education commensurate to their learning ability "great benefit must arise" from their "litirary accomplishments."[30] With the dawn of a new age, women, as well as their male counterparts, were inspired to indulge in their own literary creativity. Of the immediate war period the exertions of several women brought substantial recognition.

Most likely America's first woman professional author, Miss Hannah Adams (1758–1831) of Medfield, Massachusetts, achieved popular success with *Alphabetical Compendium of the Various Sects . . . from the Beginning of the Christian Era to the Present Day* (1784). Later works included a history of New England and also of the Jews. While growing up, Hannah Adams attended a county school for a few months out of a year, learning basic writing and arithmetic; the chief books at the school were the Bible and a psalter. Until age 20 Hannah's reading was mainly confined to "works of imagination and feeling; such as novels and poetry."[31]

Judith Sargent Murray (1751–1820), whose second husband, John Murray, founded Universalism in America, wrote in her essay, "On the Quality of Sexes" (1779, published 1790), that women's "minds are at full liberty for reflection" and "if a just foundation is early laid, our ideas will then be worthy of rational beings. If we were industrious we might easily find time to arrange them upon paper."[32] Murray's first publication in 1782 was a Universalist catechism she prepared for two orphaned children she and her husband had taken in. Soon thereafter she began what became a prodigious output of essays and poems which appeared in magazines. Her two plays (comedies), though produced, did not garner public acclaim.[33]

Annis Boudinot Stockton (1733–1801), wife of a signer of the Declaration of Independence, began writing poetry during the war. She sent two pastorals, one on the defeat of General Cornwallis and the other celebrating peace, to George Washington. The delighted commander-in-chief responded with several flowery letters, uncharacteristic of his usual style and probably penned by one of his witty aides. "The simple and beautious strains" of Mrs Stockton's poetry, Washington noted, did "great justice" to her "genius."[34]

Mercy Otis Warren (1728–1814), wife of one patriot leader and sister of another, demonstrated that women could venture into the traditional

Figure 4   Mary Otis Warren (1728–1814), a poet, playwright, and historian; sister of patriot leader James Otis. Painted by John Singleton Copley (about 1763). Bequest of Winslow Warren. *Courtesy, Museum of Fine Arts, Boston.*

male domain of politics and war. Her satirical plays, *The Adulateur* (1773) and *The Group* (1775), treated Boston events from 1765 to 1774, hurling ridicule upon Governors Thomas Hutchinson and Thomas Gage and other royal officials. Two prose farces have been attributed to her: *The Block-heads* (1776), parodying General John Burgoyne's *The Blockade*, which had

171

burlesqued the valor of patriot soldiers, and *The Motley Assembly* (1779) whereby Warren mocked the hypocrisy of Boston loyalists. Enlisting as an essayist for the Anti-federalist cause after the war, Warren moved on to her crowning achievement, *History of the Rise, Progress, and Termination of the American Revolution* (3 volumes, published in 1805), a work rendered invaluable because of its keenly eye-witnessed observations.[35]

Marriage

While there were no significant variations during the Revolutionary era as to age at marriage, republican criteria had some effect on the choice of partners and obligations within the marriage compact itself.

In New England first brides were more often to be in their early twenties and their husbands in the mid to late twenties. In Andover, Massachusetts the age at first marriage for women was 24; in Chatham, New Jersey, 1775–84, the average age at first marriage was 26 for men, and 20 for women.[36] Although substantial studies of marriage patterns in the eighteenth-century South are lacking, there is enough evidence to suggest that women married younger than their northern counterparts, in Virginia between ages of 16 and 19 not being unusual.[37]

Premarital pregnancies did not diminish. Among brides from the lower classes in Philadelphia, one-third to one-fourth were with child before marriage. Yet, in a republican society, premarital pregnancies gained a greater stigma.[38]

A trend in the late eighteenth century was for more women to remain single. Generally 10 to 15 percent never married, and among "lower sort" Philadelphians the number was 12–20 percent.[39] As Joan R. Gundersen states, most single women were widows; one-fourth of widows remarried before the Revolution, and one-fifth afterwards. Simple economic and demographic trends, more so than war-related factors, accounted for widows with reduced property or dependency, making them less desirable for marriage.[40] A study of Quakers in Rahway and Plainfield, New Jersey indicates that before 1786, 57.6 percent of women married, and afterwards 45.5 percent; the number of women unmarried by the age of 50 increased from 9.8 percent to 23 percent.[41]

Single women maintained close ties with their families. Many cared for aged parents or moved in with siblings. Those without such options lived in boarding houses.[42]

Staying single until finding a suitable husband carried no disfavor. An important change underway was greater freedom to choose spouses, to base a selection upon mutual attraction rather than parental pressure. With greater mobility, young people were more likely to marry outside their original locality and religion.[43]

The relationship between husband and wife became viewed more as a partnership than one governed by an unassailable patriarchy. Americans had revolted against their king, who, in collusion with parliament, attempted to deny his people their rights. American patriot rhetoric was replete with metaphors of the king as despot, even making war on his own family. As Americans severed patriarchal ties from abroad, it stood to reason that they should question tyranny within the home. Of course, ongoing factors contributed to effect more equality between husband and spouse, such as the growing legal protection of wives (for example, opening ways for divorce), the diffusion of population, and marrying outside one's immediate group that loosened inner family control.

Modernism and secularism were forces at work diminishing obeisance to patriarchal authority. The evangelical movement carrying over from the Great Awakening of the 1730s and 1740s threatened authority not only within a religious context but among society as a whole. The new political age, with its clarion call for democracy and equality, contributed to the removal of uncontested deference of a people toward their rulers.

An ideal marriage was to be symmetrical, an affectionate partnership. "Marriage was the very pattern from which the cloth of republican society was to be cast," writes Jan Lewis. Although a wife was expected to recognize her husband as the ultimate arbiter for the household, she could be assertive and insistent in getting across her views. An ideal for republican society as well as that for the home was to avoid conflict and subordinate individual desires for the greater good.[44]

A republican marriage was a companionate one. John Witherspoon, president of the College of New Jersey (Princeton), commented that "though beauty and personal attraction may be considered as the first motives, yet there are always supposed to be indications of something excellent in the temper within." In marriage, "if superiority and authority be given to the man, it should be used with so much gentleness and Love as to make it a state of as great equality as possible."[45] A North Carolinian, away in Philadelphia in September 1788, upon hearing of his daughter's betrothal, sent her advice for wedded bliss. A married woman's "great happiness" consists "of her being united to a Man of Virtue and Honour, who is her protector—her supporter—Affectionate friend—Bosom companion—participator in enjoyments—sharer in sorrow, and whose friendly and affectionate care will last for a lifetime." A wife should cultivate "an amiable and Virtuous disposition."[46]

Family

Average family size remained constant during the late eighteenth century, about 5–8 members. Infant mortality continued at a high level.[47] During the period of the Revolution, however, there were perceptible shifts in patterns governing childbirth and child-rearing.

Customarily women were attended at childbirth by a midwife. The whole affair was a social one, wherein the mother spent several weeks bedridden, frequently visited by female acquaintances, to the exclusion of males. From the 1760s on, however, there was a growing preference, especially among the middle class, to employ male physicians trained in obstetrics. As Catherine Scholten writes, childbirth was "transformed from an open affair to a restricted one."[48]

Most midwives additionally provided medicinal remedies for their neighbors. Midwives had an important legal function, their opinions being sought as to whether an abortion had occurred or in naming a putative father (the information being given in confidence by a birthing mother). Two midwives are known each to have assisted in about a thousand births: Elizabeth King (d. 1780) of Long Island, New York and Martha Ballard (d. 1812) of Oxford, Massachusetts and Hallowell, Maine. Ballard entered her practice of midwifery about 1776.[49]

The time between births increased, largely because of longer lactation periods. From a sample of Revolutionary War pension applications by widows, it is revealed that the spacing between births averaged 30 months.[50] Quakeress Elizabeth Drinker of Philadelphia commented upon her daughter giving birth at age 39, "that this might possibly be the last trial of this sort, if she would suckle her baby for a year to come."[51]

To the revolutionaries it was important that the family mentality was infused with republican virtue. Parents needed to instruct their children so that they could enjoy the blessings of liberty. Army chaplain Hugh Henry Brackenridge, in an oration to American troops in 1778, used the family metaphor to contrast the character between Americans and British. The people of Great Britain were like "the family of Cain, early driven to the land of Nod, sunk down to the deepest ignorance . . . debauchery and every vice," and "they labored to seduce the kindred family of Seth, which had been religiously educated and retained some degrees of moral purity and virtue." Unlike the "kindred family of Seth," Americans persevered in virtue; a voice "from the far-bending shores of America has been lifted up," determined to "enjoy freedom or die."[52] The idea of defending both a virtuous family and country is expressed in a letter from Colonel Gold Selleck Silliman to his wife in August 1776 just before the battle of Long Island:

> And I hope we shall be able to give them such a Reception as shall show Mankind that there is a difference between Troops that fight only for the Mastery and 6d. Sterling a day, and those that fight for their Religion, their Laws, their Liberties, their Wives & Children & everything else that is dear to them.[53]

Family members mutually exhibited deep affection. During the war James Allen of Philadelphia felt a sense of loss by the long separations between himself and his siblings. "There are few families who live on terms of purer love & friendship than ours," he wrote in his diary on June 6, 1777, "which is owing not only to natural affection, but the conviction of each others integrity and disinterestedness." On February 5, 1778 Allen experienced a moment that was "the most afflicting in my whole life," learning of the death of his brother, John, "the most affectionate of brothers & best of men." John Allen had exemplified the best qualities in a republican citizen:

> He was the most dutiful & affectionate son, the fondest husband & parent, the most disinterested & kindest brother & the most indulgent master that ever lived—His understanding was a very good one, his generosity, tenderness & humanity, unparall'd. He was distinguished for his courtesy, affability, modesty, humility & good-breeding; for his courage, frankness, candour, zeal & attachment to his friends . . . he had the pride & spirit of a Gentleman & no man carried his notions of Honor, & integrity higher . . . To this catalogue of positive virtues may be added, that he was perfectly free, from every moral or fashionable vice, from arrogance vanity or any seeming consciousness of his own worth.[54]

In the republican family, motherhood did not materially change, but there were higher expectations. "Women's virtue now stood for that of a nation," writes Joan R. Gundersen.[55] Affection bound the family together, with each member giving emotional support to another. Mothers could now more freely display maternal fondness. The belief in childhood depravity declined. Emphasis was placed on developing a child's mind and self-discipline.[56]

While southern gentry during colonial times had been indulgent toward their children and allowed them relative freedom of expression and action, New Englanders now were also veering in the same direction, abandoning the strict mode of attempting to break a child's will.

Portraiture of the Revolutionary era suggests the ideals of affection and equality in family relationships. Before 1775 married couples were seldom pictured together with their children; in group scenes the father is usually depicted standing and the rest of the family seated. Starting in the Revolutionary period, as Jay Fliegelman writes, "the vertical or hierarchical composition gives way to a horizontal or equalitarian composition in which all family members are shown on the same plane."[57] Siblings in the later portraits are usually touching each other, with a hand resting on another's shoulder. Mothers are holding infants. Toys, books, and useful accessories such as a map or writing utensils are shown more frequently than before.

Boys, aged 5 to 10, appear more informally clothed than in the colonial period, when they were pictured in adult attire. Teenagers are portrayed in less static positions.[58]

In 1770 Charles Willson Peale began a family group portrait (not completed until 1809) of members arranged around a table, signifying the "utmost harmony together." Peale's portraits in general expressed "such central tenets of civic republicanism as the mutual respect and affection family members owe each other, their obligations to each other and to the maintenance of harmony and order, and the responsibility of one generation for the next."[59] Social stability and continuity of responsibility were cornerstones of the new republican age.

CHAPTER TWELVE

African Americans

The war altered the lives of many bondsmen. Runaways, seeking freedom, fled to British lines, and slaves in the war zones of the South were treated as contraband. More than 50,000 slaves (one-tenth of the black population) found refuge with the British or were carried off by British military forces. Thomas Jefferson, with some exaggeration, estimated that 30,000 Virginia slaves went off to the British in 1781 alone. Twenty thousand (one-fourth of the state's black population) did the same in South Carolina, 1779–81; more than 5,000 slaves departed with the British evacuation of Savannah, Georgia; and several thousand slaves from New York City and the surrounding area and from northern New Jersey sought British protection.[1]

While black family life stabilized in the non-war zones, upon the conclusion of the war the huge western migration abetted the domestic slave trade, and migrating planters often divested themselves of some of their slaves or left them behind, causing separation of members of slave families. From 1780 to 1810, 75,000 slaves from Virginia and Maryland went to Kentucky or elsewhere on the southwest frontier, and 15,000 slaves in Georgia and South Carolina moved into the backcountry of these states or into the territories that became Alabama, Mississippi, and Louisiana.[2]

The American Revolution, as a war of liberation, challenged the rationale for the justification of slaveholding. If, as proclaimed in the Declaration of Independence, all men are imbued by natural right with a claim to freedom, then slaves should be emancipated. As Benjamin Rush wrote on the eve of the Revolution, "the plant of liberty is of so tender a nature, that it cannot thrive long in the neighborhood of slavery."[3] Although the principles of Independence did spur immediate efforts for abolition in the northern states and private manumission in the South, any general emancipation was deterred by the sheer scope of the difficulties in making large-scale compensation for loss of slave property and in providing maintenance for former slaves; most of all, emancipated slaves would form a dangerous underclass, threatening the established social order.

While the war witnessed among blacks an increase in the number of runaways, the forming of maroon communities, and participation in marauding and bandit activity, only one conspiracy for a major slave insurrection was recorded. Both opportunity for escape and the severity of slave laws served as deterrents to collective slave rebelliousness. In the long run, after the war, white–black tensions mounted, leading ultimately to widespread slave conspiracies at the turn of the century. Individual black resistance did not diminish in the postwar period. In Virginia, from 1785 to 1794, 148 blacks were arrested for murdering whites and 24 for attempted murder. The war years contrast with the period 1796–1831 in Virginia, as Philip Schwarz has shown, when some 242 capital trials occurred for insurrections or conspiracy to rebel, leading to 76 executions.[4]

The sole planned uprising recorded during the Revolution was set for July 8, 1775 among slaves in Beaufort, Pitt, and Craven counties of North Carolina's Cape Fear region. Slaves were to move from plantation to plantation, murdering whites, and then retreat into the mountains of the backcountry where they expected to found their own community under British protection. With the plot revealed during the evening before the intended uprising, authorities sent out patrols which rounded up 40 alleged leaders, one slave being killed in the process. Some of the slaves apprehended were whipped and had their ears cropped; one insurgent leader, a black pilot, was executed.[5]

Black Military Service

Five thousand free and slave blacks served in the American armies and several thousand with the British, some under arms in military units, but most as pioneers (laborers) and orderlies (waiters, cooks, and drummers). The army also used blacks as wagoners and foragers. Black seamen were distributed aboard vessels of the Continental, Royal, and state navies and on privateers. Ninety percent of the personnel in Virginia's small navy were slaves.[6]

At the start of the war, both Washington and Congress disapproved the acceptance of blacks into the Continental army. But, with British enlistment of free blacks, this policy was reversed, and Congress, in 1779, even attempted to raise a regular troop force of 3,000 blacks from South Carolina and Georgia, a scheme, however, vetoed by these state governments.[7]

Most black soldiers in the Continental army served in racially mixed units. During the summer of 1778, some 700 black troops were found throughout the army.[8] As early as July 1776, Captain Persifor Frazer wrote to his wife that among the New England troops stationed at Fort

Figure 5   Lafayette at Yorktown, 1783. Painted by Jean-Baptiste le Paon (French, *ca.* 1735–85). *Lafayette College Art Collection, Easton, Pennsylvania. Gift of Mrs John Hubbard.*

Ticonderoga there was "the strangest mixture of Negroes, Indians, and Whites, with old men and mere children, which together make a most shocking spectacle."[9] Alexander Hamilton noted in March 1779 that because of their "habit of subordination" blacks made better soldiers than whites.[10]

Slaves were recruited in Massachusetts, Connecticut, Rhode Island, and New York. In Massachusetts masters were compensated by the state for the enlistment of a slave; Rhode Island experimented with the same policy only from February to May 1778, allowing maximum compensation of £120. In Connecticut and New York slaves who enlisted had to forfeit their land bounties and part of their pay to their masters. Late in the war Maryland permitted the enlistment of slaves who had permission from their masters. Elsewhere in the South slaves were forbidden to join the army.[11] In Virginia several masters had slaves enrolled with the army as substitutes under a draft for themselves; whenever such an instance came to the attention of governmental authorities, the slave gained his freedom. The southern states, however, drafted free blacks into the army.

Three all black units were attached to the Continental army. Massachusetts sent a black company, known as the "Bucks of America," in 1778, but the actual participation of this unit is unknown. It did have the distinction that its commander, Samuel Middleton, was the only black commissioned officer in the Continental army. Connecticut also fielded a black company, commanded by white officers, in the Fourth Connecticut regiment; in 1782 the company was dissolved and its members were brought into white units. Colonel Christopher Greene commanded the nearly all black Rhode Island First Regiment, consisting of four companies. This unit won distinction in several battles. After Greene was killed in an encounter with Tory troops in Westchester County, New York in May 1781, Lieutenant-Colonel Jeremiah Olney commanded the regiment, which served until the end of the war. Free blacks entered the Continental army from southern states, serving in non-combat support capacities. In August 1778, 138 blacks were listed as serving with the Virginia troops, and 58 blacks were included in the North Carolina Line.[12]

Several dozen black veterans long after the war applied for pensions, but with mixed success. Jehu Grant of Rhode Island in the 1830s was denied a pension because he had been a slave runaway.[13]

The British army, unlike the Continental army, had few if any blacks in regular units, which were mainly recruited abroad. Although there are no estimates, it can be assumed that blacks enlisted in British provincial regiments and other loyalist detachments. Refugee blacks gave substantial aid as laborers, skilled workers, and orderlies attached to the British army.

There were occasions of black units under arms serving with British forces. Governor Lord Dunmore of Virginia, on November 7, 1775, declared "all indented Servants, Negroes, or others (appertaining to Rebels) free that are able and willing to bear Arms, they joining his MAJESTY'S Troops, as soon as may be, for the more speedily reducing this Colony to a proper Sense of their Duty, to His MAJESTY'S Crown and Dignity." By December 1 Dunmore had created the "Ethiopian Regiment," consisting of runaways and slaves brought in by fleeing Tory masters. Wearing

Figure 6   "The Bucks of America." Silk flag presented by John Hancock to the all Black military company for service in the Revolutionary War. *Courtesy of the Massachusetts Historical Society, Boston.*

the insignia "Liberty to Slaves," the black soldiers, numbering 300, made up one half of Dunmore's force and fought at the battle of Great Bridge, December 9. One half of Dunmore's Ethiopians succumbed to smallpox and other diseases; the rest, however, eventually wound up as free men in New York.[14] Like Dunmore's edict, General Henry Clinton's proclamation of June 30, 1779, issued at British headquarters in Westchester County, New York, promising freedom to black refugees, stimulated a large number of slaves in the Carolinas to seek protection behind British lines, many of whom entered service with the British army. The war in the South might have turned out differently if the British had put a large number of blacks under arms; at the war's end consideration was being given to raise 10,000 black troops, with recruits being granted freedom and bounties.[15]

The British armies incorporated whole units of African American recruits, such as the Black Guides and Pioneers. Each company had two white officers (a lieutenant and an ensign) and 60 black personnel, including three sergeants, three corporals, and 32 privates. Blacks in the authorized units received the same pay as white infantrymen—1s. per day for a sergeant, 8d. for a corporal, and 6d. for a private. Besides performing menial work, the Black Guides and Pioneers served as guards, executioners, pilots, and drummers. New York City had its "Negro barracks" at 18 Broadway, 10 Church Street, and elsewhere. In addition, the British military forces engaged runaway slaves and free blacks as "followers of the Army and Flag," who conducted guerrilla warfare, night-time raids, and foraging.

The British employed the "Negro Horse," raised in New York in 1782, with a strength of 100 men for patrol, mainly to pick up deserters. "Black Dragoons" were used by the British in the Carolinas for raids. General Nathanael Greene reported in April 1782 that 700 blacks in British service in the Carolinas were armed and in uniforms.[16]

Hessian regiments used ex-slaves in the ranks as combatants in addition to employment as servants, orderlies, and wagoners. Many of the blacks were young, aged 11–15, and employed as drummers. Blacks were assigned as musketeers and grenadiers. Most of the blacks on Hessian rosters came from the southern states, especially South Carolina. The former slaves were attracted to service with the Hessians because of the offers of freedom and wages and the lack of racial prejudice among the German troops. At the war's end, blacks in Hessian units had the choice of staying in America or going to Germany. A few such black veterans were mentioned in the records of the Hesse-Kassel region after the war, but no blacks are identified after 1830, indicating that the descendants of the ex-slave veterans assimilated into German society.[17]

Anti-slavery

Before the war any semblance of an anti-slavery movement belonged to northern Quakers. The principles for which the Revolution were fought presented a clarion call for others to become engaged in the cause of anti-slavery.

Most Americans favored curtailment of the foreign slave trade. Only South Carolina and Georgia delegates in Congress decidedly opposed retaining the clause in Thomas Jefferson's initial draft of the Declaration of Independence that condemned the British crown for fostering the "execrable commerce" upon the colonies. If men would not divest themselves of their own property in slaves, at least they could embrace the idea of freedom as a natural right by supporting a closure on imported slaves. Of course, the economic infeasibility of slavery in the northern states, fear of slave insurrection, overstocking of slaves, and depreciation in slave prices counted most in efforts to end the external slave trade. The Continental Association of 1774 called for a halt in the importation of slaves after December 1 of that year, a position reaffirmed by Congress on April 3, 1776. By 1787 all states, except South Carolina and Georgia, had passed legislation prohibiting the slave trade, and South Carolina temporarily did so in

1787–1803. Penalties for violation of slave non-importation included heavy fines and confiscation of vessels bringing in slaves. Rhode Island, for example, provided for fines of £100 per slave and £1,000 per ship.[18]

During the war substantial anti-slavery rhetoric developed, to be added to the earlier polemics of such Quaker writers as John Woolman and Anthony Benezet, both of whom had labored to establish the idea of equality relative to human attributes among the races. Thomas Paine published a short essay, signed "Justice and Humanity," in the *Pennsylvania Journal*, March 8, 1775, containing arguments that carried over to Paine's *Common Sense* of January 1776. In the earlier piece Paine attacked the slave trade as kidnapping. He asked: "Whether, then, all ought not immediately to discontinue and renounce it, with grief and abhorrence? Should not every society bear testimony against it, and account obstinate persisters in it bad men, enemies to their country, and exclude them from fellowship; as they often do for much lesser faults?"[19] Thomas Jefferson, in a model constitution he presented for consideration to the Virginia legislature in 1783, proposed that all children born of slave parents after 1800 be taught a craft and freed at age 21 for men and 18 for women, and then subsequently be deported.[20]

New England clergy attacked enslavement as sin. Reverend Levi Hart of Farmington, Connecticut, in a treatise unpublished during his lifetime, "Some Thoughts on the Freeing of the Negroes" (1775), favored "a gradual change from absolute slavery to full liberty." Hart would compensate slave owners, and ex-slaves should undergo a certain period of indentured servitude before becoming completely free.[21] Hart's gradualism would find expression in the anti-slavery legislation of the northern states.

Samuel Hopkins, pastor of the First Congregational Church in Newport, Rhode Island, in *A Dialogue Concerning the Slavery of the Africans* (1776) addressed to the Continental Congress, advocated immediate remedy. To Hopkins, abolition would provide a collective redemption. If slaveholding "be a sin of a crimson dye, which is most particularly pointed out by the public calamities which have come upon us, from which we have no reason to expect deliverance till we put away the evil of our doings, this reformation cannot be urged with too much zeal, nor attempted too soon, whatever difficulties are in the way." Hopkins urged Americans to "arise all as one man . . . with all our might, without delay" to put an end to slavery.[22]

Jacob Green, minister of the Hanover Presbyterian Church in Chatham, New Jersey, similarly issued a plea for atonement in a sermon of April 22, 1778, a day set aside by Congress for "Public Fasting and Prayer throughout the United States." Green found it difficult to believe "that a people contending for liberty should, at the same time, be promoting and supporting slavery." He asked, "Is not freedom the natural unalienable right of all?" It was hypocritical for Americans to permit slavery. "I am persuaded,"

Green declared, "these united American States must, and will groan under the afflicting hand of God, till we reform in this matter." Green predicted civil strife if slavery continued: "However we may be free from British oppression, I venture to say, we shall have inward convulsions, contentions, oppressions, and various calamities . . . till we wash our hands from the guilt of negro slavery."[23]

David Cooper's *A Serious Address to the Rulers of America*, published anonymously in 1783 was, Roger Bruns notes, "perhaps the most direct, incisive pamphlet assault on the hypocrisy of the Revolution, as applied to the black slaves, to appear during the period." A Quaker from Woodbury, New Jersey, Cooper denounced "mock patriots" who bought and sold slaves. The tract found a wide audience, and was quickly republished by Anthony Benezet. Its conclusion was addressed to Congress:

> If neither the voice of *justice*, the dictates of *humanity*, the rights of *human nature*, and establishment of *impartial liberty* now in your power, the good of your *country*, nor the fear of an *avenging God*, can restrain your hands from this *impious practice* of holding your fellow-men in *slavery* [then] let *justice, humanity, advocates for liberty*, and the sacred name of *Christians*, cease to be the *boast* of American Rulers.[24]

The anti-slavery movement received commitment from Quakers and also temporarily from Baptists and Methodists. Northern Quaker groups required members to emancipate their slaves upon penalty of disownment, and in the South many Quakers manumitted their slaves. The main concerns of Quakers in the 1780s were fair treatment for free blacks and termination of the slave trade.[25]

Separate Baptists in the South went on record against slavery. The Virginia General Committee Meeting in 1785 condemned slavery as violating the "word of God." The same body, meeting in 1790, resolved that slavery was against nature and "inconsistent with a representative government" and recommended "every legal means" to end slavery. Member associations, however, did not implement the emancipation resolution. Baptists were more interested in inculcating Christian values among slaves than in working for their freedom.[26] A major factor in deterring commitment among southern Baptists to abolition was their successful proselytizing among the planter slave-holding class. Baptists were moving into the mainstream of society, discarding an underclass identity as well as a penchant for social reform. Baptist congregations, however, permitted slaves fully to participate in worship, and one white congregation in Gloucester County, Virginia in the 1780s even had a black pastor.[27] In the post-Revolutionary period the process began of allowing blacks to have their own Baptist churches, though usually under the tutelage of a white minister.

Methodist preachers attending the Baltimore Conference of 1780 pledged to work for abolition. The Baltimore Conference, which established the Methodist Episcopal Church, in 1784 declared slavery "contrary to the laws of God, of men, and of nature" and ordered church members to free their slaves within 12 months or face expulsion. The manumission rule was withdrawn in 1800. Like the Baptists, Methodists made gains in recruiting the gentry class and overall were too busy building the denomination to be much concerned with social reform.[28]

With a long-standing opposition to slavery by Quakers before the war and many Pennsylvanians freeing their slaves it is not surprising that the first abolition society was founded in Pennsylvania. By 1780 already half of the blacks in the state were free.[29] On April 14, 1775 a group of mostly Quakers met at the Rising Sun Tavern in Philadelphia and created "The Society for the Relief of Free Negroes, unlawfully held in Bondage." The Society met only three more times in 1775, and did not reconvene during the war. Rejuvenated in 1784, the Society, led by silversmith James Starr and schoolmaster John Todd, on April 23, 1787 adopted a new constitution, styling itself the "Pennsylvania Society for Promoting the Abolition of Slavery. . . ." Benjamin Franklin was chosen president. The society assisted blacks who had been kidnapped back into slavery so that they could be "restored to liberty," helped to obtain employment and schooling for free blacks, and sent petitions to Congress and state legislatures. The Pennsylvania Abolition Society, as it was usually called, won freedom for slaves whose masters had failed to register them under the state's gradual abolition law of 1780. Ironically, during the whole of its existence, 1775–1859, the PAS had only one black member.[30]

Responding to New York merchants seizing free blacks and selling them into slavery, 20 persons in New York City in 1785 formed the "Society for promoting the Manumission of Slaves; and protecting such of them as have been or may be Liberated." John Jay was named chairman, and Alexander Hamilton was a member. Limiting its outreach, the New York Manumission Society charged high membership fees and allowed slave-holders to join. It pursued a similar agenda as that of the PAS.[31]

Anti-slavery societies cropped up in other states. In 1794 a loose federation of local societies, "The American Convention of Abolition Societies," was established in Philadelphia, with delegates from organizations in New York, Connecticut, New Jersey, Pennsylvania, Delaware, Maryland, and Virginia. Lasting until 1837, the Convention petitioned state legislatures to abolish slavery and focused much of its agenda on the improvement of life for free blacks.[32]

The anti-slavery movement of the Revolutionary era advocated mainly a national abolition of the slave trade and amelioration of the treatment of slaves and free blacks. This was a strategy that could gain commitment from the disparate, far-flung local anti-slavery societies, and the goals were achievable. The anti-slavery impulse moved from an exclusively religious to a secular arena, with slavery considered repugnant to the ideological and social values of the new Republic. By establishing a sense of collective guilt over the slave trade and the conditions under which blacks lived, the anti-slavery forces could acquire a broad base of support on which to build.

Emancipation

During the Revolutionary War all the northern states, except New York and New Jersey, provided measures to end slavery. Vermont outright forbade slavery by its 1777 Constitution. Congress, in 1787, excluded slavery from the Northwest Territory. By 1804 all states north of Maryland and Delaware had provided for some form of emancipation.

Although the pertinent records are obscure, it is probable that slaves were freed in New Hampshire by court action in accordance with the Bill of Rights of the state constitution of 1783, which declared "All men are born free." Most likely the Bill of Rights was interpreted as granting freedom for those born after the constitution went into effect. There were 150 slaves in the state in 1792. Not until July 26, 1857, however, did the New Hampshire legislature officially ban slavery.[33]

In Connecticut the legislature voted in 1777 that masters could free their slaves without liability for their support, and in 1784 a law freed all children subsequently born of slave parents when they should reach the age of 25.[34]

Rhode Island enacted a similar measure for gradual emancipation. A 1784 law freed children of slave parents born after March 1, 1784 and also declared that masters could free any slaves aged 21–40 without being obligated for their future support. Emancipation, however, did not gain complete sanction until 1843.[35]

New York in 1785 came close to adoption of a gradual abolition law. Passing both houses of the legislature it was vetoed by the Council of Revision because of objection to an amendment that denied free blacks the right to vote. New York did not institute gradual emancipation until 1799 (abolition occurred in 1827).[36] New Jersey had a similar experience. Governor William Livingston, who had freed his own slaves in 1778, sent a message to the New Jersey Assembly "to lay the foundation for their [slaves's] Manumission; but the house, thinking us rather in too critical a Situation to enter on the consideration of it at that time," prevailed upon Livingston to withdraw the proposal. "I am determined," commented Livingston to a Quaker friend, "as far as my influence extends, to push the matter till it is effected; being convinced that the practice is utterly inconsistent, both with the principles of Christianity & Humanity; & in Americans who have almost idolized liberty, peculiarly odious & disgraceful."[37]

Although Livingston did prevail upon the legislature to terminate the slave trade and to permit unrestrained private manumission, New Jersey did not have a gradual abolition law until 1804 (total abolition in 1846).

In Massachusetts there had always been doubt as to the legality of slavery going back to early colonial times. The Massachusetts *Body of Liberties* of 1641 condoned making slaves only of "lawful Captives taken in just warres," and the colony's royal charter of 1691 mentioned that settlers should "enjoy all Libertyes and Immunities of Free and Natural Subjects." But the Massachusetts experience was not really much different from that of other colonies; regular legislation protected ownership of slaves as chattels. Yet in Massachusetts before the Revolutionary War there were numerous freedom suits, some of which were successful.[38]

The Quock Walker cases of 1781–3 in Massachusetts are often viewed as establishing definitive closure of slavery in that state. In actuality, no such sweeping decision was rendered; the suits were not unlike other successful freedom litigation. Yet unquestionably the impact of the Quock Walker cases gave a heavy blow to the existence of slavery in Massachusetts. The state constitution of 1780 declared that "All men are born free and equal, and have certain natural, essential and unalienable rights." The three cases—*Walker* v. *Jennison* (1781), *Jennison* v. *Caldwell* (1781), and *Commonwealth* v. *Jennison* (1783)—grew out of Walker, a slave belonging to Nathaniel Jennison, running away and accepting employment with Jennison's neighbor, Seth Caldwell. Jennison sued Caldwell to regain possession of his slave. Walker, in turn, brought suit against Jennison for assault and battery. Jennison lost the cases, and Walker was a free man. Besides citing the Massachusetts Constitution, natural law, and the Bible, Walker's attorney, Levi Lincoln, argued that no positive law had ever given sanction to slavery in Massachusetts. Chief Justice William Cushing of the Supreme Court of Judicature, in presiding over the 1783 trial, wrote down instructions to the jury that in reference to the state constitution "every subject is entitled to liberty, and to have it guarded by the laws." There is doubt that Cushing ever delivered this charge to the jury or that he intended to strike down slavery altogether.[39] Whatever may be surmised from the incomplete records, the verdicts in the Walker cases may be regarded as punctuating the end of slavery in Massachusetts.

In spite of a strong anti-slavery presence and a relatively small slave population, 90 percent of which was thinly spread among small farms throughout the state, Pennsylvania opted for gradual rather than absolute emancipation of slaves. Pennsylvania's slave population dwindled from 6,855 (2.1 percent of the total population) in 1780 to 3,760 (0.9 percent) in 1790. The decline in the number of slaves over the decade, as in other northern states, was owing to the sale of slaves southward for a profit. The Pennsylvania "Act for the Gradual Abolition of Slavery" of March 1, 1780 provided that all children of slave mothers born after the date of the enactment of the law were to be free upon reaching age 28; thus the first slaves emancipated under the law did not occur until 1808. Total abolition in Pennsylvania came in 1848. A Pennsylvania law in 1788 prohibited sending slave women to the South to give birth.[40]

The Delaware Constitution of 1776 declared that "no person hereafter imported into this State from Africa ought to be held in Slavery under any pretence whatever; and no Negro, Indian, or mulatto slave ought to be brought into this State for sale, from any part of the world." A 1787 act permitted slave-holders to manumit slaves, aged 18–35, without being held responsible for their maintenance.[41] Slavery, however, lasted in Delaware until the implementation of the Thirteenth Amendment of the US Constitution.

More slaves in the immediate postwar period were freed by private manumission in the South than by the abolition laws of the northern states. By 1790 all southern states, except North Carolina, at least temporarily had repealed the prohibition of private manumission of slaves. A North Carolina act of April 1777 provided for manumission only by order of county courts for meritorious public service. Even Quakers in that state could not free their slaves; if they did, the ex-slaves were arrested and sold by the local governments.[42] In 1782 Virginia repealed a 1723 law that had prohibited private manumission, and allowed slaveholders to free males aged 21–5 and females aged 18–45 without liability; masters were responsible for the maintenance of any slaves freed who were above or below these age limits. Virginia had less than 2,000 free blacks in 1782; 12,866 in 1790; and 20,124 in 1800. Robert Carter III manumitted in 1791 over 500 slaves. Virginia's unrestricted manumission law was rescinded in 1806 and replaced by one that allowed a slave owner to free slaves only if they were deported out of state within a year of gaining freedom. Delaware, due to manumissions, was the only state south of the Mason-Dixon line to have a numerical decline in a number of slaves from 1775 to 1810; slaves in Delaware were reduced from 95 percent of the black population in 1775 to 70 percent in 1790 and 24 percent by 1810.[43]

Free Blacks

The number of free blacks in the United States rose from about 5,000 in 1780 to 60,000 in 1790 and 180,000 in 1810. Most of the freedmen resided in the middle states and in Maryland and Virginia.[44]

With the rise of the free black population during the Revolutionary era, a sense of black community and social organization emerged in the major urban areas of the North. Liberty, however, brought only limited benefits as to citizenship and economic opportunity. Kidnapping of free blacks and returning them to slavery was prevalent.

Free blacks found discrimination of various sorts. They faced harsh vagrancy laws. For example, by a Massachusetts law of March 26, 1788 African American newcomers who should "tarry" for more than two months in a locality were subject to imprisonment, a whipping of ten stripes, and deportation. Southern states barred immigration of free blacks. Much of the southern slave codes was applied to free blacks, for example restrictions on assembly and mobility and prevention from testifying against whites. There was also discriminatory taxation. A Maryland law of 1785 required free blacks to wear on the left shoulder a patch with the word "Free."[45] Five of the 13 states extended the vote to free blacks: New York, Pennsylvania, Delaware, Maryland, and North Carolina; this privilege, however, was withdrawn in Maryland, in 1810 and North Carolina in 1835.[46]

In urban areas, although ex-slaves began to form their own segregated communities, many freedmen lived in white households. By the 1790 census 950 black Philadelphians lived in 183 black households, while the other half of the black population in the city resided in white households. Nearly one-sixth of the Philadelphia black households were headed by women. Philadelphia blacks usually found only menial work, serving mainly as mariners, laborers, or domestic servants. One-fifth of Philadelphia's mariners were black. Only a very few of the freedmen had their own shops or were retailers. In New York City during the 1790s one-third of free blacks lived in white households. Of black males heading households in New York City, two-fifths were laborers or mariners; one-third, artisans; and 2 percent, retailers. Some free blacks engaged in selling produce from Long Island and New Jersey. More black women than men resided in the cities because, with a high demand by whites for domestic servants, women could more readily find work than in the countryside.[47]

A revolution in free black life occurred during the 1780s and 1790s with the formation of benevolent societies, schools, and churches apart from white establishments. Richard Allen became a leader of the Philadelphia black community. Born in 1760 a slave of Benjamin Chew, he was sold to a Delaware planter at the age of 10. He purchased his freedom in 1777, and while working as a teamster, woodcutter, shoemaker, and other jobs served as a Methodist preacher and circuit rider. Settling in Philadelphia in 1786, Allen became a preacher and teacher at St George's Methodist Church, a dirt-floor edifice in the poor section of the city, holding services for blacks at 5 a.m. so as not to interfere with the white worship. Along with Absalom Jones, also a former Delaware slave who had purchased his freedom, Allen founded a quasi-religious group known as the Free African Society of Philadelphia in 1787; the Society sponsored mutual aid programs for African Americans. Other mutual aid societies appeared over the next decade in Philadelphia, Providence, Rhode Island, Boston, and Charleston, South Carolina; the African Union Society of Newport, Rhode Island, founded in 1780, had been the first of such institutions. In a dispute with the white membership at St George's, Allen and blacks withdrew from the congregation. Some of the schismatics followed Absalom Jones in the founding of St Thomas Episcopal Church, the first black church in the United States; others shortly afterwards joined with Allen in establishing Bethel African Methodist Episcopal Church (July 1794). When a national denomination grew out of the Bethel church, Allen was named its first bishop.[48] The black Methodists adhered to "a theology of liberation," notes historian Benjamin Quarles. "Thus the black church was not only a spiritual fellowship; it was also a social unit, and for this reason represented a fusion of redemptions, religious and radical."[49]

Blacks had been refused membership in the Masonic Order from the time that the organization first came to America in the 1730s. A military lodge among soldiers at the British garrison in Boston in 1775 authorized 15 Boston blacks to hold their own Masonic meetings. Unable to secure a charter from the American Masonic Order, Prince Hall, the leader of the black group, applied for and received a charter from the British Grand Lodge in 1787, which led to the founding of African Lodge number 459, with Hall as master; other lodges were established in Philadelphia and Providence, and Hall became the Grand Master of African American Masonry.[50]

Educational opportunity for blacks proceeded slowly. The Quaker-sponsored Friends African School, founded in 1770 for educating slaves and free blacks, continued through the war and afterwards. Girls who were admitted learned sewing and knitting in addition to the normal curriculum of arithmetic, reading, and writing. The New York Manumission Society founded the African Free School in New York City, which began with 40 pupils. Funds left over for the relief of Quakers during the war were applied toward tuition and books for black children attending schools.[51]

Slaves gaining freedom during the Revolutionary era enhanced their individual identities by inventing family names. Gary B. Nash notes that the forenames and surnames of freedmen in Philadelphia indicate "two stages in the process of cultural self-definition: first, the symbolic obliteration of the slave past; and second, the creation of a unique Afro-American identity." Nash finds that among the names of slaves manumitted by wills or mentioned in church records before 1775, 11 percent were African names; one-sixth were classical names such as Caesar or Cato; one-sixth biblical names like Jacob or Adam; and two-fifths were Anglo-American names given by masters, often shortened to imply less than full person status, such as Ben, Tom, Dick, Fanny, Lucy, or Polly. New names commonly denoted freedom, such as Freeman and Newman; others assumed names of Revolutionary heroes, such as Washington or Jefferson; while still others gave themselves surnames referring to artisan skills, such as Cooper, Mason, or Carpenter.[52]

Toward Caste

The American Revolution increased an awareness of human behavior. Slavery came under fire as denying to one race the fundamentals of human dignity and freedom. To simply justify slavery by arguing that black bondsmen were not party to the social compact and therefore could not be citizens or be accorded the same rights as whites ignores the pervasive humanness that transcends man-made institutions and also the mutability of social conditions. Only by acknowledging the human traits of Africans as inferior to those of whites could any semblance of reason be applied to justify the institution of slavery.

As Robert Fogel writes, "Revolutionary leaders not only politicalized the issue of slavery but transformed it from a spiritual question to a rational one." The despiritualization of slavery issues, Fogel also notes, was owing to the deistical principles of the Revolutionary leaders ("52 of the 56 signers of the Declaration of Independence belonged to the Freemasons, the principal organization promoting deism in America") and "to the tendency of Revolutionary leaders to view all political issues through the prism of natural rights."[53] As the natural rights ideology was strengthened, pro-slavery advocates had to find a rationale that explained the exclusion of African Americans from the expression of enjoyment of full natural liberty.

Inferiority of blacks could be reasonably argued upon acceptance of the premises that the character of blacks had been shaped by the African environment and climate and by supposed traits inherent in the race. Even Benjamin Rush, an abolitionist, conceded in 1773 that many blacks were "inferior in Virtue, Knowledge, and the love of Liberty," which "may be explained from *Physical* causes." The heat of the African continent had caused "Indolence of Mind, and Body." But Rush considered that human nature was the same everywhere; "all the differences we perceive in its Characters in respect to Virtue and Vice, Knowledge and Ignorance, may be accounted for from Climate, Country, Degrees of Civilization, form of Government, or other accidental causes."[54] As Rush implied, blacks could be reshaped by a different environment, as were other immigrants to America.

Pro-slave advocates did not accept Rush's view as to the adaptability and changeability of the African character. Out of necessity, increasingly on through the ante-bellum period, they developed a racist ideology of black inferiority in the context of biological, cultural, and intellectual traits.

Thomas Jefferson, who preferred emancipation and subsequent deportation of slaves, felt compelled to discern pejorative traits among blacks. In his *Notes on Virginia*, written 1781, Jefferson commented that Africans lacked a talent for intellectual creativity: "nature has been less bountiful to them in the endowments of the head." Blacks have "a want of forethought." They "participate more of sensation than reflection," and "in imagination they are dull, tasteless, and anomalous." As to memory Africans "are equal to whites," but "in reason much inferior." Black men "are more ardent after their female: but love seems with them to be more an eager desire, than a tender delicate mixture of sentiment and sensation." Jefferson observed a variety of physical distinctiveness; regarding one of which he stated "they secrete less by the Kidnies, and more by the glands of the skin, which gives them a very strong and disagreeable odour."[55]

Revised slave codes enacted in the post-Revolutionary War period included language denigrating Africans as an inferior race and, out of fear of slave conspiracy and insurrection, provided for greater surveillance of slaves. The Virginia code of 1792 established a legal category of "black blood."[56]

The American Revolution stimulated a sense of guilt over slavery that brought forward an anti-slavery movement. Contrarily, independence accentuated a fear of African American freedom that caused slaveholders to become increasingly paranoid in the defense of keeping their slaves in bondage.

CHAPTER THIRTEEN

Native Americans

Native Americans, on the eve of the Revolution, were caught between two social forces: pan-Indianism and inter-tribal and intra-tribal division. Very little supra-authority affected the daily lives of the Indians, whose primary attachments were to kin, clan, and village. Bands found their turf and remained relatively isolated from other groups. From time to time a spiritual revitalization movement occurred, bringing Indians of a region together, as was evidenced, for example, among the Ohio country tribes in the Pontiac Uprising of 1763 and again during the War of 1812 period. The southern tribes, in their social organization, were much like their counterparts in the North. They, too, were beginning to experience the thrust westward of land-grabbing pioneers and speculators, despite living largely in the transmontane region. The Cherokees had fought a bloody war (1759–61) defending their eastern home territory.

From 1763 to 1775 the Indian country was at peace in relation to the British imperial and colonial governments. The Indians had all but been cleared out of the Atlantic coastal plain, affording a little breathing space before the rising intensity of white settlers crossing the mountains and beyond.

Indian populations in the area now making up the United States from the Mississippi to the Atlantic Ocean were not large. At the start of the Revolution the total Iroquois population amounted to about 11,000; the aggregate of the Ohio country and eastern Great Lakes tribes (other than the Iroquois), 18,000; Cherokees, 12,000; Creeks, 18,000; Choctaws, 8,000; and Chickasaws, 1,400.[1]

The coming of the Revolution drew Indians into military alliances with the British or Americans. Some tribes, attempting neutrality, delayed commitment until well into the war, and tribal factions had divided loyalties. But overwhelmingly the American Indians, whether directly allied or conducting war on their own, came down on the side of the British. Various factors affected this decision. Most Indians were tied to white trade networks under the auspices of the crown, and the British had the capabilities of supplying gifts and trade goods to a larger extent than could the Continental Congress or the new state governments. The British government had tried to restrain westward white advance, while the colony-state governments did not. To most Indians the British seemed the likely winners of the war. Moreover, frontier atrocities inflicted by whites on Indians necessitated revenge.

Native Americans were in a no-win situation during the war; whether either the British or Americans won, there was little that could be done to stay the flow of white westward expansion. Indeed, as the war began, the tentacles of pioneer settlement reached through the Allegheny barrier. The culmination of the American Revolution made the dispossession of Native Americans from their lands all the more inevitable.

Indian Soldiers

At first neither the Americans nor the British were willing to employ Indian auxiliaries in the war. The Americans could hope for hardly more than declared neutrality on the part of Native Americans. The British military authority feared that the Indians could not be restrained from committing atrocities, which would bring on rebel retaliation upon backcountry Tories. It did not take long, however, before the British command began to use Indians as an integral part of military operations. General Thomas Gage in 1776 ordered the British army in Canada to put Indian warriors in the field for the purpose of drawing American military forces away from a British invasion along New England's frontier. Congress responded on June 17, 1776 by authorizing Washington to employ Indians whenever he deemed necessary. Some Stockbridge (Mohican) Indians were enlisted from their western Massachusetts reservation in May 1777 to serve with the Continental troops. Several hundred Oneidas and Tuscaroras were also used in the fall of 1777 to assist the American Northern army against Burgoyne's invading force. In May 1778 Congress authorized the service of southern Indians with the Continental army.[2]

The refusal of some of the Oneidas and Tuscaroras to side with the British disrupted the unity of the Iroquois Six Nations. As a result, the Council of the Six Nations left each member tribe to decide with whom to ally. Senecas, Mohawks, Cayugas, and later also the Onondagas wholly supported the British. Actually the British had difficulty controlling their allied Iroquois troops. While the Iroquois were effective on raids, usually in conjunction with Tory rangers, they were employed officially as forward units. As the Marquis de Chastellux noted, commenting on the Iroquois:

AN INDIAN OF THE STOCKBRIDGE TRIBE

Figure 7   "Sketch of a Stockridge Indian serving with the American Army." In Joseph P. Tustin, trans. and ed., *Diary of the American War, A Hessian Journal, Captain John Ewald, Field Jäger Corps* (New Haven, CT: Yale University Press, 1979).

"As an advance guard, they are formidable, as an army they are nothing."[3] Most often Iroquois and Ohio country Indians went on the warpath in small parties for the purpose of defending their homes rather than to conquer territory.[4]

At the battle of Oriskany, August 6, 1777, 60 Oneidas fought with the rebel militia against Tory rangers and 400 Mohawks and Senecas. Iroquois Indians joined forces with Tory rangers in scouring the Mohawk and Susquehanna river valleys. At the Wyoming Valley along the Susquehanna River in Pennsylvania, July 3–4, 1778, Major John Butler's rangers and Seneca and Cayuga Indians attacked a settlement; although stories of a massacre that circulated afterwards were exaggerated, the enemy did leave with 227 scalps.[5]

On November 11, 1778 Ensign Walter Butler with Tory rangers and Delaware, Cayuga, Mohawk, Onondaga, and Tuscarora Indians attacked American pioneers at Cherry Valley on the Mohawk River. Although not the massacre rebel reports made it out to be (actually 40 Americans were killed—16 soldiers and the rest women and children and 70 captives), the event prompted the sending of a joint punitive expedition under Generals John Sullivan and James Clinton during summer 1779 deep into the Iroquois country as far west as the Genesse River. The scorched earth campaign completely destroyed Indian villages and crops. The expedition made the Iroquois more vengeful, and during 1780–1 they again conducted a series of raids in New York, Pennsylvania, and along the Ohio River. This border war finally came to a halt after Indian retreats from the battles of Johnstown and Jerseyfield (October 24 and 30, 1781).[6]

In the Ohio country atrocities committed by white ruffians, such as the murder of Cornstalk, a Shawnee chief, and his entourage while under a flag of truce, tipped the scale for the Ohio Indians to join the British. The Delawares for a while held out for neutrality, even granting the rights of passage of United States troops through their territory, but by 1778, claiming that Congress had reneged in furnishing supplies, they, too, allied with the British. Lieutenant-Colonel Henry Hamilton, the British commandant at Detroit, spurred on Indians to attack frontier stations in Kentucky. By the end of 1778 the Shawnees, Ottawas, Mingoes (Ohio Iroquois), Wyandots, Potawatomis, Delawares, and Miamis were at war with the United States.[7]

Shawnee Indians raided the Kentucky frontier successively in 1777–82, and Boonesborough in 1777–8 twice withstood siege. George Rogers Clark and Virginia troops secured the Illinois country, including the capture of Vincennes in 1779. Spaniards participated in assisting westerners in preventing British southward penetration along the Mississippi River. Indians attacked forts on the upper Ohio River, with little effective response from the Americans, although on occasion detachments of federal troops or Pennsylvania and Kentucky militia retaliated with destructive raids against Indian villages.

Only three major offensives were attempted by the British in the Ohio and Illinois country. In 1780 Captain Emanuel Hesse, with a 950-man force, consisting of a few whites and Chippewa, Ottawa, Sauk, Outgami,

Wyandot, and Sioux Indians, set out from Fort Michilimackinac and descended the Mississippi River, hopefully to reach New Orleans and then lend assistance in the recapture of West Florida from the Spaniards. Met by Spanish troops and those of Clark, and with the withdrawal of his Indian auxiliaries, Hesse had to retreat back to his base at the straits between Lakes Huron and Michigan. Meanwhile Captain Henry Bird from Detroit pushed southward into Kentucky with 150 whites and 1,000 Indians (mostly Shawnee, Wyandot, and Mingo). Ruddle's and Martin's stations were both forced to surrender. Repulsed by the savagery of the Indians toward captives, Bird ended his expedition and returned to Detroit. In 1782 Captain William Caldwell with 50 Tory rangers and 300 Indians (Shawnee, Delaware, Ojibwa, and Mingo), heading northward after an unsuccessful siege of Bryan's Station (near Lexington, Kentucky) met up with 182 Kentucky militia at Blue Licks on August 19. The Kentuckians were routed; the 77 men who were killed represented one-thirteenth of all Kentucky's militia. In November George Rogers Clark and mounted frontiersmen retaliated by crossing the Ohio and laying waste to Shawnee towns.[8]

All the major southern tribes, with the exception of the Catawbas in South Carolina, who were already on a reservation and greatly reduced by disease, came into the British fold. Cherokees, Creeks, Seminoles (Florida Creeks), Chickasaws, and Choctaws, at one time or another, fought the Americans. A Cherokee war erupted in 1776 along the Georgia and Carolina frontiers and aimed primarily at the white settlements on the Watauga and Holston rivers. Punitive militia expeditions brought the Cherokees to peace terms in the treaties of DeWitt's Corner, South Carolina (May 20, 1777) and of Long Island on the Holston River (July 20, 1777), whereby the Cherokees ceded all territory east of the Blue Ridge in North Carolina, Virginia, and eastern Tennessee.[9]

The Overhill Cherokees in 1780 again became hostile and were defeated by frontier militia under John Sevier, chiefly at the battle of Boyd's Creek on December 16, 1780. In 1782 Sevier again raided Cherokee villages and destroyed crops, cutting a swath from the Hiawassee to the Coosa rivers. Cherokee chief Dragging Canoe and a band of followers separated themselves from the Cherokee Nation and moved from the Little Tennessee and Hiawasee valleys to a site at the junction of Chickamauga Creek in northern Georgia and then to the Muscle Shoals area of the Tennessee River. The Chickamaugas, as they were now called, joined Upper Creeks in raiding on the Carolina and Georgia frontiers in 1779, and the Chickamaugas carried on warfare against the settlements on the Cumberland River in middle Tennessee in 1780 and 1781, afterwards making forays into the region lasting until the 1790s.[10]

The Creeks originally were neutral, but by 1778 Upper Creeks were attacking American frontier settlements. The British at first rejected Creek support for fear that without British leadership southern loyalists would be put in greater jeopardy. During the war Creeks and Seminoles in conjunction with British military operations fought against the Americans along the Florida/Georgia boundary. In 1778 800 Upper and Lower Creeks laid waste to settlements along the Broad River in Georgia. Creek warriors beat back South Carolina and Georgia militia at British-held Augusta on September 14–16, 1780. Creeks joined Thomas Brown's Tory rangers in raids into South Carolina. One hundred and fifty Creek warriors gave assistance against the American siege of Savannah in 1781–2. Creeks and Choctaws for a while in 1780–1 joined with the British in defending Pensacola during the Spanish siege, which ultimately succeeded.[11]

In spring 1780 Chickasaws lay siege to the Virginia Fort Jefferson, on the east bank of the Mississippi, four miles below the mouth of the Ohio River; recurring attacks forced the abandonment of the post.[12] The Choctaws, writes one author, "were virtually mercenary forces in the British service." One group of Choctaws, 122 warriors and the rest women and children, stayed with the British garrison at Savannah for almost a year until the evacuation, and, as a British official noted, behaved with "a degree of good order and regularity, not very common among savages."[13]

Savagery

Indian torture had been a ritualized affair during the course of war. Captives faced the luck of the draw: they were either adopted into a family of a tribe as replacements for lost kin or underwent hideous torture to avenge killings by an enemy. The Cherokee War of 1759–61, the French and Indian War, and Pontiac's Rebellion of 1763 gave witness to abject Indian inhumanness. The Indians seemed to be discarding cruel practices during the peaceful period of 1763–76, a trend, however, to be reversed during the Revolutionary War.

Several factors contributed to the revival of savagery by Native Americans. White ruffians on the frontier committed atrocities, against which Indians retaliated. Native Americans were brought into the bloody civil war among the whites. There was need for a harsh response in order to thwart the encroachment on Indian territory by white settlers.

The killing by Indians of an enemy, and especially so in ritualized form, had a way of affirming life. As one study notes, "identification with the aggressor by Native American men is of a quality that has as a core desire to gain the aggressor's power and eventually turn that power on the aggressor." The "acquisition of the aggressor's power has the ultimate goal of destroying the aggressor and restoring a community to a precolonization lifeworld."[14]

Women captured by Indians (and by whites for that matter) were sometimes selected for awful deaths. As Richard White comments:

In both Algonquian and backcountry attacks, women's bodies became bloody metaphors. Warriors, Indian and white, killed women more rarely than they killed men, but when they killed them, they often butchered them. Fighters who had rejected peace with its images of a common mother and common births now assailed actual mothers, ripping out their wombs. Men denied their common humanity by mutilating women.[15]

Of course, the metaphor of women as victim could be reversed. Indian women and children usually had a key role in administering torture. If the report of a soldier who escaped from the Wyoming massacre of 1778 is true, Esther Montour, a half-breed wife of an Iroquois chief, ranks as an extraordinary avenger; she lined up 15 prisoners, each held by two warriors, around a great rock and then personally tomahawked each victim one by one.[16]

It is difficult to understand why the few Indians of the Ohio Valley were involved in the waylaying and the indiscriminate killing of whites, increasingly prevalent from the war's end through to the mid-1790s. Of course, terror as a tactic by a minority population in defense of a homeland has had a measure of success throughout history. Intriguingly, there may also be psychological factors. Much like the purported propensity toward violence in today's inner cities, incidences of violence by Indians, dispossessed and living in dysfunctional communities, represented acting out what was expected of them. What was perplexing about the behavior of the Ohio Indians could be said of other Indian tribes during the Revolution. A French traveler in America in December 1780 wondered why the cruelty of the Iroquois seemed "to augment, in proportion to their decrease in numbers."[17]

People become accustomed to sanctioned ritual murder and do not question it—witness Europe's Inquisition and today's capital punishment in the United States. Occasionally courageous leaders or a turn of events arouse the public's aversion to bloodlust. One young Shawnee by the name of Tecumseh, who was destined to become the great leader of an Indian confederacy, at the age of 15 in 1783 was so enraged at witnessing the burning of a white settler by a Shawnee war party that he proclaimed his shame and declared that hereafter there would never again be such burnings— and among the Shawnee there were not.[18] Tecumseh's courage brings to mind the feat of Pitalesharo, a young Pawnee warrior, who a generation later rescued from a scaffold and carried off a Comanche girl who was about to be sacrificed to the Morning Star god; this deed brought relief to the tribe and the Morning Star sacrifice was soon abolished.[19]

Whites equaled and even exceeded Indians in committing atrocities. Johann David Schoepf, a German army surgeon who journeyed in the "Western Country" in late 1783, acknowledged that the Indians had been "inhumane," but:

A similar vengeance is practiced against the families of Indians; their dwellings are burned and their lands devastated; so that by Christian example the horrors of their wars are justified. [The Indians] hold carefully the remembrance of all the oppressions and deception, of all the numberless instances of trickery practiced against them and blood shed by the Europeans among them, treasuring it up as a warning for their descendants who may thereby demand vengeance for past encroachments and be on their guard against the future.[20]

By the eighteenth century, enemy scalps were prized trophies of war among whites as well as among the eastern Algonguian tribes and the Iroquois. Sergeant Moses Van Campen of the Pennsylvania militia had a not unique adventure when he and two companions made an escape from Indian captivity by killing their guards. "I turned my attention to scalping the Indians," Van Campen boasted. "Recovering the scalps of my father, brother and others, I strung them all on my belt for safekeeping." Upon reaching Sunbury, Pennsylvania "I was received with joy. My scalps were exhibited, the cannons were fired."[21]

Most states offered scalp bounties on enemy Indians during wartime. The problem was the difficulty in discerning whether a gruesome trophy came from a friendly or a hostile Indian, and scalps irregardless of age or gender were often accepted. South Carolina paid £75 for male Cherokee scalps; Pennsylvania allowed $1,000 for any Indian scalp. Frontier militia dug up graves at Indian villages to obtain scalps from the corpses. Sometimes a dead Indian provided other trophies. On the Sullivan expedition of 1779 several soldiers of the First New Jersey Regiment skinned two Indian bodies "from their hips down for boot legs;" one pair went to Major Daniel Piatt and another to Captain William Barton.[22]

There is no evidence that the British offered bounties for white scalps, but they paid well for prisoners brought in by their Indian allies. Undoubtedly some British commanders, such as Lieutenant-Colonel Henry Hamilton, "the Hair Buyer" at Detroit, privately endorsed scalp-taking. In any case, Indians used scalps as proof of success, whereby they were rewarded with munitions and provisions from British military storehouses.[23]

White renegades teaming up with Indians often had no hesitation in engaging in frontier atrocities. Ebenezer Allen, who fought with Iroquois Indians along the New York/Pennsylvania frontier, was one of such a breed. Mary Jemison, a white Indian herself, mentioned that at one time when Allen

> was scouting with the Indians in the Susquehannah country, he
> entered a house very early in the morning, where he found a man,
> his wife, and one child, in bed. The man, as he entered the door,

instantly sprang on the floor, for the purpose of defending himself and little family; but Allen dispatched him at one blow. He then cut off his head and threw it bleeding into the bed with the terrified woman; took the little infant from its mother's breast, and holding it by the legs, dashed its head against the jamb, and left the unhappy widow and mother to mourn alone over her murdered family.[24]

Instances of murder and torture on the Revolutionary frontier were legion. American military personnel were among the worst offenders. Fifteen Delaware warriors captured by a mixed Continental/militia force under Colonel Daniel Brodhead in April 1781 were tomahawked or speared and then scalped.[25] George Rogers Clark was especially cruel. He had five captured Indians tomahawked in front of the British garrison at Vincennes, intimating that he would give no quarter if the post did not surrender.[26] During Clark's campaign against Shawnee towns in 1780 one of the captives was an Indian woman who was killed by "ripping up her Belly & otherwise mangling her."[27]

All along the Indian frontier, north and south, there were atrocities. James Roark returned to his Kentucky home in 1780 to find that the Indians had "Scalped seven of his children and his wife."[28] At the capture of Ruddell's Station, Kentucky, June 22, 1780 Indians threw a woman and her baby into a fire.[29] Creek Indians in pursuit of Georgia militia under Colonel Elijah Clarke in September 1780 fell upon families of the militiamen: women and children were "strip'd, scalped, and suffered to welter in their gore . . . Lads obliged to dance naked between two large fires, until they were scorched to death. Men strip'd, dismembered, and scalped, afterward hung up."[30]

For most Indian groups, retributive justice was twofold: for crimes committed among members, kin of the victim were expected to exact punishment; for wrongs inflicted on Indians by outside persons justice was sought on behalf of the whole tribe. Murder was avenged in kind with added degree of suffering. One outcome of the Revolution's frontier warfare was that Indians felt they had not gained full vengeance for the destruction of lives, homes, and livelihood. Justice denied had to be postponed, accomplished in the future; the continuation of hostilities by the Shawnees and other Ohio Indians after the war attests to this attitude.

Three examples of Indian retributive justice against white people during the Revolutionary War period stand out among many such instances. The murder in April 1774 of the family of Logan, a Mingo chief, and other peaceful Indians along the Ohio River below Fort Pitt by white border ruffians called for vengeance. Especially shocking had been the stringing up of Logan's sister by her wrists and then ripping open her belly. The deed led to the short "Lord Dunmore's War," which ended after the defeat of the Indians at the battle of Point Pleasant, October 10, 1774. Still, the

Indians harbored the memory of the April 1774 atrocity. Not until April 1791 did the Indians capture a chief perpetrator of the crime, Jacob Greathouse, who along with his wife both had the lower end of their intestines tied to a tree and then forced to walk around it.[31]

As the Sullivan Indian expedition approached its furthest objective, the Seneca capital on the Genesee River, in September 1779, Lieutenant Thomas Boyd and 26 others were sent to reconnoiter in advance of the army. This detachment killed, mutilated, and scalped two Indians. Next Boyd and his party ran into an ambush that had been meant for the whole army. Boyd's Oneida scout was instantly "hewn to pieces," and the next day Boyd and Sergeant Michael Parker were subjected to the most excruciating torture, "by first plucking their nails from their hands, then spearing, cutting, and whipping them, and mangling their bodies, then cutting off the flesh from their shoulders by pieces, tomahawking and severing their heads from their bodies, and then leaving them a prey to their dogs." When Sullivan's troops came upon the scene they found Boyd's partially skinned head on a log with the mouth wide open. The bodies of 13 others of Boyd's detachment were discovered to have met a similar fate.[32]

The most horrid massacre by Pennsylvania militia under Colonel David Williamson of Moravian Christian Indians at Gnaddenhutten in northeastern Ohio on March 7, 1782 called for immediate vengeance. Ninety-six Indians, one-third of them children and one-third women, were lined up by the militiamen in two houses and systematically tomahawked one-by-one with a cooper's mallet. These Indians were falsely accused of being party to the murder of a white woman. The Gnaddenhutten massacre by the white militiamen meant to the Indians that "the blood of those innocent whom they had murdered, must be avenged in an exemplary manner."[33]

On June 4–5, 1782 Colonel William Crawford and Pennsylvania militia were defeated by Tory rangers, Delawares, and some Wyandots near present day Upper Sandusky. Some of the captives were singled out for torture, with the most terrible example to be made of Crawford, who had not been at the Gnaddenhutten slaughter; as the new militia commander replacing Williamson, however, he was scapegoated for the murders. The details of Crawford's long suffering were recorded by a witness, Dr John Knight, who was also marked for the same fate but escaped. Crawford underwent every kind of hideous torture: various kinds of beatings, burnings, mutilations, and in the end slowly roasted over a low fire.[34]

The frontier war had degenerated into orgies of merciless killings. As Robert A. Hecht writes:

> While these killings were noteworthy because of their excessive and senseless cruelty, they were sadly typical of Indian–rebel frontier fighting during the last years of the Revolution. Each atrocity committed had to be avenged in kind, until blind hatred of the

other race seemed the only motivation left for making war. . . . The frontier became not so much a battlefront, where armies plot and move against each other, as a battleground, where men locked arms with other men in grisly and mortal combat, until death or exhaustion separated them.[35]

Refugees

North American Indians since their initial contact with Europeans and on through four centuries have largely been a refugee population, dispossessed of their lands, confined to reservations, moving on away from the advance of white settlements, or even in modern times, among some Indians, finding residence in ghettoes of the inner city. From earliest times small bodies of Indians have sought refuge by joining up with other small groups or a powerful tribe. The American Revolution accentuated the shuffle of Indians into new localities.

The Iroquois long had a policy of offering refuge havens for Indian groups willing to live under their "Great Tree of Peace." The most famous of such a transition was the Tuscaroras relocating in 1714 from the Carolinas to the Iroquois domain. Laurance M. Hauptman has noted that from 1714 to 1785 there were numerous "consolidated remnant populations" settling under the protection of the Iroquois, in such towns as Oquaga, Chemango, Brotherton, Chemung, Chugnut, New Stockbridge, Oswego, Tioga, and Unandilla. Poor, displaced Indians of eastern New England and from Long Island joined together at Brotherton (just south of Clinton, New York) on a tract of land given them by the Oneidas in 1774.[36]

Those Oneidas and Tuscaroras, friendly to the Americans during the war, were established in "miserable huts" in the woods near Schenectady; they had been driven from their villages by Iroquois allied with the British. "Sometimes employed in war," these displaced Indians, whom Rev. Samuel Kirkland described as "filthy, dirty, nasty creatures—a few families excepted," subsisted almost entirely on a meatless diet of potatoes, squash, and corn, though occasionally the state of New York provided "rations of meat and sometimes flour."[37]

The great majority of the Iroquois became refugees during the war and exiles afterwards. As Colin G. Calloway has commented, "in the Revolution, American armies waged war against Indian cornfields." The Sullivan campaign, in destroying crops and 40 Indian villages, forced Indians to flee to the protection of the British at Niagara. By the end of 1779 nearly 4,000 Iroquois refugees were among the 7,365 Indian refugees, half of whom were women and children, living near Fort Niagara and receiving rations from the British. With provisions running short the British Indian superintendent persuaded some of the Iroquois to go out hunting or return to their devastated villages. At war's end 4,000–5,000 Iroquois were still found on the American side of the Canadian border, but most Iroquois were settled by the British government on the Six Nations Reserve along the Grand River in Ontario. The Mohawks had a tract six miles wide on each side of the river. Tuscaroras, Oneidas, Cayugas, and Onondagas wound up in the same area, although some of these soon migrated west to Wisconsin and elsewhere. A few small remnants of the Iroquois remained on small reservations in their old neighborhoods, principally Onondagas and Senecas, under complete jurisdiction of the United States. The Iroquois gave up millions of acres by treaty arrangements with the New York and United States governments in the 1780s.[38]

The Ohio and Illinois country was a "land filled with Ishmaels," writes William Brandon. Displaced persons from the East and South had drifted into the area. Delawares, who once inhabited New Jersey, eastern Pennsylvania and Staten Island, had been pushed westward by white settlement and the Iroquois. The Wyandots (formerly called Hurons), the traditional foe of the Iroquois, found refuge in the upper Ohio country, as did the Potawatomis and Ottawas, also fleeing the Iroquois. The Shawnees, whose name meant "Southerners," were recent arrivals in the Ohio country, having lived in the course of the century before the Revolution in South Carolina, middle Tennessee and Kentucky, and eastern Pennsylvania. About a dozen other small tribes were of similar circumstance. In addition, as Secretary at War Henry Knox reported in 1786, "outcasts of a great number of tribes," including "some fragment of the cherokee tribes," had taken refuge in southeast Ohio, where they joined "scoundrels from the Wyandots, Delawares, & mingoes."[39] Generally, reeling from destructive militia incursions during the latter part of the war, Indians of southern and eastern Ohio regrouped among tribes of northwestern Ohio and northern and central Indiana (including the Miamis, Weas, and Wyandots) to form a "multitribal world."[40]

The Moravian Delawares continued to be separate from their tribe, and, seeking isolation, after several relocations in Michigan, finally settled along the Thames River, in Ontario, Canada.[41] The Shawnee tribe split during the war; in 1780 two of the tribe's five clans—1,200 persons, including 400 warriors—moved to the area south of St Louis led by chiefs Black Stump and Yellow Hawk.[42]

Of the one southern tribe committed to the patriot side, the Catawbas, as James H. Merrell notes, paid heavily for their loyalty to the Americans. Catawba warriors fought with rebel troops at various battles in South Carolina. In 1780 the tribe took refuge from the British by fleeing to North Carolina and Virginia. When these Indians returned to South Carolina in 1781 their villages were ruined and all their livestock gone. The state of South Carolina provided only minimal relief in the form of food rations and some reimbursement for livestock.[43]

Several thousand Cherokees were left homeless during the war. With towns and crops destroyed, many of these Indians found refuge in woods, living on what provender they could find. One band of Cherokees went north to join up with the Ohio Indians, and others found sanctuary among Dragging Canoe's Chickamaugas in the Muscle Shoals area at the Tennessee/Alabama border.[44]

Social Disintegration

Divided loyalties within tribes strained kinship relations. François Marquis de Barbé-Marbois, secretary of the French legation to the United States, in 1784, while visiting an Oneida village in western New York observed that "quarrels are all the more frequent as they stem from the war that is just over." Marbois witnessed a violent fight between two brothers, age "24 or 25 years old, one of whom seemed drunk." One of the brothers had fought for the British, and the other for the Americans. Their father and several women broke up the struggle. The Indians, Marbois noticed, "adopted the names 'Whigs' and 'Tories,' which—among them as among the Americans—serve to perpetuate the division and the violence even after the war is over."[45]

The war left the Indian peoples demoralized. Mary Jemison, the white captive who became a Seneca Indian herself, wrote that "no people" were "more happy than the Indians in times of peace." From 1763–77 the "war-hoop" was heard only "on days of festivity." The Senecas carefully observed religious rites; "the moral character of the Indian was . . . uncontaminated."[46] But the war disrupted the whole fabric of Indian mores.

Indian society was increasingly bereft of a sense of sacred power and customs. John Drayton, a South Carolina legislator and governor, observed of the Catawbas at the turn of the century that "they have forgotten their antient rites, ceremonies, and manufactores."[47] The Cherokees, who had reserved war for two seasons, made war a year round matter, and gave up purification ceremonies for warriors returning to their villages. The Cherokee's six religious festivals were reduced to one, the Great Corn Festival.[48] Indians were losing their sense of relationship to the environment. The spirits did not respond to entreaties, and as William G. McLoughlin says of the Cherokees: "Forces beyond their reckoning and control continually overwhelmed them. Harmony was their highest social and religious value, yet the sense of living in harmony among themselves as well as with nature and the spirit world seemed to have been lost."[49]

Inter-tribal communication diminished. Tribes were more isolated from each other, with the opening of more western lands for white settlement during the war and its immediate aftermath and with some Indians being settled on fixed reservations. The Cherokees were soon circumscribed by American frontier communities. Even the great Warrior's Path was being blocked by settlements. No longer could northern and southern Indians easily link up with each other following either one of the Path's two branches: through the Cumberland Gap and on through Kentucky to the Ohio River or through the Shenandoah Valley on through western Maryland into Pennsylvania.[50]

Indian society had a multi-ethnic dimension. White captives were adopted; of course, there were other options for the treatment of prisoners—being killed, ransomed, or sold to an ally, such as the British. During the war two famous Kentucky frontiersmen were captured by Ohio Indians. Daniel Boone had the good fortune of attracting the favor of the Shawnee war chief, Black Fish, and was adopted by him; not unexpectedly Boone seized an opportunity to make good an escape in 1778 in time to warn Kentucky stations of Indian attack. Simon Kenton in 1779 was less fortunate, undergoing some torture and being sentenced to be burned alive. Kenton was saved twice from execution, once by the intervention of a white renegade who had influence with the Indians and on another occasion by Chief Logan; sent as a prisoner to Detroit, he escaped.

Many white captives adopted by the Indians preferred, when given a choice, to remain with the Indians. A Frenchman who settled on a New York farm just before the war marveled why whites could easily adjust to Indian life and Indians "can never be prevailed on to re-adopt European manners." There must be something in Indian society, remarked J. Hector St John Crévecoeur, that was "singularly captivating, and far superior to any thing to be boasted of among us; for thousands of Europeans are Indians, and we have no examples of even one of those Aborgines having from choice become Europeans!"[51]

Benjamin Gilbert, Jr, captured by the Indians in western Pennsylvania during the war, was not an unusual adoptee. He "was considered as the King's [head of family] Successor, and entirely freed from Restraint, so that he even began to be delighted with his Manner of Life; and had it not been for the frequent Counsel of his Fellow-Captive, he would not have been anxious for a Change."[52]

By the time of the Revolution there were many members of the Indian tribes who were not full blooded Indian. French traders had mixed freely with native women, leaving mestizo offspring. There were offspring also of the white adoptees. The southern tribes attracted an assortment of whites who came to live among them: poor whites on the fringe of civilization themselves, Tories, traders, deserters, outlaws, and renegades. The Chickamauga towns had a number of black refugees, outsiders (white and Indian), and French traders. Miscegenation was so common among the Cherokees that offspring were considered a separate social group.[53] Sequoyah (b. 1770), the inventor of the Cherokee syllabary, was the son of Colonel

Nathaniel Gist, Virginia trader and Revolutionary War officer, his mother being the sister of a Cherokee chief.

Indeed white Indians and half-breeds became leaders of Indian tribes during the Revolutionary period. Blue Jacket, the great Shawnee war chief and terror of the Ohio/Kentucky frontier, was a white Virginian by the name of Marmaduke Van Swearingen, who had been captured and adopted by the Shawnees in 1771 at the age of 17. Captain Sunfish was a black Seneca chief during the war. Alexander McGillivray, who became the powerful Creek chieftan at the end of the war, was at most one-fourth Indian: his father was a Scottish trader, and his mother a half-breed Indian princess. Joseph Brant, the great Mohawk chief, claims his biographer, "had in his veins some faint strain of white blood." Chief James Colbert, who led war parties of the Chickasaws along the Mississippi and who lay siege to Fort Jefferson in 1780, was the half-breed son of a Scottish trader.[54]

Native Americans were no less vulnerable to the white man's diseases during the Revolution than before. Smallpox ravaged the Fort Niagara refugee camps in 1779–80, and swept the Great Lakes region in 1780–1. The Wyandots were reduced to only 100 warriors. The disease claimed a heavy toll among the Senecas during the winter of 1780–1, the Creeks and Cherokees in the fall 1779 and spring of 1780, and Dragging Canoe's Chickamaugas in 1778 and 1783. Colonel Daniel Brodhead, from Fort McIntosh in April 1779, wrote to Washington that the Mingoes living along the Allegheny River "are much reduced by the small pox."[55]

As Indians were established on reservations and defeated warriors returned to a peaceful society, the problems with the abuse of alcohol became pronounced. The appetite for liquor had always been extraordinary among the Indians since the early European contact. Liquor was a staple in the Indian trade. With the coming of peace, internal aggression sublimated external aggression, as if to make war on one's own body. A traveler in 1784 noticed among the Catawbas "an universal inebriation constantly occasions a most dreadful carnage."[56] Mary Jemison, the white Seneca woman, after the war lost three sons to drunken brawls. Lieutenant John Enys, serving at Fort Niagara, pitied the exiled Indians for their alcoholism. Enys commented on Sayenqueraghta, once an influential Seneca chief: "He is a sensible old man and has been a very good Warrior in his day but like all the rest is very much addicted to Liquor, for no sooner was the council over than his Majesty was dead drunk rolling in an Outhouse amongst Indians, Squaws, Pigs, Dogs."[57]

A Conquered People

In August 1783, delegates from 35 tribes, representing Indians of the Ohio/ Illinois country, the Six Nations, and even Creeks and Cherokees from the

South, met at Sandusky and agreed at long last to establish an Indian con-federacy, pledged to keep "all invaders" out of their territories.[58] The In-dian leaders, expecting the continued support from the British in Canada, were confident for the future. Then, two months later, came news of the signing of the Treaty of Paris, ending the Revolutionary War. There was no mention in the treaty of the Indians. Technically, the Indians were still at war with the United States.

The Indians outside of states' bounds were to be treated as a con-quered people, having no rights the American government was bound to protect and certainly possessing no title to the western lands reaching to the Mississippi. The United States claimed full jurisdiction over the Indians on the public domain by transfer of sovereignty over the Indians from the British by virtue of the treaty and by the right of conquest.

Congress took charge of the national domain, which widened as states ceded western lands to the Confederation government. The Articles of Confederation gave Congress the "sole and exclusive right and power" of "regulating the trade and managing all affairs with the Indians." Congress was determined to open western lands for settlement, but only through an orderly process after land cessions by Indians, surveys, and sale. Congress decided it was cheaper and easier to deal with the Indians as foreign nations rather than as wards of the state. Thus the Northwest Ordinance of 1787 stated that "the utmost good faith shall always be observed towards the Indians; their lands and property shall never be taken from them without their consent."[59] The government, if need be, could always fall back on the right of conquest.

Significant land cessions were made by the Indians at the war's end and also a few years later. Most of the lands of the Cherokees within North Carolina were surrendered, and the Creeks also gave up a large portion of land in Georgia.[60] By the Treaty of Hopewell, November 28, 1785 the Cherokees, Chickasaws, and Choctaws recognized protection from the United States. The Cherokees gained status as a domestic dependent nation.[61]

By treaties of 1784–6 Iroquois and Ohio Indians ceded lands in present-day Ohio. Ohio country Indian leaders repudiated the treaties made on their behalf as fraudulent. Encouraged by the British retention of western posts that were supposed to have been turned over to the United States by the Treaty of Paris, delegates of the northwestern tribes met together in late 1786 and declared the American–Indian treaties void and that the Indians would act in concert as the "United Indian Nations." The Indians insisted on the Ohio River as the southern boundary of Indian territory. Supplied with British arms, several tribes mounted hostilities on settlers coming into the Ohio country by land or by boat down the Ohio River. From 1783–90, over 1,500 white pioneers were killed. Congress could only send about 700 troops, scattered among several military posts on the Ohio, to defend settlers as well as keep the white newcomers out of restricted public lands.[62]

By treaties concluded with the Iroquois and Ohio Indians at Fort Harmar in 1789, the United States renounced the principle of right of conquest, and Indians were compensated for lands ceded in the Ohio country during the 1780s; the Fort Harmar treaties confirmed the earlier cessions. If the use of right of conquest—a principle asserted by the American victory in the Revolutionary War—was to be avoided in obtaining Indian lands, it still formed a pervasive backdrop in United States–Indian negotiations, a principle that could be reinstated at any time. The United States, far into the nineteenth century, continued to acquire Indian lands by actual conquest, particularly from the Plains Indians. The hypocrisy finally ended in 1871, when Congress ordered the termination of treaty-making; all Indians became essentially wards of the state.[63]

By whatever means necessary whites divested Indians of their tribal lands. Henry Knox, the War Department head under the Confederation and the Constitution, pleaded for fair treatment of the Indians, as did other national leaders, but rhetoric and reality did not match. Knox in 1789 lamented:

> It is however painful to consider that all the Indian tribes once existing in those States, now the best cultivated and most populous, have become extinct. If the same causes continue, the same effects will happen, and in a short period the Idea of an Indian on this side the Mississippi will only be found in the pages of the historian.[64]

Henry Knox's foreboding was right on the mark. By slightly more than a generation later all the Indians who had figured in the American Revolution other than those who went to Canada had been relocated to west of the Mississippi River, except for a very few staying behind on small reservations.

CHAPTER FOURTEEN

Status and mobility

War leaves an imprint on the lives of a people who themselves sanction the contest and expect to redress wrongs and achieve certain goals. That the war aimed primarily to secure freedom from interference by an outside power, however, limited its social impact; the emphasis was governmental change, although the concern of who should rule at home suggested that inevitably there might be realization of a more deep-rooted democratic society. The conservatism of the event itself precluded any dramatic and immediate social upheaval. A slow maturing process had brought on independence. As Richard B. Morris has written, "the most remarkable fact about the American Revolution was not that there was social change, but that it was relatively so modest."[1]

Unquestionably, the American Revolution set in motion, in the long run, trends that would lead to substantial social and political reform. In the short run, during the Revolution itself, persons were affected in different ways, some finding liberation and success, while others, such as the loyalists, many of whom lost property and went into exile, left a socioeconomic vacuum to be filled through the endeavors of others. The disjunctive home front experiences, of liberty being extended and denied and patriotism versus greed underscored a desire to fashion a stable and virtuous society.

Wealth-holding Trends

Wartime opens ways for profit-making, such as taking advantage of new avenues of trade, privateering, procuring supplies for the military forces, developing war-related industries, manipulating markets, and speculating in land and government securities. Those merchants and investors reluctant to assume great risks found it difficult to get ahead. James Allen, a Philadelphia lawyer, in 1788, complained: "The estates of those who are not in business, are crumbling to pieces, by the general confusion of property, and enormous prices of everything."[2] At the same time, Samuel Adams from Boston similarly assessed the situation:

> The Spirit of Avarice prevails too much in this Town; but it rages only among the few, because perhaps, the few only are concernd at present in trade. The old substantial Merchants have generally laid aside trade & left it to Strangers or those who from nothing have raisd fortunes by privateering.[3]

Parvenus were encroaching upon the old-wealth establishments. James Bowdoin of Boston, writing in November 1783 to a former royal governor of Massachusetts who was about to return to America for a visit, advised that "when you come you will scarcely see any other than new faces." The change "has happened within the few years since the revolution itself. It seems to have anticipated the time when 'all old things shall be done away and all things become new.'"[4] James Warren of Boston complained in 1779 that "I am stil drudging at the Navy Board for a morsel of Bread, while others, and among them fellows who would have cleaned my shoes five years ago, have amassed fortunes, and are riding in chariots."[5]

While new fortunes were made in trade and commerce, merchant communities were unstable and in a state of flux. At the end of the 1780s one-half of the merchants in Boston, New York City, and Philadelphia were self-made men, many of whom obtained their wealth during the war or its immediate aftermath.[6] Despite success for some, because of war-related difficulties and intense competition, many merchants ceased business operations; bankruptcies were prevalent. Small family firms in particular could not keep up with the risk-taking in large-scale commerce, lacking capital to cover even minimum losses.

The number of merchants in urban ports, however, increased during the war. Boston had a great influx of new merchants, 63 percent of the total in 1771–80 and 46 percent in 1784. The number of merchants in Boston reached 480 by 1780, which by the mid-1780s declined to 350. Philadelphia had at least 60 percent more merchants just after the war than before. At the war's end foreign merchants flocked to American ports. One in five merchants in Philadelphia were from Europe—England, Holland, France, Germany, Denmark, and Italy. Many English firms were shipping on their own accounts, with young partners or agents in America, thereby avoiding American middlemen. The glut of imports from England and Europe at the war's end led to overstocked inventories that could not be moved. Boom turned into bust at the port cities. Thus many American merchants were forced into different occupations. In Philadelphia the number of merchants shrank by 14 percent during 1785–9.[7]

Yet great fortunes were amassed during the war. Generally merchants received 2.5–5 percent commissions from either a state or Congress for army supply contracts. Stephen Higginson and the Cabots of Boston and John Landon of Portsmouth, New Hampshire were among the most successful in privateer ventures.[8] To cite but one of numerous other examples, Samuel Smith of Maryland invested in many of the 248 privateers that sailed from Baltimore in 1778–83. Smith received letters of marque and reprisal from both the federal and state governments. In addition, Smith augmented his fortune by land speculation, including the purchase and sale of loyalist property, and by provisioning military forces.[9]

Despite the fluctuations within their own ranks, urban merchants during the war increased their share of wealth in their communities. As John W. Tyler has shown, the mean real estate assessment for merchants in 1771 was £14.5; in 1780, £145.8; and in 1784, £250.9 versus £85.6 for the general population.[10] The trend in expanded wealth for the upper classes in Boston is shown by Alan Kulikoff from the tax rolls of 1771 and 1790: the bottom 30 percent of taxpayers held 0.1 percent of the wealth in 1771 and 0.03 percent in 1790; the low middle group (30 percent of the population), 9.43 and 4.80 percent; the upper-middle group (30 percent of the population), 27.01 and 30.47 percent; and those at the top (10 percent of the population) had an increase from 63.46 to 64.70 percent share of the wealth.[11] A similar gap was noted for Chester County, Pennsylvania for the period 1760–82. The share of the wealth dropped for 90 percent of the population while it increased for the top 10 percent: the lower group (30 percent of the population), in 1760, 6.3 percent of the wealth and in 1782, 4.7 percent; the lower middle group (30 percent), 17.3 to 13.7 percent; the upper middle group (30 percent), 44.5 to 44.2 percent; and the upper group (10 percent), 33.6 to 38.3 percent.[12]

While the war encouraged domestic industry, according to one study, the "net effect of war was a sharp decline in individual income."[13] On the other hand, a merchant in Massachusetts reported in April 1777 that "there is hardly a town that has not more ratable polls" than when the war began.[14] Although caught in price and money squeezes and market manipulation, northern farmers generally held their own during the war. But debts mounted, and, without relief from the legislatures, a mood of insurgency among small farmers emerged after the war.

During the boom and bust period of 1783–5 farmers, merchants, and planters found themselves in difficult times. Many had over purchased, and prices for their goods plummeted. Joseph Hadfield, an English traveler in New England in 1785, commented on the "most horrid" and "distressing situation:" the "low state of public and private credit, owing to the numbers of failures which daily take place . . . their fisheries being almost at a stand, money very scarce, no market for their lumber of fish." Hadfield visited the Rhode Island countryside, where he found that "the peasants in general" were "miserably poor."[15]

In the deep South planters and farmers had to rebuild from the desolation of the last years of the war. In Chesapeake society there had been relief, with debts owed British creditors held in abeyance during the war. But farmers overpurchased, and a debt problem returned. Thomas Jefferson commented, "how happy a people were we during the War from the single circumstance that we could not run in debt." All that was changing at the war's end, with persons avoiding "one act of self denial, to put off buying anything till he has money to pay for it."[16]

Virginia merchants experienced setbacks during the war, hampered by interruptions of commerce, low tobacco prices, and interloping activities of northern merchants. Charles Yates, a merchant-planter near Fredericksburg, in 1778 announced that he was "No longer a Merchant but a Farmer," and like other Virginians converted to raising non-commercial crops.[17] The mercantile firm of John Banks and Company of Richmond, Virginia went bankrupt at the end of the war, having failed in speculative schemes involving the provisioning of the Southern army.[18] "The void left by the withdrawal of British merchants," writes Bruce A. Ragsdale, "was filled more frequently by traders from Philadelphia or other ports to the north than by resident Virginia merchants."[19] The Virginia congressional delegates in August 1782 wrote to Governor Benjamin Harrison that "the Balance of trade is so much against Virginia" with Philadelphia "that on every application for money on a Draught we are answerd 'we want no draught on Virginia we want money from thence.'"[20]

Virginia planters had to endure a declining price for tobacco. In France, which was the major market for American tobacco because the war had excluded the British, the Farmers General, a banking syndicate under the strict control of the government, had a monopoly on the importation of tobacco. The company forced the price of tobacco so low that in 1783 only 3,000 hogsheads of tobacco were exported to France.[21] The war certainly did not enrich Virginia planters.

Artisans and Bound Labor

American labor had an awakening experience during the Revolutionary era. Master workers, along with a large number of their journeymen, assumed a radical role in protest actions that put the colonists on the road to rebellion. Being involved with the Sons of Liberty, workers learned tactics of collective action and militancy. By serving on the committees of correspondence and the extra-legal committees of safety and provincial assemblies they acquired organizational techniques. Importantly, too, artisans rejected the inferior status that had been conferred upon them by the elite of society.[22]

During the war workers further developed into a conscious constituency, demanding equal opportunity and rights. Increasingly artisans identified with merchants and sought to avoid the restraints of responsibility for the welfare of journeymen and apprentices. As Sharon V. Salinger notes, regarding Philadelphia: "Master craftsmen donned their leather aprons and picked up their tools less often. Instead, they became primarily employers and merchant capitalists."[23]

Contracts between master craftsmen and their journeymen and apprentices were amended, making for a more cash-wage system. Whereas master craftsmen had contracted with apprentices to provide keep, clothing, and education, now the obligations were cast in money values. Journeymen were expected to move out of the master's household and provide their own room and board; they began to change jobs frequently. Several factors contributed to these labor trends. The wartime conditions placed a premium on quantity rather than quality. Master craftsmen branched out into wider retail activity. Some shops became small factories, requiring less skilled labor, and, especially in textiles, employers depended increasingly on employees who were women and the poor.[24]

The traffic in indentured servants ceased during the war, and afterwards the rate of bound immigrants arriving in the United States was one half to two-thirds of that just before the war.[25] The continued commercialization of labor relations and the entry into the labor force of servants who had completed the terms of their indentures led to less demand for white bound labor. The enlistment of many servants into the armed forces, whereupon they gained their freedom, was a factor in the reduction of the number of indentured persons during the war.

In the South indentured servants were being replaced by slaves. "The war forced a fundamental reorientation in Baltimore's workforce," writes Tina H. Sheller, "by eliminating white servants from the town's labor market." With so many white servants going into the Continental army, master craftsmen replaced them with slaves. The number of slaves at a Baltimore shipbuilding site rose from 65 in 1776 to 276 in 1783.[26]

Artisans became less likely to be servant owners. In 1775 in Philadelphia 40 percent of artisans employed indentured servants; in 1789, only 20 percent. Merchants, however, purchased more servants. The demand for contract labor as domestic servants increased just after the war.[27] Regulations concerning duties and privileges of indentured servants did not change materially during or after the war. Most states, however, at the urging of Congress, prohibited the entry of convict servants.[28] An interesting development in Pennsylvania was the anti-slave law of 1780, which offered black slaves born after the passage of the act indentured status as the first step to freedom.[29]

After the war, most servants arriving in America came from Germany and Ireland. The shift from England as a source was owing in part to parliament's laws prohibiting the emigration of skilled workers as well as the transportation on English ships of servants bound because of debt.[30] George Washington, in 1783–4, was on the lookout for two "redemptioners, or Indented (Germans or Irish)," who would serve as "a House joiner and Bricklayer." Having difficulty in procuring such workers, Washington wrote to his business agent and former aide-de-camp, Tench Tilghman, that the servants need not be "Palatines." If "they are good workmen, they may be of Asia, Africa, or Europe. They may be Mahometans, Jews, or Christian of any Sect—or they may be Athiests." Washington preferred the servants to be middle-aged.[31]

There was a growing feeling that holding white persons in bondage, even for a short while, contradicted the virtuous ideals of the new Republic. A meeting of New York citizens in January 1784 called for the end of "traffic in white people" because this practice did not comport with "the idea of liberty this country has so happily established."[32]

Although the servant trade revived in the 1780s (for example, 25,000 redemptioners and indentured servants arrived in Pennsylvania during 1783–9), it continued to dwindle. A sluggish American economy probably had some effect in discouraging servant immigration. Eventually, when the economy greatly picked up, ocean fares were drastically reduced, allowing persons to come to America without having to enter indentured contracts.[33]

Occupational Mobility

The Revolutionary War stimulated occupational mobility. Vertically, persons moved upward and downward on the fortune-making scale. In complementary mobility, businessmen, craftsmen, planters, and farmers branched out to take advantage of supplying war needs. Horizontally, migrants sought out new opportunities at different geographical locations.

Upward mobility, of persons rising from humble origins to affluence and influence, is a characteristic story in the making of early America. During the war artisans, grocers, mariners, and shopkeepers entered the wholesale business and also expanded their retailing by buying and selling large quantities of domestic and imported goods.[34]

A sure way to get rich was to conduct transactions backed by public funds and to have the government as the primary customer. Robert Morris became the prince of high finance in public–private dealings. Already wealthy by the time of the Revolution as a partner in a Philadelphia mercantile firm, Morris greatly added to his fortune during the war. From the vantage point of being a member of Congress and also successively as a member of Congress's Secret Committee of Correspondence, Secret Committee on

Trade, and Marine Committee, and finally as the Confederation's Superintendent of Finances, Morris constructed an extensive network in commodity trading with Europe and the West Indies. He had a sharp advantage over other American merchants: being privy to inside information, using public funds in arranging financial contacts, and presiding over large sales to the United States government. Persons employed by Morris for public purchasing were also used by him for his private transactions. William Bingham, also a Philadelphia merchant and an agent for Morris in the West Indies during the war, achieved a great fortune.[35] Unlike Morris, who would eventually be financially ruined, Bingham had continued success in commercial enterprise and large-scale land speculation after the war, becoming America's first millionaire.

The case of Paul Revere best serves as a single example of how a craftsman branched out during the war and postwar years. Revere ran Boston's premier silversmith shop left to him by his father, even while he was in military service off and on during 1776–9. Revere manufactured paper money for the Massachusetts government and the Continental Congress, and also produced coins, medals, and the first seals of the state of Massachusetts and the United States. He opened a hardware store in 1783, and a few years later established an iron and brass foundry in Boston where he produced cannon for the state and federal governments and other items such as nails and bolts. Later he established the first large-scale bell-manufactory in America, and still later, founded a copper-rolling and brass-casting mill at Canton, Massachusetts that became, and still is even today, one of American's pre-eminent manufacturing concerns.

The examples of persons establishing plants to produce war materiel, gristmills, distilleries, and the like to serve the war effort are legion. Major-General Adam Stephen established a gunworks on his northwestern Virginia plantation. Other military officers profited from the war. Of course there were staff officers such as Joseph Trumbull (1737–78). A partner in one of the largest merchant firms in Connecticut, Trumbull served as Commissary-General of Stores and Provisions for Connecticut, obtaining army provisions on a commission basis, and then in the same capacity as Commissary-General for the Continental army. Trumbull provisioned the army at its encampments, army hospitals, and Continental navy vessels. There was the widespread belief that staff officers were acquiring "the fortunes of Nabobs and Sultans" through their generous commissions and conflict-of-interest dealings.[36]

General Nathanael Greene had his hand in various ventures, mostly war related. From the commissions he received while quartermaster-general, Greene invested in shipping, privateering, land speculation, manufacturing, and provisioning the army. He was a partner in Barnabas Deane and Company, which supplied the army with food and clothing and had its own distillery. Greene joined with two assistant quartermaster-generals,

Colonels John Cox and Charles Pettit, whose investments included shares in the ironworks at Batsto, New Jersey.[37] Greene was a silent partner in John Banks and Company, which provided supplies for Greene's Southern army and raked in a hefty commission of 11–13 percent. When word leaked out of the Greene–Banks connection, Greene's reputation was significantly tarnished. Unfortunately Banks and Company went bankrupt, and Greene, who had endorsed notes for the firm, lost most of his own fortune.[38]

Besides pursuing wealth opportunities in the war economy, Americans were very much on the move. Tens of thousands of soldiers and military civilian personnel left their homes and even states for service. Trends carried over from the colonial period. Population expansion, at the rate of one-third increase each decade, and the lure of fresh lands were major causes for mobility. About 15 percent of the rural population moved each decade of the Revolutionary era.[39]

There was a heavy localized mobility. In Massachusetts only 2 percent of transients came from outside the state. At Boston and Salem, one half of arrivals journeyed from locations within a ten-mile radius. Many were ex-servants. Artisans went to the cities for better job opportunities, while at the same time unskilled workers were "pushed out."[40] One county grand jury in South Carolina, requesting a new vagrancy law in 1785, observed that numerous "strolling persons" were "allowed to pass unnoticed often to the great injury of the peaceable inhabitants."[41]

Americans from all directions moved to frontier regions. New Englanders went northeastward into Maine and also along the Connecticut and Housatonic rivers into the territory that would become Vermont, which by 1776 already had 20,000 immigrants.[42]

Pioneers sifted down from Virginia, Maryland, and Pennsylvania and into the Carolinas and Georgia. Before the war many foreign immigrants had entered the Deep South. Of Charleston's Revolutionary leaders, only one half were native born. After the war more newcomers to South Carolina were American. English and Scottish immigration, which had been 30 percent of the total before the war, was only 5 percent during the several decades following the war. The foreign immigrants during the latter period were more likely to be from France, Ireland, and Germany rather than from England and Scotland.[43]

At the war's end, migration southward from the Chesapeake area and Pennsylvania became a heavy stream. Many veterans relocated in the Carolinas and Georgia. William Murrell, a storekeeper at Camden, South Carolina recorded in his account ledgers for 1792 the names of 83 persons, 48 of whom were listed as being South Carolinians and 33 from Virginia, Maryland, and Pennsylvania. In Savannah, Georgia cricket matches had teams divided between natives and newcomers.[44]

Settlement of the trans-Appalachian west began during the war years, and immigration to the land of the "Western Waters" reached floodtide immediately after the Revolution. By January 1780 only 300 pioneers lived in Kentucky. In November of that year the Virginia government divided Kentucky into three counties—Fayette, Lincoln, and Jefferson. A steady flow of immigrants into Kentucky started in 1781; by 1784 the region had 30,000 settlers, and four years later, 62,000. Many Virginia state military warrants were exchanged for land in Kentucky, particularly south of the Green River.[45] During 1779–80 Colonel John Donelson and James Robertson led a party in founding settlements at the big bend of the Cumberland River in middle Tennessee.[46]

A study of 13,500 Revolutionary War veterans who sought pensions in their old age shows that more than one half (54 percent) moved out of the state in which they had lived at the beginning of the war. Non-veterans in New Jersey had about the same rate of outmigration.[47]

Social Standing and Style

The American Revolution made for a blurring of the manifestations of class distinctiveness. During the colonial period deferential behavior, forms of address, kinds of clothing, displays of conspicuous wealth, and affected mannerisms clearly set apart the upper classes from the "lower sort." A new republican society afforded persons at different levels of the social strata to engage in similar pretensions.

Devereux Jarratt, the famous Methodist preacher who grew up near Richmond, Virginia, noticed the change as to deference. His father was a carpenter. "None of my ancestors, on either side, were either rich or great, but had the character of honesty and industry, by which they lived in credit among their neighbors." Still, he recalled that as a youngster

> we were accustomed to look upon, what were called *gentle folks*, as beings of a superior order. For my part, I was quite shy of *them*, and kept off at a humble distance. A *periwig*, in those days, was a distinguishing badge of *gentle folk*—and when I saw a man riding the road, near our house, with a wig on, it would so alarm my fears, and give me such a disagreeable feeling, that, I dare say, I would run off, as for my life. Such ideas of the difference between *gentle* and *simple*, were I believe, universal among all of my rank and age. But I have lived to see, a vast alteration, in this respect, and the contrary extreme prevail. In our high *republican times*, there is more *levelling* than ought to be, consistent with good government.[48]

A British lieutenant, who was a prisoner of war with the captured British army (from the battle of Saratoga) interned near Charlottesville, Virginia had the same impressions as did Jarratt. Lieutenant Thomas Anburey noted that "before the war, the spirit of equality or levelling principle was not so prevalent in Virginia, as in the other provinces . . . but since the war, that principle seems to have gained great ground in Virginia." Anburey and other British captive officers were given the freedom to travel in central Virginia. Visiting Colonel Thomas Mann Randolph's "Tuckahoe" plantation in Goochland County in April 1779, Anburey was shocked at the indiscretions of "three country peasants" who called upon Randolph regarding the use of his mill. They "entered the room where the Colonel and his company were sitting, took themselves chairs, drew near the fire, began spitting, pulling off their country boots, all over mud . . ." After the farmers departed, "some one observed what great liberties they took." Colonel Randolph replied that "it was unavoidable, the spirit of independence was converted into equality, and every one who bore arms, esteemed himself upon a footing with his neighbor, and concluded with saying, 'No doubt, each of these men conceives himself, in every respect, my equal.'"[49]

Anburey also related an incident which showed "the ferociousness of the lower class." While at a tavern in Richmond, which although soon to be the state capital, resembled a raw frontier community, Dr William Foushee, a physician and the town's mayor, found himself in an argument over a game of billiards with a local ruffian, who gouged the mayor's "eye out of the socket, and while it hung upon his cheek, the fellow was barbarous enough to pluck it entirely out, but was prevented." Foushee's eye was refitted, but it is not known whether he recovered sight.[50]

If acts of violence between persons of different social standing were indeed rare exceptions, the "idea of equality" was evident in more subtle ways. A French traveler, shortly after the war, commented that

> a member of Congress sits side by side with the shoemaker who elected him and fraternizes with him; they talk together on familiar terms. None puts on important airs as people do only too frequently in France, [where] a person condemned to travel in a wretched *turgotine* [public stagecoach] is humiliated by the sight of a private carriage . . . It is therefore fortunate for America that the nature of things here prevents the use of private carriages as marks of social distinction.[51]

Robert Hunter, Jr, a young London merchant traveling in America, in October 1785 attended a ball in New Haven, Connecticut where the 170 assemblers "looked more like a parcel of farmers at a country turnpike meeting in England than anything else. Their chief and principal action in speaking was scratching their head all the time, like the cartmen with us when they address a gentleman."[52]

Yet there survived a certain respect for a natural aristocracy. John Adams, surveying Massachusetts society in 1787, said that there were persons of old established families of wealth who inspired "a degree of admiration" and respect which "bestows some influence." Such persons received a kind of deference "abstracted from all dependence, obligation, expectation, or even acquaintance."[53]

The war years brought about a sense of inclusiveness in society at large. Patriotism, the rising awareness of national identity, and the participation of persons from all walks of life in the winning war effort instilled pride of being American. Artisans gained universal respect, having a claim to equality and honor as any other citizen. Although there was still a semblance of hierarchy among persons of different trades and professions,[54] it was generally accepted that each person had an esteemed place in the new social order. The parades in the major cities celebrating the ratification of the Constitution, five years after the end of the war, underscored the social transformation. In each of the processions, farmers and all of the various kinds of tradesmen were amply represented. The Boston parade had 1,500 participants, who were joined on the march by 3,000 spectators. Five thousand persons marched in Philadelphia; 3,000 in Baltimore; and 2,800 in Charleston. New York City also held a comprehensive spectacle.[55] Ironically, common laborers were excluded from the processions.

Residential patterns helped to shape class status in the urban areas. In Philadelphia, the one-tenth of the population who were "criminals, alcoholics, vagrants, prostitutes, transients, escaped servants and slaves, the insane and incapacitated, and men, women, and children who were generally down and out" could be found in the neighborhood north of Arch Street between the Delaware River and Third Street. Mariners and laborers lived in the northern, southern, and western sections of the city. The wealthiest group resided in the area of east High Street near the Delaware River. By the end of the century, the configuration of Philadelphia was a series of "concentric rings radiating from a nucleus of wealthy people through bands of successively poorer ones."[56]

Specific forms of address for persons declined. Appellations, such as Esquire (more often reserved for justices of the peace) and Gentleman (upper gentry and wealthy merchants) now had a generic rather than a class meaning. The idea of being a gentleman related to the qualities of one's character—grace, dignity, courtesy, and willingness to accept social and political responsibility—rather than one's station. Generally, in the republican society, the single distinction was between gentlemen and ordinary people.

Benjamin Rush sized up a typical elite in a letter of April 1784 to Charles Nisbet, who had just been elected first president of Dickinson College. "The inhabitants of the town of Carlisle [Pennsylvania]," said Rush, "are in general an orderly people. Two or three general officers, who have served with reputation in our army, four or five lawyers, a regular-bred physician, and a few gentlemen in trade of general knowledge and of fair characters compose the society of the town."[57]

The war, however, did encourage one form of social address: the recognition of officer veterans by their rank. A story is told of an encounter of Brigadier-General Charles Scott of Virginia, who settled in Kentucky after the war. Scott, who later became the governor of Kentucky, had a reputation for heavy drinking. One day while Scott was in a log tavern, "a tolerably well dressed Stranger" from New England appeared and asked for a half pint of whiskey. The proprietor told him that he could not purchase whiskey in such small quantities.

> "Stranger I will join you and pay half," intervened Scott. "Therefore landlord give us a pint of your best." The whiskey was brought, and Scott, who drank first, addressed the stranger: "Colonel, your good health."
> "I am no Colonel," replied the stranger.
> "Well then," said Scott, "Major, your good health."
> "I am no Major," replied the New Englander.
> "Then your good health, Captain."
> "I am no Captain, Sir," said the stranger, "and what is more, never held a commission in my life."
> Amused, Scott explained, "Well then by heavens, you are the first man in Kentucky that ever wore a cloth coat and was not a commissioned officer."[58]

In contrast to the colonial period, the Revolutionary era ushered in a liberation from dress codes; no longer were persons required to attire themselves according to their station in society.

The spirit of sacrifice—the avoidance of carefree, luxurious, and ostentatious living mandated by government at the beginning of the war—soon wore off. Fashion was one way a person could enhance his or her persona. A man of small means, if he wished, could act the part of a dandy. In Boston it was difficult to tell "by their dress a lady worth 100 pounds from one worth 10,000," and the "spirit of dress and show" among "shopboys" made it hard to discern them from "the first merchants of the city."[59] Samuel Adams complained of the "superfluity of Dress and Ornament when it is as much as they can bear to support the Expenses of cloathing a naked army."[60]

Francisco de Miranda, who became the famous Venezuelan revolutionist, when visiting Boston in September 1784 was struck that "Extravagance, ostentation, and a bit of vanity are the predominant features" among the wealthy. "A young man who, ten years ago, wore silk stockings and satin breeches or powdered his hair needed nothing more to ruin his character forever; today, not only do they wear all of this, but they wear it even when booted and riding horseback. The women, as follows: silks, ribbons, muslins, pomades and perfumes every day."[61] In Philadelphia, to one observer it seemed that "every lady and gentleman endeavors to outdo the others in splendor and show."[62]

For a while the fashions of the colonial period characterizing gentlemen continued: the white linen shirt, short waistcoat, cut-away frock coat, white silk stockings, knee breeches, large shoebuckles, and wearing wigs or hair powdered and pulled back and tied with a ribbon. Paul Revere, who despite all his success as a craftsman and industrialist was never accepted in Boston's high society, eventually attired himself in a gentleman's finery. Revere persisted in donning such upper-class apparel the rest of his life (d. 1818), long after the style had faded, and became dubbed "one of the last of the Cocked Hats."

While gentlemen began to discard the wig, pigeon wing, and comet and adopt the tonsorial style of ancient Romans, cropping their hair "à la Brutus" or "à la Titus," some fashionable women went to an absurd extreme. During the war the "Dress à l'Independence," which had 13 curls at the neck to symbolize the 13 states, was popular. About 1780 some women began to wear their hair in a style resembling a beehive. The hair was teased out as far as it would go and then wrapped around a wire dome on the top of the head; puff, braids, and pieces of false hair were added to provide fullness. Then the whole contraption was coated with grease or curdled cream and white powder (flour, cornstarch, or Plaster of Paris). The hairdo soon turned into a horrible environment: the cream soured, and lice, spiders, and fungal scalp infections found a habitat. To prevent disturbing the hairdo, women slept half-sitting. In order to scratch an infected scalp one had to slice through the whole concoction. The fad lasted a generation, by which time middle-class women were also adopting the style.[63]

Lucy Knox, the amiable 240-pound wife of General Henry Knox, who was Secretary at War under the Confederation, prided herself as a fashion-setter. At a banquet in the capital, New York City, in 1787 she sported a "military" coiffure, which did not favorably impress the guests, at least not Reverend Manasseh Cutler:

> Mrs. Knox is very gross, but her manners easy and graceful. She is sociable, and would be very agreeable, were it not for her affected singularity in dressing her hair. She seems to mimic a military style, which to me is disgusting in a female. Her hair in front is craped at least a foot high, much in the form of a churn bottom upward, and topped off with a wire skeleton in the same form covered with black gauze, which hangs in streamers down to her back. Her hair behind is in a large braid, turned up, and confined with a monstrous large crooked comb. She reminded me of the monstrous cap worn by the Marquis La Fayette's valet—commonly called, on this account, the Marquis' *Devil*.[64]

223

Republican Society

Independence achieved by a people under arms throwing off tyrannical rule cleared the way for creating a social philosophy that extolled liberty and equality and called upon citizens to exercise their responsibilities in defending and promoting the *res publica*. As J. Hector St John Crèvecouer had pointed out, Americans could act upon new principles, and, in the words of Alexis de Tocqueville, could engage in "the great experiment" in an "attempt to construct society upon a new basis."[65]

Americans were fighting not only to reclaim liberty that had been usurped by unbridled power but also to reinforce liberty in the context of an upright and just society. Benjamin Rush declared in May 1776 that "I often anticipate the joy with which we shall welcome the establishment of liberty and the return of peace to our country—when freedom shall prevail without licentiousness, government without tyranny, and religion without superstition, bigotry, or enthusiasm."[66]

The revolutionaries wanted to obliterate pretension and exploitation in society and instill in the hearts of all a love of public virtue. Society among white persons was to consist of equals. It was an equality "not of status or origin, but of opportunity, of moral and political rights," writes Adrienne Koch.[67] Although "equality would underpin both social harmony and public virtue," notes Michael Kammen, there was a problem with the "inherent dualism" contained in the idea of equality. "For some it meant equality of opportunity, which therefore implied the existence of social distinctions. To others, however, it meant equality of condition, thereby repudiating social differences."[68] Furthermore, the republican tenets of upholding equality and of protection of acquisition of property could also be in conflict with each other.

Still, the republican agenda strove toward removing artificial distinctions derived from heredity and special preferment. Liberty would have a collective context, with the goals of social unity and harmony. Such an idealized scheme as envisioned during the war and afterwards could not match realities, as patriot leaders only too soon discovered. But to one Frenchman, himself "a refugee from despotism," visiting in Boston in 1788, the Americans were coming close to accomplishing the perfect society. Observed Brissot de Warville: "How I enjoyed watching the shopkeepers, the workmen, and the seamen at their varied tasks." The "people did not have the tense, harried look of the French, that intense preoccupation with pleasure, nor did they display the towering pride of the English. They had instead the simple and kindly but dignified look of men who are conscious of their liberty and to whom all other men are merely brothers and equals."[69]

Patriotic sentiment expressed the idea of making over society into a more pristine community. The Reverend Samuel Williams in a sermon, "A

Discourse on the Love of Our Country," presented at the First Church of Boston on the eve of the war, asked his congregation to

> show our love to our country, in every way in which we can promote its good, [namely] to inculcate that public and private virtue which is agreeable to the laws of God, and adapted to promote the interest and welfare of mankind. . . . Love to our country supposes that there is a proper community, public society formed.[70]

Victory confirmed the moral character of the patriots. No one denied, however, the corruption, greed, and manipulation for selfish purposes that had ensued during the war. Indeed public virtue, the true mainstay of a republic, was in danger of being lost if the country slipped into anarchy or rule by an oligarchy of the wealthy and powerful.

The military forces during the war had brought discipline to certain segments of society. Was a standing army necessary to protect citizens's rights and republican institutions and to thwart insurrection and invasion? On the other hand, would a peacetime standing army, given the experiences of history, be the very bane of a free society?

George Washington and other "nationalists" firmly believed in keeping a respectable army. In a proposal, "Sentiments on a Peace Establishment," he sent to Congress in April 1783, Washington declared "altho' a *large* standing Army in time of Peace hath ever been considered dangerous to the liberties of a Country, yet a few Troops, under circumstances, are not only safe, but indispensably necessary. Fortunately for us our relative situation requires but few." Congress shelved Washington's plan. The soon to be retired commander-in-chief had recommended maintaining an army of 2,631 soldiers (to be stationed at West Point and on the northern, western, and southern frontiers) and a national militia system which would enroll all males of ages 18–55, of whom those between 18 and 25 years old would submit to training.[71]

The Continental army, longtime idled by 1783, exhibited a restlessness that might prove dangerous to the Republic. Some Americans were disturbed by the "pretensions of many officers to superior social status and patriotism."[72] The officers at their winter cantonment at Newburgh, New York, 1782–3, disgusted that Congress had not fulfilled its promise to grant them a pension of one-half pay for life, dispatched a committee to Congress to demand redress, and an effort appeared at camp to take firm measures to intimidate Congress. Washington, learning of the situation, magnificently, in convening the officers together, succeeded in defusing the unrest. Congress immediately provided a commutation pension award, conferring on the officers a lump sum equal to five years' pay and on enlisted men four months' wages. On June 20, 1783, 80 troops of the Pennsylvania line from Lancaster headed for Philadelphia and joining 300 soldiers barracked there marched on the state house and briefly held Congress hostage. Congress fled, and reconvened at Princeton.[73]

Thus, along with vivid memories of the mutinies of 1781, Congress was in no mood to keep a sizeable army in peacetime. The common soldiers were permitted to go home on furloughs, and officers soon resigned. At the end of 1783 a few hundred troops stationed at West Point were all that remained of the Continental army. Congress, the next year, confronted with the Indian–settler problems in the northwest, authorized the creation of the American Regiment of 700 militia drawn from several states to be the sole landed military force of the Confederation.

If the Continental army had forfeited much of the public's respect during the waning years of the Revolution, it was still evident that some ample provision had to be made for protecting the new nation at its borders and from Indians on the frontier. Even later in the 1780s, during the ratification contest over the adoption of the Constitution, Anti-federalist opposers of the Constitution conceded as much, though fearing a standing army. *Brutus* (Robert Yates of New York?), writing in an Anti-federalist paper of January 17, 1788, though admitting a need for some military protection externally, expressed a fear of standing army. What worried him the most was that so many Americans believed "that no people can be kept in order, unless the government have an army to awe them into obedience." *Brutus* contended that a standing army had its own self-serving appeal. "An army will afford a decent support, and agreeable employment to the young men of many families, who are too indolent to follow occupations that will require care and industry, and too poor to live without doing any business." Prophetically *Brutus* predicted "we shall have a large standing army, as soon as the government can find money to pay them, and perhaps sooner."[74]

The Revolutionary War left a legacy of having a peacetime, professional army, although it would be many years before it became a large force. Indeed Americans in the 1780s pondered whether there was a contradiction between building a society of responsible, free individuals seeking implementation of public virtue and maintaining a standing army that might exact coercion upon the people. Could not a permanent military establishment become self-serving and a threat to liberty itself? In any case, republican society made room for a military component.

CHAPTER FIFTEEN

Liberty and fraternity

From the achievement of liberty, American revolutionaries embraced the Enlightenment ideal of the human capacity for progress in the betterment of society. Mankind could live in harmony and strive for the common good.

With the war all but over, an event occurred in Philadelphia on July 15, 1782 that symbolized republican fraternity. The French minister to the United States, Chevalier Anne-César de La Luzerne, treated citizens to a grand fete, celebrating the birth of a dauphin of France, Louis Joseph (born October 22, 1781). Such a party underscored the alliance of friendship between France and the United States. Dr Benjamin Rush attended with his wife along with a few family members and friends. He was astonished at "the harmony of the evening" from among 1,000 invited guests. Entering La Luzerene's residence (which had been rented from John Dickinson) at Sixth and Walnut streets:

> we saw the world in miniature. All the ranks and parties and pro-
> fessions in the city and all the officers of government were fully
> represented in this assembly. Here were ladies and gentlemen of
> the most ancient as well as modern families. Here were lawyers,
> doctors, and ministers of the gospel. Here were the learned faculty
> of the College, and with them many who knew not whether Cicero
> plead in Latin or in Greek, or whether Horace was a Roman or a
> Scotchman. Here were painters and musicians, poets and philos-
> ophers, and men who were never moved by beauty or harmony
> or by rhyme or reason. Here were merchants and gentlemen of
> independent fortunes, as well as many respectable and opulent
> tradesmen. Here were whigs and men who formerly bore the char-
> acter of tories. Here were the president and members of Congress,
> governors of states and generals of armies, ministers of finance and

war and foreign affairs, judges of superior and inferior courts, with all their respective suits of assistants, secretaries, and clerks. In a word, the assembly was truly republican.

Rush's other remarks illustrate the inherent shortcomings of republican-ism. Where were guests from among the great mass of Philadelphians who were not numbered among the elite?

> The doors and windows of the street which leads to the Minister's were lined with people, and near the Minister's house there was a collection of all the curious and idle men, women, and children of the city who were not invited to the entertainment, amounting, probably to ten thousand people. The Minister was not unmindful of this crowd of spectators. He had previously pulled down a board fence and put up a neat palisado fence before the dancing room and walks, on purpose to gratify them with a sight of the company and entertainment. He intended further to have distributed two pipes of Madeira wine and $600 in small change among them, but he was dissuaded from this act of generosity by some gentlemen of the city who were afraid that it might prove the occasion of a riot or some troublesome proceedings. The money devoted to this purpose was charitably distributed among the prisoners in the jails and the patients in the hospital in the city.[1]

The distinguishing feature of liberty in the United States, as Alexis de Tocqueville observed in his famous tome on American democracy, was the affinity to form association. This was commendable, for "if men are to remain civilized, or to become so, the art of associating together must grow and improve in the same ratio in which the equality of conditions is increased.[2] Social and reform-related clubs, mainly in urban areas, prolifer-ated in America during the entire eighteenth century. The Revolutionary War, however, disrupted the activity of some organizations.

While American revolutionaries, as did their European counterparts, repudiated the idea of a hierarchical-kinship society, they did hold to the broader meaning of kinship—the fraternity (or brotherhood) of mankind in the context of equal opportunity. As Wilson C. McWilliams writes, they "did not appeal to fraternity as a fact or as a method, but as an end in the relations of men; liberty and equality were only means."[3]

Freemasonry

Freemasonry in America received a significant boost during the Revolu-tionary War and from the war itself. As Americans veered away from the confines of a religious-based morality to acceptance of a world scheme of natural law and natural rights, the principles of Masonry had appeal. As J. M. Roberts writes, the rise of Masonry in England and America represented a digression "from the hope of building community on inherited subordination or confessional unity" and toward "a secular and voluntary community which would be a true community."[4] Masonry has been styled the civil religion of the American Revolution.[5]

Originating among medieval stoneworkers who built cathedrals, Freemasonry began in Great Britain in the seventeenth century, and in 1717 a Grand Lodge of England was formed from four London lodges. Freemasonry came to the colonies in 1731 with the founding of St John's Lodge in Philadelphia, under the auspices of the Grand Lodge in England. In 1733 St John's Grand Lodge was established in Boston. By 1776 there were 40 lodges in the colonies.[6]

Although some lodges had members almost exclusively from the upper classes, persons from all occupations were generally admitted. A sampling of brothers in Boston and Philadelphia just after the middle of the eighteenth century indicates that 60 percent of them were merchants; 14 percent in Boston and 21 percent in Philadelphia were professionals; 10 percent artisans; and the rest, retailers or sea captains. Most of the artisans had a close relationship with persons from the upper ranks of society or were in trades heavily capitalized.[7] Indeed, a major criticism of anti-Masonry which eventually became a powerful movement itself, was that a primary motivation for joining the order was to be in a circle of men loyal to each other, thereby affording mutual assistance for an individual's career or economic advancement. George Washington early in life realized the benefits of Masonic membership to his quest for leadership.

During the Revolutionary era there were two strains of Freemasonry in America; the older group, derived from the Grand Lodge of London, and the Ancients ("The Most Ancient and Honorable Fraternity of Free and Accepted Masons"). The latter had the greater appeal and success, contrasting with the Moderns (the older group) by excluding the "irreligious" from membership and by encouraging other than the elite of society to join. During the Revolutionary War the Ancients created 19 new lodges.[8]

The American lodges, with a few exceptions, overwhelmingly supported the Revolutionary movement and hence contributed an important unifying force. Remarkably during the war Freemasonry made extraordinary strides in the army. Fifteen thousand army personnel were members of military or nearby lodges. Forty percent of the generals were Masons.[9] The Masonic order helped to dampen contentiousness in the officer corps and also encouraged harmony between higher and lower grade officers. At least one military lodge included non-commissioned officers.[10] "Fraternal ties among the officers," comments Steven C. Bullock, "helped create and sustain the sense of common purpose necessary for the survival of the Continental army—and thus the winning of the war."[11]

Ten military (or field or traveling) lodges were organized, seven from warrants issued by the Pennsylvania Masonic order (three for Pennsylvania troops and one each for the North Carolina, Maryland, Delaware, and New Jersey lines), and the other three were authorized by the New York and two Massachusetts lodges.[12] Two of the more important military lodges, both organized in 1779, were Washington Lodge, with General John Paterson as Master, and Military Lodge No. 19, consisting of soldiers of Colonel Thomas Procter's Pennsylvania artillery regiment. Procter's group, as part of General John Sullivan's Indian expedition in 1779, conducted Masonic services for the internment of two officers killed by the Indians.[13]

It perhaps can be argued that the Masonic order, with membership from among the soldiery, especially of the officers, in both the British and American military forces, did much to mitigate brutality and excessive retaliation. Masonic officers who were made prisoners of war received extra favorable treatment, thanks to their brethren on the opposing side. Another example of extending brotherly friendship across the lines is seen regarding the death of a wounded British officer, Captain William Leslie, after the battle of Princeton in January 1777. Leslie was interred with full Masonic honors at Pluckemin, whereupon Washington through a flag of truce informed the British command of the event.[14]

George Washington, who was inducted into the Fredericksburg, Virginia lodge in 1752 and elevated to status of Master the following year, attended the celebrations of the order's two feast days (St. John the Baptist, June 24 and St. John the Evangelist, December 27) held at army encampments whenever he could. In Philadelphia in December 1778, the commander-in-chief, in full Masonic attire, headed the procession of 300 brothers in their procession to Christ Church.[15]

The American Union Lodge No. 1 was "the most single institutional vehicle for the Americanization of Masonry."[16] Formed in February 1776 when a group of mostly Connecticut officers at the American army encampment at Roxbury received a warrant from St John's Grand Lodge in Boston, the new lodge was authorized to function "wherever your Body shall remove on the Continent of America." The lodge ceased to meet in the fall of 1776 because so many members were casualties or made prisoners of war from the battle of Long Island and the attack on Ft Washington. Military operations further intervened, but on February 7, 1779 the lodge reconvened.[17]

The American Union Lodge met on December 27, 1779 at Morristown, New Jersey, with 40 members, including Washington, and 64 brethren from other military lodges attending. The group recommended an appointment of a Grand Master "in and over the thirteen United States of America." A "Convention" of delegates from all the military lodges on February 7, 1780 endorsed the idea of an American Grand Lodge and also proposed Washington as Grand Master. Approval was sought from the military and regular lodges of each state. The Massachusetts Grand Lodge, however, thwarted the implementation of the proposals because its members did not like the idea of Washington becoming the Grand Master of all of American Masonry. Washington himself declined to be considered for the post of national Grand Master.[18]

Like the other military lodges, the American Union Lodge broke up at the end of the war (the last meeting being at West Point on April 23, 1783). So many officers took up military bounty lands in the Ohio country, however, that it is not surprising that the American Union Lodge in 1790 was reinstated under its original charter at Marietta, Ohio. At the end of the Revolutionary War there were 187 lodges of Freemasons in America.[19]

The Reverend Ezra Stiles commented in his diary of January 31, 1784 that Scotsmen were getting control of the movement. He feared if that trend continued Masonry would lose its broad appeal and acquire such "sinister & illiberal Views" that "a storm may arise."[20]

Because of their exclusion from Masonry, many American women developed an antipathy for the organization and were later first in the ranks of anti-Masonry. Not so Mrs Hannah Mather Crocker, who in 1778 organized Boston women into St Ann's Lodge (named after the mother of Mary), dedicated to "the original principles of true ancient masonry," as far as they were "consistent for the female character." The women held lodge meetings, having their own "tokens, signs, and word." The ladies of St Ann's had as special objectives the encouragement of education and self-improvement for women. Although St Ann's Lodge was short-lived, Crocker in later life became a staunch defender of male Masonry.[21]

Society of the Cincinnati

The end of the war saw the creation of America's first veterans' organization, and a controversial one it proved to be. The Society of the Cincinnati came along at a time when officers and soldiers gave indications of mutinous attitudes. In spring 1783 Congress had not paid off the army nor made good the promise of pensions for officers. The officers had threatened not to disband with the coming of peace. Congress, acutely aware of the potential for a *coup d'état*, suddenly voted the officers a commuted pension in the form of a bonus of five years' pay and cleverly ordered indefinite furloughs for the enlisted men, knowing quite well their service would no longer be needed.

On May 10, 1783 a group of officers met at the Temple (a public building) in the Fishkill, New York cantonment to consider proposals for establishing a hereditary fraternity of officer veterans. Three days later the assembly reconvened at headquarters at Verplanck's Point and adopted the

"Institution," drafted by Major-General Henry Knox, creating the Society of the Cincinnati, so named after the fifth-century Roman general, Lucius Quinctius Cincinnatus, who twice disrupted his retirement to lead troops to victory and afterwards each time returned to the plow.

The "Institution" pledged the officers to "an incessant attention to preserve inviolate those exalted rights and liberties of human nature, for which they have fought and bled," mutual friendship, and assistance to members and their families in need and to promote among the states "that union and national honor so essentially necessary to their happiness and future dignity of the American empire." Membership would be perpetuated after death through the eldest son. All officers with three years' service or who continued to the end of the war were eligible. Upon joining, members were to pledge one month's equivalent military pay to be applied to charity. The Society had 13 chapters, one for each of the original 13 states. A national meeting was to be held annually. On the first such occasion, in June 1783, Washington was elected president-general, and Henry Knox secretary-general.

Continental army officers felt the same way as Henry Knox, who in September 1776 in a conversation with John Adams expressed the desire "for some ribbon to wear in his hair, or in his button hole, to be transmitted to his descendants as a badge and a proof that he had fought in defence of their liberties."[22] The jovial artillery general realized more than his wish, as stipulated in the founding document of the Society of the Cincinnati:

The Society shall have an Order, by which its members shall be known and distinguished, which shall be a medal of gold, of a proper size . . . suspended by a deep blue riband two inches wide, edged with white, descriptive of the union of France and America, viz.:

The principal figure,
CINCINNATUS

Three Senators presenting him with a sword and other military ensigns—on a field in the background, his wife at the door of their Cottage—near it:

A PLOUGH AND INSTRUMENTS OF HUSBANDRY.
Round the whole,
OMNI RELINQUIT SERVARE REMPUBLICAM.
On the reverse,

Sun rising—a city with open gates, and vessels entering the port—
Fame crowning CINCINNATUS with a wreath, inscribed

VIRTUTIS PRAEMIUM
Below,
HANDS JOINED, SUPPORTING A HEART,

With the motto,
ESTO PERPETUA
Round the whole,
SOCIETAS CINCINNATORIUM INSTITUTA
A. D. 1783[23]

French army and naval officers who served in the American war had eligibility for joining the Society of the Cincinnati. Louis XVI, December 18, 1783 at Versailles, by decree established the order in France. The king, as he did for the Royal and Military Order of Saint Louis, decided upon the French applications for membership in the Society of the Cincinnati.[24]

As the only national organization other than Congress, the Society of the Cincinnati served to some extent as a veterans' lobby, pressing Congress to open lands in the west for military land bounties, to grant pensions for all Revolutionary War veterans, and to compensate veterans for the difference in price between what they sold their pay and bonus certificates for and the stated value. As Minor Meyers notes, the Society of the Cincinnati offered "a constructive alternative to an ultimatum from an army refusing to lay down its arms until paid." Within a year the 13 societies were established, with membership of 2,150 from the 5,500 officers who were eligible. Twenty-three of the original members were among the 65 signers of the Constitution.[25]

The founders of the Society of the Cincinnati did not anticipate the fury of opposition that soon mounted against the organization. Many of the Cincinnati, wrote Mercy Warren, "knew not enough of the world, and of history and character of man, to suspect any latent mischief or any concealed object that must not yet be divulged."[26] But the very idea of a military hereditary society grated on republican ears—having the potentiality in time to evolve into an American nobility.

Judge Aedanus Burke's *Considerations on the Society or Order of Cincinnati . . . Proving that it creates a Race of Hereditary Patricians, or Nobility* (published in Charleston on October 10, 1783 and in successive editions in English, French, and German) aroused widespread and intense hostility toward the Society. Burke, an Irishman who settled in South Carolina and who once studied for the Catholic priesthood, had already irritated the South Carolina political establishment by championing backcountry interests and leniency toward Tories. He himself was a few months short of Revolutionary War military service to qualify for Cincinnati membership. Burke claimed that "this Order is planted in a fiery, hot ambition, and thirst for power; and its branches will end in tyranny." The Society, if prevailing, "would give a fatal wound to civil liberty thro' the world." To Burke, South Carolina already had an aristocracy, which the Society of the Cincinnati would make complete.[27]

Soon prominent revolutionaries joined in the chorus of protest. John Adams said the Society of the Cincinnati was "the first step taken to deface the beauty of our Temple of Liberty."[28] Elbridge Gerry of Massachusetts referred to the Society as an attempt to create "an *imperium in imperio*."[29] Samuel Adams, in April 1784, said that he considered the Society "to be as rapid a Stride towards a hereditary Military Nobility as was ever made in so short a time."[30] John Quincy Adams, in the summer of 1787, predicted the Society, if not reformed, "will infallibly become a body dangerous, if not fatal to the Constitution."[31] Several state legislatures passed resolutions condemning the Society, and in Rhode Island it was declared that no member of the organization could hold office in the state.[32]

George Washington, having accepted the highest office in the Cincinnati, was alarmed that people might think he was associated with a monarchical/aristocratic order. On April 8, 1784 he asked Thomas Jefferson, "if with frankness, and the fullest latitude of a friend, you will give me your opinion of the Institution of the Society of the Cincinnati, it would confer an acceptable favor upon me."[33] Jefferson welcomed the opportunity, and advised the former commander-in-chief to "stand on ground separated from it;" the Society was against constitutional government and "the natural equality of man." "Experience has shown," Jefferson said further, "that the hereditary branches of modern governments are the patrons of privilege and prerogatives."[34]

Washington, as president-general, at the national meeting of the Society in May 1784, presented an address calling for specific changes in the Society's "Institution:" to "strike out every word, sentence and clause which has a political tendency;" to abolish "the hereditary part in all its connexions *absolutely*;" to do away with general meetings; to "admit no more honorary Members;" and to refuse to accept donations from non-citizens.[35]

The delegates at the national meeting voted to eliminate the hereditary requirement, but for the change to become operative, it had to be approved by all 13 state chapters. Several states refused to give ratification of the change. Newspapers reported the acceptance of the amended "Institution" by the national gathering, but failed to follow up its negation on the state level. Hence public opposition became less vocal. The Society for the remainder of the century refrained from officially taking political positions, although it was no secret that the organization supported strong central government, ratification of the Constitution, and in the 1790s the Federalist Party.[36] On the eve of Shays's Rebellion, however, the Society in July 1786 at its national meeting resolved: "May the enemies of public faith, public honor and public justice hold no place in the Councils of America." Most of the officers leading government troops against Shaysite insurgents were Cincinnati members.[37]

With so many of the Cincinnati relocating in the West on military bounty lands and renewed popular opposition in the 1790s inspired by the

French Revolution, the Society by 1800 was moribund; by 1832 only six state chapters had survived. Toward the end of the nineteenth century the Society picked up again, with the hereditary principle intact but now broadened to allow collateral descent. Today, the Society, with national headquarters at a splendid 50-room mansion in the nation's capital, thrives, with 3,500 active members in America and France.[38] The Society's resources are used to promote historical programs, preservation, and research.

"Private Societies"

The "private society," a term used by Anthony Ashley Cooper, Earl of Shaftesbury, in 1709 to describe new voluntary associations in England, became a common feature in eighteenth-century America. Associations formed out of a common interest and without any government connection. As David S. Shields writes: "In private society persons took part in—and were transformed by the great project of civility."[39] Joining the Masons and Cincinnati in this category were many other groups, often informally organized. It is estimated that more societies or clubs appeared between 1776 and 1789 than during all of the colonial period.[40] Some groups, however, suspended activities during at least part of the war.

Brissot de Warville, visiting America after the war, commented on the club scene in Boston. Most groups were small, one to two dozen members, gathering at an individual's home alternately, with each member allowed to bring one guest. Warville, who undoubtedly was somewhat misinformed, claimed that there were no coffeehouses in either Boston, New York City, or Philadelphia. Moreover, "clubs no longer meet in taverns, and this is a blessing," the Frenchman said, "for people drink less, drinks are cheaper, and less money is spent. The need to save cash, which was felt at the end of the war, probably led to this change in custom to the benefit of public morals."[41]

Women had their own social outlets. Francisco de Miranda, in Boston during September 1784, noted that "the married women have a club that meets every Saturday, at which six or eight families gather to eat," often out in the countryside. Unmarried women "have tea parties with each other as their only school for manners, customs, elegance, etc. and therefore they are highly deficient in those respects and have a self-preoccupation such as I have never seen."[42]

The Tea Assembly, organized in 1781 in Boston, brought men and women together every other week. The club's members drank tea or wine, danced, and played cards at 40 tables set up in the Concert Hall. Most members were young, upwardly mobile gentry and professionals. Older and more proper Bostonians, such as John Hancock and Samuel Adams, had no liking for the organization. Boston newspapers denounced the Assembly for promoting "effeminacy," "prostituting all our glory . . . for new modes of pleasure . . . injurious to virtue and totally detrimental to the well being of society," and corrupting character more so than in "an evening spent in a *back chamber* of a tavern among a group of wretches." In 1785 a three-act play, *Sans Souci. Alias Free and Easy: or an Evening's Peep into a polite Circle* (probably written by Mercy Warren) was published; its theme depicted how the young through card playing and the like were being seduced into the pursuit of luxury similar to that which had been destructive of morality in English society.[43]

Dancing assemblies were common. Miranda belittled such a group in Boston. "The old and the young dance together, grossly as a rule." It was sad, Miranda noted, "that the list of subscribers has not been offered to any officer of the American army, with the result that not one of them can attend. See here the envy of the mercantile corps and the ingratitude of the people in general."[44] In 1781 a French officer in Boston "spent some moments" at a "ladies' hall or school where the young ladies meet to dance from noon until two o'clock . . . I found nearly all the women extremely handsome, but at the same time extremely awkward. It would be impossible to dance with less grace or to be worse dressed (although with a certain extravagance)."[45]

In Charleston during the British occupation "gentlemen's clubs" flourished, often with the participation of British officers. Among the social groups were the Charleston Hunt Club and St Cecilia (musical) Society, and philanthropic organizations, such as St George's Society, German Friendly Society, St Andrews' Society, and Friendly Sons of St Patrick. Less respectable were the Knights Terrible who met weekly at a local tavern.[46] Johann David Schoepf reported on the "exclusive private societies" in Charleston. "There are as many as 20 different Clubs, and most of the residents are members of more than one. These social unions give themselves strange names at times: Mount Sion Society, Hell-fire Club, Marine Anti-Britannic Society, Smoking Society, and the like."[47]

Philadelphia boasted the largest number and variety of social clubs. Fifteen fire companies, neighborhood based, usually represented ethnic origins and occupational status. Three-fourths of the companies were made up of non-wealthy members. The Hand and Hand Fire Company drew from the upper level of society—merchants, gentlemen, and professionals. The Union Fire Company consisted mainly of Quakers. The city abounded with dining clubs, such as the Krout and Turtle, Sub Rosa, Black Friars, and Yorkshire Club.[48] Popular sporting groups in Philadelphia were the Gloucester Fox Hunting Club, the Jockey Club, and the fishing societies, namely the Colony in Schuylkill (reformed in 1782 as the Schuylkill Fishing Company in the State of Schuylkill), Society of Fort St David Colony, which merged with the Schuylkill club, and the Mount Regale Fishing

Company. The Schuylkill fishing club suspended activity during most of the war, but was revived in 1781; it is still a going concern today.[49]

Ethnic groups in Philadelphia had their organizations: St Andrew's Society (which before and during the war included officers of British army units, the Royal Highlanders and Royal Americans, as members); German Society of Pennsylvania; Society of the Sons of St George; Welsh Society of Ancient Britons; Friendly Sons of St Patrick; Scots Thistle Society; and Hibernian Society. The ethnic societies by and large sided with the American cause. A Pennsylvania newspaper on March 6, 1776 carried a notice that Dr John Kersley was being expelled from the St Geroge Society "having shown himself inimical to the Liberties of this Country."[50]

Other cities had many of the same clubs. In addition to the usual ethnic organizations, New York City had an Irish Club and a French Club. Sons of St Tammany societies sprung up in the colonies in 1765–74, and some of the chapters continued in existence during and after the war, with the New York City organization evolving into a political club. On May 1 each year, Tammany members celebrated "Saint Tammany's Day" (the Society's patron saint was Tamanand, or Tammany, a Delaware Indian chief who lived in the late seventeenth century) with what has been regarded as a "festival of the common people."[51]

John Marshall, later the Chief Justice, belonged to the Sons of St Tammany in Richmond, Virginia. Marshall was also a member of the Quoit Club (formed in the 1780s and later renamed the Barbecue Club), which admitted only prominent persons of the community. The convivial group met at Buchanen's Springs just outside the city: "Quoits was the game, and toddy, punch and mint julep the beverages, to wash down a plain substantial dinner, without wines or dessert."[52]

Library societies (for example, Massachusetts incorporated one in June 1780) and literary, art, and music clubs appeared. The Massachusetts legislature chartered the American Academy of Arts and Sciences in May 1780, "animated by the generous principles, which liberty and independence inspire." The American Philosophical Society in Philadelphia, disrupted by the war, revived in 1779. The Connecticut Society of Arts and Sciences was founded in May 1786.[53]

Everywhere, even in Kentucky, societies for "promoting useful knowledge" were established, as well as organizations for stimulating development and investment in manufacturing and encouraging agriculture.[54]

Working-class citizens continued to expand organizational activity. The Patriotic Society of Philadelphia (founded 1772 and revived 1778) served as a watchdog over Tories and exercised political clout. Two new artisan clubs were established in Charleston: the Palmetto Society (1777) and the Carpenters Society (1783). The General Society of Mechanics and Tradesmen, chartered by New York state in 1785, representing various trades, was typical of new workingmen's fraternal and benevolent societies.[55]

Progress in Humanity

The sufferings and cruelties experienced during the war by civilians and soldiers alike and the strains placed upon already inadequate welfare systems awakened Americans to the need for social reform. War itself was the greatest bane to progress in humanity, and by securing the blessings of peace a more compassionate society could be accomplished. During the war Anthony Benezet, the Quaker teacher and philanthropist, set the groundwork for a future peace movement; in 1776 he published a small anti-war tract, *Thoughts on the Nature of War*, and also similarly two years later, *Serious Reflections Affectionately Recommended*.[56] Benjamin Rush after the war became a powerful leader in the cause.

The war stimulated a renewal of the conception of the American experience as a world mission, a "City upon a Hill," now, however, recast in the secular context of an enlightened and virtuous people. If Americans truly believed in natural law and natural rights the time had come to demonstrate the commitment.

While educational institutions were disrupted and not much expansion occurred during the war, afterwards schools and academies proliferated, even with some attention to the ideal of universal public learning, although the broad realization of this goal was long in the future.

Only in New England was there a general public education system, at the elementary and secondary levels, long rooted in the colonial past. The revolutionaries became increasingly aware that a virtuous Republic required an educated citizenry. Thomas Jefferson, from a state where the elite for a century and a half had been determined to keep education away from the masses, in a "Bill for the More General Diffusion of Knowledge," which he proposed to the Virginia legislature in December 1777 and again in June 1780, advocated at least a partial general education program for Virginia. Although ahead of his time for any success, Jefferson forced the issue. Jefferson's plan would guarantee free education for all white male and female children in county schools for three years. Afterwards a weeding out process at the grammar-school level would leave only one student from the whole state to go on to study tax-free at the College of William and Mary.[57]

The colleges endured hard times during the Revolution. "Dislocation, dispossession, and damage afflicted many institutions at one time or another, and physical distress usually heightened politicalization," writes David W. Robson.[58]

The Harvard building was used by the Americans during the siege of Boston, and the college was moved to Concord, returning to Cambridge in June 1776. One hundred and fifty students enrolled in 1783. Yale's students were dismissed for the term in July 1779 as British troops operated near New Haven; the college, however, was soon back on its feet, with 270 students matriculating in 1783.[59]

In April 1776 the New York Committee of Safety ordered King's College in New York City to be used as a hospital, and the library and other materials were deposited at City Hall. Benjamin Moore, president *pro tempore* of the college, tried to keep the school functioning at a house on Wall Street, but it closed in June 1777. The British also appropriated the college building for military use. Under a charter from the state, King's College was revived in 1784, renamed Columbia College.[60]

With British forces occupying the campus, Queen's (Rutgers) College was closed from December 2, 1776 to June 22, 1777. It resumed operations for 1778–9 at a site on the North Branch of the Raritan River in Somerset County. In the fall of 1779 the college returned to New Brunswick.[61] The College of Philadelphia (University of Pennsylvania) shut its doors for two years (1776–8) while the campus served as a barracks first for American militia and then for British troops.[62]

With its building used as a barracks for American militia and then as a French army hospital, Rhode Island College (Brown) remained closed from late 1776 to mid 1782. From December 1776 until 1782 studies were disrupted at the College of New Jersey (Princeton). British troops first occupied the college, and cannon fire from the battle of Princeton, January 3, 1777 heavily damaged Nassau Hall and the church. American troops for a while were barracked at the college, which was then used as a military hospital until November 1778. Dartmouth, located away from the military campaigns, escaped injury. Its president, Eleazar Wheelock, sent an agent into Canada to enlist Indians for the American cause, for which a grateful Congress paid Wheelock $900 for expenses, the first "defense contract" with an American college. The College of William and Mary closed in June 1781 when Cornwallis's army passed through Williamsburg and remained shut during the siege of Yorktown when the French army used its buildings for a hospital.[63]

The war left an impact on the colleges in other ways. Curricula reflected more emphasis on history and mathematics. Several states attempted to take over private colleges. From 1784 to 1787 title to Columbia College was held by the regents of the University of the State of New York. The Pennsylvania legislature in 1779 removed the trustees of the College of Philadelphia and renamed the institution the University of the State of Pennsylvania. The school enrolled 250 students in 1780 and four years later, 400. In 1789 the Pennsylvania assembly restored the old trustees, but retained the new name.[64]

States conferred land grants for the purpose of founding colleges. In Kentucky, Transylvania Seminary (re-named Transylvania University in 1799), incorporated by Virginia in 1783 and opened in 1785, received 20,000 acres.[65]

Charters for new colleges after the Revolution stressed republican virtue and civic responsibility. Two state universities were chartered shortly after the war—University of Georgia in 1785 and University of North Carolina in 1789. Of ten colleges founded before 1776, only one was non-sectarian; for two decades after the war, ten of 14.[66]

Besides Transylvania, four colleges came into existence during the war years. Hampden-Sydney started out as an academy in 1776, and in 1783 was granting college degrees. Liberty Hall Academy (originally founded as Augusta Academy in 1749 and renamed in 1776), also in Virginia, received a charter as a college in December 1782, the first degrees being granted three years later; renamed Washington College in 1798, today the school is Washington and Lee University. Washington College at Chestertown on Maryland's Eastern Shore opened in 1782. Dickinson College at Carlisle, Pennsylvania was chartered by Pennsylvania in 1783; Benjamin Rush expected that this new Presbyterian institution would be a "bulwark of the blessings obtained by the Revolution" and just as importantly might deter Scots–Irish emigration out of the western Pennsylvania counties.[67]

The achievement of a virtuous republican society required more than expanding educational advantage. As Alice F. Tyler writes, "there was a fundamental incompatibility between the social forces of the American Revolution and the criminal codes of the colonial era. If the equality proclaimed in the Declaration of Independence meant anything at all, it meant equality before the law."[68]

The war underscored the brutality and capriciousness in the administration of capital punishment. So much retribution had been taken just in the hangings of Tories and spies and in the bloodbath of the partisan war in the South. The close possibility that Washington would have an innocent 19-year-old British captain, Charles Asgill, hanged in retaliation for the wanton execution of Captain Joshua Huddy, a New Jersey militiaman, by a group of the Associated loyalists, was shocking; through Congress's and the French government's intercession Asgill was spared. The hanging of two elderly Quakers in Philadelphia in 1778 for collaboration with the enemy was one of many events that pointed to excesses in the enforcement of capital penalties.

Americans had already become familiar with European writers of the Enlightenment and their appeal for more humane criminal codes, especially Cesare Beccaria's *Essays on Crimes and Punishment* (English translation 1767 and first American edition in Philadelphia, 1778), which stressed certainty of punishment as a better deterrent than severity.[69] For a republican society, the unevenness in the rate of handing down capital sentences did not make sense. As Melvin Yazawa writes, "capital punishment was so contrary to humanity" that juries often chose "to acquit a criminal rather than to execute him. As a result, the system of punishment became unpredictable and the efficacy of all laws was undermined."[70]

Henry Knox spoke for other revolutionary leaders in expressing the hope that "dispassionate and enlightened minds" would prevail to bring about a reduction in the number of capital penalties; otherwise the capital laws "will be recited to sully the purity of our cause."[71] Benjamin Rush would go further and eliminate all corporal and public punishments. "I cannot help entertaining the hope," Rush wrote in his *Enquiry into the Effects of Public Punishments upon Criminals* (1787), "that the time is not very far distant when the gallows, the pillory, the stocks, the whipping post and the wheelbarrow will be connected with the history of the rack, the stake, as marks of barbarity."[72]

While Americans debated over the fitness of retaining capital penalties for numerous crimes, reform came slowly. The penal codes of the colonies reflected the severity of the British legal system, which contained capital penalties for 160 crimes; the colonies, however, had a far smaller number. By 1776 New York had 16 crimes punishable by death, Connecticut 15, Delaware 20, Pennsylvania 13, and the other colonies in the same range.[73] Thomas Jefferson, having returned from Congress to sit in the Virginia House of Delegates, proposed a bill in 1776 for a revised criminal code, which would provide death only for murder and treason. The legislature balked, as it did also in 1785, largely due to the problem of horse-thievery, and not until 1796 did Jefferson's code pass.[74]

Meanwhile Pennsylvania led the way in actual reform. The state constitution of 1776 called for a more humane revision of the criminal code. From 1779 to 1789 50 persons in Pennsylvania were executed: for burglary 20; for robbery 23; for rape 4; for counterfeiting 1; for arson 1; and for crime against nature 1. In 1783 five persons were executed for one robbery. A Pennsylvania enactment of 1786 abolished the death penalty for robbery, burglary, and crime against nature, and subsequent legislation of 1790, 1791, and 1794 resulted in first-degree homicide as the only capital offense. Hard labor "publicly and disgracefully imposed" became the punishment for most felonies.[75]

Some reactionary tendencies, however, were evident. A Massachusetts act of 1785 made six crimes punishable by death, including robbery, rape, burglary, and sodomy. But in time in Massachusetts executions decreased. In the 1780s, 29 persons were executed, of whom 24 were put to death for burglary. It is interesting that in early America the high tide of executions for crimes against property occurred during the Revolutionary era. In the three decades after 1790, Massachusetts executed 17 persons, of whom only one was for robbery. North Carolina in its revised code of 1837 had 22 capital crimes. Slaves benefited almost nothing at all from criminal code reforms. In Virginia after the war, for example, slaves faced execution for 71 crimes from which white persons were exempt.[76]

A movement began to ameliorate the suffering of prisoners. During the colonial period there were few jails. Punishment of criminals was largely corporal—whipping, the stocks, the pillory, branding, and mutilation (for example, ear cropping). The more affluent culprits normally could make amends by paying fines. During the Revolutionary era there was a trend to substitute imprisonment for corporal punishment. The major problem, however, was the lack of jail space. The infamous underground prison, in copper mines, at Simsbury, Connecticut held regular convicts as well as detained Tories. Usually a log cabin or one or two rooms in a house served as a jail. To prevent escape, prisoners were often shackled, usually with ball and chain. Such was the fate of Lieutenant-Colonel Henry Hamilton, who was captured by George Rogers Clark at Vincennes and wound up being held incommunicado for several months at the Williamsburg, Virginia jail. During the war, the Henrico County jail in Richmond, Virginia consisted of two small rooms, each ten feet square and each holding as many as 11 prisoners. Commonly jails everywhere housed an aggregate of humanity— men, women, children, profligate criminals, debtors, runaway servants and slaves, and often temporarily detained deserters of both armies.[77]

On February 7, 1776 the Philadelphia Society for Assisting Distressed Prisoners came into being. It ceased functioning during the British occupation, but was revived in 1787 as the Pennsylvania Society for Alleviating the Miseries of Public Prisons. This prison society took the lead in a movement to prevent "undue and illegal suffering" and to seek "means of restoring our fellow creatures to virtue and happiness." Specific objectives of the reformers were substituting hard labor for corporal punishment, ending idleness, and segregating different kinds of inmates. One problem with the reforms, as evident at Philadelphia's Walnut Street Jail, was that prisoners performing outdoor public labor aroused friction with citizens. Another alternative emerged, the building of a large facility, serving a whole state, whereby prisoners would be kept in solitary cells and have intramural employment. The first small step toward a penitentiary system was taken by the Pennsylvania legislature in 1790 when it ordered the erection of a building in the Walnut Street jailyard; the new facility would have solitary cells for the most "hardened and atrocious offenders."[78] By the turn of the century several states were committed to the penitentiary system.

Not surprisingly, the Revolution sparked a movement for the abolition of imprisonment for debt. Many Americans were caught in the web of debt. Virginia planters were substantially in debt to British creditors at the start of the war; the state tried to collect these obligations in escrow, with settlement coming after the war. Virginia during 1783–4 halted all collection of debts owed British creditors, and, indeed, payment was never realized, with the United States government eventually making compensation. Many Americans who ventured into privateering and market speculation found themselves steeped in debt. Scarcity of money and the depreciation and repudiation of paper currency contributed to the inability to pay off debts. Thus it was not difficult to find sympathy for debtors who were forced into incarceration by their creditors.

States generally limited jail sentences for debt. New Hampshire in 1782 typically enacted a law providing for the release of poor persons after 60 days of imprisonment for debt unless creditors were willing to pay the costs of detainment. A study of Massachusetts for 1785–1800 notes that only 35 of 1,905 debtors were imprisoned longer than a year, and most were jailed for no more than two weeks. The constitutions of North Carolina, Pennsylvania, and Vermont of 1776–7 stated that debtors could be imprisoned only on a strong presumption of fraud. The North Carolina Constitution forbade jailing of debtors after their property had been assigned to creditors. By the 1780s most states prohibited imposing involuntary servitude on debtors. Generally there was a trend to abolish imprisonment for debtors owing small amounts, war veterans, and women. The imprisonment for debt would remain a heated issue into the nineteenth century. One problem was that state measures for curtailing imprisonment for debt were often not accompanied by enabling legislation.[79]

While minimum aid was available on the local level to destitute persons or needy soldiers's families, the extensiveness of wartime suffering and the ideals of republican society gave some impetus to paying more attention to the needs of the deserving poor. Poor relief was a helter-skelter affair, varying according to communities. A very few towns and counties had almshouses, some started in the colonial period. The Pennsylvania almshouse in Philadelphia saw a vast increase in admissions from 1782 to 1787. Unfortunately the almshouse became a catchall for all kinds of the poor. A Boston committee reported that the city's almshouse after the war was the only place known, "where persons of every description and disease are lodged under the same roof."[80]

States became more involved in requiring standards of care for the poor. As David M. Schneider writes, in New York the Revolutionary War period was "important in the development of public welfare primarily because it witnessed the first participation of the state in poor-relief administration." This change resulted from the collapse of civil authority and armed conflict which "deprived many localities of the mechanisms for the collection and distribution of the poor rates" and New York City's unemployment and refugee problems.[81] North Carolina and Georgia were the only two states where there were no almshouses at the time of the Revolution. This soon changed in North Carolina, however, when the legislature in 1785 required such institutions to be established locally through county taxation. By the early nineteenth century most North Carolina counties had almshouses.[82] Pennsylvania in the 1790s started a system of poorhouses.[83]

Treatment for the mentally ill progressed slowly. The first state asylum exclusively for the insane was established at Williamsburg, Virginia in 1773; it closed in 1782 and reopened in 1786. Unfortunately care was custodial rather than remedial. General hospitals in Philadelphia and New York

City had separate wards where the mentally sick were treated. Other than the Pennsylvania Hospital erecting a wing to be used for caring for the mentally ill in 1796, further development in providing public institutions for the treatment of the insane belonged to the next century.[84]

Private endeavors supplemented public welfare. In Philadelphia the Quakers still operated the Bettering House, despite its original buildings being used by the military during part of the war. The institution housed "vagabonds, wrongdoers, and prostitutes" who were forced to work until release. Importantly new societies, supported by voluntary contributions, appeared to address the needs of those in distress. In Philadelphia the Society for Inoculating the Poor Gratis, founded in 1774, gave free medicine to the poor; it ceased to function during the war but was revived in 1787. The city also had the Dispensary, which provided medicines to the poor for a minimal fee.[85] Among the mutual aid societies, such as the ethnic and trades organizations, which provided relief to families of constituents, in Philadelphia about 200 ship captains were subscribers to the Society for the Relief of Poor Distressed Masters of Ships, Their Widows and Children.[86]

Voluntarism was the fiber that bound Americans to the new Republic. They had combined together to repudiate British rule. From social contract they had reinvented their own governments, and they had joined together in military combat to confirm their own freedoms, by which they could pursue untrammeled the course of their own lives. Benjamin Rush was confident "that a revolution is soon to take place in favour of human happiness."[87] It was incumbent upon citizens to break away from a European mold and accomplish a moral reformation effecting equality of opportunity and public virtue. Associations of men of goodwill would help realize expectations of building as near a perfect society as was within the capability of man. As Thomas Paine wrote in 1776: "We have it in our power to begin the world over again."[88]

The war opened vistas for new opportunity. As Benjamin Rush declared on the eve of the Federal Constitutional Convention in 1787: "There is nothing more common than to confound the terms of the American Revolution with those of the late American War. The American War is over: but this is far from being the case with the American Revolution."[89] It remained to be seen if the participation in the Revolutionary War, the challenges faced on the home front in enduring wartime conditions, and the restructuring of a new political and social order prepared Americans for the difficult task ahead of consummating liberty, equality, and social harmony.

Notes

Abbreviations Used in the Notes

AHR   *American Historical Review.*

AWP   W. W. Abbot et al. (eds), *The Papers of George Washington*, Revolutionary War Series, 7 vols to date; Confederation Series, 6 vols. Charlottesville, VA, 1983–97. Notes refer to Revolutionary War Series unless otherwise indicated.

FP   Leonard W. Labaree et al. (eds), *The Papers of Benjamin Franklin*, vols 1–28. New Haven, CT, 1959–90.

FWW   John C. Fitzpatrick (ed.), The *Writings of George Washington*, 39 vols. Washington, DC, 1931–44.

GHSC   *Collections of the Georgia Historical Society.*

JCC   C. Ford Worthington (ed.), *Journals of the Continental Congress, 1774–1789*, 34 vols. Washington, DC, 1904–37.

LD   Paul H. Smith (ed.), *Letters of Delegates to Congress, 1774–1789*, 24 vols. Washington, DC, 1973–96.

LP   Stanley J. Idzerda (ed.), *Lafayette in the Age of the American Revolution: Selected Letters and Papers, 1775–1790*, 5 vols. Ithaca, NY, 1977–83.

MHSC   *Collections of the Massachusetts Historical Society.*

MHSP   *Proceedings of the Massachusetts Historical Society.*

NCHR   *North Carolina Historical Review.*

NEQ   *New England Quarterly.*

NG   Richard K. Showman et al. (eds), *The Papers of Nathanael Greene*, 9 vols to date. Chapel Hill, NC, 1976–97.

PMHB   *Pennsylvania Magazine of History and Biography.*

SCHM   *South Carolina Historical Magazine.*

VMHB   *Virginia Magazine of History and Biography.*

WL   Carl E. Prince et al. (eds), *The Papers of William Livingston*, 5 vols. Trenton and New Brunswick, NJ, 1979–88.

WMQ   *William and Mary Quarterly*.

Chapter One

1. Edmund Burke to the Committee &c. of New York, April 6, 1774, Lucy S. Sutherland (ed.), *The Correspondence of Edmund Burke* (Chicago, 1960), 2: 527.
2. William Duane (ed.), *Extracts from the Diary of Christopher Marshall . . . 1774–1781* (Albany, NY, 1877), June 1, 1774, 6; "Correspondence in 1774 and 1775 between a Committee of the Town of Boston and Contributors of Donations. . . ," *MHSC*, 4th Ser., 4: 149n.
3. Winthrop Sargent (ed.), "Letters of John Andrews, 1772–1776," *MHSP*, 8 (1864–5), June–July 1774, 328 and 335–6; Carl Bridenbaugh, *Cities in Revolt: Urban Life in America, 1743–1776* (New York, 1964, orig. pub. 1955), 234; Henry J. Cadbury, *Quaker Relief during the Siege of Boston* (n. pl., 1938), 44.
4. Sargent (ed.), "Letters of Andrews," July 1774, 337; Richard D. Brown, *Revolutionary Politics in Massachusetts: The Boston Committee of Correspondence and the Town, 1772–1774* (Cambridge, MA, 1970), 220–2; James A. Henretta, "Economic Development and Social Structure in Colonial Boston," *WMQ*, 3rd Ser., 22 (1965): 75–92; Jackson T. Main, *The Social Structure of Revolutionary America* (Princeton, NJ, 1965), 39.
5. Franklin B. Dexter (ed.), *The Literary Diary of Ezra Stiles* (New York, 1901), August 17, 1774, 1: 454.
6. *JCC*, October 10, 1774, 1: 59.
7. "Correspondence in 1774 and 1775 . . . Contributors of Donations," Bucks County Committee, December 15, 1774, 149n.; Sydney James, *A People Among Peoples: Quaker Benevolence in Eighteenth Century America* (Cambridge, MA, 1963), 259–60; Cadbury, *Quaker Relief*, 48 and 58.
8. Gov. James Wright to Earl of Dartmouth, April 24, 1775, Kenneth G. Davies (ed.), *Documents of the American Revolution, 1770–1783* (Dublin, Ire., 1975), 9: 10; *Virginia Gazette* (Rind), August 25, 1774 in Nan Netherton et al., *Fairfax County, Virginia: A History* (Fairfax, VA, 1978), 95; "Correspondence in 1774 and 1775 . . . Contributors of Donations," *passim*; Kenneth Coleman, *The American Revolution in Georgia, 1763–1789* (Athens, GA, 1958), 53.
9. *Rivington's Gazette*, March 9, 1775 in Frank Moore (comp.), *The Diary of the American Revolution, 1775–1781* (New York, 1967), 8–10; Richard Buel, Jr, *Dear Liberty: Connecticut's Mobilization for the Revolutionary War* (Middletown, CI), 27; Brown, *Revolutionary Politics*, 216–17.

10. Handbill Notices, May 16, 1774, Peter Force (ed.), *American Archives* (Washington, DC, 1837), 4th Ser., 1: 293n; Paul A. Gilje, *The Road to Mobocracy: Popular Disorder in New York City, 1763–1834* (Chapel Hill, NC, 1987), 60–2; Staughton Lynd, "The Mechanics in New York Politics, 1774–1785," in Staughton Lynd (ed.), *Class Conflict, Slavery, and the United States Constitution* (Indianapolis, IN, 1967), 82–90; Edward Countryman, *A People in Revolution: The American Revolution and Political Society in New York, 1760–1790* (New York, 1989, orig. pub. 1981), 137–8.

11. Duane (ed.), *Diary of Marshall*, 6–7; Arthur M. Schlesinger, *The Colonial Merchants and the American Revolution, 1763–1776* (New York, 1968, orig. pub. 1917), 360; John A. Silver, *The Provisional Government of Maryland, 1774–1777* (Baltimore, MD, 1898), 7.

12. Jack P. Greene (ed.), *The Diary of Colonel Landon Carter of Sabine Hall, 1752–1778* (Charlottesville, VA, 1965), June 3, 1774, 2: 815.

13. Silver, *Provisional Government of Maryland*, 7–9; Lindley Butler, *North Carolina and the Coming of the American Revolution* (Raleigh, 1976); Richard F. Upton, *Revolutionary New Hampshire* (Hanover, NH, 1936), 36–37; Larry R. Gerlach, *Prologue to Independence: New Jersey in the Coming of the American Revolution* (New Brunswick, NJ, 1976), 212–13.

14. Walter J. Fraser, Jr, *Patriots, Pistols and Petticoats: "Poor Sinful Charles Town during the American Revolution* (Columbia, SC, 1993, orig. pub. 1945), 58 and 65; E. Stanley Goldbold and Robert H. Woody, *Christopher Gadsden and the American Revolution* (Knoxville, TN, 1982), 118–19; George E. Frakes, *Laboratory for Liberty: The South Carolina Legislative Committee System, 1719–1776* (Lexington, KY, 1970), 120–1; Schlesinger, *Colonial Merchants*, 464–7.

15. Agnes Hunt, *The Provincial Committees of Safety of the American Revolution* (Cleveland, OH, 1904), 11–15; David J. Toscano et al., "A Shift in Strategy: The Organization of Military Struggle," in Walter Conser et al. (eds), *Resistance, Politics and the American Struggle for Independence, 1765–1775* (Boulder, CO, 1986), 437 and 443–6; e.g. *WL*, 1: 33n.

16. Benjamin Franklin to Thomas Cushing, July 7, 1773, *FP*, 20: 273; Town Meeting, Providence, May 17, 1774, Force, *American Archives*, 4th Ser., 1: 333–4.

17. *JCC*, 1: 31–7.

18. John Adams to Abigail Adams, September 18, 1774, L. H. Butterfield (ed.), *Adams Family Correspondence* (Cambridge, MA, 1963), 1: 157.

19. *JCC*, 1: 77–9.

20. Roger J. Champagne, *Alexander McDougall and the American Revolution in New York* (Schenectady, NY, 1975), 74 and 77–8; Ronald G. Killion and Charles T. Waller (eds), *Georgia and the Revolution* (Atlanta, GA, 1978), "Association. . . ," January 18, 1775, 117–19.

21. In Committee at New Bern, May 31, 1775, *The Proceedings of the Revolutionary Committee of the Town of New Bern and the County Craven, North Carolina 1775* (Chicago, 1938), 4.

22. David L. Ammerman, "The Continental Association: Economic Resistance and Government by Committee," in Conser et al. (eds), *Resistance*, 247–9; James K. Martin, *Men in Rebellion: Higher Government Leaders and the Coming of the American Revolution* (New York, 1976), 194; Peter D. G. Thomas, *Tea Party to Independence: The Third Phase of the American Revolution, 1773–1776* (New York, 1991), 221.

23. Duane (ed.), *Diary of Marshall*, May 2, 1775, 22.

24. Extract of a Letter from Exeter, New Hampshire, January 2, 1775, Nathaniel Bouton (ed.), *Documents and Records relating to the Province of New Hampshire* (Nashua, NH, 1873), 7: 424–5.

25. Joseph Reed to Earl of Dartmouth, December 10, 1774, William B. Reed, *Life and Correspondence of Joseph Reed* (Philadelphia, 1847), 1: 88.

26. Todd Cooper, "Trial and Triumph: the Impact of the Revolutionary War on the Baltimore Merchants," in Ernest M. Eller (ed.), *Chesapeake Bay and the American Revolution* (Centerville MD, 1981), 250; Leila Sellers, *Charleston Business on the Eve of the American Revolution* (New York, 1970, orig. pub. 1934), 229.

27. James F. Shepherd, "British America and the Atlantic Economy," in Ronald Hoffman et al. (eds), *The Economy of British America . . . The Revolutionary Period* (Charlottesville, VA, 1988), 40.

28. *JCC*, May 17, 1775, 2: 54.

29. Thomas Gage to Lord Barrington, September 25, 1774, Clarence E. Carter (ed.), *The Correspondence of General Thomas Gage . . .* (New Haven, CT, 1931–3), 2: 654–5.

30. John Adams to Abigail Adams, September 18, 1774, Butterfield (ed.), *Adams Family Correspondence*, 1: 159.

31. *Newport Mercury*, December 12, 1774, in William B. Clark (ed.), *Naval Documents of the American Revolution* (Washington, DC, 1964), 1: 14–15; Extract of letters to Gentlemen in New York, December 16–17, 1774, Bouton (ed.), *Documents . . . New-Hampshire*, 7: 423.

32. In other colonies the first war action also consisted of taking public munitions, e.g. in Charleston, April 20, 1775; Savannah, May 10, 1775; and at Turtle Bay near New York City, June 12, 1775.

33. Sargent (ed.), "Letters of John Andrews," October 5, 1774, 373.

34. *JCC*, July 18, 1775, 1: 187–8.

35. New Hampshire Committee of Safety, October 12, 1775 and An Act of Assembly, Equipping, &c . . . (Connecticut Assembly), April 26, 1775, Force, *American Archives*, 4th Ser., 1: 3 and 2: 411, resp.; Philip V. Fithian, *Journal, 1775–1776 . . .* , eds Robert G. Albion and Leonidas Dodson (Princeton, NJ, 1934), July 6, 1775, 24; Gerlach, *Prologue*, 259.

36. Allen French, *The First Year of the American Revolution* (New York, 1938, orig. pub. 1934), 41 and n.

37. John D. McBride, "The Virginia War Effort; 1775–1783: Manpower Policies and Practices", PhD diss., University of Virginia, 1977, 2–3.

38. John Shy, *A People Numerous and Armed: Reflections on the Military Struggle for American Independence* (New York, 1976), 222.

39. *New York Journal*, May 18, 1774, in *Archives of the State of New Jersey*, 31: 132.

40. Resolution of the House of Burgesses, May 24, 1774 and excerpt from Thomas Jefferson's "Autobiography," *JP*, 1: 105–7 and n.

41. *JCC*, June 12, 1775, 2: 87–8; Philip Davidson, *Propaganda and the American Revolution, 1763–1783* (Chapel Hill, NC, 1941), 96; Walter H. Conser, Jr, "Religion and the Development of Political Resistance in the Colonies," in Conser et al. (eds), *Resistance*, 398.

42. Quoted in John W. Tyler, *Smugglers and Patriots* (Boston, MA, 1986), 219.

43. "Government Corrupted by Vice," quoted in Frank Moore, *The Patriot Preachers of the American Revolution, 1766–1783* (New York, 1860), 67 and 71.

44. Edward H. Tatum, Jr (ed.), *The American Journal of Ambrose Serle, Secretary to Lord Howe, 1776–1778* (San Marino, 1940), September 3, 1776, 89; quoted in Robert M. Calhoon (ed.), *Religion and the American Revolution in North Carolina* (Raleigh, NC, 1976), 16.

45. Amos Farnsworth, "Diary kept during part of the Revolutionary War. . . ," *MHSP*, 2nd ser., 12: 79.

46. See Alice M. Baldwin, *The New England Clergy and the American Revolution* (Durham, NC, 1928), *passim*; Klaus Wust, *The Virginia Germans* (Charlottesville, VA, 1969), 80.

47. North Carolina Delegates to the Presbyterian Ministers of Philadelphia, 3–8? July 1775 and to Elihu Spencer, December 8, 1775, *LD*, 1; 575–6 and 2: 459 and 461, resp.

48. Dexter (ed.), *Literary Diary of Stiles*, November 17, 1774, 1: 480.

49. William Heath, *Memoirs of Major General William Heath* (ed.), William Abbatt (New York, 1901, orig. pub. 1798), 10.

50. Extract of a letter from a Surgeon of one of His Majesty's ships at Boston, May 26, 1775, Margaret W. Willard (ed.), *Letters on the American Revolution, 1774–1776* (Boston, MA, 1925), 120.

51. For example, Caroline County Committee, April 13, 1775 and Amelia County Committee, May 3, 1775, Robert L. Scribner and Brent Tarter (eds), *Revolutionary Virginia: The Road to Independence* (Charlottesville, VA, 1977), 3: 41 and 43n.

52. Schlesinger, *Colonial Merchants*, 517 and 524.

53. Richard Walsh, *Charleston's Sons of Liberty: A Study of the Artisans, 1763–1789* (Columbia, SC, 1959), 74–5.

54. Schlesinger, *Colonial Merchants*, 492.
55. *Pennsylvania Gazette*, March 18 and 22, 1775; *Pennsylvania Journal*, August 9, 1775, in Moore, *Diary*, 61–2; Ammerman, "Continental Association," 251.

Chapter Two

1. *JCC*, 3: 318–19, 326–7, and 403–4.
2. John Adams to James Warren, November 5, 1775, *LD*, 2: 306.
3. *JCC*, 4: 342 and 357–8.
4. Oliver Wolcott to Samuel Lyman, May 16, 1776, *LD*, 4: 16–17.
5. SALUS POPULI, March 1776, Force, *American Archives*, 4th Ser., 5: 182.
6. "The Constitution of the Commonwealth of Massachusetts," 1780, Francis W. Thorpe (ed.), *The Federal and State Constitutions . . .* (St Clair Shores, MI, 1977, orig. pub. 1909), 3: 1888–9.
7. Quoted in Thad W. Tate, "The Social Contract, 1774–1787: Revolutionary Theory as a Conservative Instrument," *WMQ*, 3rd Ser., 22 (1965): 379.
8. "The People are the Best Governors," in Frederick Chase, *A History of Dartmouth College and the Town of Hanover, New Hampshire* (Cambridge MA, 1891), 1: 654 and 656.
9. "The Interest of America," *c.* June 1776, Force, *American Archives*, 4th Ser., 6: 840.
10. "Four Letters on Interesting Subjects," Jack P. Greene (ed.), *Colonies to Nation, 1763–1789: A Documentary History of the American Revolution* (New York, 1975, orig. pub. 1967), 315.
11. John Adams to Abigail Adams, July 3, 1776, *LD*, 4: 374–5.
12. "Address to the Convention . . . of Virginia," (1776), Greene (ed.), *Colonies to Nation*, 321–2.
13. Mark Philip (ed.), [Thomas Paine], *Rights of Man, Common Sense, and other Political Writings* (New York, 1995) ("Common Sense"), 19.
14. "Rights of Man" (1792), in Philip (ed.), *Rights of Man*, 230–2.
15. "Virginia Declaration of Rights," Greene (ed.), *Colonies to Nation*, 332–4.
16. Quoted in Robert J. Dinkin, *Voting in Revolutionary America: A Study of Elections in the Original Thirteen States, 1776–1789* (Westport, CT, 1982), 50–1.
17. Roger Atkinson to Samuel Pleasants, November 23, 1776, "Letters of Roger Atkinson, 1769–1776," *VMHB*, 15 (1907): 357.
18. Jackson T. Main, "Government by the People: The American Revolution and the Democratization of the Legislatures," *WMQ*, 3rd Ser., 23 (1966), 400–6.

19. Jackson T. Main, *The Upper House in Revolutionary America, 1763–1788* (Madison, WI, 1967), *passim*.

20. Martin, *Men in Rebellion*, 184.

21. David Hawke, *The Colonial Experience* (Indianapolis, IN, 1966), 346.

22. Quotes in Margaret B. Macmillan, *War Governors in the American Revolution* (Gloucester, MA, 1965, orig. pub. 1943), 106–7.

23. Marquis de Chastellux, *Travels in North America in the Years 1780, 1781 and 1782* (Chapel Hill, NC, 1963), ed. Howard C. Rice, Jr, 1: 161.

24. Alexander Hamilton to Robert Morris, August 13, 1782, Harold C. Syrett (ed.), *The Papers of Alexander Hamilton* (New York, 1962), 3: 135.

25. Thomas Jefferson, *Notes on the State of Virginia* (Chapel Hill, NC, 1954), ed. William Peden, 120.

26. Jerome J. Nadelhaft, "'The Snarls of Invidious Animals': The Democratization of Revolutionary South Carolina," in Ronald Hoffman and Peter J. Albert (eds), *Sovereign States in an Age of Uncertainty* (Charlottesville, VA, 1981), 80.

27. David Ramsay to Benjamin Rush, July 11, 1783, Robert L. Brunhouse (ed.), *David Ramsay, 1749–1815: Selections from His Writings* (Philadelphia, 1965), 75.

28. George Mason to William Cabell, May 6, 1783, Robert A. Rutland (ed.), *The Papers of George Mason, 1725–1792* (Chapel Hill, NC, 1970), 2: 768.

29. Thomas Paine, "Prospects on the Rubicon," Philip S. Foner (ed.), *The Complete Writings of Thomas Paine* (New York, 1945), 2: 624.

30. [Washington's] Circular Letter to the States, June 8, 1783. Greene (ed.), *Colonies to Nation*, 438–9.

31. Alexander Hamilton to James Duane, August 23, 1780, Syrett (ed.), *Papers of Hamilton*, 2: 407; Thomas Paine, "Public Good" (1780), Foner (ed.), *Writings of Paine*, 2: 332.

32. John Mathews to George Washington, January 31, 1781, *LD*, 16: 648.

33. James Madison, "Vices of the Political System of the United States" (April 1787), Greene (ed.), *Colonies to Nation*, 514–19.

Chapter Three

1. Washington to Joseph Reed, April 1, 1776, *FWW*, 4: 456.

2. Quoted in Wallace Brown, *The Good Americans: The Loyalists in the American Revolution* (New York, 1969), 110.

3. N. E. H. Hull, "Choosing Sides: A Quantitative Study of the Personality Determinents of Loyalist and Revolutionary Political Affiliations in New York," *Journal of American History*, 65 (1978): 347.

4. William H. Nelson, *The American Tory* (London, 1961), 86.

5. George W. Corner (ed.), *The Autobiography of Benjamin Rush* (Philadelphia, 1945), 118.

6. Anne Hulton, *Letters of a Loyalist Lady . . . Anne Hulton* (Cambridge, MA, 1927), 26.

7. Quoted in Robert M. Calhoon, *The Loyalists in Revolutionary America, 1760–1781* (New York, 1973), 104.

8. Samuel Seabury, *Letters of a Westchester Farmer, 1774–1775*, ed. Clarence H. Vane (New York, 1970, orig. pub. 1930), 61.

9. *JCC*, January 2, 1776, 1: 18–20 and March 14, 1776, 4: 205.

10. *JCC*, November 27, 1777, 9: 971.

11. Paul H. Smith, "The American Loyalists: Notes on Their Organization and Numerical Strength," *WMQ*, 3rd Ser., 25 (1968): 266–7; Paul H. Smith, *Loyalists and Redcoats: A Study in British Revolutionary Policy* (Chapel Hill, NC, 1964), 60–1; Calhoon, *Loyalists in Revolutionary America*, 502.

12. Cornwallis to Lt.-Col. Nisbet Balfour, July 3, 1780, quoted in Robert S. Lambert, *South Carolina Loyalists in the American Revolution* (Columbia, SC, 1987), 156.

13. Staughton Lynd, "The Tenant Uprising at Livingston Manor, May 1777," *New York Historical Society Quarterly*, 48 (1964): 163 and 171; Philip Ranlet, *The New York Loyalists* (Knoxville, TN, 1986), 130–2.

14. Harold B. Hancock, *The Delaware Loyalists* (Boston, MA, 1972, orig. pub. 1940), 13 and 38–9; North Callahan, *Royal Raiders: The Tories of the American Revolution* (Indianapolis, IN, 1963), 188–9.

15. Diary of Robert Honyman, March 4, 1777, Library of Congress, microfilm edn, 185 and 187; Calhoon, *Loyalists in Revolutionary America*, 469.

16. Dorothy M. Quynn, "The Loyalist Plot in Frederick," *Maryland Historical Magazine*, 40 (1945): 201–9.

17. Patricia G. Johnson, *William Preston and the Allegheny Patriots* (Pulaski, VA, *c.* 1976), 252; McBride, "Virginia War Effort," PhD diss., 214 and 220.

18. Mary Beth Norton, *The British-Americans: The Loyalist Exiles in England, 1774–1789* (Boston, MA, 1972), 54.

19. Phyllis R. Blakeley, "Loyalist Military Settlement in Nova Scotia and Prince Edward Island," in Robert S. Allen (ed.), *The Loyal Americans: The Military Role of the Loyalist Provincial Corps and Their Settlement in British North America, 1775–1784* (Ottawa, 1983), 73; Alexander C. Flick, *Loyalism in New York during the American Revolution* (New York, 1970, orig. pub. 1901), 191.

20. Blakeley, "Loyalist Military Settlement," 76; Wallace Brown, "Military Settlement in New Brunswick," in Allen (ed.), *Loyal Americans*, 82; North Callahan, *Flight from the Republic: The Tories of the American Revolution* (Indianapolis, IN, 1967), 7–37.

21. Ellen G. Wilson, *The Loyal Blacks* (New York, 1976), 67–70 and 75; Charles R. Ritcheson, *Aftermath of Revolution: British Policy Toward the United States, 1783–1795* (Dallas, TX, 1969), 71; Sylvia R. Frey, *Black Resistance in a Revolutionary Age* (Princeton, NJ, 1991), 106 and 182.

22. Norton, *British-Americans*, 230–4; Stuart E. Brown, Jr, *Virginia Baron: The Story of Thomas 6th Lord Fairfax* (Berryville, VA, 1965), 198–9; Robert O. DeMond, *The Loyalists in North Carolina during the Revolution* (Durham, NC, 1940), 207; Isaac Harrell, *Loyalism in Virginia: Chapters in the Economic History of the Revolution* (Durham, NC, 1926), 104–10.

23. Hugh E. Egerton (ed.), *The Royal Commission on the Losses and Services of American Loyalists, 1783 to 1785* (New York, 1971, orig. pub. 1915), xxxi–xl; Eugene R. Fingerhut, "Uses and Abuses of the American Loyalists' Claims: a Critique of Quantitative Analyses," *WMQ*, 3rd Ser., 25 (1968): 246–7.

24. *JCC*, January 14, 1784, 26: 23–8; Ritcheson, *Aftermath of Revolution*, 60–8; Merrill Jensen, *The New Nation: A History of the United States during the Confederation, 1781–1789* (New York, 1950), 266–77.

25. Lambert, *South Carolina Loyalists*, 268 and 277.

Chapter Four

1. Henry J. Young, "Treason and Its Punishment in Revolutionary Pennsylvania," *PMHB*, 90 (1966): 293: Bradley Chapin, *The American Law of Treason: Revolutionary and Early National Origins* (Seattle, WA, 1964), 183.

2. Otis G. Hammond, *Tories of New Hampshire in the War of the Revolution* (Boston, MA, 1972), 202.

3. Richard C. Haskett, "Prosecuting the Revolution," *AHR*, 59 (1954): 580.

4. Leonard W. Levy, *Origins of the Fifth Amendment: The Right Against Self Incrimination* (New York, 1968), 413.

5. Claude W. Van Tyne, *The Loyalists of the American Revolution* (Gloucester, MA, 1959, orig. pub. 1959), 220.

6. Thomas Jefferson to James Innes, May 2, 1781, *JP*, 5: 593.

7. Arthur J. Mekeel, *The Relation of the Quakers to the American Revolution* (Lanham, MD, 1979), 177.

8. Quoted in *NG*, 5: 193n.–4n.

9. Nathanael Greene to Benjamin Lindsley, December 22, 1779, *NG*, 5: 198–99 and 193n.–4n.; Harry M. Ward, *General William Maxwell and the New Jersey Continentals* (Westport, CN, 1997), 140.

10. Allison Reppy, "The Specter of Attainder in New York," *St. John's Law Review*, 23 (1948): 22–3, 26 and 185; Robert A. Rutland, *The*

Birth of the Bill of Rights, 1776–1791 (Chapel Hill, NC, 1955), 96–7; Chapin, *American Law of Treason*, 78–9.

11. Chapin, *American Law of Treason*, 78–80.

12. Chapin, *American Law of Treason*, 42, 47, 63–4, and 132; Henry C. Black, *Black's Law Dictionary*, 4th ed (St Paul, MN, 1968), 1261.

13. Frederick B. Wiener, *Civilians Under Military Justice: The British Practice since 1689 Especially in North America* (Chicago, 1967), 96–8; Thomas Jones, *History of New York during the Revolutionary War* (New York, 1968, orig. pub. 1879), 2: 152.

14. Chapin, *American Law of Treason*, 51–4 and 64; Calhoon, *Loyalists in Revolutionary America*, 411.

15. Catherine S. Crary (ed.), *The Price of Loyalty: Tory Writings for the Revolutionary Era* (New York, 1973), 238–9 and 285.

16. *JCC*, October 6, 1775, 3: 280.

17. Frank Diffenderffer, "Lancaster County Loyalists," *Journal of the Lancaster County Historical Society*, 12 (1908): 248; Van Tyne, *Loyalists*, 204–5.

18. Crary (ed.), *Price of Loyalty*, 216–17; Michael Kammen, "The American Revolution as a *Crise de Conscience*: The Case of New York," in Richard Jellison (ed.), *Society, Freedom and Conscience: The American Revolution in Virginia, Massachusetts, and New York* (New York, 1976), 167; Tom Martin, "Simsbury Mines, Connecticut," in Richard L. Blanco (ed.), *The American Revolution, 1775–1783: An Encyclopedia* (New York, 1993), 2: 1525–6.

19. Kammen, "American Revolution as a *Crisis de Conscience*," 148–9; Van Tyne, *Loyalists*, 215 and 220; Frederic G. Mather, *The Refugees of 1776 from Long Island to Connecticut* (Albany, NY, 1913), 168–71 and 187–93.

20. William W. Hening, comp., *The Statutes at Large: Being a Collection of All the Laws of Virginia* (Richmond, VA, 1822), 10: 309–15; letters of Charles Lee and Robert Howe and proceedings of the Virginia Convention, May 1776, Scribner and Tarter (eds), *Revolutionary Virginia*, 6: 280–1 and 7, pt. 1: 92, 96–7, 157–9, 267n., and 285; Van Tyne, *Loyalists*, 227.

21. *JCC*, August 26, 1777 and September 6 and 8, 1777, 8: 678–9, 718–19, and 722–3, respectively.

22. Theodore Thayer, *Israel Pemberton: King of the Quakers* (Philadelphia, 1943), 216–17 and 224–5; Isaac Sharpless, *A Quaker Experiment in Government, Part II: The Quakers in the Revolution* (Philadelphia, 1902), 151–68; Thomas Gilpin, *Exiles in Virginia: with Observations on the Conduct of the Society of Friends . . . 1777–1778* (Philadelphia, 1848), 40–4.

23. Chapin, *American Law of Treason*, 29–36.

24. *JCC*, June 24, 1776, 5: 475–6.

25. Chapin, *American Law of Treason*, 44.
26. Henry J. Young, "Treason and Its Punishment in Revolutionary Pennsylvania," *PMHB*, 90 (1966), 295 and 297.
27. Crary (ed.), *Price of Loyalty*, 230–1.
28. Don Higginbotham, *The War of American Independence: Military Attitudes, Policies, and Practice, 1763–1789* (New York, 1971), 280.
29. Robert Morris to William Livingston, November 10, 1777, *WL*, 2: 111–15 and 115n.–118n.
30. Calhoon, *Loyalists in Revolutionary America*, 400–1; Crary (ed.), *Price of Loyalty*, 236–7.
31. *JP*, 5: 640–3, includes petition of Mann Page, May 13, 1781 and "Court Proceedings."
32. Harry M. Ward and Harold E. Greer, Jr, *Richmond During the Revolution, 1775–1783* (Charlottesville, VA, 1977), 148–50.
33. Jefferson, *Notes on the State of Virginia*, ed. Peden, 155.
34. Chapin, *American Law of Treason*, 70–1.
35. Chapin, *American Law of Treason*, 41, including quote; James W. Hurst, *The Law of Treason in the United States: Collected Essays* (Westport, CN, 1971), 122–3.
36. McBride, "Virginia War Effort," PhD diss., 217; Hurst, *Law of Treason*, 102, including quote.
37. Hurst, *Law of Treason*, 102 and 123n.
38. Jefferson to William Preston, March 21, 1780, *JP*, 3: 325.
39. *JCC*, January 2, 1776, 4: 18–19; Leonard W. Levy, *Emergence of a Free Press* (New York, 1985), 177.
40. Young, "Treason and Its Punishment," 290–1.
41. Van Tyne, *Loyalists*, 199–200.
42. Louisa County Court, Virginia, May 15, 1777, Revolutionary War Records, photostats, microfilm edition, National Archives.
43. David Ramsay, *The History of the American Revolution* (New York, 1968, orig. pub. 1789), 2: 319.
44. Philip Davidson. *Propaganda and the American Revolution, 1763–1783* (Chapel Hill, NC, 1941), 394.
45. Francis Hopkinson, *The Miscellaneous Essays and Occasional Writings of Francis Hopkinson* (Philadelphia, 1972), Two Letters [1776], 1: 135.
46. Levy, *Emergence of a Free Press*, 181–3; Richard Buel, Jr, "Freedom of the Press in Revolutionary America: The Evolution of Libertarianism, 1760–1820," in Bernard Bailyn and John B. Hench (eds), *The Press and the American Revolution* (Worcester, MA, 1980), 81–2.
47. Levy, *Emergence of a Free Press*, 186, 191, 196–7, and 213–14.
48. Levy, *Emergence of a Free Press*, 206–11; Joseph T. Wheeler, *The Maryland Press, 1777–1790* (Baltimore, MD, 1938), 27–8 and 32–3.
49. Richard F. Hixson, *Isaac Collins: A Quaker Printer in Eighteenth Century America* (New Brunswick, NJ, 1968), 95–8.

50. William D. Sloan and Julie H. Williams, *The Early American Press, 1690–1783* (Westport, CN, 1994), 178–9 and 186; Frank L. Mott, *American Journalism: A History of Newspapers in the United States through 250 Years* (New York, 1941), 87–8.

51. Willi Paul Adams, "The Colonial German-language Press and the American Revolution," in Bailyn and Hench (eds), *The Press and the American Revolution*, 215–16.

52. Janice Potter and Robert M. Calhoon, "The Character and Coherence of the Loyalist Press," in Bailyn and Hench (eds), *The Press and the American Revolution*, 233.

53. Kenneth Scott (ed.), *Rivingston's New York Newspaper: Excerpts from a Loyalist Press, 1773–1783* (New York, 1973), 17–19; Catherine S. Crary, "The Tory and the Spy: The Double Life of James Rivington," *WMQ*, 3rd Ser., 16 (1959): 67; Mott, *American Journalism*, 84–6.

54. Levy, *Emergence of a Free Press*, 175; Mott, *American Journalism*, 82–3; Jones, *History of New York*, 1: 63–5.

55. Fred S. Siebert, "The Confiscated Revolutionary Press," *Journalism Quarterly*, 13 (1936): 179–81.

56. W. Bird Terwilliger, "William Goddard: Victory for the Freedom of the Press," *Maryland Historical Magazine*, 36 (1941): 141–7; Ward L. Miner, *William Goddard, Newspaperman* (Durham, NC, 1962), 150–71.

Chapter Five

1. Otto Hufeland, *Westchester County during the American Revolution, 1775–1783* (White Plains, NY, 1926), 180–3; William S. Hadaway (ed.), *The McDonald Papers* (White Plains, NY, 1926), pt. 2: 3–5; Stephen Jenkins, *The Story of the Bronx* (New York, 1912), 152.

2. Crary (ed.), *Price of Loyalty*, 173–5; Catherine S. Crary, "Guerrilla Activities of James DeLancey's Cowboys in Westchester County: Conventional Warfare or Self-Interested Freebooting?", in Robert A. East and Jacob Judd (eds), *The Loyalist Americans: A Focus on Greater New York* (Tarrytown, NY, 1975), 10; Jones, *History of New York*, 1: 301.

3. DeLancey to Guy Carleton, April 3, 1783, quoted in Crary, "Guerrilla Activities," 20.

4. George F. Scheer (ed.), *Private Yankee Doodle: Being a Narrative of Some of the Adventures, Dangers and Sufferings of a Revolutionary Soldier,* by Joseph Plumb Martin (Boston, MA, 1962), 219–21.

5. William Heath to Gov. George Clinton, March 17, 1781, *Public Papers of George Clinton* (Albany, NY, 1902), 6: 44–5.

6. John L. Romer (ed.), *Historical Studies of the Romer, Van Tassel Allied Families and Tales of the Neutral Ground* (Buffalo, NY, 1917), 20–24.

7. Timothy Dwight, *Travels in New England and New York*, ed. Barbara M. Solomon (Cambridge, MA, 1969), 3: 345.

8. Morton Pennypacker, *General Washington's Spies on Long Island and in New York* (Brooklyn, NY, 1939), 240–1.

9. Harry M. Ward, *Charles Scott and the "Spirit of '76"* (Charlottesville, VA, 1988), 63–4.

10. James F. Collins, "Whaleboat Warfare on Long Island Sound," *New York History*, 25 (1944): 196–7; Jones, *History of New York*, 1: 362–3.

11. Jones, *History of New York*, 1: 301–2.

12. Lydia M. Post, *Recollections of the American Revolution: A Private Journal*, ed. Sidney Barclay (Port Washington, NY, 1970, orig. pub. 1859), 78, 106–7, and 164.

13. Post, *Recollections of the American Revolution*, 84–5.

14. Post, *Recollections of the American Revolution*, 75–6.

15. Benjamin Tallmadge, *Memoir of Colonel Benjamin Tallmadge* (New York, 1968, orig. pub. 1858), 32–3; Crary (ed.), *Price of Loyalty*, 197; Jones, *History of New York*, 2: 33–4.

16. Samuel W. Eager, *An Outline History of Orange County* (Newburgh, NY, 1846–7), 556.

17. Eager, *Orange County*, 556–7: Henry C. Beck, *Tales and Towns of Northern New Jersey* (New Brunswick, NJ, 1988, orig. pub. 1964), 115–23; Claire K. Tholl, "The Career of Claudius Smith," *The North Jersey Highlander*, 4: 4 (1968): 3–4.

18. Eager, *Orange County*, 562; Claire K. Tholl, "The Confession of William Cole," *The North Jersey Highlander*, 4: 4 (1968): 10–17; Lorenzo Sabine, *Biographical Sketches of Loyalists of the American Revolution* (Baltimore, MD, 1979, orig. pub. 1864), 2: 315.

19. Sabine, *Biographical Sketches*, 2: 400–1.

20. Theodore M. Banta, *A Frisian Family: The Banta Genealogy* (New York, 1893), 68–70; Adrian C. Leiby, *The Revolutionary War in the Hackensack Valley: The Jersey Dutch and the Neutral Ground* (New Brunswick, NJ, 1980), 188–98, 207, 210, 260, and 295–6.

21. Ward, *William Maxwell*, 145–9 and 213n.; James Thacher, *Military Journal of the American Revolution* (Hartford, CT, 1862 edn), 200.

22. David J. Fowler, "Egregious Villains, Wood Rangers and London Traders: The Pine Robber Phenomenon in New Jersey during the Revolutionary War," PhD diss., Rutgers University, 1987, 115–6, 125–7, 131, 145, 162, 213, 234, 238, 274, 294, 311, and 340; Beck, *Tales and Towns*, 114; *New Jersey Gazette*, February 3 and September 29, 1779 and August 8, 1781, in *Archives of the State of New Jersey*, 2nd Ser., 3: 53, 641 and 649 and 5: 282, respectively.

23. James Moody, *Lieut. James Moody's Narrative of his Exertions and Sufferings . . .* (New York, 1968, from 2nd edn, 1783), *passim*; Richard Sampson, *Escape in America: The British Convention Prisoners, 1777–*

1783 (Chippenham, Eng., 1995), 3–5; *WL*, 4: 3–5; Alfred E. Jones, *The Loyalists of New Jersey: Their Memorials, Petitions, Claims, Etc. from English Records* (Bowie, MD, 1988, orig. pub. 1926), 143–5; Leiby, *Hackensack Valley*, 279.

24. John F. Reed, "Rogues of the Revolution: The Story of the Doane Renegades," *Bulletin of the Historical Society of Montgomery County, Pennsylvania*, 18 (1968): 5.

25. Reed, "Rogues of the Revolution", 6–14 and 20–28; John P. Rogers, *The New Doane Book: Bucks County's Bandit Tories of the Revolution* (Doylestown, PA, 1952), *passim*.

26. John Wilson to Patrick Henry, May 20, 1778, Executive Communications, Library of Virginia; Adele Hast, *Loyalism in Revolutionary Virginia: The Norfolk Area and the Eastern Shore* (Ann Arbor, MI, 1982), 96–8; Hugh P. Leaming, *Hidden Americans: Maroons of Virginia and the Carolinas* (New York, 1995), 239.

27. Levin Joynes to Col. William Davies, September 10, 1781, Executive Papers, Library of Virginia.

28. Edmund Randolph to James Madison, August 30, 1782, William T. Hutchinson and William M. E. Rachal (eds), *The Papers of James Madison* (Chicago, 1967), 5: 91 and 93n.

29. Quoted in Lambert, *South Carolina Loyalists*, 222.

30. Thomas Bee to Gov. John Matthews, December 9, 1782, quoted in Jerome J. Nadelhaft, *The Disorders of War: The Revolution in South Carolina* (Orono, ME, 1981), 129.

31. William Stevens, *A History of Georgia* (Philadelphia, 1859), 2: 376–7.

32. Richard M. Brown, *The South Carolina Regulators* (Cambridge, MA, 1963), 28 and 184n.

33. David Ramsay, *History of South Carolina* (Spartanburg, SC, 1968, from 1858 edn), 1: 259.

34. Brown, *South Carolina Regulators*, 91, 103, 204n.–5n., quoted 205n.; Leaming, *Hidden Americans*, 411.

35. Prisoners sent to Charleston [Jan. 1776] by Col. Richardson and Francis Salvador to William Drayton, July 18, 1776, Robert W. Gibbes (ed.), *Documentary History of the American Revolution* (Spartanburg, SC, 1972, orig. pub. 1855 and 1857), 1: 249–53 and 2: 24, respectively; Tom Hatley, *The Dividing Paths: Cherokees and South Carolina Through the Era of Revolution* (New York, 1993), 188–9 and 197; Lambert, *South Carolina Loyalists*, 46–52.

36. Quoted in Leaming, *Hidden Americans*, 436.

37. William Moultrie, *Memoirs of the American Revolution* (New York, 1968, orig. pub. 1802), 203n.

38. Rachel N. Klein, *Unification of a Slave State: The Rise of the Planter Class in the South Carolina Backcountry, 1760–1808* (Chapel Hill, NC, 1990), 95; Ronald G. Killion and Charles T. Waller, *Georgia and the*

American Revolution (Atlanta, GA, 1975), 51–3; Brown, *South Carolina Regulators*, 205n.

39. Klein, *Unification of a Slave State*, 98.
40. Klein, *Unification of a Slave State*, including quote, 116.
41. Address to the Upper and Commons Houses of Assembly, February 27, 1781, James Wright to Lord Germain, April 2, 1781, and Joseph Clay to John Lewis Gervais, September 22, 1779, *Collections of the Georgia Historical Society*, 3: 339 and 345 and 8: 146–7, respectively.
42. Nathanael Greene to Robert Howe, December 29, 1780, *NG*, 7: 17.
43. Joseph B. Lockey, "The Florida Banditti 1783," *Florida Historical Quarterly*, 24 (1945): 97.
44. Klein, *Unification of a Slave State*, 99.
45. Klein, *Unification of a Slave State*, including quote.
46. Robert S. Davis, "Daniel McGirth," in Blanco (ed.), *American Revolution . . . Encyclopedia*, 2: 997–8; Lockey, "Florida Banditti," 89 and 93–6.
47. Klein, *Unification of a Slave State*, 118 and 354–5; Nadelhaft, *Disorders of War*, 131–2.

Chapter Six

1. William Livingston to Washington, December 21, 1778, *WL*, 2: 519; Washington to William Maxwell, December 21, 1778 and to Joseph Reed, February 12, 1779, *FWW*, 13: 444 and 14: 101–2, respectively.
2. From the Essex Grand Jury, August 13, 1777 and William Livingston to Washington, December 21, 1778 and to Henry Lee, November 24, 1779, *WL*, 2: 27 and 519 and 3: 230, respectively; General Orders, July 9 and 17 and August 4 and 8, 1776, *AWP*, 5: 245–6n., 352, 556 and 618, respectively.
3. William Maxwell to Washington, December 25, 1778, Washington Papers, Library of Congress.
4. General Orders, April 5, 1781, *FWW*, 22: 461.
5. General Orders, June 28, 1781, *FWW*, 22: 270.
6. General Orders, July 10, 1781, *FWW*, 22: 356.
7. General Orders, August 1, 1781, *FWW*, 22: 444.
8. *Valley Forge Orderly Book of General George Weedon* (New York, 1971, orig. pub. 1902), 136; Allen Bowman, *The Morale of the American Revolutionary Army* (Port Washington, NY, 1964 orig. pub.1943), 79.
9. Alexander McDougall to Washington, August 19, 1776, *ASP*, 6: 77–8.
10. John Bakeless, *Turncoats, Traitors and Heroes* (Philadelphia, 1959), 252–9.
11. *The Journal of Lieut. William Feltman of the First Pennsylvania Regiment* (Philadelphia, 1853), January 22, 1781, 37.

12. Congressional Committee, April 1777 and *New-York Journal*, July 19, 1779, in Moore, *Diary*, 216 and 378, respectively; Sylvia R. Frey, *The British Soldier in America: A Social History of Military Life in the Revolutionary Period* (Austin, TX, 1981), 78–9; Varnum L. Collins, *A Brief Narrative of the Ravages of the British and Hessians at Princeton 1776–77* (Princeton, NJ, 1906), 4–20.

13. Washington to Fisher Gay, September 4, 1776 and General Orders, September 4, 1776, *ASP*, 6: 214–15 and 212, respectively; General Orders, June 30, 1778, *FWW*, 12: 132 Washington to William Heath, May 10, 1777, "William Heath Papers," *MHSC*, 5th Ser., 4 (1878), 53.

14. *JCC*, May 27, 1778, 11: 541; Fred A. Berg, *Encyclopedia of Continental Army Units: Battalions, Regiments and Independent Corps* (Harrisburg, PA, 1972), 132–3; John B. B. Trussell, *The Pennsylvania Line: Regimental Organization and Operations* (Harrisburg, PA, 1977), 230–1; Charles P. Neimeyer, *American Goes to War: A Social History of the Continental Army* (New York, 1996), 50–1 and 182n.

15. General Orders, October 11, 1778, *FWW*, 13: 61–2.

16. Instructions to Captain Bartholomew von Heer, October 11, 1778, *FWW*, 13: 68.

17. Quoted from John Lamb's Orderly Book, October 11, 1778, in Holly A. Mayer, *Belonging to the Army: Campfollowers and Community during the American Revolution* (Columbia, SC, 1996), 48.

18. Nathanael Greene to James Abeel, December 21, 1779 and to Benjamin Lindsley, December 22, 1779, *NG*, 5: 190 and 198.

19. Albert C. Myers (ed.), *Sally Wister's Journal . . . A Quaker Maiden's Account of Her Experiences with Officers of the Continental Army, 1777–1778* (Philadelphia, 1902), October 19, 1777, 76–8.

20. William Maxwell to Greene, December 24, 1779, *NG*, 5: 206–7.

21. Samuel Holden Parsons to Greene, December 8, 1779, *NG*, 154.

22. Wayne K. Bodle and Jacqueline Thibaut, *Valley Forge Research Report* (Valley Forge, PA, 1980), 3: 78–9 and 90.

23. John W. Jackson, *With the British Army in Philadelphia, 1777–1778* (San Rafael, CA, 1979), 5: Ewald G. Schaukirk, *Occupation of New York City by the British [extracts of a diary]* (New York, 1969), 5.

24. Crane (ed.), *Diary of Drinker*, January–March 1778, 1: 239, 266, 271, 273, and 289–90.

25. Josiah Bartlett to John Langdon, July 13, 1778, *LD*, 10: 268.

26. Crane (ed.), *Diary of Drinker*, 1: 218 and n. 222 and n. and 383n.

27. John Adams to Abigail Adams, August 24, 1777, Butterfield (ed.), *Adams Family Correspondence*, 2: 328; *Valley Forge Orderly Book*, August 23, 1777, 19.

28. Janet Schaw, *Journal of a Lady of Quality*, ed. Charles M. Andrews (New Haven, CT, 1921), 190.

29. *Journal of Feltman*, June 22, 1781, 5.

30. Orderly Book of Brig.-Gen. Anthony Wayne, 1781, quoted in Mayer, *Belonging to the Army*, 75n.

31. *Pennsylvania Journal*, July 9, 1777, *Pennsylvania Evening Post*, July 24, 1777, and *New-Jersey Gazette*, March 3, 1779, in Moore, *Diary*, 228–30 and 346–7.

32. General Greene's Orders, May 18, 1776, *NG*, 1: 215.

33. For example, General Orders, July 2, 1778, *FWW*, 12: 147 and John W. Jordan (ed.), "Orderly Book of the Second Pennsylvania Continental Line," May 14, 1778, *PMHB*, 36 (1912): 246.

34. Meyers (ed.), *Sally Wister's Journal*, June 7, 1778, 179.

35. Meyers (ed.), *Sally Wister's Journal*, November 2, 1777 and June 3, 1778, 108 and 158.

36. John Chilton to Leven Powell, July 8, 1777, "The Old Virginia Line in the Middle States during the American Revolution," *Tyler's Quarterly*, 12 (1931): 125.

37. Ebenezer David to Nicholas Brown, January 8, 1776, Jeanette D. Black and William G. Roelker (eds), *A Rhode Island Chaplain in the Revolution: Letters of Ebenezer David to Nicholas Brown, 1775–78* (Providence, RI, 1949), 7.

38. Ebenezer Huntington to Jabez Huntington, February 22, 1776, G. W. F. Blanchfield (ed.), *Letters Written by Ebenezer Huntington* (New York, 1914), 29.

39. *The Journal of Nicholas Cresswell, 1774–1777* (Port Washington, NY, 1968, orig. pub. 1924), May 21, 1777, 221.

40. "Diary of Lieutenant James McMichael of the Pennsylvania Line," *PMHB*, 16 (1892): 146, August 3, 1777.

41. Mayer, *Belonging to the Army*, 147.

42. Edward Pinkowski, *Washington's Officers Slept Here* (Philadelphia, 1953), 102.

43. Crane (ed.), *Diary of Drinker*, April 6, 1778, 297.

44. Quoted in Darlene E. Fisher, "Social Life in Philadelphia during the British Occupation," *Pennsylvania History*, 37 (1970): 246–7.

45. Walter J. Fraser, Jr, *Patriots, Pistols and Petticoats: "Poor Sinful Charles Town" during the American Revolution* (Columbia, SC, 1993, orig. pub. 1945), 145.

46. E. A. Benians (ed.), *A Journal by Thos: Hughes . . . 1778–1789* (Cambridge, Eng., 1947), 80.

47. Subscription List, *NG*, 5: 408; Samuel S. Smith, *Winter at Morristown, 1779–1780: The Darkest Hour* (Monmouth Beach, NJ, 1979), 22–5; Chastellux, *Travels*, December 14, 1789, 1: 177; Simon V. Anderson, "American Music during the War for Independence, 1775–1783," PhD diss., University of Michigan, 1965, 110; James T. Flexner, *The Young Hamilton: A Biography* (Boston, MA, 1978), 270 and 276.

48. General Orders, June 4, 1777 and July 20, 1781, *FWW*, 8: 181–2 and 22: 398.

49. Washington to Sullivan, December 20, 1778 *FWW*, 13: 440.

50. John Adams to Abigail Adams, July 5, 1777, Butterfield (ed.), *Adams Family Correspondence*, 2: 274–5; Kenneth Silverman, *A Cultural History of the American Revolution* (New York, 1987), 356–8. For various public occasions in which military bands participated, see Raoul F. Camus, "The Military Band in the United States Army Prior to 1834", PhD diss., New York University, 1969.

51. Silverman, *Cultural History*, 355–6.

52. Johann Döhla, *A Hessian Diary of the American Revolution*, ed. Bruce E. Burgoyne (Norman, OK, 1990), 115.

53. James McHenry to Washington, July 14, 1782 and Washington to the Secretary at War, July 18, 1778, *FWW*, 24: 432 and n.

54. Thomas Pollock, *The Philadelphia Theater in the Eighteenth Century* (Philadelphia, 1933), 37; Silverman, *Cultural History*, 350; Anderson, "American Music," PhD diss., 114.

55. Reminiscence of Dr William Read, Gibbes (ed.), *Documentary History*, 2: 262.

56. *JCC*, October 16, 1778, 12: 1018.

57. Pollock, *Philadelphia Theater*, 38–9; Silverman, *Cultural History*, 365–6.

58. Gordon E. Beck, "British Military Theatricals in New York City during the Revolutionary War," PhD diss., University of Illinois, 1964, 13, 16–24, and 43; Oscar T. Barck, *New York City during the War for Independence* (New York, 1931), 170–4; Schaukirk, *Occupation of New York City*, June 5, 1780, 12; Silverman, *Cultural History*, 292.

59. Jackson, *With the British Army*, 196, 199–200, and 235–49; Fisher, "Social Life in Philadelphia," 249–52; Pollock, *Philadelphia Theater*, 34–5; Crane (ed.), *Diary of Drinker*, May 18, 1778, 1: 306.

60. Ray W. Pettengill (trans.), *Letters from America, 1776–1779: Being Letters of Brunswick Hessian and Waldeck Officers with the British Army during the Revolution* (Port Washington, NY, 1964, orig. pub. 1924), 150–1; Frey, *British Soldier*, 67–8.

61. William Livingston to Ephraim Harris, February 16, 1783, *WL*, 4: 511.

62. George S. McGowen, Jr, *The British Occupation of Charleston, 1780–82* (Columbia, SC, 1972), 26–33; Frederic B. Wiener, *Civilians under Military Justice: The British Practice since 1689 Especially in North America* (Chicago, 1967), chapters 5 and 6; Lambert, *South Carolina Loyalists*, 193; Barck, *New York City . . . Independence*, 49–73 and 95–144.

63. Milton M. Klein and Ronald W. Howard (eds), *The Twilight of British Rule in Revolutionary America: The New York Letter Book of General James Robertson, 1780–1783* (Cooperstown, NY, 1983), 47; Jones, *History of New York*, 1: 164 and 341.

64. James G. Bradsher, "Preserving the Revolution: Civil–Military Relations during the American War for Independence, 1775–1783," PhD diss. University of Massachusetts, 1984, 540 and 548–51.

65. *JCC*, September 20, 1776, 5: 795.

66. General Orders, February 24, 1779, *FWW*, 13: 140.

67. Washington to Gov. George Clinton, October 8, to the Magistrates and Selectmen of Norwalk, October 15, and to Henry Lee, November 29, 1778, *FWW*, 50, 81, and 351, respectively.

68. Ward, *William Maxwell*, 115–16.

69. Jefferson to Lafayette, March 19, 1781, *JP*, 5: 180.

70. *JCC*, September 17, 1778, 8: 752; Donald Jackson (ed.), *The Diaries of George Washington* (Charlottesville, VA, 1978), May 1781, 3: 356; Victor L. Johnson, *The Administration of the American Commissariat during the Revolutionary War* (Philadelphia, 1941), 92–3.

71. Washington to the President of Congress, January 5, 1780, *FWW*, 17: 357–8; S. Sydney Bradford, "Hunger Menaces the Revolution, December, 1779–January, 1780," *Maryland Historical Magazine*, 61 (1966): 13; Erna Risch, *Supplying Washington's Army* (Washington, DC, 1981), 15–16.

72. George Mason to Jefferson, May 14, 1781, *JP*, 5: 647; E. Wayne Carp, *To Starve the Army with Pleasure: Continental Army Administration and American Political Culture* (Chapel Hill, NC, 1984), 77.

73. Jordan (ed.), "Orderly Book . . . Pennsylvania Line," May 15, 1778, 37.

74. Nathanael Greene to Col. John Cox, November 28, 1779, *NG*, 5: 123.

75. Elizabeth Cometti, "Impressment during the American Revolution," in Vera Largent (ed.), *The Walter Clinton Jackson Essays in the Social Sciences* (Chapel Hill, NC, 1942), 103, 106, and 108.

76. John Lucas to Ferdinand Huddleston, November 7, 1783, in Stephen Conway, "To Subdue America: British Army Officers and the Conduct of the Revolutionary War," *WMQ*, 3rd Ser., 43 (1986): 407.

77. Merrill Jensen, *The New Nation: A History of the United States during the Confederation, 1781–89* (New York, 1950), 376–7; Risch, *Supplying Washington's Army*, 22–3.

Chapter Seven

1. Samuel Adams to James Warren, January 7, 1776, Cushing (ed.), *Writings of Samuel Adams*, 3: 250.

2. *JCC*, June 14 and 15, 1775, 2: 89 and 91.

3. *JCC*, September 16, 1776 and November 12, 1776, 5: 762 and 6: 944–5.

4. James Duane's Notes, February 27, 1776, *LD*, 3: 295.

5. *JCC*, September 16, 1776, 5: 763.

6. William Hull to William Heath, March 8, 1781, "Heath Papers," *MHSC*, 7th Ser., 5: 179; Jonathan Smith, "How Massachusetts Raised Her Troops in the Revolution," *MHSP*, 55 (1921–2): 351; Arthur J. Alexander, "How Maryland Tried to Raise Her Continental Quotas," *Maryland Historical Magazine*, 42 (1947): 188.

7. Heath to Washington, December 21, 1779 and April 30, 1780, "Heath Papers," *MHSC*, 7th Ser., 4: 336–7 and 5: 60.

8. John Paterson to Heath, March 31, 1780 and October 30, 1780, "Heath Papers", *MHSC*, 7th Ser., 5: 44 and 114–15.

9. Samuel Shaw to Nathaniel Shaw, August 10, 1780, Josiah Quincy (ed.), *The Journals of Samuel Shaw* (New York, 1968, orig. pub. 1847), 76.

10. Washington to Gov. Nicholas Cooke, February 2, 1777, *FWW*, 7: 89.

11. *JCC*, August 26, 1776 and February 25, 1783, 5: 702–5 and 24: 145–7.

12. William H. Glasson, *Federal Military Pensions in the United States* (New York, 1918), 67 and 81–3.

13. Scheer (ed.), *Private Yankee Doodle*, 283.

14. Edward D. Papenfuse and Gregory A. Stiverson, "General Smallwood's Recruits: The Peacetime Career of the Revolutionary Private," *WWQ*, 3rd Ser., 30 (1973): 124.

15. Richard J. Buel, *Dear Liberty: Connecticut's Mobilization for the Revolutionary War* (Middletown, CT, 1980), 39.

16. Douglas L. Jones, "The Strolling Poor: Transiency in Eighteenth-Century Massachusetts," in James K. Martin (ed.), *Interpreting Colonial America* (New York, 1978), 290; Neimeyer, *America Goes to War*, 17–18.

17. Shy, *A People Numerous and Armed*, 172–3.

18. Mark E. Lender, "The Social Structure of the New Jersey Brigade: The Continental Line as an American Standing Army," in Peter Karsten (ed.), *The Military in America* (New York, 1980), 34; Neimeyer, *America Goes to War*, 15 and 19.

19. John R. Sellers, "The Common Soldier in the American Revolution," in Stanley J. Underhal (ed.), *Military History of the American Revolution* (Washington, DC, 1976), 154.

20. Jefferson to Benjamin Harrison, December 11, 1780, *JP*, 4: 199.

21. Steuben to Jefferson, December 28, 1780, *JP*, 4: 245.

22. *The Diary of Frederick Mackenzie* (Cambridge, MA, 1930), 1: 111–12.

23. Thomas Balch (ed.), *The Journal of Claude Blanchard, 1780–1783* (Albany, NY, 1876), June 28, 1781, 115.

24. William Heath to Caleb Davis, March 16, 1781, "Heath Papers," *MHSC*, 7th Ser., 5: 181.

25. Bowman, *Morale*, 14.

26. Trussell, *Pennsylvania Line*, 244–5.
27. Neimeyer, *America Goes to War*, 16.
28. Mark E. Lender, "The Enlisted Line: The Continental Soldiers of New Jersey," PhD diss., Rutgers University, 1975, 111.
29. Sellers, "Common Soldier," 154.
30. Mayer, *Belonging to the Army*, 58 and 191.
31. Washington to the President of Congress, May 13, 1777, *FWW*, 8: 56.
32. *Journal of Cresswell*, March 3, 1777, 186.
33. Bradsher, "Preserving the Revolution," 354.
34. Lender, "Social Structure of the New Jersey Brigade," 34.
35. *LD*, 10: 686n.–87n.
36. Elliott W. Hoffman, "The German Soldiers in the American Revolution," PhD diss., University of New Hampshire, 1982, 503.
37. Baron Curt von Stedingk to King Gustavus III, January 18, 1780, in Adolph B. Benson, *Sweden and the American Revolution* (New Haven, CT, 1926), 165.
38. Bernard Bailyn, *Voyagers to the West: A Passage in the Peopling of America on the Eve of the Revolution* (New York, 1986), 26, 36–7, and quote on p. 40.
39. Charles J. Stillé, *Major-General Anthony Wayne and the Pennsylvania Line in the Continental Army* (Port Washington, NY, 1968, orig. pub. 1893), 248–9; Papenfuse and Stiverson, "General Smallwood's Recruits," 120, 125, and 126–7.
40. Joseph A. Goldenberg et al., "Revolutionary Ranks: An Analysis of the Chesterfield Supplement," *VMHB*, 87 (1979): 184 and 186; Michael A. McDonnel, "The Politics of Mobilization in Revolutionary Virginia: Military Culture and Political and Social Relations, 1774–1783," DPhil, University of Oxford, 1995, 71.
41. Henry M. M. Richards, *The Pennsylvania-Germans in the Revolutionary War, 1775–1783* (Baltimore, MD, 1991, org. pub. 1908), 4; Trussell, *Pennsylvania Line*, 249–50.
42. Mark E. Lender and James K. Martin (eds), *Citizen Soldier: The Revolutionary Journal of Joseph Bloomfield* (Newark, NJ, 1982), August 28, 1776, 102.
43. Washington to Col. Samuel Griffin, December 24, 1776, *AWP*, 7: 429.
44. *JCC*, January 17, 1776, 4: 63; Lender, "Enlisted Line," 79–80.
45. Charles Royster, *A Revolutionary People at War: The Continental Army and American Character, 1775–1783* (New York, 1979), 84.
46. Alexander Graydon, *Memoirs of His Own Time . . .* , ed. John S. Littell (New York, 1969, orig. pub. 1846), 133–4.
47. Graydon, *Memoirs of His Own Time*, 135–6.
48. Durand Echeverria and Orville T. Murphy (eds), "The American Revolutionary Army: A French Estimate in 1777," *Military Analysis of the Revolutionary War* (Millwood, NY, 1977), 209.

49. Francis Johnston to Anthony Wayne, November 17, 1776, in Stillé, *Anthony Wayne*, 44.

50. Ebenezer Fox, *The Adventures of Ebenezer Fox* (Boston, MA, 1838), 57–8.

51. John Claspy deposition (1833) in John C. Dann (ed.), *The Revolution Remembered: Eyewitness Accounts of the War for Independence* (Chicago, 1980), 365–6.

52. Washington to William Grayson, May 3, 1777, *FWW*, 13: 14; Royster, *Revolutionary People at War*, 133.

53. *JCC*, July 31, 1777, 8: 593–4; Circular to the States, August 4, 1777, *FWW*, 9: 16.

54. Lender, "Enlisted Line," 78.

55. William Davies to Jefferson, March 18, 1781, *JP*, 5: 174.

56. Jefferson to J. P. G. Muhlenburg, April 12, 1780, *JP*, 3: 351.

57. Washington to Patrick Henry, May 17, 1777, *FWW*, 8: 77–8; Royster, *Revolutionary People at War*, 43.

58. Jefferson to John Adams, May 16, 1777, *JP*, 2: 18.

59. *JCC*, April 14, 1777, 7: 262–3.

60. Robert A. Gross *The Minutemen and Their World* (New York, 1976), 147; Jean F. Hankins, "Conscription for the Continental Army," in Blanco (ed.), *American Revolution . . . Encyclopedia*, 364.

61. *JCC*, February 26, 1778, 10: 200–2.

62. Scheer (ed.), *Private Yankee Doodle*, 60–1.

63. Richard Henry Lee to Jefferson, April 29, 1777, *JP*, 2: 13–14.

64. Hugh F. Rankin, *The North Carolina Continentals* (Chapel Hill, NC, 1971), 179.

65. Gross, *Minutemen*, 147–8.

66. John R. Van Atta, "Conscription in Revolutionary Virginia: The Case of Culpeper County, 1780–1781," *VMHB*, 92 (1984), 265–7.

67. Rankin, *North Carolina Continentals*, 135.

68. McBride, "Virginia War Effort," 118.

69. William Davies to Col. William Preston, July 29, 1781, "Preston Papers," *VMHB* (1920): 112.

70. Paul V. Lutz, "Greetings, or Do I Feel a Draught," *American Heritage*, 17: 5 (August 1966): 112.

71. McBride, "Virginia War Effort," 116.

72. Van Atta, "Conscription in Revolutionary Virginia," 278.

73. Mark E. Lender, "The Conscripted Line: The Draft in Revolutionary New Jersey," *New Jersey History*, 103 (1985), 34.

74. McDonnell, "Politics of Mobilization . . . Virginia," 107.

75. Session of Virginia Council of State, February 27, 1778, Hutchinson and Rachal (eds), *Papers of Madison*, 1: 23–32; Loudoun County Order Book, May 12, 1778, Library of Virginia.

76. Westmoreland County Orders, 1776–1786, August 5, 1778, 63–4, Library of Virginia microfilm; Northumberland County, January 13, 1778, Revolutionary War Records, National Archives, Library of Virginia microfilm.

77. Stillé, *Anthony Wayne*, 267.

78. Hening, *Statutes*, October 1780 session, 10: 334–5; McDonnell, "Politics of Mobilization . . . Virginia," 98–100.

79. John Taylor to Jefferson, December 5, 1780, *JP*, 4: 180.

80. Thomas Gaskins to Jefferson, February 23, 1781, *JP*, 693; Northumberland County Order Book, 1773–1783, January 8–March 13, 1781, 441–54, Library of Virginia; McBride, "Virginia War Effort," 261–2; McDonnell, "Politics of Mobilization . . . Virginia," 93–4.

81. Virginia Board of War, March 1781, *JP*, 5: 212n.

82. Garrett Van Meter to Jefferson, April 20, 1781, *JP*, 513–14; General Court Martial, Leeds Town (Richmond County, VA), June 1781, Executive Papers, Library of Virginia; McBride, "Virginia War Effort," 261–7.

83. Col. John Cropper to Gov. Nelson, September 30, 1781 and John Cropper to County Lieutenant of Accomac, October 1, 1781, Executive Papers, Library of Virginia; Commissioners for Collecting Taxes in Accomac County to Jefferson, May 15, 1781 and George Corbin to Jefferson, August 31, 1781, *JP*, 5: 653–4 and 6: 44–5; Hast, *Loyalism in Revolutionary Virginia*, 152–7.

84. Deposition on April 23, 1781 riot, enclosed in Col. Cropper to Gov. Nelson, September 30, 1781, Executive Papers, Library of Virginia.

85. Col. Samuel Brown to Col. William Davies, April 14, 1782, William P. Palmer (ed.), *Calendar of Virginia State Papers* (Richmond, VA, 1883), 3: 130.

Chapter Eight

1. Joseph P. Tustin (ed.), *Diary of the American War: A Hessian Journal; Captain Johann Ewald, Field Jäger Corps* (New Haven, CT, 1979), 68 and 489n.; Wiener, *Civilians under Military Justice*, 87.

2. Mayer, *Belonging to the Army*, 133.

3. Washington to the Superintendent of Finance, January 29, 1783, *FWW*, 26: 78–9.

4. A. W. Lauber (ed.), *Orderly Books of the Fourth New York Regiment, 1778–1780; The Second New York Regiment, 1780–1783*, by Samuel Tallmadge (Albany, NY, 1932), October 10, 1781, 610.

5. Harry E. Wildes, *Anthony Wayne* (New York, 1941), 232.

6. *Diary of Mackenzie*, 146.

7. Quoted in Mayer, *Belonging to the Army*, September 20, 1780 (possibly Elias Parker), 126.
8. Scheer (ed.), *Private Yankee Doodle*, 197–8.
9. Hannah Winthrop to Mercy Warren, November 11, 1777, *Warren–Adams Letters: Chiefly Correspondence among John Adams, Samuel Adams, and James Warren*, MHSC, 73 (1925): 451.
10. General Orders, July 1, 1777, Joseph B. Turner (ed.), *The Journal and Order Book of Captain Robert Kirkwood of the Delaware Regiment of the Continental Line* (Port Washington, NY, 1970, orig. pub. 1910), 94.
11. General Orders, August 4, 1777, *FWW*, 9: 17.
12. General Orders, August 23, 1777, *FWW*, 126.
13. General Orders, July 4, August 27, and September 13, 1777 and June 19, 1781, *FWW*, 8: 347, 9: 139 and 213, and 22: 233, respectively.
14. For example, *Valley Forge Orderly Book*, January 29, 1778, 215; Turner (ed.), *Journal of Kirkwood*, May 21, 1777, 63.
15. *Major [John] André's Journal . . .* (New York, 1968, reprint of 1930 edn), June 22, 1777, 30.
16. Thomas Anburey, *Travels through the Interior Parts of America in a Series of Letters* (New York, 1969, orig. pub. 1789), 1: 436–7.
17. John T. White, "The Truth about Molly Pitcher," in James K. Martin and Karen R. Stubaus (eds), *The American Revolution: Whose Revolution?* (New York, 1977), 103–4.
18. Frey, *British Soldier*, 76.
19. *JCC*, June 29, 1779, 14: 805; Paul Eagle, *Women in the American Revolution* (Chicago, 1976), 27–8; Trussell, *Pennsylvania Line*, 202–3.
20. John B. Landis, "Investigation into American Tradition of a Woman Known as 'Molly Pitcher,'" *Journal of American History*, 5 (1911): 88; Samuel S. Smith, "The Search for Molly Pitcher," *Daughters of the American Revolution Magazine*, 109 (1975): 295; Scheer (ed.), *Private Yankee Doodle*, 132; Trussell, *Pennsylvania Line*, 100 and 201.
21. Much of this discussion is based on William F. Norwood, "Deborah Sampson: Alias Robert Shirtliff, Fighting Female of the Continental Line," *Bulletin of the History of Medicine*, 31 (1957): 147–61. See Herman Mann, *The Female Review: Life of Deborah Sampson* (New York, 1972, orig. pub. 1797), 1857 edn, with notes and introduction by John A. Vinton.
22. Sandra G. Treadway, "Anna Maria Lane: An Unknown Soldier of the American Revolution," *Virginia Calvacade*, 37: 3 (1988): 134–43.
23. Robert Fridlington, "A 'Diversion' in Newark: A Letter from the New Jersey Continental Line, 1778," *New Jersey History*, 105 (1987): 75–8.
24. Holly A. Mayer, "Women Soldiers," in Blanco (ed.), *America Revolution . . . Encyclopedia*, 2: 1795–7.

25. General Orders, August 24, 1777, *FWW*, 9: 129–30; Lynn Montross, *Rag, Tag, and Bobtail: The Story of the Continental Army* (New York, 1952), 45.

26. Rebecca D. Symmes (ed.), *A Citizen-Soldier in the American Revolution: The Diary of Benjamin Gilbert in Massachusetts and New York* (Cooperstown, NY, 1980), May 7, 1778, 31.

27. Report of a Court of Enquiry, November 1, 1777, *NG*, 2: 188.

28. Symmes (ed.), *Diary of Gilbert*, 30–2; Bonnie S. Stadelman, "Amusements of the American Soldiers during the Revolution," PhD diss., Tulane University, 1969, 184; Walter H. Blumenthal, *Women Camp Followers of the American Revolution* (Philadelphia, 1952), 39 and 67; Mayer, *Belonging to the Army*, 111.

29. Anderson, "American Music during the War for Independence," 39.

30. Sally S. Booth, *The Women of '76* (New York, 1973), 187; Frey, *British Soldier*, 61–2; Humphrey, *From King's College to Columbia*, 206.

31. Edward Bangs (ed.), *Journal of Lieutenant Isaac Bangs, April 1 to July 29, 1776* (New York, 1968, orig. pub. 1890), 29; James Neagles, *Summer Soldiers: A Survey & Index of Revolutionary Courts-Martial* (Salt Lake City, UT, 1986), 22.

32. Quoted, June 17, 1776 in Douglas S. Freeman, *George Washington: A Biography* (New York, 1951), 4: 85.

33. Bangs (ed.), *Journal of Bangs*, April 25, 1776, 30.

34. Charles I. Bushell (ed.), *Journal of Solomon Nash, 1776–1777* (New York, 1861), April 25, 1776, 13.

35. Frey, *British Soldiers*, 62.

36. *Continental Journal and Weekly Advertiser*, July 30, 1778, quoted in George F. Scheer and Hugh F. Rankin, *Rebels and Redcoats* (Cleveland, OH, 1957), 327.

37. John Shy (ed.), *Winding Down: The Revolutionary War Letters of Lieutenant Benjamin Gilbert of Massachusetts, 1780–1783* (Ann Arbor, MI, 1989), March 1, 1783, 86–7.

38. *Valley Forge Orderly Book*, January 26, 1778, 210; Bolton, *Private Soldier*, 81.

39. General Orders, September 2, 1775, *NG*, 1: 112.

40. John W. Kruger, "Troop Life at the Champlain Valley Forts during the American Revolution," PhD diss., State University of New York, 1981, 225.

41. Oliver Wolcott to Matthew Griswold, November 18, 1776 and Matthew Thornton to Meshech Weare, December 25, 1776, *LD*, 5: 513 and 667.

42. *JCC*, September 20 and November 9, 1776, 5: 794, 800, and 937–9.

43. Edward C. Boynton (ed.), *General Orders of George Washington Issued at Newburgh on the Hudson, 1782–1783* (Harrison, NY, 1973), May 16, 1782, 20; *The Order Books of Colonel William Henshaw, October 1,*

1775, Through October 3, 1776 (Worcester, MA, 1948), August 16, 1776, 219.

44. General Orders, June 11, 1777, *FWW*, 8: 226.
45. General Orders, November 14, 1775, *ASP*, 2: 369
46. General Orders, November 1, 1777, *FWW*, 9: 491.
47. Turner (ed.), *Journal of Kirkwood*, March 30, 1777, 53.
48. For example, Worthington C. Ford (ed.), *General Orders Issued by Major-General Israel Putnam when in Command of the Highlands . . . 1777* (Brooklyn, NY, 1893), July 22 and August 23, 1777, 35 and 61.
49. General Orders, September 1782, *FWW*, 25: 130; Carp, *To Starve the Army*, 192.
50. *Valley Forge Orderly Book*, February 1778, 228.
51. Proclamation, July 10, 1781, *FWW*, 22: 351–2.
52. Washington to William Livingston, March 3, 1779, *FWW*, 14: 185–6; Ford (ed.), *General Orders of Putnam*, August 7, 1777, 51; *Order Book Kept by Peter Kinnan, July 7–September 4, 1776* (Princeton, NJ, 1931), July 26, 1776, 32–3.
53. Nathanael Greene to Col. Nicholas Long, January 18, 1781, *NG*, 7: 140.
54. Risch, *Supplying Washington's Army*, 160–1, 315, 324, 329–30.
55. Howard L. Applegate, "Constitutions Like Iron: the Life of the American Revolutionary War Soldiers in the Middle Department, 1775–1783," PhD diss., Syracuse University, 1966, 166; John C. Fitzpatrick, "Bread and the Superintendence of Bakers of the Continental Army," *Daughters of the American Revolution Magazine*, 56 (1922): 514–17.
56. Nathanael Greene to Gov. Jonathan Trumbull, July 20, 1779, *NG*, 4: 248; Risch, *Supplying Washington's Army*, 158; Mayer, *Belonging to the Army*, 206.
57. Lauber (ed.), *Orderly Books . . . New York Regiment*, October 10, 1781 and April 19, 1782, 610 and 677.
58. For example, August 8, 1775, *NG*, 1: 105n.
59. "Troop Life at the Champlain Valley," 166–7.
60. Memorial of the Fishkill Carpenters and Wheelwrights, January 6, 1779, Nathanael Greene to Udny Hay, February 10, 1779, to Col. Morgan Lewis, February 10, 1779, and to Udny Hay, February 20, 1779, *NG*, 3: 150, 226, 227 and 277, respectively.
61. Washington to the Board of War, June 15, 1778 and to Greene, April 19, 1779, *FWW*, 12: 65 and 14: 410.
62. Greene to Washington, February 24, 1779, *NG*, 3: 296–7.
63. *JCC*, May 14, 1777, 7: 357–9; Risch, *Supplying Washington's Army*, 71 and 75.
64. Carp, *To Starve the Army*, 62; Risch, *Supplying Washington's Army*, 91.
65. James Abeel to Greene, October 22, 1778, *NG*, 3: 9; Jacob Weiss to Thomas Anderson, March 28, 1781, Melville J. Boyer (ed.), "The

Letter Book of Jacob Weiss, Deputy Quartermaster General of the Revolution," March 28, 1781, *Proceedings of the Lehigh Historical Society*, 2 (1956): 121; Applegate, "Constitutions Like Iron," 180–1; Carp, *To Starve the Army*, 62–3.

66. Sidney Berry to Moore Furman, December 7, 1778, *NG*, 2: 298n.

67. Jacob Weiss to John Lerch, January 24, 1781, Boyer (ed.), "Letter Book of Weiss," 116.

68. Jacob Weiss to Thomas Anderson, October 29, 1778, Boyer (ed.), "Letter Book of Weiss," 38.

69. Arthur D. Graeff, "Henry Vanderslice, Wagon-Master, 1777–1778," *Historical Review of Berks County*, 2 (1937): 67–9.

70. "Journal of Joseph Joslin, Jr. of South Killingly: A Teamster in the Continental Service, March 1777–August 1778," *Collections of the Connecticut Historical Society*, 7 (1899): 311–29.

71. *JCC*, July 18, 1780, 17: 615; Carp, *To Starve the Army*, 194.

Chapter Nine

1. Russell Siebert, "The Treatment of Conscientious Objectors in War Time, 1775–1920," PhD diss., Ohio State University, 1936, 30 and 82.

2. Record of Revd Christopher Schultz, May 2, 1777, in "The Conduct of the Schwenkfelders during the Revolutionary War," *The Pennsylvania German*, 11 (1910): 690.

3. Quoted in Ruth Blackwelder, "The Attitude of the North Carolina Moravians Toward the American Revolution," *NCHR*, 9 (1932): 15.

4. John Ettwein to Henry Laurens, January 15, 1778, in Kenneth Hamilton, "John Ettwein and the Moravian Church during the American Revolution," *Transactions of the Moravian Historical Society*, 12 (1940): 265.

5. Richard K. MacMaster et al. (eds), *Conscience in Crisis: Mennonite and Other Peace Churches in America, 1739–1939* (Scottdale, PA, 1979), 365–6.

6. Peter Brock, *Pacifism in the United States from the Colonial Era to the First World War* (Princeton, NJ, 1968), 201–2.

7. John Bayley to Thomas Wharton, July 27, 1777, in MacMaster et al. (eds), *Conscience in Crisis*, 317.

8. Arthur J. Mekeel, *The Relation of the Quakers to the American Revolution* (Washington, DC, 1979), 202, 212, 252, 262, and 266–73.

9. Siebert, "Treatment of Conscientious Objectors," 75; Brock, *Pacifism*, 272–5.

10. Baurmeister to Col. Friedrich Christian von Jungkenn, May 10, 1778, in Bernhard A. Uhlendorf and Edna Vosper (eds), *Letters from Major Baurmeister to Colonel von Jungenn Written during the Philadelphia Campaign, 1777–1778* (Philadelphia, 1937), 57; Brock, *Pacifism*, 240–1.

11. "Suffering of William Davis as related by himself," June 20, 1779, University of Virginia Library.

12. MacMaster et al. (eds), *Conscience in Crisis*, 258–9.

13. Brock, *Pacificism*, 223–7.

14. Crane, *Diary of Drinker*, October 10 and 11, 1777, 1: 242.

15. Quoted New Garden Friends, March 30, 1781, in Dorothy G. Thorne, "North Carolina Friends and the Revolution," *NCHR*, 38 (1961): 337–8; Greene to Members of the New Garden Monthly Meeting, March 26, 1781, *NG*, 7: 469–70.

16. James H. Edmonson, "Desertion in the American Army during the Revolutionary War," PhD diss., Louisiana State University, 1971, 342.

17. Edmonson, "Desertion in the American Army," 331–2; Thaddeus W. Tate, "Desertion from the American Revolutionary Army," MA Thesis, University of North Carolina, 1948, 59; *The Journal and Order Book of Capt. Robert Kirkwood* (Wilmington, DE, 1910), 17.

18. Edmonson, "Desertion in the American Army," 327–8; Arthur J. Alexander, "Desertion and Its Punishment," *WMQ*, 3rd Ser., 3 (1946), 392.

19. Edmonson, "Desertion in the American Army," 291.

20. Tate, "Desertion . . . Revolutionary Army," 42–3.

21. Tate, "Desertion . . . Revolutionary Army," 12–14; Edmonson, "Desertion in the American Army," 236–9 and 252; Bowman, *Morale*, 72.

22. Edmonson, "Desertion the American Army," 231.

23. Washington to the President of Congress, September 24, 1776, *FWW*, 6: 110–11.

24. Washington to John Armstrong, May 5, to John Sullivan, May 23, and to William Smallwood, May 26, 1777, *FWW*, 7: 251 and 8: 106–7 and 128, respectively; Tate, "Desertion . . . Revolutionary Army," 64–8.

25. *Valley Forge Orderly Book*, November 1, 1777, 114.

26. Edmonson, "Desertion in the American Army," 277–9.

27. For example, New Kent County, 28 of 104, Edmonson, "Desertion in the American Army," 29.

28. William Davies to Jefferson, March 18, 1781, Executive Papers, Library of Virginia.

29. *JCC*, July 31, 1777, 8: 593–4.

30. Hening, *Statutes*, May 1777, 9: 289–90; Tate, "Desertion . . . Revolutionary Army," 39.

31. Alexander, "Desertion and Its Punishment," 396–7.

32. Washington to Joseph Reed, April 28, 1780, *FWW*, 18: 311.

33. Joseph Reed to Washington, March 15, 1780, quote in Bowman, *Morale*, 86.

34. Alexander, "Desertion and Its Punishment," 396; Tate, "Desertion . . . Revolutionary Army," 72; Bowman, *Morale*, 85; McBride, "Virginia War Effort," 249.

35. *Journal of the House of Delegates*, 1778 (Richmond, VA, 1827), 48.

36. Intelligence by Micah Townshend, April 10, 1781, in James B. Wilbur, *Ira Allen: Founder of Vermont, 1751–1814* (Boston, 1928), 1: 185–6.

37. Washington to Joseph Jones, July 10, 1781, *FWW*, 22: 354.

38. Washington to Stirling, December 9, 1782 and to President of Congress, January 20, 1783, *FWW*, 25: 408 and 26: 54 and n.; *JCC*, November 27, 1782, 23: 756.

39. Washington to Joseph Jones, February 11, 1783, *FWW*, 26: 123; Michael A. Bellesiles, *Revolutionary Outlaws: Ethan Allen and the Struggle for Independence on the Early American Frontier* (Charlottesville, VA, 1993), 214–15; *JCC*, December 5, 1780, 23: 765–6; *LD*, 19: 426n. and 623n.

40. Joseph Jones to Washington, February 27, 1783, *LD*, 19: 746–7.

41. Benjamin Rush to Washington, December 26, 1777, Butterfield (ed.), *Letters of Rush*, 1: 180; Charles H. Lesser (ed.), *The Sinews of Independence: Monthly Strength Reports of the Continental Army* (Chicago, 1976), 36, 38, and 54–5; Richard L. Blanco, *Physician of the American Revolution: Jonathan Potts* (New York, 1979), 94.

42. Gen. Johann de Kalb to Count Charles Francis de Broglie, December 25, 1777, in Henry S. Commager and Richard B. Morris (eds), *The Spirit of 'Seventy-Six* (Indianapolis, IN, 1958), 1: 647.

43. James E. Gipson, *Dr. Bodo Otto and the Medical Background of the American Revolution* (Springfield, IL, 1937), 81.

44. *JCC*, July 27, 1775, 2: 209–11; Richard L. Blanco, "Continental Army Hospitals and American Society, 1775–1781," in Maarten Ultee (ed.), *Adapting to Conditions: War Society in the Eighteenth Century* (University, AL, 1986), 155 and 158.

45. Mary C. Gillett, *The Army Medical Department, 1775–1818* (Washington, DC, 1981), 69, 75, 85, and 98: Risch, *Supplying Washington's Army*, 375.

46. Allison P. Clark III, "Military Medicine, in Blanco (ed.), *American Revolution . . . Encyclopedia*, 2: 1033–4; Gillett, *Army Medical Department*, 117–20; Risch, *Supplying Washington's Army*, 403–4 and 411.

47. Quoted in Louis C. Duncan, *Medical Men in the American Revolution, 1775–1783* (Carlisle Barracks, PA, 1931), 170–1.

48. Gillett, *Army Medical Department*, 90; Gipson, *Otto*, 153.

49. Dr Barnabas Binney to Greene, May 18 and Erastus Van Harlingen to Greene, May 18, 1779, *NG*, 4: 42 and 46–7.

50. John W. Jordan, "The Military Hospitals of Bethlehem and Lilitz during the Revolution," *PMHB*, 12 (1888): 385–406; 13: 71–90, and 20: 137–57.

51. Blanco, *Potts*, 182, quoted 168.

52. Benjamin Rush to Washington, December 26, 1777 and to Thomas Henry, July 22, 1783, Butterfield (ed.), *Letters of Rush*, 1: 180–1 and 358–60.

53. Duncan, *Medical Men*, 170–1, quote Dr L. Young.

54. Benjamin Rush to John Adams, October 21, 1777, Butterfield (ed.), *Letters of Rush*, 1: 161.

55. Linda K. Kerber, *Women of the Republic: Intellect and Ideology in Republican America* (Chapel Hill, NC, 1980), 58–9.

56. Washington to John Hancock, September 14, 1776, *AWP*, 6: 309; Linda G. De Pauw, "Women in Combat: The Revolutionary War Experience," *Armed Forces and Society*, 7 (1980–1): 214.

57. *JCC*, June 20, 1777, May 1, 1783, October 14, 1783, April 20, 1784, February 8, 1785, and April 27, 1785, 8: 485, 25: 321–2 and 680, 26: 253–5, 28: 51–2 and 310, respectively; Berg, *Continental Army Units*, 54–5; Elizabeth D. Schafer, "Corps of Invalids," in Blanco (ed.), *American Revolution . . . Encyclopedia*, 1: 808–9.

58. William R. Lindsey, *Treatment of American Prisoners of War during the Revolution* (Emporia, KA, 1973), 9.

59. Lindsey, *Treatment of American Prisoners*, 10–11, including quote.

60. Quoted in Duncan, *Medical Men*, 152.

61. Duncan, *Medical Men*, 152–3; David L. Sterling (ed.), "American Prisoners of War in New York: A Report by Elias Boudinot," *WMQ*, 3rd Ser., 13 (1956): 381; Richard H. Amerman, "Treatment of American Prisoners during the Revolution," *Proceedings of the New Jersey Historical Society*, 78 (1960): 266.

62. Albert Greene (ed.), *Recollections of the Jersey Prison Ship by Capt. Thomas Dring* (Bedford, MA, 1992, orig. pub. 1829), 74.

63. Lindsey, *Treatment of American Prisoners*, 20–1.

64. Wiener, *Civilians under Military Justice*, 156.

65. Jerome J. Nadelhaft, *The Disorders of War: The Revolution in South Carolina* (Orono, ME, 1981), 67; Larry G. Bowman, *Captive Americans: Prisoners During the American Revolution* (Athens, OH, 1976), 101–2; Harold Campbell, "Execution of Isaac Hayne," in Blanco (ed.), *American Revolution . . . Encyclopedia*, 2: 746–8.

66. Richard Sampson, *Escape in America: The British Convention Prisoners, 1777–1783* (Wiltshire, Eng., 1995), 175.

67. Sampson, *Escape in America*, 173.

68. Tustin (ed.), *Diary of the American War*, xxi.

69. *JCC*, December 11, 1782, 23: 785; Charles H. Metzger, *The Prisoner in the American Revolution* (Chicago, 1971), 146–7.

70. Ralph Wood (ed.), *The Pennsylvania Germans* (Princeton, NJ, 1942), 23 and 231.

71. Tustin (ed.), *Diary of the American War*, July 14, 1783, 349 and 435n–36n.
72. George A. Boyd, *Elias Boudinot: Patriot and Statesman, 1740–1821* (Princeton, NJ, 1952), 66.
73. Döhla, *Hessian Diary*, 201 and 208.

Chapter Ten

1. Dexter (ed.), *Diary of Stiles*, September 22, 1777, 2: 209–10; Elizabeth Cometti, "Women in the American Revolution," *New England Quarterly*, 20 (1947): 337.
2. Ebenezer Huntington to Joshua Huntington, May 3, 1779, *Letters Written by Ebenezer Huntington during the American Revolution* (New York, 1915), 81.
3. Andrew M. Davis, "The Limitation of Prices in Massachusetts, 1776–1779," *Publications of the Colonial Society of Massachusetts*, 10 (1904–6): 126; Oscar and Mary F. Handlin, "Revolutionary Economic Policy in Massachusetts," *WMQ*, 3rd Ser., 4 (1947): 15–16.
4. Davis, "Limitation of Prices," 125.
5. Alexander D. Flick et al., *The American Revolution in New York: Its Political, Social and Economic Significance* (Albany, NY, 1926), 200.
6. Cometti, "Women in the American Revolution," 334–5.
7. John Hanson to Philip Thomas, June 21, 1780, *LD*, 315–55; Washington to Joseph Reed, June, 25, 1780, Esther Reed to Washington, July 4, 1780, and Washington to Mrs Esther Reed, August 10, 1780, *FWW*, 19: 71n., and 350–1 and n.; Edith P. Meyer, *Petticoat Patriots of the American Revolution* (New York, 1976), 132–4.
8. Washington to Mrs Ann Francis et al., February 13, 1781, *FWW*, 21: 221.
9. Washington to Col. Samuel Miles, December 23, 1780, *FWW*, 5.
10. Mary Dagworthy to Washington, July 17, 1780, *FWW*, 19: 72n; *Pennsylvania Packet*, July 8, 1780, in Edmund J. James, "Some Additional Information concerning Ephraim Martin," *PMHB*, 36 (1912): 148.
11. Signed "Machaon," September 1, 1780, Jersey Camp, *Archives of the State of New Jersey*, 2nd Ser., 4: 640–2.
12. *JP*, 3: 533n.
13. Washington to Mrs Mary [Thomas Sim] Lee, October 11, 1780, *FWW*, 20: 168.
14. Lafayette to Greene, April 17, 1781 and Lafayette to Washington, April 18, 1781, *LP*, 4: 38 and 45; Louis Gottschalk, *Lafayette and the Close of the American Revolution* (Chicago, 1942), 217–18.
15. Coleman, *American Revolution in Georgia*, 231–2; Mekeel, *Relation of the Quakers*, 301 and 304.

16. Crane (ed.), *Diary of Drinker*, May 30, 1778, 1: 308.
17. Lillian B. Miller (ed.), *The Selected Papers of Charles Willson Peale and His Family* (New Haven, CT, 1983), Diary 6, part 1, July 13, 1779, 325 and n.
18. Washington to William Maxwell, May 10, 1779, *FWW*, 15: 33.
19. Ebenezer Huntington to James Huntington, December 21, 1778, *Letters of Huntington*, 78.
20. Gen. John Twiggs to Greene, October 30, 1781, *NG*, 9: 500.
21. Howard K. Sanderson, *Lynn in the Revolution* (Boston, MA, 1908), 113.
22. Steven Rosswurm, *Arms, Country, and Class: The Philadelphia Militia and "Lower Sort" during the American Revolution, 1775–1783* (New Brunswick, NJ, 1987), 137.
23. Hanover County (Virginia) Court Order Book, no. 1, January 7, 1782, Library of Virginia.
24. John J. McClusker and Russell R. Menard, *The Economy of British America, 1607–1789* (Chapel Hill, NC, 1985), 361–3; Jackson T. Main, *The Sovereign States, 1775–1783* (New York, 1973), 220–31.
25. Anburey, *Travels*, August 4, 1779, 2: 426–7; Victor S. Clark, *History of Manufactures in the United States* (New York, 1929 edn), 1: 223.
26. David L. Salay, "Arming for War: The Production of War Material in Pennsylvania for the American Armies during the Revolution," PhD diss., University of Delaware, 1977, 34; Neil L. York, *Mechanical Metamorphosis: Technological Change in Revolutionary America* (Westport, CT, 1985), 71.
27. Chastellux, *Travels*, ed. Rice, 1: 76–7.
28. Merrill Jensen, "The American Revolution in American Agriculture," *Agricultural History*, 43 (1969): 113; Robert A. East, *Business Enterprise in the American Revolutionary Era* (Gloucester, MA, 1964, orig. pub. 1938), 101 and 175.
29. James L. Abrahamson, *The American Homefront: Revolutionary War, Civil War, World I, World War II* (Washington, DC, 1983), 22–3.
30. Davis, "Limitation of Prices," 126; Broadus Mitchell, *The Price of Independence: A Realistic View of the American Revolution* (New York), 1974, 97.
31. Arthur C. Bining, *Pennsylvania Iron Manufacture in the Eighteenth Century* (Harrisburg, PA, 1938), 180–1; Clark, *History of Manufactures*, 1: 219.
32. Bining, *Pennsylvania Iron Manufacture*, 180.
33. Salay, "Arming for War," 32; Lafayette to Greene, April 17, 1781, *LP*, 4: 38.
34. Bining, *Pennsylvania Iron Manufacture*, 180; Clark, *History of Manufactures*, 1: 222.
35. Richard B. Morris, *Government and Labor in Early America* (New York, 1947), 301–2; York, *Mechanical Metamorphosis*, 68.

36. York, *Mechanical Metamorphosis*, 37.
37. York, *Mechanical Metamorphosis*, 65–7; Harry M. Ward and Harold Greer, *Richmond during the Revolution, 1775–1783* (Charlottesville, VA, 1977), *passim*.
38. Anthony Noble to Adam Stephen, October 21, 1777, Adam Stephen Papers, Library of Congress.
39. John Taylor to Meshech Weare, September 25, 1782, *LD*, 19: 209; Anne Bezanson, *Prices and Inflation during the American Revolution, Pennsylvania, 1770–1790* (Philadelphia, 1951), 322–3; Gross, *Minutemen*, 140.
40. Flick, *American Revolution in New York*, 196–7.
41. Quoted in Ralph V. Harlow, "Aspects of Revolutionary Finance, 1775–1783," *AHR*, 35 (1930): 57.
42. Harlow, "Aspects of Revolutionary Finance," 57; Morris, *Government and Labor*, 94 and 103, including quote.
43. Harlow, "Aspects of Revolutionary Finance," 57; Main, *Sovereign States*, 237–9.
44. Elizabeth Cometti, "The Labor Front during the American Revolution," *West Georgia College Studies in the Social Sciences*, 15 (1976): 79–90; Nevins, *American States*, 617; Morris, *Government and Labor*, 100.
45. *JCC*, November 22, 1777 and June 4, 1778, 9: 956–7 and 11: 569; Morris, *Government and Labor*, 103 and 105; Davis, "Limitation of Prices," 124–5.
46. Barck, *New York City during War of Independence*, 99, 102, and 106; Morris, *Government and Labor*, 126; Willard O. Mishoff, "Business in Philadelphia during the British Occupation, 1777–1778," *PMHB*, 61 (1937): 169–70.
47. Barbara C. Smith, "Food Rioters and the American Revolution," *WMQ*, 3rd Ser., 51 (1994): 5 and 37.
48. David J. Mays, *Edmund Pendleton, 1721–1803: A Biography* (Cambridge, MA, 1952), 2: 48; Scribner and Tarter (eds), *Revolutionary Virginia*, 4: 13.
49. *The Journal of Nicholas Cresswell, 1774–1777* (New York, 1924), November 20, 1776, 132; Oscar and Lilian Handlin, *A Restless People: Americans in Rebellion, 1770–1787* (Garden City, NY, 1982), 147; Edward Countryman, *A People in Revolution: The American Revolution and Political Society in New York, 1766–1790* (New York, 1989), 182; Smith, "Food Rioters," 35.
50. Smith, "Food Rioters," 18.
51. Countryman, *People in Revolution*, 182–3; Hadaway, *McDonald Papers*, part 1: 35–7.
52. Abigail Adams to John Adams, April 20, 1777, Butterfield (ed.), *Adams Family Correspondence*, 2: 218–19; "Boyle's Journal of Occurrences in Boston," *New England Historical and Genealogical Register*, 85

(1931): April 19, 1777, 128; R. S. Longley, "Mob Activities in Revolutionary Massachusetts," *NEQ*, 6 (1933): 126; Dirk Hoerder, *Crowd Action in Revolutionary Massachusetts, 1763–1780* (New York, 1777), 359.

53. "A Notification" from *Boston Gazette*, April 21, 1777, *Publications of the Colonial Society of Massachusetts*, 8 (1907): 97–101.

54. Smith, "Food Rioters," 27 and 36; Meyer, *Petticoat Patriots*, 137; East, *Business Enterprise*, 203.

55. Abigail Adams to John Adams, July 31, 1777, Butterfield (ed.), *Adams Family Correspondence*, 2: 296.

56. Smith, "Food Rioters," 16–17; Kerber, *Women of the Republic*, 44n.

57. Crane (ed.), *Diary of Drinker*, May 26, 1777, 1: 355.

58. John K. Alexander, "The Fort Wilson Incident of 1779: A Case Study of the Revolutionary Crowd," *WMQ*, 3rd Ser., 31 (1974): 588, 601–2, and 605–7; Rosswurm, *Arms, Country, and Class*, 215–16 and 220.

59. Crane (ed.), *Diary of Drinker*, 1: 393 and n.

60. Crane (ed.), *Diary of Drinker*, May 8, 1781, 1: 387; Rosswurm, *Arms, Country, and Class*, 166; Philip S. Foner, *Labor and the American Revolution* (Westport, CT, 1976), 187–8.

61. Alexis de Tocqueville, *Democracy in America*, abridged edition, ed. Andrew Hacker (New York, 1972), 285.

62. Jefferson to William Fleming, June 8, 1779, *JP*, 2: 288.

63. James Murray to Elizabeth Murray, September 1, 1777, Eric Robson (ed.), *Letters from America, 1773 to 1780; Being the Letters of a Scots Officer, Sir James Murray* (New York, 1951), 48.

64. *Valley Forge Orderly Book*, September 5, 1777, 34.

65. Robert Hanson Harrison to Washington, September 11, 1777, Washington Papers, Library of Congress.

66. Edmund Pendleton to James Mercer, October 4, 1777, David J. Mays (ed.), *Letters and Papers of Edmund Pendleton, 1734–1803* (Charlottesville, VA, 1967), 1: 226.

67. Quincy (ed.), *Journals of Shaw*, June 28, 1779, 58.

68. Ebenezer Huntington to Andrew Huntington, July 7, 1780, *Letters of Huntington*, 87–8.

69. Schaukrik, "Occupation of New York City," December 16, 1780, 17.

70. Diary of Honyman, May 31, 1778, 233–4.

71. Mann Page, Jr to Richard Henry Lee, April 13, 1779, Revolutionary Lee Papers, Library of Virginia microfilm.

72. Joseph Reed to Nathanael Greene, September—, 1779, in George W. Greene, *The Life of Nathanael Greene* (Freeport, NY, 1972, from 1867–71 edn), 2: 344.

73. William Peartree Smith to Elias Boudinot, April—, 1783, "Letters from William Peartree Smith to Elias Boudinot," *Proceedings of New Jersey Historical Society*, 1st Ser., 4 (1849): 122.

74. Washington to Col. Lewis Nicola, May 22 and Nicola to Washington, May 22, 1782, *FWW*, 24: 272–3 and 273n.

75. Henry Young to William Davies, June 9, 1781, *JP*, 6: 84 and 85n.–86n.; Richard Henry Lee to James Lovell, September 12, 1781, James C. Ballagh (ed.), *The Letters of Richard Henry Lee* (New York, 1914), 2: 237; Jefferson, *Notes on the State of Virginia*, ed. Peden, 126–7 and 284n.–85n.

76. Archer Robertson Petition, June–July 1781, transcribed by Edmund Ruffin, #20670, Library of Virginia.

Chapter Eleven

1. Sylvia R. Frey and Marian J. Morton (eds), *New World, New Roles: A Documentary History of Women in Pre-Industrial America* (Westport, CT, 1986), 122.

2. Joan R. Gundersen, *To Be Useful to the World: Women in Revolutionary America, 1740–1790* (New York, 1996), 114.

3. Ramsay, *History of South Carolina*, 2: 229.

4. Abigail Adams to John Adams, March 31, 1776, Butterfield (ed.), *Adams Family Correspondence*, 1: 370.

5. John Adams to Abigail Adams, April 14, 1776, Butterfield (ed.), *Adams Family Correspondence*, 382.

6. John Adams to John Sullivan, May 26, 1776, *LD*, 4: 473–4.

7. Rosemary Keller, *Patriotism and the Female Sex: Abigail Adams and the American Revolution* (Brooklyn, NY, 1994), 94–5; Gundersen, *To Be Useful*, 48.

8. Carole Shammas et al., *Inheritance in America from Colonial Times to the Present* (New Brunswick, NJ, 1987), 67 and 72–3; Joan R. Gundersen and Gwen V. Gampel, "Married Women's Legal Status in Eighteenth-Century New York and Virginia," *WMQ*, 3rd Ser., 39 (1982): 114–34; Marylynn Salmon, "Republican Sentiment, Economic Change and the Property Rights of Women in American Law," in Ronald Hoffman and Peter J. Albert (eds), *Women in the Age of the American Revolution* (Charlottesville, VA, 1989), 449; Kerber, *Women of the Republic*, 146.

9. Marylynn Salmon, *Women and the Law of Property in Early America* (Chapel Hill, NC, 1986), 63–4.

10. Nancy F. Cott, "Divorce and the Changing Status of Women in Eighteenth-Century Massachusetts," *WMQ*, 3rd Ser., 33 (1976): 605; Steven Mintz and Susan Kellogg, *Domestic Revolutions: A Social History of American Family Life* (New York, 1988), 61; Gundersen, *To Be Useful*, 49.

11. Merril D. Smith, *Breaking the Bonds: Martial Discord in Pennsylvania, 1730–1830* (New York, 1991), 19; Kerber, *Women of the Republic*, 181; Gunderson, *To Be Useful*, 49.

12. Kerber, *Women of the Republic*, 149–50.

13. Constance B. Schulz, "Daughters of Liberty: The History of Women in the Revolutionary War Pension Records," *Prologue: Journal of the National Archives*, 16 (fall 1984), April 1, 1837, Scott County, Kentucky, 146.

14. Janet Schaw, *Journal of a Lady of Quality . . . 1774 to 1776*, ed. Evangeline W. Andrews (New Haven, CT, 1927), 178–9.

15. James A. Henretta, "The War for Independence and American Economic Development," in Ronald Hoffman et al. (eds), *The Economy of Early America: The Revolutionary Period, 1763–1789* (Charlottesville, VA, 1988), 76.

16. Carole Shammas, "The Female Social Structure of Philadelphia in 1775," *PMHB*, 107 (1983): 70–2, 75, and 82.

17. Quoted in Henretta, "War for Independence," 63–4.

18. Cometti, "Women in the American Revolution," 332–3; Kathleen Bruce, "Massachusetts Women of the Revolution," in Albert B. Hart (ed.), *Commonwealth History of Massachusetts* (New York, 1929), 3: 326.

19. Hannah Adams, *Memoir of Miss Hannah Adams, with Additional Notices by a Friend* (Boston, MA, 1832), 10; Laurel Thacher Ulrich, "Wheels, Looms, and the Gender Division of Labor in Eighteenth-Century New England," *WMQ*, 3rd Ser., 55 (1998): 6, 13, 16, 18 and 20–1.

20. Cometti, "Women in the American Revolution," 333.

21. Laurel T. Ulrich, "Martha Ballard and Her Girls: Women's Work in Eighteenth-Century Maine," in Stephen Innes (ed.), *Work and Labor in Early America* (Chapel Hill, NC, 1988), 84.

22. Eugenie A. Leonard, *The Dear-Bought Heritage* (Philadelphia, 1965), 463; Julia C. Spruill, *Women's Life and Work in the Southern Colonies* (New York, 1972, orig. pub. 1938), 264–5; Gundersen, *To Be Useful*, 73.

23. John H. Jackson (ed.), *Margaret Morris: Her Journal* (Philadelphia, 1949), June 14, 1777, 72–3; Elizabeth Evans, *Weathering the Storm: Women of the American Revolution* (New York, 1975), 106.

24. Leonard, *Dear-Bought Heritage*, 476; Meyer, *Petticoat Patriots*, 97.

25. Kenneth A. Lockridge, *Literacy in Colonial New England* (New York, 1974), 38–44; Nancy F. Cott, *The Bonds of Womanhood: "Women's sphere" in New England, 1780–1835* (New Haven, CT, 1977), 103; Joan M. Jensen, *Loosening the Bonds: Mid-Atlantic Farm Women, 1750–1850* (New Haven, CT, 1986), 169 and 189; Kerber, *Women of the Republic*, 193; Gundersen, *To Be Useful*, 81 and 87–8.

26. Gundersen, *To Be Useful*, 83, 86, and 174.

27.   *JP*, 2: 527–8.

28.   Noah Webster, "On the Education of Youth" (1798), in Frederick Rudolph (ed.), *Essays on Education in the Early Republic* (Cambridge, MA, 1965), 68–71.

29.   Benjamin Rush, "Thoughts upon Female Education . . ." and "A Plan for the Establishment of Public Schools," Rudolph (ed.), *Essays on Education*, 28–32 and 21.

30.   Abigail Adams to John Adams, August 14, 1776, Butterfield (ed.), *Adams Family Correspondence*, 2: 94.

31.   Hannah Adams, *Memoir*, 3 and 10.

32.   "On the Equality of the Sexes," Sharon M. Harris (ed.), *Selected Writings of Judith Sargent Murray* (New York, 1995), 7.

33.   Sheila L. Skemp, *Judith Sargent Murray: A Brief Biography with Documents* (Boston, MA, 1998), 5 and 131.

34.   Carla Mulford (ed.), *Only for the Eye of a Friend: The Poems of Annis Boudinot Stockton* (Charlottesville, VA, 1995), 1–2, 5–6, 106–12, and 121–30; Washington to Annis Boudinot Stockton, July 22, 1782, September 2, 1783, and February 18, 1784, *FWW*, 24: 437–8 and 27: 127–9 and 337–8, respectively.

35.   Lester H. Cohen, "Explaining the Revolution: Ideology and Ethics in Mercy Otis Warren's Historical Theory," *WMQ*, 3rd Ser., 37 (1980): 203 and 210; Jeffrey H. Richards, *Mercy Otis Warren* (New York, 1995), 86–106; Silverman, *Cultural History of the American Revolution*, 212–13 and 255–6.

36.   Carl N. Degler, *At Odds: Women and the Family in America from the Revolution to the Present* (New York, 1980), 8; Donald W. White, *A Village at War: Chatham, New Jersey and the American Revolution* (Rutherford, NJ, 1979), 156.

37.   Spruill, *Women's Life and Work*, 140; Gundersen, *To Be Useful*, 39.

38.   Smith, *"Lower Sort,"* 178; Gundersen, *To Be Useful*, 173.

39.   Smith, *"Lower Sort,"* 177; Degler, *At Odds*, 8.

40.   Gundersen, *To Be Useful*, 46.

41.   Robert V. Wells, "Quaker Marriage Patterns in Colonial Pennsylvania," *WMQ*, 3rd Ser., 29 (1972): 426–7.

42.   Terril Premo, *Winter Friends: Women Growing Old in the New Republic, 1785–1835* (Urbana, IL, 1990), 43.

43.   Gordon S. Wood., *The Radicalism of the American Revolution* (New York, 1992), 147.

44.   Jan Lewis, "The Republican Wife: Virtue and Seduction in the Early Republic," *WMQ*, 3rd Ser., 44 (1987): 689–711; Smith, *Breaking the Bonds*, 50.

45.   Jack Scott (ed.), *An Annotated Edition of Lectures on Moral Philosophy by John Witherspoon* (Newark, DE, 1982), 134.

46. A. Jocelyn to his daughter, September 1788, in Nancy F. Cott et al. (eds), *Roots of Bitterness: Documents of the Social History of American Women* (Boston, MA, 2nd edn, 1972), 92–3.
47. Philip G. Greven, Jr, "The Average Size of Families and Households in the Province of Massachusetts in 1764 and in the United States in 1790: An Overview," in Peter Laslett (ed.), *Household and Family in Past Time* (Cambridge, Eng., 1978), 551–66; Smith, "Lower Sort," 180–1.
48. Catherine Scholten, *Childbearing in American Society, 1650–1850* (New York, 1985), 48–49; Judith W. Leavitt, *Brought to Bed: Childbearing in America, 1750 to 1950* (New York, 1986), 31 and 38–9.
49. Leonard, *Dear-Bought Heritage*, 475–6; Laurel T. Ulrich, *A Midwife's Tale: The Life of Martha Ballard, Based on Her Diary, 1785–1812* (New York, 1990), 5 and 11.
50. Robert V. Wells, *Revolutions in Americans' Lives* (Westport, CT, 1982), 44–5; Schulz, "Daughters of Liberty," 151.
51. Crane (ed.), *Diary of Drinker*, 2: 1227.
52. David Marder (ed.), *A Hugh Henry Brackenridge Reader, 1770–1815* (Pittsburgh, 1970), from *United States Magazine*, 1779, 94–7.
53. Joy Day and Richard Buel, Jr, *The Way of Duty: A Woman and Her Family in Revolutionary America* (New York, 1984), 114.
54. "Diary of James Allen, Esq. of Philadelphia, Counsellor at Law, 1770–1778," *PMHB*, 9 (1885): 284 (June 6, 1777) and 433 (February 27, 1778).
55. Ruth H. Bloch, "The Gendered Meanings of Virtue in Revolutionary America," *Signs: Journal of Women in Culture and Society*, 13 (Autumn 1987): 116; Gundersen, *To Be Useful*, 173.
56. Mintz and Kellogg, *Domestic Revolutions*, 47–8.
57. Jay Fliegelman, *Prodigals and Pilgrims: The American Revolution against Patriarchal Authority, 1750–1800* (Cambridge, Eng., 1982), 10.
58. Stephen Brobeck, "Images of the Family: Portrait Paintings as Indices of American Family Culture, Structure and Behavior, 1730–1860," *Journal of Psychohistory*, 5 (1977): 85 and 89–92.
59. Lillian B. Miller, *The Peale Family: Creation of a Legacy, 1770–1870* (Washington, DC, 1996), 43 and 48.

Chapter Twelve

1. Sylvia R. Frey, *Water from the Rock: Black Resistance in a Revolutionary Age* (Princeton, NJ, 1991), 211n.; Gary B. Nash, *Race and Revolution* (Madison, WI, 1990), 60–1.
2. Frey, *Water from the Rock*, 221; Robert Olwell, "Slavery and the American Revolution," in Blanco (ed.), *American Revolution . . . Encyclopedia*, 2: 1532; Allan Kulikoff, "Uprooted Peoples: Black Migrants in the

Age of the American Revolution," in Ira Berlin and Ronald Hoffman (eds), *Slavery and Freedom in the Age of the American Revolution* (Charlottesville, VA, 1983), 144–5, 148, and 156.

3. Quoted Benjamin Rush, "An Address . . . upon Slave Keeping" (1773), in David B. Davis, *The Problem of Slavery in the Age of Revolution, 1770–1823* (Ithaca, NY, 1975), 283.

4. Frey, *Water from the Rock*, 225; Philip J. Schwarz, *Slave Laws in Virginia* (Athens, GA, 1996), 81.

5. Herbert Aptheker, *American Negro Slave Revolts* (New York, 1963), 202–3; Nicholas Halasz, *The Rattling Chains: Slave Unrest and Revolt in the Antebellum South* (New York, 1966), 52–3; Jeffrey J. Crow, *The Black Experience in Revolutionary North Carolina* (Raleigh, NC, 1977), 58; Jeffrey J. Crow, "Slave Rebelliousness and Social Conflict in North Carolina, 1775 to 1802," *WMQ*, 3rd Ser., 37 (1980): 84–5.

6. Philip S. Foner, *Blacks in the American Revolution* (Westport, CI, 1976), 70; Benjamin Quarles, *The Negro in the American Revolution* (Chapel Hill, NC, 1961), ix.

7. Peto Maslowski, "National Policy Toward the Use of Black Troops in the Revolution," *SCHM*, 73 (1972): 2–11.

8. Paul F. Dearden, *The Rhode Island Campaign of 1778* (Providence, RI, 1980), 24.

9. Persifor Frazer to his wife, July 25, 1776, "Some Extracts from the Papers of General Persifor Frazer," *PMHB*, 31 (1907), 134.

10. Alexander Hamilton to John Jay, March 14, 1779, Syrett (ed.), *Papers of Hamilton*, 2: 18.

11. David O. White, *Connecticut's Black Soldiers, 1775–1783* (Chester, CT, 1973), 21 and 31–2; Quarles, *Negro in the American Revolution*, 54–7; Dearden, *Rhode Island Campaign*, xiii.

12. Robert A. Selig, "The Revolution's Black Soldiers," *Colonial Williamsburg* (Summer 1997): 20; Quarles, *Negro in the American Revolution*, 65 and 74–5; White, *Connecticut's Black Soldiers*, 31; Arthur Zilversmit, *The First Emancipation: The Abolition of Slavery in the North* (Chicago, 1967), 119; Berg, *Continental Army Units*, 105–6.

13. John C. Dann (ed.), *The Revolution Remembered: Eye-Witness Accounts of the War for Independence* (Chicago, 1980), 226–9.

14. John E. Selby, *The Revolution in Virginia, 1775–1783* (Williamsburg, VA, 1988), 66–7; Sidney Kaplan, *The Black Presence in the Era of the American Revolution, 1770–1800* (New York, 1973), 62.

15. Quarles, *Negro in the American Revolution*, 150–1.

16. Paul A. Gilje and William Penack, *New York in the Age of the Constitution, 1775–1780* (Rutherford, NJ, 1992), 31–3; Philip R. N. Katcher, *Encyclopedia of British, Provincial, and German Army Units, 1777–1783* (Harrisburg, PA, 1973), 92; Nadelhaft, *Disorders of War*, 129; Kaplan, *Black Experience*, 87.

17. Selig, "The Revolution's Black Soldiers," 20; David L. Valuska, "Black Hessians," in Blanco (ed.), *American Revolution . . . Encyclopedia*, 1: 119–20.

18. W. E. B. Du Bois, *The Suppression of the African Slave-Trade in the United States of America, 1638–1870* (New York, 1970, orig. pub. 1896), 41–51; Dwight L. Dumond, *Antislavery: The Crusade for Freedom in America* (Ann Arbor, MI, 1961), 29–34.

19. *Pennsylvania Journal*, March 8, 1775, in Robert Bruns (ed.), *Am I Not a Man and a Brother: The Antislavery Crusade in Revolutionary America, 1688–1788* (New York, 1977), 376–9.

20. Draft of a Fundamental Constitution for the Commonwealth of Virginia, June 1783, *JP*, 6: 298; Douglas R. Egerton, *Gabriel's Rebellion: The Virginia Slave Conspiracies of 1800 and 1802* (Chapel Hill, NC, 1993), 12.

21. Bruns (ed.), *Am I Not a Man*, 365–6.

22. Bruns (ed.), *Am I Not a Man*, 397–426.

23. Quoted in White, *Village at War, Chatham*, 111–12.

24. Bruns (ed.), *Am I Not a Man*, 475–86.

25. Sydney V. James, *A People among Peoples: Quaker Benevolence in Eighteenth-Century America* (Cambridge, MA, 1963), 228; Jean R. Soderlund, *Quakers and Slavery: A Divided Spirit* (Princeton, NJ, 1985), 177.

26. Frey, *Water from the Rock*, 247–9.

27. W. Harrison Daniel, "Virginia Baptists and the Negro in the Early Republic," *VMHB*, 80 (1972): 62.

28. Donald G. Mathews, *Slavery and Methodism: A Chapter in American Morality, 1780–1815* (Princeton, NJ, 1965), 8, 10, and 12; Harry V. Richardson, *Dark Salvation: The Story of Methodism as It Developed among Blacks in America* (New York, 1976), 53–5: Frey, *Water from the Rock*, 245.

29. Edward R. Turner, "The First Abolition Society in the United States," *PMHB*, 36 (1912): 92.

30. Turner, "The First Abolition Society," 95–6; Bruns (ed.), *Am I Not a Man*, 384n. and 570; Soderlund, *Quakers and Slavery*, 185.

31. Robin Blackburn, *The Overthrow of Colonial Slavery, 1776–1848* (London, 1988), 120; Bruns (ed.), *Am I Not a Man*, 504n.

32. Duncan J. MacLeod, *Slavery, Race and the American Revolution* (London, 1974), 44–5; Dumond, *Antislavery*, 48; Zilversmit, *The First Emancipation*, 174.

33. Zilversmit, *The First Emancipation*, 117.

34. White, *Connecticut's Black Soldiers*, 48.

35. Zilversmit, *The First Emancipation*, 121.

36. Zilversmit, *The First Emancipation*, 147–8.

37. William Livingston to Samuel Allison, July 25, 1778, *WL*, 2: 403.

38. Massachusetts Charter, in Jack P. Greene (ed.), *Settlements to Society, 1584–1763* (New York, 1966), 207; George L. Haskins, *Law and Authority in Early Massachusetts* (New York, 1960), 229; Lorenzo J. Greene, *The Negro in Colonial New England* (New York, 1968, orig. pub. 1942), 63.

39. William Cushing's charge to the Jury, July 1783, Bruns (ed.), *Am I Not a Man*, 474–5; Zilversmit, *The First Emancipation*, 113; Robert M. Spector, "The Quock Walker Cases (1781–3)—Slavery, Its Abolition, and Negro Citizenship in Early Massachusetts," *Journal of Negro History*, 53 (1968): 12–32; William O'Brien, "Did the Jennison Case Outlaw Slavery in Massachusetts?" *WMQ*, 3rd Ser., 17 (1960): 219–41.

40. Edward R. Turner, "The Abolition of Slavery in Pennsylvania," *PMHB*, 36 (1912): 138 and 142–3; Davis, *Problem of Slavery*, 89n.; Gary B. Nash and Jean R. Soderlund, *Freedom by Degrees: Emancipation in Pennsylvania and Its Aftermath* (New York, 1991), 7 and 32.

41. Monte A. Calvert, "The Abolition Society of Delaware, 1801–1807," *Delaware History*, 10 (1962–3): 296.

42. Don Higginbotham (ed.), *The Papers of James Iredell* (Raleigh, NC, 1976), 1: 83n.; Nash, *Race and Revolution*, 17 and 19; Allan Nevins, *The American States during and after the Revolution, 1775–1789* (New York, 1969, orig. pub. 1924), 447.

43. Virginia Manumission Law, Bruns (ed.), *Am I Not a Man*, 470–1; Louis Morton, *Robert Carter of Nomini Hall: A Virginia Tobacco Planter in the Eighteenth Century* (Charlottesville, VA, 1945), 251; William H. Williams, *Slavery and Freedom in Delaware, 1639–1865* (Wilmington, NC, 1966), 141.

44. Duncan J. MacLeod, "Toward Caste," in Berlin and Hoffman (eds), *Slavery and Freedom*, 234.

45. Winthrop D. Jordan, *White over Black: American Attitudes Toward the Negro, 1550–1812* (Chapel Hill, NC, 1968), 408–11.

46. Benjamin Quarles, "The Revolutionary War as a Black Declaration of Independence," in Berlin and Hoffman (eds), *Slavery and Freedom*, 209–10; Frey, *Water from the Rock*, 241.

47. Gary B. Nash, *Forging Freedom: The Formation of Philadelphia's Black Community, 1720–1840* (Cambridge, MA, 1988), 73–6; Shane White, "'We Dwell in Safety and Pursue Our Honest Callings:' Free Blacks in New York City, 1783–1810," *Journal of American History*, 75 (1988): 451–3 and 456–7; Jacqueline Jones, "Race, Sex, and Self-Evident Truths: The Status of Slave Women during the Era of the American Revolution," in Hoffman and Albert (eds), *Women in the Age of the American Revolution*, 331.

48. Charles H. Wesley, *Richard Allen: Apostle of Freedom* (Washington, DC, 1935), 9 and 16–35; James O. and Lois E. Horton, *In Hopes of*

Liberty: Culture, Community, and Protest Among Northern Free Blacks, 1700–1800 (New York, 1997), 137–9; Nash, *Forging Freedom*, 96–9.

49. Quarles, "The Revolutionary War as a Black Declaration of Independence," 295.

50. Quarles, "The Revolutionary War as a Black Declaration of Independence," 298–9; Horton and Horton, *In Hopes of Liberty*, 126.

51. James, *A People Among Peoples*, 236–9; Horton and Horton, *In Hopes of Liberty*, 22; Peter M. Bergman, *The Chronological History of the Negro in America* (New York, 1969), 65.

52. Nash, *Forging Freedom*, 80–1 and 84–5.

53. Robert W. Fogel, *Without Consent or Contract: The Rise and Fall of American Slavery* (New York, 1989), 242–3.

54. Quoted in Jordan, *White over Black*, 287.

55. Jefferson, *Notes on the State of Virginia* (ed.), Peden, 139–43.

56. Frey, *Water from the Rock*, 235–6.

Chapter Thirteen

1. Report of Sir James Wright to Lord Dartmouth, September 20, 1773, *GHSC*, 3 (1873): 167–9; Henry Knox to Washington, July 6 and 7, 1789, *American State Papers . . . Indian Affairs* (Washington, DC, 1832), 1: 15–16, 38, and 49; J. Leitch Wright, Jr, *Creeks & Seminoles: The Destruction and Regeneration of the Muscogulge People* (Lincoln, NE, 1986), 288; Kathryn D. H. Braund, *Deerskins & Duffels: The Creek Indian Trade with Anglo-America, 1685–1815* (Lincoln, NE, 1993), 9 and 198n.; Colin G. Calloway, *The American Revolution in Indian Country: Crisis and Diversity in Native American Communities* (Cambridge, Eng., 1995), 182. Widely varying Indian census estimates provided by contemporaries for 1775 and before and after are given in Evarts E. Greene and Virginia D. Harrington, *American Population Before the Federal Census of 1790* (New York, 1932), 194–206.

2. Jack M. Sosin, "The Use of Indians in the War of the American Revolution: A Re-Assessment of Responsibility," *Canadian Historical Review*, 46 (1965): 120; Arrell M. Gibson, *The American Indian: Prehistory to the Present* (Lexington, MA, 1980), 251–2; Walter H. Mohr, *Federal Indian Relations, 1774–1785* (Philadelphia, 1933), 38–9.

3. Chastellux, *Travels*, ed. Rice, 1: 209; James E. Seaver (ed.), *A Narrative of the Life of Mary Jemison* (New York, 1925), 395.

4. Richard White, *The Middle Ground: Indians, Empires, and Republics in the Great Lakes Region, 1650–1815* (Cambridge, Eng., 1991), 407.

5. Barbara Graymount, *The Iroquois in the American Revolution* (Syracuse, NJ, 1972), 170–2; Howard Swiggett, *War Out of Niagara: Walter Butler and the Tory Rangers* (Port Washington, NY, 1963, orig. pub. 1933), 91.

6. Jack M. Sosin, *The Revolutionary Frontier, 1763–1783* (New York, 1967), 188–9; Christopher Ward, *The War of the Revolution* (New York, 1952), 2: 651–2; Graymount, *Iroquois in the American Revolution*, 184.

7. Gregory E. Dowd, *A Spirited Resistance: The North American Indian Struggle for Unity, 1745–1815* (Baltimore, MD, 1992), 73; Solon J. and Elizabeth H. Buck, *The Planting of Civilization in Western Pennsylvania* (Pittsburgh, PA, 1939), 195–6.

8. Robert A. Hecht, *Continents in Collision: The Impact of Europe on the North American Indian Societies* (Washington, DC, 1980), 117; Dale Van Every, *A Company of Heroes: The American Frontier, 1775–1783* (New York, 1977, orig. pub. 1962), 241 and 245–6; Ted F. Belue, "Battle of Blue Licks, Kentucky, August 19, 1782," in Blanco (ed.), *American Revolution . . . Encyclopedia*, 1: 133–6; Gibson, *American Indian*, 256.

9. James H. O'Donnell, *Southern Indians in the American Revolution* (Knoxville, TN, 1973), 40–7; Gregory E. Dowd, "Paths of Resistance: American Indian Religion and the Quest for Unity, 1745–1815," PhD diss., Princeton University, 1986, 397–8; Hecht, *Continents in Collision*, 113; Mohr, *Federal Indian Relations*, 51.

10. Samuel C. Williams, *Tennessee During the Revolutionary War* (Knoxville, TN, 1974, orig. pub. 1944), 92–9, 175–7, and 187–90; Dowd, *Spirited Resistance*, 54–5; Mohr, *Federal Indian Relations*, 57; O'Donnell, *Southern Indians in the American Revolution*, 107.

11. David H. Corkran, *The Creek Frontier, 1540–1783* (Norman, OK, 1967), 309, 315–16, and 321; Dowd, *Spirited Resistance*, 56.

12. Dowd, "Paths of Resistance," 406–8; Williams, *Tennessee During the Revolutionary War*, 171–2; Calloway, *American Revolution in Indian Country*, 227–8.

13. Quoted in J. Russell Snapp, *John Stuart and the Struggle on the Southern Frontier* (Baton Rouge, LA, 1996), 202–3.

14. Eduardo and Bonnie Duran, *Native American Postcolonial Psychology* (Albany, NY, 1995), 37–8.

15. White, *Middle Ground*, 388.

16. Joseph R. Fischer, *A Well-Executed Failure: The Sullivan Campaign Against the Iroquois, July–September 1779* (Columbia, SC, 1997), 28 and 233n.; Graymount, *Iroquois in the American Revolution*, 171–2 and 174.

17. Chastellux, *Travels*, ed. Rice, December 27, 1780, 1: 209.

18. Alvin M. Josephy, Jr, *The Patriot Chiefs* (New York, 1969), 142.

19. George E. Hyde, *The Pawnee Indians* (Norman, OK, 1974), 157 and 160–1.

20. Alfred J. Morrison (trans. and ed.), *Travels in the Confederation [1783–1784] from the German of Johann David Schoepf* (New York, 1968, orig. pub. 1788), 1: 282.

21. Frederick Drimmer (ed.), *Captured by the Indians: 15 Firsthand Accounts, 1750–1870* (New York, 1985, orig. pub 1961), 106 and 110–12.

22. "Journal of Lieut. William Barton," August 30, 1779, in Frederick Cook (comp.), *Journals of the Military Expedition of Major General John Sullivan against the Six Nations of Indians in 1779* (Freeport, NY, 1972, orig. pub. 1887), 8; Van Every, *Company of Heroes*, 72, 194n., 221, and 240; Calloway, *American Revolution in Indian Country*, 49.

23. Thomas S. Abler (ed.), *Chainbreaker: The Revolutionary War Memoirs of Governor Blacksnake* (Lincoln, NE, 1987), 73 and 270n.; Isabel T. Kelsay, *Joseph Brant, 1743–1807; Man of Two Worlds* (Syracuse, NY, 1984), 303–4; Van Every, *Company of Heroes*, 194n.

24. Seaver (ed.), *Narrative of Jemison*, 91.

25. C. A. Weslager, *The Delaware Indians: A History* (New Brunswick, NJ, 1972), 314.

26. John D. Barnhart (ed.), *Henry Hamilton and George Rogers Clark in the American Revolution with the Unpublished Journal of Lieut. Gov. Henry Hamilton* (Crawfordsville, IN, 1951), 75 and 182–3.

27. White, *Middle Ground*, 388.

28. Quoted in Eric Hindertaker, *Elusive Empires: Constructing Colonialism in the Ohio Valley, 1673–1800* (Cambridge, Eng., 1997), 223.

29. Allan W. Eckert, *The Frontiersmen: A Narrative* (Boston, MA, 1967), 219–20.

30. Extract of a letter, Elijah Clarke to - - - -, December 1780, in "Preston Papers," *VMHB*, 27 (1919): 316.

31. Eckert, *Frontiersmen*, 79–80 and 357.

32. "Journal of Lieut. Col. Adam Hubley," in Cook (comp.), *Journals of Sullivan*, 162–3; Seaver (ed.), *Narrative of Jemison*, 70–3; Kelsay, *Joseph Brant*, 266–7.

33. John Heckewelder, *A Narrative of the Mission of the United Brethren among the Delaware and Mohegan Indians* (New York, 1971, orig. pub. 1820), 321–35 and 341; Dowd, "Paths of Resistance," 450.

34. Knight's account in Bernard W. Sheehan, *Seeds of Extinction: Jeffersonian Philanthropy and the American Indian* (Chapel Hill, NC, 1973), 185–6.

35. Hecht, *Continents in Collison*, 118.

36. Walter Pilkington (ed.), *The Journals of Samuel Kirkland* (Clinton, NY, 1980), 134 and 148n.; Lawrence M. Hauptman, "Refugee Havens: The Iroquois Villages in the Eighteenth Century," in Christopher Vecsey and Robert Venables (eds), *American Indian Environments: Ecological Issues in Native American History* (Syracuse, NJ, 1980), 129–30; Gibson, *American Indian*, 97; Kelsay, *Joseph Brant*, 86–7.

37. Chastellux, *Travels*, ed. Rice, December 27, 1780, 208 and 349n.–350n.; Kirkland quote in Graymount, *Iroquois in the American Revolution*, 286.

38. Lewis H. Morgan, *League of the Ho-De-No Sau-Nee or Iroquois* (New Haven, CT, 1954, orig. pub. 1901), 1: 27–31; Robert Hunter, *Quebec to Canada in 1785–1786, Being the Travel Diary and Observations of Robert Hunter, Jr., a Young Merchant of London*, ed. Louis B. Wright (San Marino, CA, 1943), 95; Kelsay, *Joseph Brant*, 267–71 and 416; Calloway, *American Revolution in Indian Country*, 47, 130, 135, and 155; Swiggett, *War out of Niagara*, 48; Abler, *Chainbreaker*, 117.

39. Henry Knox to Major Winthrop Sargent, March 5, 1786 and March 21, 1786, Sargent Papers, 1: 11 and 20, Ohio State Historical Society; William Brandon, *Indians* (Boston, MA, 1961), 137–8, 156, and 196; Josephy, *Patriot Chiefs*, 137–9.

40. Calloway, *American Revolution in Indian Country*, 287–8.

41. Weslager, *Delaware Indians*, 319–20; R. Pierce Beaver, *Church, State, and the American Indians* (St Louis, MO, 1966), 58.

42. Richard R. Juday, *The Battle of Piqua: Revolutionary Encounter in Ohio* (Dayton, OH, 1976), 8–9.

43. James H. Merrell, *The Indians' New World: Catawbas and Their Neighbors from European Contact through the Era of Removal* (Chapel Hill, NC, 1989), 216–17.

44. Samuel Montgomery, "Journey Through the Indian Country Beyond the Ohio, 1785," ed. David I. Bushnell, *Mississippi Valley Historical Review*, 2 (1915–16): 212 and n.; James P. Pate, "The Chickamaugas: A Forgotten Segment of Indian Resistance of the Southern Frontier," PhD diss., Mississippi State University, 1969, 128 and 164–5; R. S. Cotterill, *The Southern Indians: The Story of the Civilized Tribes before Removal* (Norman, OK, 1954), 44 and 55; Erminie Wheeler-Voegelin, *Indians of Ohio and Indiana Prior to 1795: Ethnohistory of Indian Use and Occupancy in Ohio and Indiana Prior to 1795* (New York, 1974), 536–7, 574, 578, 583, and 653; O'Donnell, *Southern Indians in the American Revolution*, 52.

45. Barbé de Marbois's Journal of His Visit to the Territory of the Six Nations, September 23, 1784, *LP*, 5: 250.

46. Seaver (ed.), *Narrative of Jemison*, 46 and 63–7.

47. Quote John Drayton (1803) in Merrill, *Indians' New World*, 227.

48. Calloway, *American Revolution in Indian Country*, 62.

49. William G. McLoughlin, *Cherokee Renascence in the New Republic* (Princeton, NJ, 1986), 3–4.

50. Corkran, *Creek Frontier*, 148; Tom Hatley, *The Dividing Paths: Cherokees and the South Carolinians Through the Era of Revolution* (New York, 1993), 224; Thomas Clark, *Frontier America* (New York, 1959), 107.

51. J. Hector St John Crèvecoeur, *Letters from an American Farmer* (New York, 1904, orig. pub. 1782), 306.

52. Frank H. Severance (ed.), *The Captivity and Suffering of Benjamin Gilbert and His Family, 1780–1783* (Cleveland, OH, 1904), 109.

53. Hatley, *Dividing Paths*, 225; McLoughlin, *Cherokee Renascene*, 31.

54. Williams, *Tennesee During the Revolutionary War*, 171; Eckert, *Frontiersmen*, 19–21 and *passim*; Ward, *William Maxwell*, 135; Kelsay, *Joseph Brant*, 109.

55. Daniel Brodhead to Washington, April 3, 1779, Louise P. Kellogg (ed.), *Frontier Advance on the Upper Ohio, 1778–1779* (Madison, WI, 1916), 273; Hatley, *Dividing Paths*, 227; Calloway, *American Revolution in Indian Country*, 58; Russell Thornton, *American Indian Holocaust and Survival: A Population History since 1492* (Norman, OK, 1987), 81.

56. John F. D. Smyth, *A Tour of the United States of America* (New York, 1968, orig. pub, 1784), 1: 187.

57. Elizabeth Cometti (ed.), *The American Journals of Lt. John Enys* (Syracuse, NJ, 1976), 144.

58. Weslager, *Delaware Indians*, 318; Kelsay, *Joseph Brant*, 344–8.

59. *JCC*, September 22, 1783, 25: 602; Clarence E. Carter (ed.), *The Territorial Papers of the United States* (Washington, DC, 1934), 2: 47; Francis P. Prucha, *The Great Father: The United States Government and the American Indians* (Lincoln, NE, 1984), 1: 43.

60. Cotterill, *Southern Indians*, 57–9; Calloway, *American Revolution in Indian Country*, 284.

61. Francis P. Prucha, *The Indians in American Society: From the Revolutionary War to the Present* (Berkeley, CA, 1985), 31; McLoughlin, *Cherokee Renascence*, 21.

62. Henry Knox to Washington, May 5, 1785, Washington Papers, Library of Congress; Reginald Horsman, *Matthew Elliott, British Indian Agent* (Detroit, 1964), 51–2; Gibson, *American Indian*, 265–6.

63. Gibson, *American Indian*, 263 and 397.

64. Report of Henry Knox, July 7, 1789?, Knox Papers, Mass. Hist. Soc.

Chapter Fourteen

1. Richard B. Morris, "Class Struggle and the American Revolution," *WMQ*, 3rd Ser., 19 (1962): 22.

2. "Diary of James Allen Esq. of Philadelphia, Counsellor-at-Law, 1770–1778," *PMHB*, 9 (1885): 440.

3. Samuel Adams to Francis Lightfoot Lee, 1778, Cushing (ed.), *Writings of Samuel Adams*, 4: 19.

4. James Bowdoin to Thomas Pownall, November 20, 1783, *The Bowdoin and Temple Papers*, MHSC, 7th Ser., 6 (1907): 22.

5. James Warren to John Adams, June 13, 1779, Worthington C. Ford (ed.), *Warren–Adams Letters*, MHSC, 7th Ser., 73 (1925): 105.

6. Allan Kulikoff, "The Progress of Inequality in Revolutionary Boston," *WMQ*, 28 (1971): 404–8; Edward Pessen, *Riches, Class, and Power before the Civil War* (Lexington, MA, 1973), 81.

7. John W. Tyler, "Persistence and Change within the Boston Business Community," in Conrad E. Wright and Katheryn P. Viens (eds), *Entrepreneurs: The Boston Business Community, 1700–1850* (Boston, MA, 1997), 102–3; Merrill Jensen, *The New Nation: A History of the United States during the Confederation, 1781–1789* (New York, 1950), 183–4; Peter J. Coleman, "The Insolvent Debtor in Rhode Island, 1745–1828," *WMQ*, 3rd Ser., 22 (1965): 426–34; Peter D. Hall, *The Organization of American Culture, 1700–1900: Private Institutions, Elites, and the Origins of American Nationality* (New York, 1982), 32; Thomas M. Doerflinger, *A Vigorous Spirit of Enterprise: Merchants and Economic Development in Revolutionary Philadelphia* (Chapel Hill, NC, 1986), 244–5.

8. Main, *Social Structure of Revolutionary America*, 247.

9. Main, *Social Structure of Revolutionary America*, 247; John S. Pancake, *Samuel Smith and the Politics of Business, 1752–1839* (University, AL, 1972), 27 and 30.

10. Tyler, "Persistance and Change," 105.

11. Kulikoff, "Progress of Inequality," 381 and 383.

12. Gary B. Nash, *Class and Society in Early America* (Englewood Cliffs, NJ, 1970), 177.

13. John J. McCusker and Russell R. Menard, *The Economy of British America, 1607–1789* (Chapel Hill, NC, 1985), 366–7.

14. April 4, 1777, quoted in William B. Weeden, *Economic and Social History of New England, 1620–1789* (Williamstown, MA, 1978, orig. pub. 1890), 2: 779.

15. Douglas S. Robertson (ed.), *An Englishman in America, 1785, being the Diary of Joseph Hadfield* (Toronto, 1933), September 15, 1785, 185 and 219.

16. Thomas Jefferson to James Currie, August 4, 1787, *JP*, 11: 682.

17. Bruce A. Ragsdale, *A Planters' Republic: The Search for Economic Independence in Revolutionary Virginia* (Madison, WI, 1996), 255.

18. Hutchinson and Rachal (eds), *Papers of Madison*, 5: 287n.

19. Ragsdale, *Planters' Republic*, 255.

20. Virginia Delegates to Benjamin Harrison, August 27, 1782, Hutchinson and Rachal (eds), *Papers of Madison*, 5: 85.

21. E. James Ferguson (ed.), *The Papers of Robert Morris* (Pittsburgh, 1975), 2: 46n.; Jensen, *New Nation*, 202–4.

22. Philip S. Foner, *Labor and the American Revolution* (Westport, CT, 1976), 202; Richard Walsh, *Charleston's Sons of Liberty: A Study of the Artisans, 1763–1789* (Columbia, SC, 1959), 109–11.

23. Sharon V. Salinger, *"To Serve Well and faithfully:" Labor and Indentured Servants in Pennsylvania, 1682–1800* (Cambridge, Eng., 1987), 134.

24. Salinger, *"To Serve Well and faithfully,"* 161; Foner, *Labor and the American Revolution,* 200–1; Ronald Schultz, *The Republic of Labor: Philadelphia Artisans and the Politics of Class, 1720–1780* (New York, 1993), 40.

25. Eric Foner, *Tom Paine and Revolutionary America* (New York, 1976), 43–5.

26. Tina H. Sheller, "Freeman, Servants, and Slaves: Artisans and the Craft Structure of Revolutionary Baltimore Town," in Howard B. Rock et al. (eds), *American Artisans: Crafting Social Identity,* (1750–1856), 27.

27. Salinger, *"To Serve Well and faithfully,"* 137–8.

28. Jensen, *New Nation,* 137.

29. William Miller, "The Effects on the American Revolution on Indentured Servitude," *Pennsylvania History,* 7 (1940): 133.

30. David W. Galenson, *White Servitude in Colonial America: An Economic Analysis* (Cambridge, Eng., 1981), 179; Salinger, *"To Serve Well and faithfully,"* 145.

31. Washington to Clement Biddle, August 13, 1783 and June 30, 1784, *FWW,* 27: 102 and 429; Washington to Tench Tilghman, March 24, 1784, *ASP,* Confederation Series, 1: 232.

32. *Independent Journal,* January 24, 1784, quoted in Foner, *Labor and the American Revolution,* 200.

33. Evarts B. Greene, *The Revolutionary Generation, 1763–1790* (New York, 1950), 308–9; Galenson, *White Servitude,* 179–80.

34. Doerflinger, *A Vigorous Spirit,* 50–5.

35. Doerflinger, *A Vigorous Spirit,* 236–8; E. James Ferguson, *The Power of the Purse* (Chapel Hill, NC, 1961), 78–9; Clarence L. Ver Steeg, *Robert Morris: Revolutionary Financier* (New York, 1972, orig. pub. 1954), 21.

36. Carp, *To Starve the Army,* 105.

37. *NG,* 4: 310n. and 341n., 5: 374n., 6: 122n. and 241n.; Freeman, *Washington,* 5: 505–10.

38. Theodore Thayer, *Nathanael Greene: Strategist of the American Revolution* (New York, 1960), 415–20; Harry M. Ward, *Charles Scott and the "Spirit of '76"* (Charlottesville, VA, 1988), 84–5.

39. Main, *Social Structure of Revolutionary America,* 193.

40. Douglas L. Jones, "The Strolling Poor: Transiency in Eighteenth-Century Massachusetts," in James K. Martin (ed.), *Interpreting Colonial America* (New York, 1978), 295–6.

41. Klein, *Unification of a Slave State,* 116.

42. Oscar and Lilian Handlin, *A Restless People: Americans in Rebellion, 1770–1787* (Garden City, NY, 1982), 120–1 and 129.

43. Arthur H. Shaffer, *To Be an American: David Ramsay and the Making of the American Consciousness* (Columbia, SC, 1991), 138–9.

44. Joyce E. Chaplin, *An Anxious Pursuit: Agricultural Innovation and Modernity in the Lower South* (Chapel Hill, NC, 1993), 287–93.

45. Lowell H. Harrison, *Kentucky's Road to Statehood* (Lexington, KY, 1992), 7–11 and 24; Charles R. Staples, *The History of Pioneer Lexington, 1779–1806* (Lexington, KY, 1996, orig. pub. 1939), 7.

46. Harriet S. Arnow, *Seedtime on the Cumberland* (New York, 1960), chapter 9.

47. Theodore J. Crackel, "Revolutionary War Pension Records and American Mobility, 1780–1830," *Prologue: Journal of the National Archives*, 16 (fall 1984), 155, 162, 164, 166–7.

48. Devereux Jarratt, *The Life of Devereux Jarratt* (New York, 1969, orig. pub. 1806), 12–15.

49. Anburey, *Travels,* April 10, 1779, 2: 370–1; William H. Gaines, Jr, *Thomas Mann Randolph: Jefferson's Son-in-Law* (Baton Rouge, LA, 1966), 10.

50. Anburey, *Travels,* February 12, 1779, 2: 347–8; Harry M. Ward, *Richmond: An Illustrated History* (Northridge, CA, 1985), 43–5.

51. J. P. Brissot de Warville, *New Travels in the United States of America,* ed. Durand Echeverria (Cambridge, MA, 1964), August 1788, 153.

52. Louis B. Wright and Marion Tinling (eds), *Quebec to Carolina in 1785–1786: Being the Travel Diary and Observations of Robert Hunter, Jr., Young Merchant of London* (San Marino, CA, 1943), October 21, 1785, 146.

53. Adams quote in Richard L. Bushman, "'This New Man:' Dependence and Independence, 1776," in Richard L. Bushman et al. (eds), *Uprooted Americans* (Boston, MA, 1979), 84.

54. Smith, *"Lower Sort,"* 4–5.

55. Whitfield J. Bell, Jr, "The Federal Processions of 1788," *New-York Historical Society Quarterly*, 46 (1962): 5–39; Paul A. Gilje, "The Common People and the Constitution: Popular Culture in New York City in the Late Eighteenth Century," in Paul A. Gilje and William Pencak (eds), *New York in the Age of the Constitution, 1775–1800* (Rutherford, NJ, 1992), chapter 2.

56. Smith, *"Lower Sort,"* 21 and 163.

57. Benjamin Rush to Charles Nisbett, April 19, 1784, Butterfield (ed.), *Letters of Rush*, 1: 323.

58. The Scott passage is mainly verbatim from Ward, *Charles Scott*, 98–9, adapted from "Interview of Herman Bowman," Draper Collection, 13CC172, State Historical Society of Wisconsin.

59. Quoted in Norman Jacobson, "Class and Identity in the American Revolution," in Reinhard Bendix and Seymour M. Lipset (eds), *Class Status and Power: A Reader in Social Stratification* (New York, 1961), 549.

60. Quoted in Handlin and Handlin, *A Restless People*, 209.

61. John S. Ezell (ed.), *The New Democracy in America: Travels of Francisco de Miranda in the United States, 1783–1784* (Norman, OK, 1963), 162.

62. Quoted in Stephen Brobeck, "Changes in the Composition and Structure of Philadelphia Elite Groups, 1756, 1790," PhD diss., University of Pennsylvania, 1973, 195.

63. Handlin and Handlin, *A Restless People*, 58; Patsy McLaughlin, "Why Washington Stopped Wearing Pink Satin," in the "Inventing America: Philadelphia and the Making of the Constitution" section of *The Philadelphia Inquirer*, April 28, 1987, 16–17.

64. William P. and Julia P. Cutler, *Life and Correspondence of Rev. Manasseh Cutler* (Cincinnati, OH, 1888), July 7, 1787, 1: 231.

65. Quoted in Adrienne Koch, *Power, Morals and the Founding Fathers: Essays in the Interpretation of the American Enlightenment* (Ithaca, NY, 1961), 125.

66. Benjamin Rush to Mrs Rush, May 29, 1776, Butterfield (ed.), *Letters of Rush*, 1: 99.

67. Koch, *Power, Morals and the Founding Fathers*, 127.

68. Michael Kammen, *People of Paradox: An Inquiry Concerning the Origins of American Civilization* (New York, 1972), 234.

69. Brissot de Warville, *New Travels*, July 30, 1788, 84.

70. Samuel Williams, "A Discourse on the Love of Our Country," December 15, 1774, in Greene (ed.), *Colonies to Nation*, 378 and 384.

71. "Sentiments on a Peace Establishment [to] . . . Committee of Congress on the Peace Establishment," enclosed in Washington to Hamilton, May 2, 1783, *FWW*, 26: 374–98.

72. Royster, *Revolutionary People at War*, 358.

73. Harry M. Ward, *Department of War* (Pittsburgh, PA, 1962), 27–30.

74. "Essays of Brutus," Herbert J. Storing (ed.), *The Compete Anti-Federalist* (Chicago, 1981), 2: 411.

Chapter Fifteen

1. Benjamin Rush to Elizabeth Greene Ferguson, July 16, 1787, Butterfield (ed.), *Letters of Rush*, 1: 278–9.

2. De Tocqueville, *Democracy in America*, ed. Hacker, 185.

3. Wilson C. McWilliams, *The Idea of Fraternity in America* (Berkeley, CA, 1973), 4.

4. J. M. Roberts, *The Mythology of the Secret Societies* (New York, 1972), 17.

5. David Van Biema, "Endangered Conspirators, Freemasons. . . ," *Time* (May 25, 1998): 64.

6. Mary Ann Clawson, *Constructing Brotherhood: Class, Gender, and Fraternalism* (Princeton, NJ, 1989), 51; Catherine Albanese, *Sons of the*

Fathers: The Civil Religion of the American Revolution (Philadelphia, 1976), 129–30; Sidney Kaplan, "Veteran Officers and Politics in Massachusetts, 1783–1787," *WMQ*, 3rd Ser., 9 (1952): 31.

7. Clawson, *Constructing Brotherhood*, 59.

8. Dorothy A. Lipson, *Freemasonry in Federalist Connecticut* (Princeton, NJ, 1977), 32 and 38n.; Melvin M. Johnson, *The Beginnings of Freemasonry in America* (New York, 1924), 22–3, 377, and 383; Stephen C. Bullock, *Revolutionary Brotherhood: Freemasonry and the Transformation of the American Social Order, 1730–1840* (Chapel Hill, NC, 1996), 113.

9. Bullock, *Revolutionary Brotherhood*, 122; Albanese, *Sons of the Fathers*, 130–1.

10. Bullock, *Revolutionary Brotherhood*, 126.

11. Bullock, *Revolutionary Brotherhood*, 122.

12. Bullock, *Revolutionary Brotherhood*, 128.

13. "Journal of William Rogers," June 23 and July 29, 1779, in Cook (comp.), *Journals of Expedition against Six Nations*, 248 and 254.

14. Julius F. Sachse, *Old Masonic Lodges of Pennsylvania: "Modern" and "Ancient," 1730–1800* (Philadelphia, 1912–13), 1: 367.

15. Freeman, *Washington*, 1: 267 and n.; Albanese, *Sons of the Fathers*, 131; Henry J. Parker, *Army Lodges during the Revolution* (Boston, MA, 1884), 4.

16. Lipson, *Freemasonry in Federalist Connecticut*, 56.

17. Lipson, *Freemasonry in Federalist Connecticut*, 56–7; Parker, *Army Lodges*, 3; Charles S. Plumb, *The History of the American Union Lodge No. 1. Free and Accepted Masons, 1776 to 1933* (Marietta, OH, 1934), 82.

18. Parker, *Army Lodges*, 5; Lipson, *Freemasonry in Federalist Connecticut*, 58–61; Charles H. Callahan, *Washington: The Man and the Mason* (Washington, DC, 1913), 267–9; Albert H. Heusser, *George Washington's Map Maker: A Biography of Robert Erskine* (New Brunswick, NJ, 1966, orig. pub. 1928), 206; Norris S. Barratte and Julius F. Sachse, *Freemasonry in Pennsylvania, 1727–1907* (Philadelphia, 1908), 399–410; Bernard Fay, *Revolution and Freemasonry, 1680–1800* (Boston, MA, 1935), 246–7.

19. Parker, *Army Lodges*, 7–9.

20. Dexter (ed.), *Diary of Stiles*, January 30, 1784, 3: 104–6.

21. Lipson, *Freemasonry in Federalist Connecticut*, 199; Bullock, *Revolutionary Brotherhood*, 160–2; Janet W. James, "Hannah Mather Crocker," in Edward T. James (ed.), *Notable American Women, 1607–1950: A Biographical Dictionary* (Cambridge, MA, 1971), 1: 406–7.

22. "Notes of a Tour through Holland and the Rhine Valley," March 16, 1788, *JP*, 13: 11.

23. Minor Meyers, Jr, *Liberty without Anarchy: A History of the Society of the Cincinnati* (Charlottesville, VA, 1983), 258–63.

24. Edgar E. Hume, *Lafayette and the Society of the Cincinnati* (Baltimore, MD, 1934), 8.

25. Charles M. Holloway, "Society of the Cincinnati, Borrowing from the Past . . . ," *Colonial Williamsburg* (summer 1997): 23, 26, and 28; Meyers, *Liberty without Anarchy*, 24.

26. Warren, *History . . . American Revolution*, 3: 282.

27. Aedanus Burke, "Considerations on the Society or Order of Cincinnati" (October 10, 1783), in Greene (ed.), *Colonies to Nation*, 459; John C. Meleney, *The Public Life of Aedanus Burke: Revolutionary Republican in Post-Revolutionary South Carolina* (Columbia, SC, 1989), 87.

28. Hume, *Lafayette and the Society of the Cincinnati*, 20.

29. Wallace E. Davies, "The Society of the Cincinnati in New England, 1783–1800," *WMQ*, 3rd Ser., 5 (1948): 11.

30. Samuel Adams to Elbridge Gerry, April 23, 1784, Cushing (ed.), *Writings of Samuel Adams*, 4: 301.

31. John Quincy Adams to John Adams, June 30, 1788, Worthington C. Ford (ed.), *Writings of John Quincy Adams* (New York, 1913), 1: 33.

32. Davies, "Society of the Cincinnati in New England," 12; Warren, *History . . . American Revolution*, 3: 291.

33. Washington to Jefferson, April 8, 1784, *FWW*, 27: 388.

34. Jefferson to Washington, April 16, 1784, *JP*, 7: 105–7.

35. Washington to the Society of the Cincinnati, May 4, 1784, *FWW*, 27: 393–6.

36. Edgar E. Hume, *Early Opposition to the Cincinnati*, reprint from article in *Americana* (1936), 18–28; Davies, "Society of the Cincinnati in New England," 15–16.

37. Richard Severo and Lewis Milford, *The Wages of War: When American Soldiers Came Home—From Valley Forge to Vietnam* (New York, 1989), 63.

38. Richard F. Saunders, "The Origin and Early History of the Society of the Cincinnati: The Oldest Hereditary and Patriotic Association in the United States," PhD diss., University of Georgia, 1969, 230 and 267; Sarah Conroy, "The Glory of the Gilded Age: Anderson House," *Washington Post*, "Styles," December 18–25, 1997, 23–4.

39. David S. Shields, *Civil Tongues & Polite Letters in British America* (Chapel Hill, NC, 1997), xiii.

40. Jensen, *New Nation*, 140–1.

41. Brissot de Warville, *New Travels*, July 30, 1788, 90–1.

42. Ezell (ed.), *Miranda*, 162.

43. William M. Fowler, Jr, *The Baron of Beacon Hill: A Biography of John Hancock* (Boston, MA, 1979), 256–7; Silverman, *Cultural History of the American Revolution*, 509–10.

44. Ezell (ed.), *Miranda*, September 17, 1784, 162.

45. "Diary of a French Officer 1781," *Magazine of American History* 4 (1880): June 14, 1781, 214.

46. George McCowen, Jr, *The British Occupation of Charleston*, 123–6; George C. Rogers, Jr, *Charleston in the Age of the Pinckneys* (Norman, OK, 1969), 6.

47. Schoepf, *Travels in the Confederation*, January 1784, 2: 168–9.

48. Robert J. Gough, "Towards a Theory of Class and Social Conflict: A Social History of Wealthy Philadelphians, 1775 and 1790," PhD diss., University of Pennsylvania, 1977, 421–2; Eleanor B. Scott, "Early Literary Clubs in New York City," *American Literature: A Journal of Literary, History, Criticism, and Bibliography*, 5 (1933–4): 3; Darlene E. Fisher, "Social Life in Philadelphia during the British Occupation," *Pennsylvania History*, 37 (1970): 244–5.

49. Nicholas B. Wainwright, *The Schuylkill Fishing Company of the State of Schuylkill, 1732–1982* (Philadelphia, 1982), 1–18; Gough, "Towards a Theory of Class and Social Conflict," 426.

50. Daniel R. Gilbert, "Patterns of Organization and Membership in Colonial Philadelphia Club Life, 1725–1755," PhD diss., University of Pennsylvania, 1952, 159–60; Gough, "Towards a Theory of Class and Social Conflict," 429.

51. Dixon Wecter, *The Saga of American Society: A Record of Social Aspiration, 1607–1937* (New York, 1937), 255–6; Edgar E. Hume, "The Society of the Cincinnati and the Tammany Society," *New York Genealogical and Biographical Record*, 68 (1937): 45 and 49.

52. Samuel Mordecai, *Richmond in By-Gone Days* (Richmond, VA, 1946, from 2nd edn of 1860), 261.

53. Dexter (ed.), *Diary of Stiles*, 2: 436, 486, and 487n.; Brooke Hindle, *Pursuit of Science in Revolutionary America, 1735–1789* (Chapel Hill, NC, 1956), 264 and 273.

54. Shaffer, *To Be an American . . . Ramsay*, 140; Hindle, *Pursuit of Science*, 273–5; Robert A. East, *Business Enterprise in the American Revolutionary Era* (Gloucester, MA, 1964, orig. pub. 1938), 312–13.

55. Doerflinger, *A Vigorous Spirit*, 276; Schultz, *Republic of Labor*, 51; Howard B. Rock, "'All Her Sons Join as One Social Band:' New York City's Artisanal Societies in the Early Republic," in Howard B. Rock et al., *American Artisans: Crafting Social Identity, 1750–1850* (Baltimore, MD, 1995), 161–2.

56. Brookes, *Anthony Benezet*, 127; Carl and Jessica Bridenbaugh, *Rebels and Gentlemen: Philadelphia in the Age of Franklin* (New York, 1942), 259.

57. "A Bill for the General Diffusion of Knowledge," *JP*, 2: 526–33 and 534n.–5n.; Jefferson, *Notes on the State of Virginia*, ed. Peden, 146–7.

58. David W. Robson, *Educating Republicans: The College in the Era of the American Revolution, 1750–1800* (Westport, CT, 1985) 103.

59. Robson, *Educating Republicans*, 111–12; "Diary of a French Officer 1781," 213.

60. Humphrey, *King's College to Columbia*, 153–4, 270–4, and 285.

61. William M. S. Demarest, *A History of Rutgers College, 1766–1924* (New Brunswick, NJ, 1924), 103–5 and 118–23; Stephen Brobeck, "Changes in the Corporation and Structure of Philadelphia's Elite Group, 1756–1790," PhD diss., University of Pennsylvania, 1973, 198.

62. James E. Cronin (ed.), *The Diary of Elihu Hubbard Smith* (Philadelphia, 1973), 2; Whitfield J. Bell, Jr, "Some Aspects of the Social History of Pennsylvania, 1760–1790," *PMHB*, 62 (1938): 291.

63. Robson, *Educating Republicans*, 103 and 112.

64. Whitfield, J. Bell, Jr, "Science and Humanity in Philadelphia, 1775–1790," PhD diss., University of Pennsylvania, 1947, 105–7.

65. Robson, *Educating Republicans*, 46–7 and 66.

66. Robson, *Educating Republicans*, 324; Harvey Wish, *Society and Thought in Early America* (New York, 1950), 207.

67. Benjamin Rush to John Armstrong, March 19, 1783, Butterfield (ed.), *Letters of Rush*, 1: 295–6 and 297n.; Bell, "Some Aspects," 291; David W. Robson, "College Founding in the New Republic," *History of Education Quarterly* (fall 1983): 329; Ollinger Crenshaw, *General Lee's College: The Rise and Growth of Washington and Lee University* (New York, 1969), 12–14.

68. Alice F. Tyler, *Freedom's Ferment: Phases of American Social History from the Colonial Period to the Outbreak of the Civil War* (New York, 1944), 265.

69. Michael Kraus, "Eighteenth Century Humanitarianism Collaboration between Europe and America," *PMHB*, 60 (1936): 271–2.

70. Melvin Yazawa, "The Impact of the Revolution on Social Problems: Poverty, Insanity, and Crime," in Jack P. Greene and J. R. Pole (eds), *The Blackwell Encyclopedia of the American Revolution* (Cambridge, MA, 1991), 425.

71. Henry Knox to Alexander Hamilton, July 24, 1782, Syrett (ed.), *Papers of Hamilton*, 3: 118.

72. Quoted in John Woestendiek, "Searching for Dignity, Inventing America" section, *Philadelphia Inquirer*, April 28, 1987, 14.

73. Nevins, *American States*, 452–3.

74. Jefferson, *Notes on the State of Virginia*, ed. Peden, 144–5; Jensen, *New Nation*, 138.

75. Jensen, *New Nation*, 137; Nevins, *American States*, 454; Butterfield (ed.), *Letters of Rush*, 1: 416n.–17n.

76. David B. Davis, "The Movement to Abolish Capital Punishment in America, 1787–1861," *AHR*, 63 (1957): 27n.; Nevins, *American States*, 455; Yazawa, "Impact of the Revolution on Social Problems," 426.

77. Harry E. Barnes, *The Evolution of Penology in Pennsylvania* (Indianapolis, IN, 1927), 72, 135, and 163–5; Harry M. Ward and Harold E. Greer, Jr, *Richmond during the Revolution, 1775–83* (Charlottesville, VA, 1977), 118.

78. Barnes, *Evolution of Penology*, 80–1; Kraus, "Eighteenth Century Humanitarianism," 273; Orlando F. Lewis, *The Development of American Prisons and Prison Customs, 1776–1845* (Albany, NY, 1922), 13–14; Blake McKelvey, *American Prisons: A Study in American Social History Prior to 1915* (Chicago, 1936), 5.

79. Peter J. Coleman, *Debtors and Creditors in America: Insolvency, Imprisonment for Debt and Bankruptcy, 1607–1900* (Madison, WI, 1974), *passim*; Jonathan M. Chu, "Debt Litigation and Shays's Rebellion," in Robert A. Gross (ed.), *In Debt to Shays: The Bicentennial of an Agrarian Rebellion* (Charlottesville, VA, 1993), 84–5.

80. Robert W. Kelso, *The History of Public Poor Relief in Massachusetts, 1620–1920* (Boston, MA, 1922), 116; Schultz, *Republic of Labor*, 116.

81. David N. Schneider, *The History of Public Welfare in New York State, 1609–1866* (Chicago, 1938), 95–109.

82. Benjamin J. Klebaner, "Some Aspects of North Carolina Poor Relief, 1700–1800," *NCHR*, 31 (1954): 482.

83. William C. Heffner, *History of Poor Relief Legislation in Pennsylvania, 1682–1913* (Cleona, PA, 1913), 139–45.

84. Brissot de Warville, *New Travels*, 179–80; Tyler, *Freedom's Ferment*, 300–1; David J. Rothman, *The Discovery of the Asylum: Social Order and Disorder in the New Republic* (Boston, MA, 1971), 141.

85. Bell, "Some Aspects," 302–3; Jensen, *New Nation*, 146; Brissot de Warville, *New Travels*, 262.

86. Smith, *"Lower Sort,"* 214.

87. "A Discourse delivered before the College of Physicians of Philadelphia," February 6, 1787, quoted in Bell, "Science and Humanity," 246.

88. Thomas Paine, "Common Sense," appendix, in Philp (ed.), *Thomas Paine*, 53.

89. "On the Defects of the Confederation," in Dagebert D. Runes (ed.), *The Selected Writings of Benjamin Rush* (New York, 1947), 26.

Index